Tank Warfare on the Eastern Front 1943–1945

Tank Warfare on the Eastern Front 1943–1945

Red Steamroller

Robert A. Forczyk

Pen & Sword
MILITARY

First published in Great Britain in 2016
and reprinted in 2016 by
PEN & SWORD MILITARY
An imprint of
Pen & Sword Books Ltd
47 Church Street
Barnsley, South Yorkshire
S70 2AS

Copyright © Robert A Forczyk, 2016

ISBN 978 1 78346 278 0

Typeset in Ehrhardt by
Mac Style Ltd, Bridlington, East Yorkshire

Printed and bound in England
By CPI Group (UK) Ltd, Croydon, CR0 4YY

Pen & Sword Books Ltd incorporates the Imprints of Aviation, Atlas,
Family History, Fiction, Maritime, Military, Discovery, Politics, History,
Archaeology, Select, Wharncliffe Local History, Wharncliffe True Crime,
Military Classics, Wharncliffe Transport, Leo Cooper, The Praetorian Press,
Remember When, Seaforth Publishing and Frontline Publishing.

For a complete list of Pen & Sword titles please contact
PEN & SWORD BOOKS LIMITED
47 Church Street, Barnsley, South Yorkshire, S70 2AS, England
E-mail: enquiries@pen-and-sword.co.uk
Website: www.pen-and-sword.co.uk

Contents

List of Plates

T-34 tanks on the production line.

Vyacheslav Malyshev was the Soviet engineer tasked by Stalin with running the Soviet Union's tank industry.

A Lend-Lease Matilda tank with a tank unit in the Central Front, January 1943.

An Su-122 self-propelled gun negotiates its way down a very muddy trail.

German preparations for Operation Zitadelle were extensive.

A Soviet tank company commander briefs his platoon leaders on their next operation.

The turret of a Panther Ausf D after an internal explosion had shattered the interior.

A German StuG-III assault gun pauses by a burning T-34/76 Model 1942 in the summer of 1943.

This is the same burning T-34 as in the previous photo.

A Tiger positioned next to a knocked-out KV-1.

Crewmen of a Panther loading 7.5-cm ammunition in a hurried, haphazard manner which begs for an accident.

T-34 with its turret blown off after a massive explosion.

The crew of an SU-76M assault gun in action.

Soviet T-34s enroute to Zhitomir, November 1943.

A Soviet KV-85 tank captured during the German counter-attack near Radomyschyl in early December 1943.

Soviet Lend Lease Churchill tanks entering Kiev, November 1943.

T-34s advance with infantry across a frozen field, winter 1943/44.

A German Pz IV advancing with an infantry section.

The recapture of Zhitomir in late November 1943 was a minor tactical victory, but von Manstein's armored counter-offensive failed to destroy Rybalko's 3 GTA or recover Kiev.

A Kampfgruppe from 1.

German infantry ride atop a Pz IV tank during the winter of 1944.

A German grenadier with a Panzerfaust observes a burning T-34 in a village.

A late-model Pz IV alongside a knocked-out late-model T-34/76 in the Ukraine, early 1944.

A Panther from SS-*Wiking* in a wood line in Poland, September 1944.

A Lend-lease Sherman in Red Army service.

A JS-2 lies disabled in the streets of an East Prussian town.

Another JS-2 has come to grief in a German city street, which was far too narrow for armoured operations.

List of Maps

Glossary

ABTU	*Auto-Bronetankovoe Upravlenie* (Main Tank Directorate), 1934–40.
AFV	Armoured Fighting Vehicle
AOK	*Armeeoberkommando (Army)*
AP	Armour Piercing
APCBC	Armour Piercing Composite Ballistic Cap (steel core)
APCR	Armour Piercing Composite Rigid (tungsten core)
APHE	Armour Piercing High Explosive
C^2	Command & Control
cbm (m³)	Cubic meter of fuel, equivalent to 1,000 litres or 744 kg
Desantniki	Russian term for troops who rode mounted on tanks or other AFVs into battle
GABTU	*Glavnoe Avto-Brone-Tankovoe Upravlenie* (Chief Department of Autos and Armoured Vehicles), 1940–45.
GAU KA	*Glavnye Artilleryiskye Upravlenue Krasnoy Armii* (Main Artillery Directorate of Red Army)
Gefechtstroß	Combat Trains, including ammunition trailers
Gepäcktroß	Baggage Train, including field kitchens
GCC	Guards Cavalry Corps
GKO	*Gosudarstvennij Komitet Oboroniy* (State Defence Committee)
GMC	Guards Mechanized Corps
Großtransportraum	Large Transport (GTR)
GTC	Guards Tank Corps
HE-FRAG	High Explosive, Fragmentation
HEAT	High Explosive Anti-tank
HKL	*Hauptkampflinie* (main line of resistance)
HVAP	High Velocity Armour Piercing (Tungsten core)
Instandsetzungsgrupe	Repair Group
Kradschützen	Motorcycle infantry
KwK	*Kampfwagenkanone* (Fighting vehicle cannon)
LSSAH	*Leibstandarte SS Adolf Hitler*
MC	Mechanized Corps
MD	Military District
NKO	*Narodnyi Kommissariat Oborony* (the People's Commissariat of Defence)
NKTP	*Narodnyi Kommissariat Tankovoy Promyslennosti* (the People's Commissariat of the Tank Industry)

NKVD   *Narodnyi Kommisariat Vneshnykh Del* (People's Commissariat of Internal Affairs)

OKH   *Oberkommando des Heeres* (German, Army High Command)

OTB   *Otdel'nyye tankovyye batal'ony* (Separate Tank Battalion)

OTTPP   *Otdel'nyye Tyazhelij Tankovij Polk Proriva* (Independent Heavy Tank Breakthrough Regiment)

PaK   *PanzerAbwehrKanone* (anti-tank gun)

PP   *podderzhka pekhoty* (infantry support tanks)

Pz.Rgt   Panzer Regiment

PzAOK   Panzerarmee

RKKA   *Raboche-Krest'yanskaya Krasnaya Armiya* (the Army of Workers and Peasants/the Red Army)

RVGK   *Rezerv Verkhovnogo Glavnokomandovaniya* (Reserve of Supreme High Command)

SAP   *Samokhodno-Artillerijskij Polk* (Self-Propelled Artillery Regiment)

SPW   Schützenpanzerwagen [Armoured Infantry Vehicle or APC]

SR   Schützen-Regiment [Motorized Infantry]

TA   Tank Army

TC   Tank Corps

TSAP   *Tyazhelij Samokhodno-Artillerijskij Polk* (Heavy Self-Propelled Artillery Regiment)

TTPP   *Tyazhelij Tankovij Polk Proriva* (Heavy Tank Breakthrough Regiment)

UABTTS   *Uchebnyy Avtobronetankovyy Tsentr* (Tank Automotive Training Centre)

UMM   *Upravlenie Motorizatzii i Mekhanizatzii RKKA* (Directorate of Mechanization and Motorization of the Red Army), 1929–1934. Re-named ABTU.

VA   *vozdushnaya armiya* (Air Army)

VAMM   *Voennaya Akademiya Mekhanizatzii i Motorizatzii RKKA* (Military Academy of Mechanization and Motorization of the Red Army)

V.S.   *Verbrauchssatz*

VVS   *Voenno-Vozdushnye Sily* (Military Air Forces) i.e. the *Soviet Air Force*

Vorausabteilung   Vanguard battalion (abbrev. V.A.)

Preface

It was hot and dry, as I stood in the turret of 'Godzilla-II' and scanned across the flat horizon with my binoculars, looking for any indications of the adversary – but there were none. My tank company had been out on manoeuvres for a week in the desert and our battalion commander – who rarely graced us with his presence in the field – had ordered us to spend a day conducting company-size tactical drills. One particular favourite of his was the so-called 'thirteen-on-one' scenario, in which one tank from the company would assume a hull-down defensive position and the other thirteen tanks would then manoeuvre to engage and destroy the one hidden tank. We were informed that the mission had to be conducted with urgency and that we would be provided no air, artillery or infantry support, nor could we try to bypass the defending tank. This was the kind of mental inflexibility that usually leads to disaster. When I tried to point out that this kind of tank–pure assault across flat desert terrain had not worked in the Western Desert in 1941–42 or on the steppes of Russia in 1941–43, all common sense was dismissed with a curt, 'Do as you are ordered'.

So we spent the day fruitlessly attacking that single tank, over and over again. We had to cross over 3 kilometres of flat ground that lacked anything more than the occasional tumbleweed. Standard overwatch tactics – which were actually frowned upon by our battalion commander as 'slowing down' the operational tempo – were useless, since there was no cover at all. At first we tried a 'tank charge' with all three platoons moving as rapidly as possible, almost on line – but the MILES lights were blinking on all thirteen tanks after just 1,500 metres – indicating that all were notionally destroyed. We never even saw the hull-down tank until it was too late. Then we tried a variety of different methods, but there really was nowhere to manoeuvre and the adversary – whom I knew to be a very experienced combat veteran – could see every move we made. I knew he was chain-smoking cigarettes in his turret, peering through his primary daylight sight and laughing at the stupidity of it all. We even tried dismounting with a few troops and low-crawling with an AT-4 light anti-tank weapon, but we were spotted and the adversary fired upon us with his .50 calibre machine-gun. Eventually, on around the fourth try, we got a bit luckier and found a few spots that were almost dead space; we deliberately sacrificed two tank platoons in order to draw fire off to one flank and one tank out of thirteen survived long enough to spot the black smoke of the adversary's diesel engine – every time he pulled up to fire there was a puff of smoke that gave away his position – but it could only be seen from about 400 metres. The last tank was able to close and engage the adversary when he moved up to fire. Our chain of command seemed unconcerned that we had suffered something like 400 per cent losses in order to knock out one adversary tank, but were more upset that we had taken so many hours to accomplish this seemingly simple task. They would have made fine commanders in the Red Army. Not one of these men actually spent any time in a tank or bothered to look at the terrain. Nor did they seem aware – despite their West Point credentials – that von Clausewitz had written that everything in war is simple, but actually accomplishing it is not.

When I read about single German Panther or Tiger tanks in 1943–44 engaging masses of T-34 tanks and destroying a dozen of them, I think back to my own experiments with armoured mass versus armoured firepower. Modern armour aficionados – few of whom ever served on tanks – tend to ascribe this kind of achievement to the innate superiority of German tanks over Soviet models, without considering that any hidden, hull-down tank has a huge advantage against tanks moving across the open. Other folks, perhaps taken in by lingering Nazi-era propaganda, tend to regard the Third Reich and its weaponry with a certain romanticism that blinds them to its numerous faults. For years, German veterans have harped on the notion of the Soviet 'Steamroller', achieving victory only by dint of massive numbers, but my experiences with tanks taught me that mass is ephemeral and that victory is achieved not by dint of numbers, but by bold and effective use of combined arms tactics. This was proven again in the Golan in 1973 and Iraq in 1991, where masses of Syrian and Iraqi tanks proved completely at a loss against better-led Israeli and Coalition tanks.

In 1941–42, the German panzer forces were victorious because they successfully used combined arms tactics and the Red Army tankers did not. Instead, in the first two years of the war on the Eastern Front Red Army tankers relied primarily upon mass and suffered defeat after lop-sided defeat. Red Army tank commanders were hounded by political commissars and Stavka representatives to attack prematurely and under unfavourable conditions, often ignoring doctrine and military common sense. The results were predictable – heavy losses and frustration. However, in November 1942 the balance of armoured warfare on the Eastern Front began to change as the Red Army improved its methods, and these changes accelerated in 1943. The badly-depleted Wehrmacht had fewer and fewer resources to conduct true combined arms tactics and was less able to achieve its missions, while the Red Army leadership became less focussed on mass and more on adopting the kind of combined arms tactics that had worked so well for their adversary at the outset of the war.

Chapter 1

The Opposing Armoured Forces in 1943

Efficiency Hypothesis
This work is the second part of a two-volume study of armoured operations on the Eastern Front in the Second World War. The first volume, *Tank Warfare on the Eastern Front 1941–1942 Schwerpunkt* (2014), covered the initial two years of the war during the period when the Germans usually had the initiative. This volume covers the second half of the war, as the Red Army gained the initiative after Stalingrad and kept it all the way to Berlin. These two volumes are not intended to be a comprehensive chronological account of every action involving armour in four years of conflict, which would require many more volumes. Rather, my intent is to attempt to identify the reasons for the eventual outcome in the dynamics of operational and tactical armoured operations. Oftentimes, I choose to focus on battles that lie outside the standard orthodoxy about the war, since there are too many pre-conceived notions about certain well-known battles, while other important actions are completely ignored. A case in point is the well-known Battle of Kursk in July 1943 and the virtually unknown German counter-offensive on the Mius River, which occurred just a few weeks later.

My working hypothesis for this study revolves around relative war-making efficiency. In the first volume, I outlined how German armoured operations in the first part of the war were generally successful because they had superior efficiency in terms of training and use of combined arms tactics. The Wehrmacht of 1940 was tailored to Germany's limited resources, but the Wehrmacht of 1941–42 was not. In order to mount an operation on the scale of *Barbarossa*, the Third Reich had to confiscate thousands of captured vehicles from Western Europe as well as captured fuel stocks – but this was a one-time plus-up. Hitler's Blitzkrieg Army was designed to win before internal weakness made it grind to a halt. Yet when *Barbarossa* failed, the Germans were not prepared for a protracted war – unlike the Soviet Union – and the inefficiencies in their system, such as low tank production, limited personnel replacements, inadequate theatre logistics and inter-service rivalries began to emerge as serious problems within six months of the start of the war. Thereafter, the German military effort on the Eastern Front – particularly their conduct of armoured warfare that was at the core of their operational-level doctrine – became less and less efficient as the war dragged on.

In contrast, the Red Army started at a very low level of efficiency due to the Stalinist purges and rapid pre-war expansion, but began to gain its footing by late 1942. However, thanks to the pre-war industrialization of the Five Year Plans, the Soviet Union and the Red Army were well prepared for protracted war. This volume begins in January 1943, as the relative efficiency of the German mechanized forces was beginning to decline and the Red Army's tank armies were finally ready to begin spearheading large-scale offensives. While other works about the Eastern Front have suggested that this or that battle decided the outcome, be it Smolensk, Moscow, Stalingrad or Kursk, this study looks at the decline of German panzer forces and the rise of Soviet tank forces as a holistic process, not a solitary event. Furthermore, it was a process driven just as much by industrial decisions, as by battlefield ones.

German Armoured Units on the Eastern Front

At the start of 1943, the German Army (Heer) and Waffen-SS had five primary types of armoured units:

- Panzer-Divisionen, intended to spearhead mobile combined arms operations. These units comprised one Panzer-Regiment with 1–2 Panzer-Abteilungen (nominally 152 tanks), two motorized infantry regiments with four battalions (one mounted in SPW halftracks), a motorized artillery regiment with three battalions (24 10.5cm and 12 15cm howitzers), a reconnaissance battalion, a Panzerjäger Bataillon (with 14 Marder-type self-propelled tank destroyers), a motorized engineer battalion, plus signal and support troops.
- Panzer-Grenadier-Divisionen, intended to supplement the Panzer-Divisionen with additional infantry. The Panzergrenadiers either had one Panzer-Abteilung or a Sturmgeschütz-Abteilung, but had a total of six infantry battalions.
- Independent schwere-Panzer-Abteilungen (Heavy Tank Battalions) assigned as corps-level units for breakthrough operations. The original 'Organization D' of August 1942 consisted of a battalion with two companies, each with nine Tigers and 10 Pz III tanks, but this was replaced with the 'Organization E' scheme in March 1943, which had three companies each with 14 Tigers.[1]
- Sturmartillerie units to provide direct support to infantry units. Each battalion consisted of three batteries, with an authorized total of 22 StuG III and nine StuH 42.
- Self-propelled Panzerjäger units to provide general anti-tank support across a wide front. The earlier Panzerjäger-Abteilungen usually consisted of three companies equipped with 27 Marder-type tank destroyers, but the new schwere Panzerjäger-Abteilungen introduced in 1943 were authorized 45 Hornisse tank destroyers each.

On 1 January 1943, the Germans had a total of 21 Panzer-Divisionen and six Panzer-Grenadier-Divisionen committed to the Eastern Front, which altogether contained 41 Panzer-Abteilungen (battalions).* In addition, there were elements of two schwere-Panzer-Abteilungen, with a total of 40 Tiger tanks and 40 Pz III tanks, as well as a few odd company-size tank detachments. Altogether, on paper these battalions had an authorized strength of almost 3,200 tanks. However, after six months of intensive combat, the German Panzer-Divisionen were much reduced in both equipment and personnel strength. Ostensibly, according to numbers provided by Thomas J. Jentz, at the start of the New Year the Germans had 1,475 operational tanks on the Eastern Front, or about 46 per cent of their authorized strength, along with another 1,328 tanks awaiting repairs, which means that total write-offs (*Totalausfalle* in German terminology) amounted to just 12 per cent.[2]

Yet these numbers do not reflect the woeful state of Germany's armoured forces on the Eastern Front and appear to be inflated. Only two Panzer-Divisionen, the newly-arrived 7.Panzer-Division and the veteran 9.Panzer-Division, had 100 or more operational tanks. Most of the remaining German Panzer-Divisionen at the front were *ausgebrannt* (burnt out) and had been reduced to just 30–40 operational tanks, meaning that they were closer to 25 per cent of their authorized armoured strength. Some particularly decimated units, such as the 3., 4., 8. and 13. Panzer-Divisionen, had barely a dozen operational tanks each. Furthermore, three Panzer-Divisionen (14., 16. and 24.) and three Panzer-Grenadier-Divisionen (3., 29., 60.) – comprising a total of 12 Panzer-Abteilungen – were encircled with the 6.Armee (AOK 6) at Stalingrad. While these trapped divisions still had 94 operational tanks and 31 assault guns, they were virtually out of fuel and on the verge of annihilation.[3] Thus, the actual number of operational German tanks at the front was likely fewer than 800. Unlike the beginning of the War in the East in June 1941, by 1943 Germany no longer had a mechanized *masse de manoeuvre*.

At the start of 1943, the main German tanks in use were the Pz III Ausf L and Ausf M models, equipped with the long-barreled 5cm KwK 39 L/60 gun and the Pz IV Ausf G armed with the long-barreled 7.5cm KwK 40 L/43 gun. Under favourable circumstances, both of these medium tanks were capable of defeating their primary opponent – the Soviet T-34 medium tank – at typical battlefield ranges, although the Pz III's modest level of armoured protection was a liability. Unlike the T-34's advanced sloped armour, the German medium tanks could only increase their protection by adding bolt-on plates, which increased their weight. As it was, the Pz III and Pz IV were noticeably inferior to the T-34

---

* In late 1942, the Waffen-SS had already re-designated their motorized infantry divisions, each of which were equipped with at least one Panzer-Abteilung, as 'Panzergrenadier-Division', but the Heer did not similarly re-designate their motorized infantry divisions as such until mid-1943. In the interest of avoiding confusion, I will use the term Panzer-Grenadier-Division for the Heer units in aggregate, but continue to use 'Infanterie-Division (mot.)' when referring to specific Heer divisions prior to mid-1943.

in terms of mobility, since both used the Maybach HL 120 TRM petrol engine, capable of producing up to 300hp against the Soviet tank's powerful V-2 diesel engine, which could produce up to 500hp. In addition, neither the Pz III's torsion bar suspension, nor the Pz IV's leaf spring suspension, could compare with the T-34's Christie suspension over cross-country terrain. Furthermore, Germany's best two medium tanks comprised only 42 per cent of their operational front-line strength – approximately 300 tanks. Nearly one-third of German armour still consisted of older Pz III and Pz IV models armed with short-barreled 5cm and 7.5cm guns, which were greatly-outclassed by the T-34, but these older tanks were kept on hand because newer models were still in very short supply. Another 20 per cent of German armoured strength consisted of obsolete Pz II light tanks and Pz 38t Czech-built light tanks, both of which were no longer useful on the front line. Thus, German armoured strength on the Eastern Front was really built around a remarkably small number of up-to-date medium tanks. While the Tiger heavy tank was on hand in very small numbers and the new Panther medium tank was just entering production in January, it would be many months before they could influence the armoured balance on the Eastern Front.

In addition to the Panzer-Divisionen, Germany had 22 Sturmgeschütz-Abteilungen (assault gun battalions) and 7 Panzerjäger-Abteilungen (tank destroyer battalions) deployed in the Soviet Union. These battalions theoretically comprised another 900 armoured tank-killing weapons, but seven of these battalions were trapped at Stalingrad and the remainder were reduced to 30–50 per cent operational numbers, or roughly 250 assault guns and tank destroyers. Furthermore, while these weapons added to the defensive anti-tank capabilities of German infantry formations, they were not well-suited to the kind of fast-moving manoeuvre warfare favoured by German mechanized doctrine since 1940.

The onslaught of two powerful Soviet counter-offensives – Operations Mars at Rzhev and Operation Uranus at Stalingrad – had caused the Germans to concentrate their armoured strength on the Eastern Front in just two commands: with the 9.Armee defending the Rzhev salient (five Panzer-Divisionen, one Panzergrenadier-Division and three Sturmgeschutz-Abteilungen) and Heeresgruppe Don (six Panzer-Divisionen, two Panzergrenadier-Divisionen and two Sturmgeschutz-Abteilungen). Generaloberst Walter Model's 9.Armee had just succeeded in repulsing a massive Soviet attempt to sever the Rzhev salient with Operation Mars in November–December 1942, but this effort had necessitated massing virtually all of Heeresgruppe Mitte's armour in this one sector. Generalfeldmarschall Erich von Manstein's Heeresgruppe Don was still seized in crisis as the New Year began, attempting to stop the Soviets from advancing to Rostov and cutting off the retreat route of Heeresgruppe A from the Caucasus. Von Manstein enjoyed absolute priority for replacements and would retain this advantage throughout 1943. The rest of the German front was largely denuded of armoured reserves, particularly in the north around

Leningrad and in the centre around Orel. Although the Germans still had four nominal 'Panzer Armies' on the Eastern Front, these had been reduced to little more than empty husks, with none possessing more than 100 operational tanks.

Between July and December 1942, the German armoured units on the Eastern Front had lost 1,256 tanks as *Totalausfalle**, while receiving 1,365 replacement tanks – so German tank strength had actually increased slightly during the 1942 campaign. Indeed, when the Soviets began their winter counter-offensives in November 1942, the Germans had 40 per cent more operational tanks than they had possessed at the start of Case Blau in July. However, the Panzer units on the Eastern Front only received 67 per cent of the tanks built in the period July–December 1942 and this percentage actually dropped to just 60 per cent in the final three months of the year due to the crisis in North Africa.[4] The remaining 33–40 percent of German tank production was not going to the Eastern Front, but to other fronts or retained for training new units. Thus, the Panzer-Divisionen on the Eastern Front received just enough replacements to maintain their authorized strength, with no real theatre reserves of replacements. A normal rule of thumb is that a mechanized army should try to maintain a 10 per cent over-strength of key weapons, like tanks, in a category called 'Operational Readiness Floats', which are in-theatre spares to replace losses. Without a reserve of spares, natural attrition meant that German Panzer-Divisionen at the front could not be kept at authorized strength levels. Nevertheless, if German theatre logistics had been adequate, this approach might have sufficed.

The OKH Panzer Reserve was located at Sagan in Silesia. After acceptance from the manufacturers in Germany, new panzers typically arrived by rail at Sagan, where they were either forwarded on to front-line units in Russia or kept temporarily in holding depots at Vienna. The OKH decided the priority of where new tanks would be sent, but the logic employed was arcane; for example, sending Tigers to the Leningrad Front where terrain was clearly unfavourable for the use of heavy tanks. Normally, replacement tanks were sent in small groups, usually 10–20, to specific Panzer-Divisionen. This method of injection kept combat units going and spread the resources around, but prevented them from ever getting back up to full strength.

Furthermore, the weakness of German theatre-level supply greatly undermined German armoured strength on the Eastern Front, which was built on a logistical house of cards. The advances of 1941–42 had brought the German Panzer-Divisionen very far from their logistical support bases in Eastern Europe and the homeland, which greatly complicated field and depot-level repairs on vehicles. In the Caucasus for example, Heeresgruppe A was dependent upon a single-track rail line to supply Panzerarmee 1 (PzAOK 1), which was grossly inadequate for receiving regular supplies of fuel and spare parts. At Rzhev, the main rail line from Vyazma was never converted to standard

---

* Total loss, meaning that the tank was beyond repair.

gauge, so the 9.Armee was forced to fight off Zhukov's Operation Mars offensive while receiving no more than two supply trains per day.

The lack of standardization in spare parts was a particular disadvantage for German armour, compared to the standardization witnessed in the Soviet and Anglo–American tank fleets. When units lacked adequate spare parts to restore damaged vehicles they were wont to resort to cannibalization (also known as 'controlled substitution': taking parts from one or more damaged tanks to repair at least one tank) to keep tanks running, but cannibalization resulted in tanks being stripped for parts. Normally, tanks in heavy use should receive some kind of depot-level service every three to six months to restore their systems, particularly the suspension and engine-train. Field-level maintenance can keep tanks running for weeks or months, but minor problems will gradually escalate into major problems that cannot be readily fixed in the field – like a ruptured fuel cell. Certain types of combat damage could also be repaired in the field and some tanks were 'knocked out' multiple times, but usually depot-level maintenance was required to restore a tank to full fighting trim. Sending a damaged tank back to Germany for depot-level maintenance meant that it might be gone for many weeks and in the meantime, the unit was down another tank. Consequently, German under-strength Panzer units tended to keep large numbers of non-operational tanks up-front with them, hoping that through cannibalization and various field expedients they could keep a reasonable number of tanks operational. For example, if a tank had the electrical motor for its turret traverse burned out and there were no spare motors available, the tank could still use manual traverse – even though this put the crew at much greater risk in a tank engagement. The result was that tanks kept at the front, operating in 'degraded mode', were rather fragile. When winter arrived, the 'degraded' tanks tended to be the first to fall out.

The German logistic infrastructure supporting their panzers tended to fail whenever units were forced to retreat any great distance, when snow/ice/mud turned the Russian roads into glue, or when Soviet partisans succeeded in interfering with the lines of communication. This weakness was particularly apparent when the Soviets broke through Heeresgruppe B's front along the Don in late 1942. German supply bases were overrun and often had to be abandoned due to lack of transport. This lack of operational mobility – insufficient trains, long-haul trucks and air transport planes – proved to be the Achilles' heel that nearly brought German armoured strength to its knees in the winter of 1942–43. Essentially, German theatre logistics on the Eastern Front had no leeway and even minor disruptions could halt or delay the timely delivery of critical spare parts, ammunition and fuel to forward areas.

Guderian to the Rescue?

On 28 February 1943, Hitler appointed Generaloberst Heinz Guderian as *Inspekteur der Panzertruppen*. Guderian had been unemployed in the Führer-

Reserve since Hitler had relieved him of command in December 1941, but now Hitler needed Guderian's organizational talents to restore the depleted Panzer units on the Eastern Front. Guderian demanded a broad authority over all armoured units, included those belonging to the Waffen-SS and the Luftwaffe. However, Guderian lost the bureaucratic battle with the Sturmartillerie branch, which blocked his efforts to gain control over their assault guns, and the Panzerjäger branch also managed to retain considerable autonomy. Guderian wasted no time in drawing up a lengthy memorandum for Hitler on how to rejuvenate the Panzer-Divisionen, which was presented to the Führer on 9 March 1943.

In its main points, Guderian's memorandum stated:

> The task for 1943 is to provide a certain number of Panzer-Divisionen with complete combat efficiency capable of making limited objective attacks. A Panzer-Division only possesses complete combat efficiency when the number of its tanks is in correction proportion to its other weapons and vehicles. German Panzer-Divisionen were designed to contain 4 Panzer-Abteilungen with a total of roughly 400 tanks per division....at the moment, we unfortunately have no Panzer-Divisionen which can be said to possess complete combat efficiency. Our success in battle this year, and even more so next year, depends on the recreation of that efficiency. So the problem is this: without delay, and regardless of all special interests, to recreate Panzer-Divisionen with complete combat efficiency.[5]

Hitler agreed with many of Guderian's points and respected his technical expertise, but failed to back him in the various inter-service and intra-service bureaucratic battles. While Guderian was able to achieve some limited successes in organizational reform and training, his belief in the necessity of rebuilding the Heer Panzer-Divisionen on the Eastern Front met with negligible success. Above all, Guderian's sound argument for the creation of a sizeable strategic armoured reserve under the control of the Oberkommando des Heeres (OKH) was a complete failure. Yet it should also be noted that in many respects, Guderian was overly attached to a dated, tank-heavy conception of what a Panzer-Division should look like, in that a 100-tank battalion was far too unwieldy and providing a 1943 Panzer-Division with 400 medium tanks was both impractical and unnecessary. In contrast, even a full-strength Soviet tank corps in late 1943 was only equipped with 200 T-34 medium tanks in three tank brigades.

Armour Deployed to the Western Front

The Third Reich had three-quarters of its armour deployed on the Eastern Front, with only small mobile forces deployed in the Western Front. Since the OKH lacked a strategic reserve – unlike the Red Army – the only armoured reserves that it could draw upon to deal with unexpected contingencies were either tired veteran units rebuilding in the West or new, inexperienced formations in training. There were no full-strength, combat-ready panzer units sitting around in reserve – everything was deployed at the front. Inside Germany, the Panzertruppenschule I at Munster and the Panzertruppenschule II at Wünsdorf had a cadre of experienced officers and NCOs, as well as tanks for training, which were not supposed to be used as a pool for forming operational tank units – but that rule would be broken late in 1943. Each Panzer-Division also maintained a Panzer-Ersatz-Abteilung to train replacements in its home Wehrkreis; these too would be tapped for use as ad hoc combat units later in the war.

Up until the end of 1942, Hitler had been able to avoid deploying Panzer-Divisionen to guard Western Europe, since the threat of Allied invasion had appeared negligible. Throughout 1942, France was regarded as a rear-area training zone, where decimated armoured units could be rested and rebuilt for about six months, before heading back to the Eastern Front. During the rebuilding phase, these units had not been required to maintain much ready combat capability and many of their vehicles were sent to depot-level maintenance while the troops were rotated home on leave. Panzertruppen resting in France were more interested in wine, women and sunshine, than in intensive training or coastal defence duties. However, that perception began to change when Commonwealth forces conducted the Dieppe Raid in August 1942, which included landing part of a battalion of Churchill tanks. Although a costly failure, the Dieppe Raid indicated that larger Allied amphibious landings, with much more armour, were a distinct possibility in the not-so-distant future. Emphasizing this growing vulnerability, the Anglo-American Operation Torch in North Africa in November 1942 indicated that Hitler would soon have to commit at least a few Panzer-Divisionen to protect both the Atlantic and Mediterranean coastlines. Consequently, the 1.Panzer-Division, which was pulled out of the Rzhev sector in December 1942, was first sent to France, but in May 1943 it was sent to cover the Greek coast for five months. As the threat of unexpected Allied amphibious landings increased throughout 1943, Hitler directed that a Panzer-Reserve would be created to cover contingencies in Western Europe.

In order to fulfill Hitler's requirement, in July–August 1943 the Ersatzheer (Replacement Army) simply collected several of its Panzer-Ersatz Abteilung (Tank Replacement Battalions) and assorted other training units and cobbled them together into three new Reserve-Panzer-Divisionen. The 155. and 179. Reserve-Panzer-Divisionen were assigned to France and the 233.Reserve-Panzer-Division was sent to Denmark. These divisions could continue to train replacements, but were also tasked with providing a contingency reserve to oppose Allied landings. Although the 155.Reserve-Panzer-Division had 60 older Pz III and Pz IV tanks, none of these Reserve Divisions had much combat capability and they diverted precious training resources away from supporting the Eastern Front.[6]

In addition to the Reserve-Panzer-Divisionen, the OKH had begun forming two new Panzer-Divisionen in 1942, but priority was low so their formation occurred over an extended period. The 26.Panzer-Division was formed in Belgium from the battered 23.Infanterie-Division and Panzer-Regiment 202, but it would be mid-1943 before the division would be equipped and trained for battle. Due to Hitler's paranoid fear of Allied landings in Norway, the 25.Panzer-Division had been pulled together in Oslo from various garrison units and a Panzer-Abteilung equipped with captured French tanks, but it barely amounted to a brigade-size Kampfgruppe before mid-1943. By September 1943, the 25.Panzer-Division was approaching full strength and was transferred to France. Even before the loss of the 14.,16 and 24.Panzer-Divisionen at Stalingrad, Hitler directed the OKH to set aside resources to rebuild these divisions and by spring 1943 this project would divert even more personnel and equipment away from the Eastern Front. Guderian bitterly opposed the formation of these new Panzer-Divisionen since they were depriving him of the resources to restore the divisions on the Eastern Front, but he was over-ruled.[7]

North Africa: Reinforcing Failure
Russian historians have often attempted to downplay the role of the Western Allies in the defeat of Germany – particularly the Anglo-American campaigns in North Africa – and criticized the lack of an earlier 'Second Front' to divert German resources from the Eastern Front. In fact, the North African 'sideshow' diverted significant German reinforcements from being sent to Russia and acted as a sinkhole for the limited pool of German armoured replacements, which were needed far more in the East. By January 1943, Generalfeldmarschall Erwin Rommel's Deutsche Afrika Korps (DAK), which had the 15. and 21.Panzer-Divisionen, had been badly defeated by the British at the Battle of El Alamein in Egypt in November 1942 and was in full retreat into Libya. With the Americans and British having landed in Morocco and Algeria, it was clear that the Axis strategic position in North Africa was rapidly becoming untenable. Rommel recommended pulling these veteran troops back to mainland Europe where they could be re-equipped and provide a formidable mobile reserve for Western Europe.

However, in one of his more foolish strategic decisions, Hitler rejected the idea of evacuating Africa and instead ordered strong armoured reinforcements, including the refurbished 10.Panzer-Division and the newly-formed s.Panzer-Abteilung 501, to be transported to Tunisia to reinforce Rommel's retreating forces. While this decision delayed the inevitable for five months, Hitler's decision to send more than 300 tanks (including 31 Tigers) to Tunisia when the German Panzer-Divisionen in the East were reduced to threadbare strength represented a colossal mistake. Had these forces been sent eastward, von Manstein's 'Backhand Blow' counter-offensive at Kharkov in February 1943 would have been nearly doubled in strength. Guderian opposed the diversion of this much armour to North Africa, particularly the Tigers, but he was ignored. Instead, by May 1943 all these reinforcements sent to North Africa would be eliminated, costing Germany three Panzer-Divisionen and a Panzergrenadier-Division, losses that would also have to be replaced out of hide. Like Stalingrad, German losses in North Africa were 100 per cent of equipment. Only small numbers of Panzertruppen were evacuated by air.

Diversion of Armour to the Waffen-SS and Luftwaffe

While the Heer panzer units were being bled to death in Russia and were often forced to make do with obsolete weapons, Reichsführer-SS Heinrich Himmler successfully lobbied Hitler to divert an enormous amount of men and equipment to convert three of his own Waffen-SS divisions to Panzergrenadier-Divisionen. Up to this point in the war, the Waffen-SS divisions had served as motorized infantry units, each with a battery of attached assault guns, and had limited experience with armoured operations. In 1942 the SS-*Wiking* Division had been given a single SS-Panzer-Abteilung, which was employed in the Caucasus. Yet Himmler did not want his troops to be used merely as a support force for the Heer, and sought to build up his best divisions into a mobile strike force capable of independent operations. During the winter of 1942–43, the SS-Panzergrenadier-Divisionen *Leibstandarte Adolf Hitler (LSSAH)*, *Das Reich* and *Totenkopf* were refitted in France and each received a newly-created SS-Panzer-Regiment with two full-strength battalions. At a time when half of the Heer Panzer-Divisionen only had a single under-strength Panzer-Abteilung, Himmler ensured that his troops received the best; over 317 tanks went to outfit these six SS-Panzer-Abteilungen, including brand-new Pz III and Pz IV medium tanks. Himmler even connived to get each of these three Waffen-SS divisions its own schwere-Panzer Kompanie with 10 Tiger tanks. Once completed in early 1943, these three divisions were grouped into the I.SS-Panzerkorps and began preparing to transfer back to the Eastern Front.

There is no doubt that the I.SS-Panzerkorps was a powerful strike force, but the amount of effort put into creating it was enormously detrimental to the revitalization of the Heer Panzer-Divisionen; the Germans were robbing from Peter to pay Paul. Furthermore, it is important to note that at the start of 1943 the Heer had far more experience with the use of tanks in combined arms warfare than the Waffen-SS commanders, who had no direct experience with leading large tank formations. Instead, the Waffen-SS simply appropriated experienced tankers from the Heer as needed; for example, Oberst Herbert Vahl, commander of the Panzer-Regiment 29, was transferred to take over the SS-*Das Reich* Division's new SS-Panzer-Regiment. Guderian argued against lavishing resources on the creation of Waffen-SS armoured units. However, Hitler was enamoured of the idea of an armoured 'Praetorian Guard' and even granted Himmler permission to form three more Waffen-SS Panzergrenadier Divisions; both the first three and the next three would soon be referred to as SS-Panzer-Divisionen. In another year, Himmler would be suggesting the creation of an 'SS-Panzer-Armee' to Hitler. By this concession to Himmler, Hitler allowed a rivalry for resources to develop between the Waffen-SS and the Heer, which would eventually reduce the regular Panzer-Divisionen to second-rate status.

Not to be outdone by Himmler, Reichsmarschall Hermann Göring lobbied to get the Luftwaffe's Division Hermann Göring converted into a Panzer-Division; by late 1942 this plan was a reality and the division sent a regimental-size Kampfgruppe to Tunisia. In short order this unit was destroyed, but the rest of the division fitted out in Italy. Like the Waffen-SS units, Göring ensured that his new division was provided with a two-battalion Panzer-Regiment and that it only received new-build tanks. However, Göring did not get authorization for Tiger tanks for the HG Division, and instead it received its own Sturmgeschütz-Abteilung. Since the Luftwaffe had virtually no officers or troops experienced in armoured combat, Göring used his influence to pressure the Heer into transferring a number of experienced panzer crews to the new outfit. Thus, between the Waffen-SS and the Luftwaffe, Germany had to find the resources to create eight new Panzer-Abteilungen – a total of over 420 tanks and assault guns. Like Himmler, Göring was not satisfied with controlling a single Panzer-Division and would soon be lobbying for more – all to the detriment of the Heer Panzer-Divisionen at the front. In March 1943, Guderian visited the Hermann Göring Division and was incensed to discover that the Luftwaffe had gathered 34,000 troops into this formation. Guderian later wrote that, 'the majority of this large number of men were leading a pleasant life in Holland. In view of our replacement problem this was intolerable, even in 1943.'[8] Nevertheless, Guderian utterly failed to prevent either the Waffen-SS or the Luftwaffe from diverting resources from his programme of revitalizing the Heer Panzer-Divisionen.

German Tactical and Doctrinal Changes

The German *Bewegungskrieg* (manoeuvre warfare) doctrine that had worked so well during 1940–42 was built around a combined arms team comprised of tanks, mechanized infantry, motorized engineers, self-propelled artillery and other elements, supported by abundant Luftwaffe close air support. In operational terms, the German preference for *Bewegungskrieg* was to conduct deliberate offensives under the most favourable circumstances – i.e. with full-strength units in fair weather. German armoured strength was to be applied to enemy weakness – an open or vulnerable flank or a poorly-guarded sector like the Ardennes – in order to achieve overwhelming combat power at the *Schwerpunkt* or decisive point. By focusing priority of tactical effort against a single *Schwerpunkt*, a decisive breakthrough could be achieved and the mechanized forces would pour into the enemy's rear and then envelop his main body. After that, it was merely a matter of mopping up the encircled enemy in a *Kessel* (cauldron) battle.

While the Germans were able to achieve this standard with Operation *Barbarossa* in 1941, and with *Fridericus, Trappenjagd* and *Blau* in 1942, by 1943 the Germans were being forced to violate their own doctrine and conduct offensives without proper combined arms tactics and with less regard for the *Schwerpunkt* concept. During Operation *Wintergewitter,* the Stalingrad relief effort in December 1942, Hoth's panzers had attacked with virtually no infantry and negligible air support. From that point onward, Soviet offensives would force the Germans to mount major armoured operations in winter until the end of the war – usually to save encircled units – and typically conducted as hasty attacks with understrength units. By mid-February 1943, von Manstein would be forced to conduct counter-attacks with Heer Panzer-Divisionen that had been reduced to fewer than a dozen operational tanks and this tended to become increasingly commonplace throughout much of 1943. The necessity of conducting mobile operations even in winter and under less-than-favourable circumstances led to doctrinal modifications.

The foremost modification to German *Bewegungskrieg* was a realization that Luftwaffe close air support was no longer a given. While the Luftwaffe could still occasionally muster substantial numbers of Ju-87 Stukas and bombers for a major operation like *Zitadelle* in mid-1943, most relief efforts would receive modest air support at best. The declining ability of the Luftwaffe to support offensive operations meant that manoeuvre units required more organic firepower in order to blast their way through stout defences. At the beginning of the war, German Panzer-Divisionen relied upon speed to accomplish their missions, not firepower or armoured protection. The Pz II, Pz III and Pz IV had been adequate, even against the occasional T-34 or KV-1, as long as the Luftwaffe was available. Indeed, the units that normally formed the Panzer-Division's *Vorausabteilung* (advance guard) were the divisional Aufklärungs-Abteilung (Reconnaissance Battalion) and Kradschützen-Abteilung, equipped primarily with armoured cars and motorcycles. However, the increase in Soviet defensive capabilities by late 1942 meant that thin-skinned German tanks and motorcycle units could no longer easily penetrate the enemy's front line as they had in the past. Thus, due to the shortfall in close air support and improved Soviet defences, German tactics shifted from an emphasis upon speed and mobility, to tactics based upon shock effect and firepower.

Reflective of this trend, in January 1943 the organization of Panzer-Divisionen was modified and all Kradschützen-Abteilungen and the Aufklärungs-Abteilungen were supposedly merged into a new Panzer-Aufklärungs-Abteilung, although it took most of 1943 to implement this new structure. The Panzer-Aufklärungs-Abteilung was a powerful armoured force, authorized 122 halftracks and 18 armoured cars, which gave it the ability to 'fight for intelligence' rather than act merely as scouts. As this new structure was introduced, the reconnaissance battalions in German Panzer and Panzergrenadier Divisionen became de facto manoeuvre units and were often used as such. German tactical doctrine was revised to assign a variety of potential missions to these versatile units, including advance guard, rearguard and even counter-attacks.

Another major modification to German manoeuvre doctrine was an increased emphasis upon zone defence, decentralized operations and local counter-attacks. Although German doctrine preferred to maintain a *Hauptkampflinie* (HKL or main line of resistance) with infantry divisions and to keep Panzer-Divisionen in reserve in the rear, this was no longer possible by January 1943. By that point, most Panzer-Divisionen in Heeresgruppe A and B were forced to hold their own sector of the front, which deprived the army commander of mobile reserves. When a Soviet breakthrough in another sector occurred, local infantry corps commanders would demand that the nearest Panzer-Division respond by dispatching a Kampfgruppen to launch a counter-attack; the inevitable result was that Panzer-Divisionen in defence were parcelled out into small Kampfgruppen to support various hard-pressed infantry units, losing mass and being diluted into the 'driblets' that Guderian had decried in 1939–40. Rather than being used properly as an independent manoeuvre force, German panzers were increasingly likely to be used to stiffen infantry units in the defence or mount company-size counter-attacks.

Of course, German tanks and other armoured vehicles were evolving rapidly by 1943, based upon two years of combat experience on the Eastern Front. Several painful encounters with the superior Soviet T-34 and KV-1 tanks had caused the Germans to question the value of their existing tanks and to seek a technical solution that would ensure German armoured superiority. The resulting OKH Panzer Commissions of July and October 1941 began the process of defining the requirements for a new medium tank which resulted in the development of the Panther tank in 1942.[9] As 1943 began, the Pz V Panther was about to begin serial production and was expected to re-equip one tank battalion in each Panzer-Divisionen as soon as possible. While the Pz V had far superior gunnery capabilities compared to earlier German models, it was a medium tank in name only and its 44-ton bulk would be far too heavy to cross existing tactical bridges. The Panther was also a fuel-hog that used double the amount of fuel to move 100km compared to a Pz III and, like the 54-ton Tiger, it was difficult to recover on the battlefield. Taken together, the shift to reliance upon heavily-armoured and up-gunned tanks like the Panther and Tiger meant that previous German mobile tactics became impractical; these tanks could not slash cross-country, covering up to 100km in a day, and would have to rely upon shock effect rather than manoeuvre.

The introduction of so many turret-less assault guns and thin-skinned Panzerjäger like the Marder series also caused the Germans to revise their armoured doctrine. In the first two years of combat on the Eastern Front, German medium tanks – often outgunned by the T-34 – had learned to manoeuvre in close and seek the opportunity for flank shots. These aggressive tactics usually succeeded for a number of reasons and often resulted in Soviet positions being overrun. Yet while tanks could still overrun an enemy-held position in 1943, it was usually inadvisable to attempt this with assault guns or Panzerjäger, which were better suited for defensive combat. The real threat was concealed enemy anti-tank guns, which were very difficult to spot from a vehicle like a StuG-III assault gun. Instead, the Germans increasingly began to favour long-range, stand-off engagements so that their assault guns and Panzerjäger would not be put at risk from enemy anti-tank guns or infantry ambushes, but this removed a great deal of the shock effect from German armoured operations.

German Tank Training

In the first years of the Second World War, Germany was able to maintain very high standards of training for its Panzertruppen, which gave them an enormous tactical edge over their opponents. However, the edge was beginning to dull as casualties mounted in 1941–42 and the German training system could not keep pace with losses. For example, during the Caucasus Campaign in 1942, the three Panzer-Divisionen (3., 13., 23.) in von Kleist's 1.Panzerarmee were suffering an average of 600–1,200 casualties per month, including 150–300 killed.[10] Over the course of four months from July–October 1942, this amounted to 3,000 casualties for 3.Panzer-Division, including 600 dead or missing. Throughout 1942, the 23.Panzer-Division suffered a total of 6,569 casualties, including 2,079 dead or missing; 16.8 per cent of these casualties were in Panzer-Regiment 201 (including 331 dead or missing).[11] Although Panzertruppen losses were much lower than the Panzergrenadiers, a much higher proportion of tanker casualties were officers or NCOs. Nor were losses only due to enemy action; in addition to frostbite casualties in the long winter months, diseases such as typhus inflicted significant losses on German Panzertruppen – one Panzer Kompanie in Panzer-Regiment 35 suffered 12 dead from this cause.[12] Approximately two-thirds of all wounded returned to duty with their units. Thus while losses could vary greatly depending upon the operational tempo, the average Panzer-Division on the Eastern Front required something like 400–500 replacement tankers per year in order to keep a 960-man Panzer-Regiment up to authorized strength.

Replacements for the Panzer-Divisionen on the Eastern Front came from the affiliated Panzer-Ersatz-Abteilung in their home Wehrkreis. For example, the 23.Panzer-Division received its Panzertruppen replacements from Panzer-Ersatz-Abteilung 7 in Wehrkreis V (Stuttgart). In theory, a replacement unit like this could train up to about 1,000 new enlisted recruits per year – well above the loss rates on the Eastern Front – but many fewer officers and NCOs. Yet not all recruits passed basic training (some were reassigned to other branches) and even among graduates, not all went to replace combat losses. Obergefreiter Armin Bottger spent two years in a replacement battalion along with a number of his fellow tankers, ferrying tanks to railheads and working at the OKH tank depot at Sagan, before finally going to the front.[13] By mid-war, the Heer had a long logistical tail and replacements were siphoned off to a myriad of other training and non-combat duties. When the 12 Panzer-Abteilungen were destroyed at Stalingrad, thousands of replacements were diverted to rebuild these units – at the expense of the units in the East. Consequently, the front-line Panzer-Regiments on the Eastern Front generally received 1:1 replacements for enlisted tank crewmen, but an insufficient number of junior officers and NCOs.

German Panzer-Ersatz-Abteilungen used obsolete tanks like the Pz I and Pz II for driver training and initial panzer familiarization, but recruits then moved on to obsolescent short-barreled versions of the Pz III and Pz IV tanks for manoeuvre and gunnery training. The Germans made a particular fetish of producing skilled tank drivers, something to which Soviet training attached no great value. During initial basic training, selected recruits could earn a driver permit for tanks up to 10 tons, but required another four weeks of training to earn the permit for tracked vehicles over 10 tons.[14] Experience had shown that a good tank driver had to acquire a good deal of situational awareness in moving across the battlefield, using cover and concealment to avoid enemy observation and to keep the tank oriented toward the direction of threat. A good driver was also capable of making his own tactical selection of route, without being constantly told what to do; in contrast, Soviet tank drivers often expected to be told exactly where and when to move. Nevertheless, both fuel and time allotted for driving training in 1943 were much reduced compared to previous years and, in particular, the rush to get units equipped with Tiger tanks to the Eastern Front led to Tiger crews receiving insufficient driver training at Paderborn, which resulted in numerous accidents at the front.[15]

In 1943, the Heer was forced to shorten basic training for Panzer crewmen from 16 to 12 weeks by introducing a *Kurzausbildung* (abbreviated training).[16] By this measure, the Heer intended to increase replacement output by one-third. The new training regime placed greatest emphasis on tank gunnery and teaching 'battle drills' that prepared a tank crew for combat in conditions that were as realistic as possible. All classroom training was cut to an absolute minimum and recruits were expected to spend most of their time in a field training environment. Most of the inculcation of old-style Prussian military discipline through marching and drill was abandoned. After basic training, the most promising recruits were sent to NCO training for 4–6 weeks and gunners were sent to advanced gunnery training at sites such as the Putlos range. German gunnery training was very advanced and began with training gunners to conduct a proper boresight of the main gun. Usually strings or wire were affixed in a cross pattern across the muzzle and the loader would look through the open breech and visually lay the gun on a target board approximately 800–1,200 metres distant. Then the gunner would adjust the elevation and deflection knobs on his primary sight, to put the gun tube and sight in synch, followed by a zeroing fire with 3–5 rounds. The zero fire confirmed the accuracy of the boresight and enabled final corrections to the gunner's primary sight. With a good boresight, a tank crew could be reasonably certain that a gunner had a 25–30 per cent chance of hitting a target at the normal combat boresight ranges of 800–1,200 meters. Boresighting and zeroing were key characteristics that distinguished German from Soviet tankers and enabled them to have a much higher probability of achieving hits. However, boresighting and zeroing required discipline and good small unit leadership, since it needed to be conducted soon after any long tactical road march or movement over rough terrain. It is easy, after a night movement in the rain, to put off such details, but it was the kind of detail that made all the difference on the battlefield.

Soviet tankers were astounded to discover in 1945 that German gunnery ranges included both moving and pop-up targets.[17] German tank gunnery employed a number of different drills, employing armour-piercing (*Panzergranate*) against stationary, frontal tank-size targets and moving targets moving obliquely to the tank. Crews were also trained to use high-explosive (*Sprenggranate*) rounds against anti-tank guns and machine-guns against troop targets. While the ammunition used for training was limited and often not the same calibre that would be used by the crew in actual combat, a panzer crew in 1943 could expect to fire the equivalent of a basic load of ammunition during the course of training. After hard experience in Russia, German tank gunnery training also emphasized low-visibility and night training scenarios to accustom crews to the reality that combat did not always occur under the best conditions.

By 1943, most of the junior panzer officers were former enlisted men or NCOs who were awarded reserve commissions after attending Panzertruppenschule I or II. The term 'reserve officer' suggests a callow, hastily-trained officer with limited ability to lead troops in the field, but Germany's wartime reserve officers were anything but '90-day wonders'. Rather, these men usually had the advantage of prior combat service, often in tanks, although some candidates came from other branches as well. One example was 20-year-old Leutnant der Reserve (d.R.) Otto Carius, who had served as a tank loader in the opening weeks of Operation *Barbarossa*, then was promoted to Unteroffizier in August 1941 before receiving his commission in 1942. By the time he was assigned to schwere Panzer-Abteilung 502 as a platoon leader in January 1943, Carius was a veteran tanker and would ably prove himself as a leader at the front.[18]

The introduction of the Tiger tank in late 1942 and the Panther tank in early 1943 forced the Germans to make major adjustments to their tank training programmes. Even veteran panzer crews and the unit-level mechanics required extensive training on the new vehicles, since they were so different from the existing Pz III and Pz IV medium tanks. A special unit, Panzer-Ersatz-Abteilung 500, was established at Paderborn to train all Tiger tank crews and mechanics; this unit could train 24 crews at a time. However, the demand for Tigers at the front was so extreme in 1943 that most crews passed through the training course in 4–6 weeks, which was barely sufficient. In March 1943, the Panther Lehrgänge (Training Course) was established at Erlangen, which provided convenient technical support from the manufacturer MAN in Nurnberg. Manoeuvre and gunnery training for Panther crews was conducted at Grafenwöhr, but like the Tiger training, the Panther training was rushed. Important items, such as training crews how to recover a 45- or 54-ton tank on the battlefield, received minimal time. Since the Germans intended to convert one Panzer-Abteilung in each Panzer-Division to the Panther, there was great pressure to push crews rapidly through the training, which would soon cause major problems in combat. Furthermore, neither the Waffen-SS nor the Luftwaffe had their own training structure for Panzertruppen and simply borrowed the Heer's – which seriously interfered with the introduction of the Panther in 1943.

Impact of Fuel and Spare Parts Shortages
By 1943, shortages of fuel and spare parts at the front were seriously reducing the operational readiness of Germany's Panzer-Divisionen. The Third Reich went to war with the Soviet Union with completely inadequate fuel reserves and exhausted nearly half its stockpile during Operation *Barbarossa* in 1941. Although Germany made great efforts to increase synthetic fuel production, during 1942 monthly military consumption of fuel exceeded production in seven out of 12 months. At the end of 1942, Germany's reserve stockpile of motor gasoline was down to 313,000 tons, equivalent to less than three months' worth. By 1943, minus civilian consumption, Germany was producing about 136,000 tons of motor gasoline per month and consuming about 120,000 tons – enabling a slight increase in the strategic reserve. In addition, about 47,500 tons of diesel oil per was produced per month.[19] Thus, Germany's military machine was living a hand-to-mouth existence that left little or no room for unanticipated losses of production due to enemy action, such as Allied bombing. Nor could the Germans really afford to continue to mount large-scale manoeuvre operations like *Barbarossa* and *Blau* without further depleting their reserves; the new norm shifted to mount short-objective operations measured in weeks, not months.

German fuel logistics were measured in *Verbrauchssatz* (abbreviated to V.S.); 1 V.S. was the amount of fuel required to move every vehicle in a unit 100km. German doctrine stated that a Panzer-Division should possess at least 4 V.S. prior to the start of offensive operations. The amount of fuel in 1 V.S. varied considerably depending upon the type of vehicles in use; the German tanks of 1941–42 were much more economical than the heavier tanks and self-propelled guns of 1943–45. In 1941, 1 V.S. of fuel for a Panzer-Division was roughly 150,000 litres (measured in cubic metres, cbm, with 1 cbm equivalent to 1,000 litres) or 150 cbm or 111 tons of fuel. Yet while it only required between 340–360 litres of fuel to move a Pz III or Pz IV 100km, it required 720 litres for the Panther and 711 litres for the Tiger. Likewise, equipping the Panzer-Division with more tracked vehicles such as self-propelled artillery and more SPW halftracks nearly doubled the amount of fuel required for operations. Increased armament and increased armoured protection resulted in much more fuel being consumed, which became something of a vicious circle for the Panzerwaffe.

In order to keep some kind of strategic fuel buffer, panzer units training in Germany and Western Europe were given only modest amounts of fuel for training. Basic driver training on the Pz I was essentially unaffected since this obsolete light tank was fairly fuel efficient, but it had a major impact on the Panther and Tiger conversion courses. Drivers were given less training time on these fuel hogs in order to save fuel for the front, but this meant that many of the new Panther drivers did not get sufficient cross-country experience. Units sent to train in France were shocked to find that there was no stockpile of fuel and ammunition available there for training. One newly-formed unit, the schwere Panzerjäger-Abteilung 560, equipped with the new Hornisse tank destroyer, was sent to France to train in April 1943 but received no fuel and only ten rounds of 8.8cm ammunition per company. Soon afterwards, the unit deployed to the Eastern Front with no driver training and only a familiarization fire for the gunners.

An additional complication with fuel supplies was actually getting the fuel to the forward areas in the Soviet Union, which was a laborious process and fraught with risks from bad weather, partisan activity and Soviet air attacks on rail centres and fuel storage areas. In the first winter on the Eastern Front, about 80 per cent of the Deutsche Reichsbahn's (DR) trains suffered mechanical failures in the extreme cold, which reduced daily supply deliveries to one-third of required demand. Due to the destruction of railroad bridges over the Dnepr River, the Germans were also forced to send trains on a circuitous route to reach Heeresgruppe Süd during the 1942 campaign. The situation eased a bit in 1943, since the Germans were no longer gaining significant amounts of ground and were able to re-gauge most rail lines so trains could run up fairly close to the front, which helped reduce distribution problems. Nevertheless, the general weakness of the captured Soviet rail net made it difficult for the Germans to achieve the necessary throughput, with the result that trains carrying fuel and spare parts often did not arrive in a timely manner or with the quantities required. In addition to transportation difficulties, the OKH assigned priority of supplies to the main effort, which usually lay in the Heeresgruppe Süd portion of the front; units assigned to Heeresgruppe Mitte and Nord did not have priority and were allotted much less fuel, ammunition and spare parts.

The German Panzer-Divisionen on the Eastern Front were regularly plagued by shortages of spare parts for tanks, as well as wheeled vehicles. Over 1,000 panzers were awaiting repair at the start of 1943. One root cause of these shortages was the lack of standardization, resulting in trying to operate equipment from multiple manufacturers and countries – this was a severe problem in the 1941 campaign. Yet by 1943 virtually all of the Czech-made Pz 38t tanks and French-made trucks were gone, and there were usually adequate amounts of Pz III and Pz IV spare parts reaching the front. Many of the inoperative tanks would be repaired, once the overworked repair units were able to focus on something other than retreating. However, the introduction of the Tiger and Panther complicated the spare parts situation again. First, the *Heereswaffenamt* (Army Weapons Department) had ordered very few spare parts for the two new tank models, instead preferring to concentrate on production. Consequently, the schwere-Panzer-Abteilung received only one spare engine and one spare transmission for every ten Tiger tanks.[20] The spare parts situation with the Panther was also quite severe in mid-1943, when faulty components such as the fuel pump malfunctioned more frequently than expected. Normally, it is best not to commit a new weapon system into battle until an adequate stock of spare parts can be accumulated at the front, but Hitler pressured the OKH into prematurely sending both tanks into combat. Nor did it help that the Tiger and Panther used different size road wheels and track, as well as different engines, transmissions and armaments than the Pz III and Pz IV tanks, so the possibility of using any existing parts was almost nil. Taken together, the spare parts crisis hit the new tank models the hardest in 1943, ensuring lower-than-expected operational readiness rates, while the proven Pz IV had a relatively stable logistical pipeline in place.

German Tank Production

After three years of operating well below capacity, the Third Reich finally got serious about increasing its tank production output after the reality of the Stalingrad debacle began to sink in. Prior to Stalingrad, in September 1942, Hitler had ordered production of tanks and Sturmgeschütz (assault guns) tripled from 380–400 units per month over the next two years, which was rather a leisurely build-up. Yet once the 6.Armee was surrounded at Stalingrad and the relief operation had failed, it became increasingly clear to even Hitler and his inner circle that Germany was facing a real crisis and needed to quickly restore its combat power on the Eastern Front as well as preparing for the increased likelihood of a Western Front.

On 22–23 January 1943, Hitler met with *Reichsminister für Bewaffnung und Munition* Albert Speer, who had gained his position after the death of the less-than-efficient Fritz Todt in February 1942. Hitler now ordered Speer to increase the production of Armoured Fighting Vehicles (AFV) five-fold by the end of 1944. The so-called 'Adolf Hitler Panzer Program' that Speer hastily developed called for a monthly production quota of between 1,100 AFVs by early 1944 and 2,000 or more by the end of the year. Yet in January 1943, German factories still built only 248 tanks, including 35 Tigers and 163 Pz IV medium tanks, plus 130 assault guns and 140 tank destroyers; a total of 518 AFVs. In contrast, Soviet industry built 1,433 tanks in January, including 1,030 T-34, plus 57 self-propelled guns. The main German tank, the Pz IV Ausf G, was being out-built 6–1 by its main competitor, the T-34; this production imbalance handicapped the Panzer-Divisionen on the Eastern Front since they were always fighting at a huge numerical disadvantage.

Speer was not without talent, but as economic historian Adam Tooze has noted, his highly-touted 'production miracle' was part propaganda and unsustainable improvisations.[21] The two levers that determined German tank production output were the availability of labour and steel, which were both constrained resources in the Third Reich's wartime economy. Speer was able to temporarily get more steel for the Adolf Hitler Panzer Program, but as Tooze notes, this still only amounted to 15 per cent of the steel allotted for German armaments production; instead, the lion's share of the monthly steel allotment went to ammunition and aircraft production. Speer was also able to get forced labor from the occupied countries. In 1941, there were fewer than 50,000 employees working in the entire German tank industry and its sub-contractors, but this was increased to 160,000 in late 1943. One-third of the new workers were low-skill and unmotivated foreign workers.[22] Furthermore, Germany's industrial priorities kept shifting between aircraft, ammunition, tanks, U-Boats, the Atlantic Wall project and other flavour-of-the-month projects like the V-2 rocket, which made it difficult to establish consistent levels of output. Shortages of copper and rubber also made it difficult to increase tank production; Germany imported most of its copper and a large percentage of it went for ammunition production, but each Pz IV required 195 kg of copper.[23] Likewise, tanks needed rubber for their road wheels and by 1943, German factories were forced to make a new type of roadwheel that used 50 per cent less rubber; it worked, but it was noisier and wore out more quickly.[24]

Speer had Hitler's full backing in centralizing Germany's armaments industry and increasing AFV production. An easy decision, taken late in 1942, was to terminate Pz III production and instead have the Alkett factory focus exclusively upon StuG III Sturmgeschütz production. By early 1943, Speer's organizational reforms were beginning to bear some fruit as German tank and assault gun production slowly began to increase, but it would be March before Pz IV monthly production broke the 200-mark and October before it went over 300. Guderian cooperated closely with Speer in trying to increase German tank production and both realized that the only efficient way for Germany to narrow the gap with Soviet tank output was to focus on one or two proven designs. Guderian favored focusing on boosting Pz IV production to at least 400 per month and delaying the introduction of the Panther until it was thoroughly tested and its technical defects remedied. He was ignored.

Hitler respected Guderian, but had limited tolerance for his brash opinions. On the other hand, Dr Ferdinand Porsche, who had developed the Volkswagen in 1936, had Hitler's ear – even though that project had only been a propaganda success.[25] Porsche not only joined the Nazi party, but the SS as well, and Hitler recognized him as a 'great German engineer'. Once the war began, Porsche sought ways to contribute to the military effort – and to stay in Hitler's inner circle – so he connived to get himself appointed as *Hauptausschusses Panzerwagen und Zugmaschinen*, in charge of managing tank production – but he was a dismal failure. Next, Porsche decided to try his hand at designing tanks, despite the fact that he had no technical experience at all in designing armoured vehicles. Porsche developed his concepts of tank design from his imagination, not from practical requirements based upon combat experience or the needs of front-line tankers. Indeed, Porsche was particularly enamoured of gargantuan-size tanks, even though these were inconsistent with the German Army's *Bewegungskrieg* manoeuvre doctrine – of which he was ignorant. However, what Porsche lacked as a tank designer, he made up for as a sycophant, being able to convince Hitler that his ridiculous projects deserved priority.

The three largest German tank manufacturers in terms of total output in 1943 were the *Nibelungenwerke* in St Valentin, Austria, VOMAG in Plauen, Saxony and the *Krupp-Grusonwerk* in Magdeburg. These three plants employed about 9,000 workers and built 52 per cent of Germany's tanks in 1943. However, the largest manufacturer of AFVs was Alkett in Berlin, which had 3,500 employees and built over 2,000 assault guns in 1943. Altogether, seven German firms with about 25,000 employees assembled almost all of the tanks, assault guns and tank destroyers for the Wehrmacht. Although skilled workers were a critical bottleneck in expanding tank production, particularly welders and electricians, German industry had far greater access to raw materials than their opposite numbers in Soviet industry. Due to the German conquests of 1941–42, the Soviet Union had lost control over more than half of its critical resources such as aluminum, iron ore and coal. Indeed, the Germans were able to send manganese back from the captured mines at Nikopol and Krivoy Rog, which was used in the production of armour plate for German tanks.[26] Consequently, by 1943 Germany was out-producing the Soviet Union by 4–1 in steel production. The difference was that Germany was also building U-Boats, halftracks and a wide variety of different equipment that the Soviet Union simply opted not to build. Consequently, German industry lost the production battle to Soviet industry in 1942–43 and bears a large portion of the responsibility for the eventual defeat of the Panzer-Divisionen. Why was German tank production decisively out-stripped by Soviet tank production?

A classic example of German inefficiency in tank production is the *Nibelungenwerke* in Austria, which was built from scratch between 1939–41 at the cost of RM 65.7 million and was intended to produce 150 Pz IV tanks per month in 1942. However, just as the plant was reaching initial operational capability (IOC) in January 1942, the OKH decided to escalate the long-dormant heavy tank program. The *Nibelungenwerke* was directed to work with Porsche in developing and building his VK 4501(P) Tiger prototype, while Henschel built its own VK 4501 (H) project. Despite the fact that Porsche's design was plagued with technical problems, the Nazi hierarchy ensured that it was assigned higher priority than Pz IV production and the two largest workshops at the *Nibelungenwerke* were given over to Dr Porsche's project. Enter Karl Otto Saur, Speer's deputy in the *Reichsminister für Bewaffnung und Munition*. Saur was also an ardent Nazi and issued orders to both Henschel and Porsche that they would complete their prototypes for the Tiger competition by Hitler's birthday on 20 April 1942. Remarkably, the *Nibelungenwerke* was able to meet this arbitrary schedule and assemble a single VK 4501(P) prototype, but this came at the cost of restricting Pz IV production to just 2–8 tanks per month for the first five months of the year. Adding insult to injury, Speer recognized that the VK 4501(P) prototype was technically unreliable and terminated the programme, awarding the production contract for the Tiger to Henschel instead. However, Porsche continued to be one of Hitler's favourites, so he was handed a consolation prize: the *Nibelungenwerke* would build 90 VK 4501(P) hulls, which Porsche would convert into an as-yet-undesigned Ferdinand heavy tank destroyer. Just as the *Nibelungenwerke* was ramping up to build 32 Pz IV tanks in November 1942, the staff were informed that the Ferdinand now had top priority and assembly had to be completed by April 1943. Half the workspace of Workshop VII, intended for Pz IV assembly, was handed over to Porsche for his Ferdinand project. Consequently, thanks to Porsche and Saur's Nazi cronyism, the *Nibelungenwerke* only built the miniscule total of 186 Pz IV tanks during 1942 instead of the 1,800 planned. The Ferdinand programme prevented any significant increase in Pz IV production for months and it was not until June 1943 that the *Nibelungenwerke* was able to raise its monthly output to 120 Pz IV Ausf H. Since the *Nibelungenwerke* was also responsible for producing spare road wheels for the Pz IV, this output was also significantly impaired until spring 1943.[27] Stalin never tolerated this kind of disruption of critical war production, but it was commonplace in the Third Reich.

Nor were the problems at the *Nibelungenwerke* unique. In addition to his faulty VK 4501(P) prototype, Porsche wanted to build a super-heavy tank and built a wooden prototype, which was demonstrated to Hitler, Guderian and other dignitaries on 1 May 1943. Porsche intended to build a 188-ton tank, mounting the new 12.8cm Pak gun. Guderian rejected this concept as ridiculous, but Hitler liked the idea and authorized a production run of 150 units, to be known as the Maus. Both Krupp and Alkett were ordered to provide production space and technical personnel to assist Porsche on his fool's errand of constructing the largest tank in the world. Not to be left behind in the super-heavy field, Henschel began development of its own version of a 140-ton tank armed with a 12.8cm gun in June 1943. Indeed, Hitler was so impressed with the firing trials of the 12.8cm gun that he ordered that it should be mounted on a future variant of either the Tiger or Panther – this was despite the fact that the 7.5cm KwK 42 and 8.8cm KwK 36 were more than adequate to defeat Soviet tanks. Hitler's whimsical decision meant that just as the *Nibelungenwerke* was ramping up Pz IV production after Kursk, it was ordered to devote resources to design and produce a new heavy tank destroyer, which would become the Jagdtiger.

The ripple effect of Porsche's unrealistic designs and Hitler's love of 'gigantic' weapons hit the German tank industry hard throughout 1943–44, diverting resources from the production of proven designs in favour of experimentation gone wild.

As if Porsche's experimentation was not a big enough distraction, most of the German tank plants were still operating well below capacity even after Stalingrad. In Kassel, the Henschel plant, the sole manufacturer of the Tiger tank, continued to devote two-thirds of its production space to the construction of locomotives, not tanks. While it was supposedly ramping up for full-scale production of the new Panther tank, the MAN factory in Nurnberg continued to produce trucks, because they were regarded as 'essential for the company's survival in the post-war economy'. Speer's deputy, Saur, kept trying to get MAN to shut down its truck line in order to expand Panther production, but the company management just ignored him.[28] Heading into 1943, German manufacturing procedures were still not really geared toward mass assembly of tanks. Many businessmen were concerned that Hitler could shift armaments priorities on a whim – as he had decided to do at the start of *Barbarossa* in 1941 – and were reluctant to invest capital in developing excess production capacity in military factories when they were assured by the regime once again in 1942 that victory was imminent. At mid-war, most German tank plants were still not operating at full capacity due to severe labour shortages and Speer was astounded that the plants were not running a second shift.[29] Henschel was the first to institute two 12-hour shifts in late 1942 and by early 1943 Speer pressed the other companies into following suit. However, the only way to quickly add additional shifts was to boost reliance on foreign forced labor, including prisoners of war, which further reduced efficiency in the factories.

Another factor that hindered a significant increase in German tank production in 1943 was the over-engineered nature of German tanks and the finicky criteria retained by the Heereswaffenamt inspectors to evaluate completed tanks. For decades, most sources have claimed that the Tiger tank required 300,000 man hours to complete, or roughly double the time required to build a Panther. Yet other sources state that the Panther required 55,000 man hours, and another authoritative source states that a single complete Panther could be built in just 2,000 man hours.[30] In fact these numbers are over-simplistic, because the production rate of Panther tanks at various German factories varied considerably – there was no standard rate. However, by 1944 the MAN factory employed 4,483 employees directly involved in tank manufacture and assembly, who together spent roughly 1.6 million man hours per month on this task. Since MAN's production of Panthers in 1944 topped off at 140–155 Panthers per month, this means than a single late-model Panther required at least 10,400–11,500 man hours to complete.[31] Obviously the early Panther Ausf D, plagued by technical faults, required many more hours than the late-run Panther, but the same could be said about the T-34 or any other tank. It is clear that as German tanks became more sophisticated after 1942, the amount of time and effort required to build just one of them greatly exceeded the amount of time and effort that Soviet industry needed to construct several T-34s. Even after Stalingrad, the Heereswaffenamt inspectors at the *Nibelungenwerke* were rejecting completed tanks due to 'un-polished welds' and 'non-standard painting' – i.e. for aesthetics. This kind of nonsense continued until mid-1943 until the Battle of Kursk, after which Speer pushed factories to expedite production by simplifying construction procedures and lowering standards; these changes resulted in much greater output in 1944. Yet based on the numbers from MAN, it is clear that even after Speer's improved efficiencies, a Panther still required three times as much labour effort as a T-34 to produce.

Allied strategic bombing also had some effect on German tank production, although Alkett was the only factory that was seriously disrupted in 1943. Panther production was temporarily reduced in August 1943 when the MAN plant was bombed twice.[32] The Henschel plant in Kassel was bombed by the RAF in October 1943 and also suffered some disruption in Tiger tank production.[33] In November 1943, a major RAF raid on Berlin left much of Alkett's Berlin- Borsigwalde plant in ruins, which severely disrupted StuG III production for about six weeks. Reacting hastily, Hitler decided in December 1943 to terminate Pz IV production at the Krupp-Grusonwerk AG plant and instead use Pz IV hulls to build the new Jagdpanzer IV assault gun. Guderian opposed this decision, pointing out that Alkett would soon restore StuG III production and that Hitler had already authorized a new tank destroyer to be built on the Panther hull (the Jagdpanther), armed with an 8.8cm Pak 43. It made little sense for Germany to further reduce its tank output in order to produce another assault gun variant, but again he was ignored.

The RAF bombing of the Ruhr in March–June 1943 also caused the *Zulieferungskrise* (sub-component crisis) in which delays in the arrival of sub-components delayed AFV construction at the main plants.[34] For example, a Pz IV assembled at the *Nibelungenwerke* received its turret from Magdeburg, its main gun from Dusseldorf, its engine from Friedrichshafen and various other sub-components from across the Reich. Allied bombing increasingly disrupted rail yards in central Germany, causing delay in the internal transport network. Without a large stockpile of critical sub-components on hand, the main tank plants became increasingly vulnerable to transportation disruptions. Allied bombing also induced second- and third-ordered effects, by causing distribution problems with raw materials and damaging the myriad of small manufacturers who built unique items for tanks.

The Red Army's Tank Forces
In 1943, the Red Army had six different kinds of armoured units with a variety of missions committed on the Eastern Front:

- Tank Armies, intended to be capable of large-scale mobile operations. Although the Red Army had created five tank armies in 1942, both the 1st and 4th Tank Armies were disbanded after suffering crippling combat losses in August 1942. At the start of 1943, the 2nd, 3rd and 5th Tank Armies were still active. These formations were supposed to consist of two tank corps and one mechanized corps with about 500 tanks, but the tank armies were still rather improvised in nature.
- Tank Corps (consisting of three tank brigades and a motorized rifle brigade), were intended for either independent mobile operations or as part of a larger Tank Army. As defined by Stalin's Order No.325 in October, the primary purpose of the Soviet Tank Corps was to destroy enemy infantry, not fight enemy tank formations. At authorized strength, the Corps should have 159 tanks (96 T-34 and 63 T-70) in six tank battalions and 3,200 infantry in six motorized infantry battalions and one motorcycle battalion. However, fire support was limited to a single Guards Mortar Battalion with eight BM-13 multiple rocket launchers, which was a serious deficiency.
- Mechanized Corps (consisting of three mechanized brigades and usually a tank brigade or two tank regiments) were intended to act primarily as a breakthrough and pursuit force for the front-level commander. A full-strength mechanized corps should have 170–200 tanks in five tank regiments and almost 6,000 motorized infantrymen in nine battalions. The mechanized corps had additional fire support that the tank corps lacked, including three light artillery battalions (each with 12 76.2mm guns) and additional mortars. However, the mechanized corps was critically short of trucks to move its infantry brigades and was forced to mount a good portion of its infantry on tanks. By late 1944, the arrival of large numbers of Lend-Lease trucks would alleviate this shortage and greatly enhance the mobility of Soviet mechanized corps.[35]
- Tank Brigades (consisting of two tank battalions and a motorized rifle battalion), were the basic building-block of Soviet manoeuvre warfare. For most of 1943, a tank brigade was authorized 32 T-34 medium tanks and 21 T-70 light tanks (or Lend-Lease equivalents). A medium tank battalion was usually led by a Kapetan or Major and had two tank companies, each with 10 T-34 tanks, plus one for the commander. In terms of support, the tank battalion was authorized a 27-man supply platoon, which was supposed to have 13 trucks (including three for fuel and two for ammunition).[36] The brigade had only modest reconnaissance capability (a scout platoon with three armoured cars) and no fire support – it was not a combined arms team but rather a tank-heavy formation. Consequently, Soviet Tank Brigades were best used as sub-components in a larger formation, but they could and did serve as independent infantry support units as well. By 1943, the trend was increasingly to incorporate tank brigades into larger formations in order to maximize their shock power.

- Tank Regiments were separate formations used in either the breakthrough or infantry support role, and often equipped with heavy tanks. In January 1943 the tank regiment consisted of either 32 T-34 and seven T-70 or 21 KV-series heavy tanks. Unlike the tank brigade, the tank regiment had no organic infantry component and its armour was usually employed as individual companies, not battalions.[37] Most of the KV-series tanks were being assigned to newly-formed Guards Heavy Tank Regiments.
- Independent Tank Battalions (OTB) were usually separate formations tasked with the infantry support role. The OTBs were extremely heterogeneous in composition and could include up to five KV-series heavy tanks, 11 T-34s or equivalent Lend-Lease tanks and 20 light tanks. A few OTBs were equipped with flamethrower tanks or captured German tanks. A full-strength OTB had 36 tanks, but these units tended to stay at the front for long periods of time and typical strength was more like 10–20, with some reduced to just a handful of operational tanks.[38] By 1943, these units were being phased out since they were a relic of the improvisation days of 1941.

On 1 January 1943, the Red Army had a total of 20 tank Corps, 11 Mechanized Corps, 120 tank brigades, 91 tank regiments and 68 OTBs. According to Krivosheev's data, at that time the Red Army had 20,600 tanks on hand, of which 7,600 were medium tanks (T-34 or M3 Grant) and 2,000 were KV-series heavy tanks. The remaining 11,000 tanks were light T-60s and T-70s or Lend-Lease Matildas, Valentines, Lees and Stuarts.[39] A small number of American M4A2 Shermans had arrived via the Persian Corridor in late 1942, but were just beginning to be fielded. Some of the Soviet armoured units that had been heavily engaged in the December 1942 fighting, such as the 24th and 25th Tank Corps, had very few tanks operational, but most Soviet tank units had at least 50 per cent of their tanks operational. Unlike the Germans, the Red Army did not divert sizeable amounts of armour to quiet fronts; in 1943 there were some 2,500 tanks (mostly obsolete T-26 and BT-7 light tanks) deployed in the Far East and a few hundred on the Turkish-Iranian borders. The Stavka's Reserve (RVGK) contained two tank corps, four tank brigades, three tank regiments and three OTBs, amounting to about 700 tanks. In addition, there were over 2,000 tanks in the Moscow, Volga and Trans-Baykal Military Districts. This left approximately 14,000 Soviet tanks at or near the front, with perhaps 7–8,000 operational. This meant that the roughly 1,000 operational German tanks and assault guns on the Eastern Front were outnumbered by more than 7:1, which far exceeded the textbook 3:1 numerical advantage required for a successful attack.

However, only 30 per cent of the Red Army's armour was deployed in large-scale tank and mechanized corps, while the rest was still employed in smaller units geared toward the infantry support role. The *Narodnyi Kommisariat Oborony* (NKO or People's Commissariat of Defence), which directed organizational changes, was acting to change this imbalance by gradually phasing out many of the OTBs and consolidating more brigades within corps-size structures, but this would not be fully realized until 1944. Thus, the maintenance of so many smaller tank units tended to make it difficult for the Soviet fronts to mass decisive combat power and to maintain it through a protracted battle of attrition. Brigade size and smaller tank units could be consumed in a single action, which often caused Soviet offensive pulses to lose momentum at critical moments.

At the start of 1943, the Red Army's tank units relied primarily upon the T-34/76 medium tank (known to Soviet tankers as the *Tridtsat'chetverka*), which had the excellent V-2 diesel engine, sloped armour and the decent 76.2mm F-34 gun. Yet while the T-34 had been an impressive weapon in 1941–42, it had seen only modest evolutionary improvement during the first two years of the war due to the NKO's desire to achieve maximum production, rather than tinker with the design. The basic ammunition load, typically 75 OF-350 HE-Frag rounds and 25 BR-350A APHE rounds indicated that the T-34/76 was primarily intended to attack soft targets, not other tanks. A new hexagonal turret had been introduced in 1942, along with slightly thicker armoured protection, but there was no change in firepower and crew ergonomics – particularly for the commander – were suboptimal. The lack of a commander's cupola, which German tanks had, seriously reduced the situational awareness of T-34 tank commanders. The T-34 did receive one upgrade in 1943 that made a real difference: more and better tactical radios. Stalin had not appreciated the value of the electronics industry, so it had a low priority in the pre-war Five Year Plans. Consequently, Soviet industry was not able to manufacture enough radios for each tank and during 1941–42 only platoon leaders and above received a radio in their tank. Furthermore, the NKO failed to evacuate pre-war electronics factories eastward in 1941, so Soviet domestic manufacture of tank radios fell off sharply in 1942. However, in 1943 the British began supplying radio components in large quantities to the Soviet Union, which was able to introduce an improved 9R radio for the T-34 and by late 1943, most Soviet tanks were equipped with a radio or at least a receiver.[40] Brigade and higher-level communications remained problematic throughout 1943, since the Tank Brigade command post was only provided with two 12-RP radio sets with a range of only 8km.[41]

The Red Army's other two domestically-built tanks, the KV-1 heavy tank and the T-70 light tank, added little to overall armoured capabilities. Since the beginning of the war, the KV-1 heavy tank had failed to properly fulfill its role as a breakthrough tank due to persistent mobility issues with its inadequate transmission – it was unable to keep up with other Soviet tanks. In order to improve mobility, the KV-1S tank was introduced in December 1942, which was five tons lighter than previous models; this increased off-road speed from 13 to 24km/hour but at the cost of reducing armoured protection by 30 per cent. Consequently, the KV-1S was only marginally faster, but significantly more vulnerable. Recognizing that the KV-1 series was a technological dead-end, the NKO decided to relegate KV-1 tanks to separate heavy tank regiments and to cease production as soon as a better alternative was available. Finally, the ubiquitous T-70 light tank was in most Soviet tank units from battalion to corps as a filler, until more medium tanks were available. The NKO knew that the T-70 could not stand up to even the German Pz III series tanks, but there was little alternative. What the T-70 lacked in firepower and armoured protection, it made up for in sheer numbers.

Unlike the German Heer, the Red Army had failed to make a significant investment in halftracks, which negatively affected the mobility of the mechanized infantry units within tank formations and impaired their logistic support capabilities in mud and snow. There was no Soviet equivalent of the German Sd. Kfz. 250/251 type armoured personnel carriers and the limited number of U.S. M2 and M5 halftracks delivered under Lend-Lease were usually used as command vehicles or prime movers for artillery, not to transport infantry. Instead, the Red Army continued to rely upon tanks to transport a significant amount of infantry on their decks in the *desant* role. Soviet industry had developed the ZIS-22 halftrack (based upon the ZIS-5 truck) and the GAZ-60 halftrack in the mid-1930s, but only about 1,100 were built before the German invasion and most were lost in the first year of the war. In 1942, the ZIS-42 halftrack entered large-scale production, but this vehicle's mobility in snow and mud was very poor. Consequently, the Red Army's tank units were not provided with either the quantity or quality of German tracked support vehicles – an important but often ignored deficiency.

Soviet Tactical and Doctrinal Changes
On 16 October 1942, Stalin had issued Order No.325, which outlined a host of problems noted in the Red Army's use of tanks in combat. Foremost was a lack of coordination between tanks and supporting infantry, artillery, engineers and aviation, which led to an inability to conduct the kind of combined arms warfare employed by German panzer units. A second significant problem was a failure of tank commanders to conduct proper reconnaissance or to use terrain properly; consequently, Soviet tank units had tended to 'wander onto the battlefield', unsure of where the enemy was located and ignorant of obstacles, including minefields. Finally, Soviet tank commanders at brigade and above often attempted to exercise Command and Control (C^2) over their units from fixed command posts and did not rely on radios, since they had few. Instead, Soviet tank commanders issued a rigid operations order with a very simplistic scheme of manoeuvre – usually a frontal attack – and expected subordinate battalions and brigades to fulfill it to the letter. This rigid Soviet tactical C^2 style was the polar opposite of the German doctrine, which relied upon front-line leadership and flexibility through radio-coordinated operations. Consequently, Soviet tank units had been routinely bested by smaller German panzer units, due to their inherently rigid style of battle command. Although he made a fairly

accurate assessment of shortfalls in Soviet armoured operations, Stalin failed to note that he was often responsible for causing many of these problems, by bullying commanders to prematurely start offensives and depriving them of time to coordinate with other units or to conduct proper reconnaissance.[42]

Order No.325 began the process of Red Army tankers learning from their mistakes and trying to close the gap in capabilities between them and their German opponents. The order stressed the importance of a well-planned artillery preparation and close-infantry tank coordination in the attack. Instead of tangling with German tanks – as had often happened in 1941–42 – Soviet tank corps were ordered to focus on destroying the enemy infantry, leaving artillery and anti-tank units to deal with German tanks. The order also stressed proper terrain reconnaissance and the use of surprise and deception (*maskirovka*) to catch the enemy off guard. Of course, it was easy for Stalin to dictate orders, but this standard became the doctrinal guidepost for the Red Army's tankers heading into 1943.

One of the foremost tactical and doctrinal changes that the Red Army did begin to adopt in 1943 was the introduction of the *Samokhodnaya Ustanovka* (SUs or self-propelled guns), which were modelled on the German Sturmgeschütz. The Su-76, which mounted the reliable 76.2mm ZIS-3 anti-tank gun on a lengthened T-70 chassis, could be built in great quantity. The Su-122, mounting a 122mm howitzer on a T-34 chassis, offered Soviet mechanized infantry units a real boost in direct fire support. Altogether, the creation of regimental-size units equipped with SUs reflected a desire within the Red Army to hand off much of the infantry support mission to AFVs other than tanks. Although early technical problems slowed the introduction of the SU-equipped regiments in 1943, this step would gradually free more tanks to conduct offensive manoeuvre warfare rather than being tied to infantry units. Those tanks that remained in the infantry support role were increasingly assigned to the new separate tank regiments.

In 1942, the Red Army had created tank armies and tank corps, but they were really just large collections of tanks with little in the way of supporting arms. This began to change in 1943, as the Red Army absorbed combat lessons learned from the Germans at great cost in 1941–42 and laboured to create their own balanced combined arms formations in line with Stalin's Order 325. In January 1943, the NKO moved to strengthen Tank Corps by adding a mortar regiment with 36 120mm mortars and an SU Regiment equipped with 8 SU-76 and 8 SU-122s. Furthermore, in order to improve the staying power of the Tank Corps, it was authorized an additional 33 T-34 and seven T-70 as spares; the addition of an extra battalion's worth of tanks would give Red Army tankers an edge in attritional battles like Kursk. In February 1943, the engineer component in the Tank Corps was upgraded from a company-size unit to a battalion. In March, the same increase occurred with the integral signal unit and an anti-aircraft regiment with 16 37mm guns was added. In April, the NKO decided to increase the anti-tank component of the Tank Corps in response to the improvement of German armoured capabilities, particularly the Tiger tank; each Tank Corps was authorized an anti-tank regiment, which had a mix of 20 45mm, 57mm and 76.2mm guns, and a separate anti-tank battalion with 12 towed 85mm 52-K AA guns. The decision to employ the 85mm 52-K AA gun to counter German heavy armoured vehicles would substantially add to Soviet defensive capabilities at Kursk.

Although a number of Red Army leaders recognized the need to go beyond the tactical prescriptions of Order No.325, and that larger, better-equipped tank and mechanized formations might actually be able to execute something akin to the pre-war Deep Battle (*glubokiy boy*) doctrine, the risk of failure inclined them towards conservative progress toward this goal, rather than a rapid shift in doctrine. Noticeably, Order 325 really only addressed the tactical breakthrough battle and said very little about operational art. Key leaders in the Red Army, such as Georgy Zhukov and Vasilevsky, recognized the need to improve operational technique rather than just to rely upon mass, which had rarely prevailed in the counter-offensives of 1941–42. The best minds in the Red Army knew that mass was not enough to defeat an opponent as skillful as the Wehrmacht. One of the first steps toward a doctrinal shift at the operational level was the increased use of echelonment in both offensive and defensive formations. Whereas the Germans tended to employ everything they had from the outset of an operation, Red Army leaders were beginning to learn the value of feeding fresh formations in at critical moments in order to keep up momentum. Previously, Soviet offensives had tended to commit all or most of their armour up front, as at Kharkov in May 1942, incurring huge losses and rapid loss of capability. For short periods of time, the Germans demonstrated that they could defeat Soviet mass, but echeloned offensive operations enabled the Red Army to conduct protracted offensives that gradually exhausted a German-style defence. Use of echelonment enabled Soviet commanders to use their numerical advantages to best effect. Echelonment would also be used in defence, at Kursk.

Another subtle change in Soviet armoured doctrine was a growing realization that there would have to be increased emphasis on 'push' logistics, i.e. getting fuel and ammunition resupply to fast-moving tank units at the front in order to sustain the pace of advance, rather than just waiting for the rear echelons to arrive. Up to November 1942, the Red Army had spent more time retreating than advancing and had been able to rely upon resupply from nearby railheads. Yet it was the lack of emphasis upon forward logistics that marred the Red Army's first execution of Deep Operations (*glubokaya operatsiya*) with the Tatsinskaya Raid in December 1942; the 24th Tank Corps succeeded in capturing this important German airfield, but the Southwest Front was unable to resupply the immobilized corps, which became encircled by two German Panzer-Divisionen and was virtually annihilated. In order to make this change, more trucks, radios and support troops would have to be allocated to Soviet armoured units and the haphazard style of staff planning drastically improved. Thus, the improvement of logistical sustainment over long distances and the staff planning processes to make this occur when and where it was most needed were an essential requirement for the Red Army to begin conducting large-scale advances westward. These changes did not come easily.

Soviet Tank Training

During the first two years of the war, the Red Army had been desperate to crank out as many tankers as possible and had created a plethora of training units. Prior to the war, the Red Army had operated a number of Tank Training Schools (STU, *Tankovoye Uchilishche*) to train officers; by 1943 there were still more than a dozen STU with two each in Gorky, Kazan and Ulyanovsk and three in Saratov. Each STU could train about 500 tank commanders in a six-month long course. In addition, there were also higher-level courses for battalion and regimental commanders at the VAMM, which was initially evacuated to Tashkent but brought back to Moscow in 1943. Most of the tank training units were stationed near the factories that built the tanks, which simplified the creation of replacement crews. A number of Tank Automotive Training Centres (UABTTS or *Uchebnyy Avtobronetankovyy Tsentr*) were created around the tank factories to coordinate and supervise subordinate tank training regiments and battalions. Training battalions were broken down by type of tank (heavy, medium and light) and there were separate units to train crews on American or British tanks. The Chelyabinsk UABTTS was the largest and its subordinate units could generate over 2,500 replacement crews in six months. A typical training battalion had about 1,190 students and 171 staff, while the training regiments had over 4,000 trainees.

Early in the war, the NKO had raided tank schools to harvest trained cadre for front-line service, which greatly impacted the quality of training in 1942. However, the situation began to improve when the NKO issued Order 003 on 3 January 1943 to rationalize and improve tank training by combining various separate tank training battalions into tank training brigades. Cadre with frontline experience – often wounded – were sent to revitalize the training schools, but the quality of Soviet tanker training still remained problematic throughout much of 1943. Even the T-34 training battalions still used obsolete T-26 and BT-7 light tanks for training. Most of the instruction for crewmen was rote in nature, producing drivers and gunners who had attained only a modest level of familiarity with their tanks. In the training schools, there was virtually no realistic field training and tanks were taught merely to move using simple line and column tactics. Leytenant Pavlov V. Bryukhov, who trained at the Kurgan Tank Training School from January to April 1943, described training as 'very weak'. Bryukhov said that, 'they only taught us the basics – starting the engine and driving straight. We had tactical training, but it was mostly walking about on foot imitating the manoeuvreing of tanks'. Soviet tank platoon leaders were not even trained to read maps, which became a real problem once the Red Army began advancing westward.[43] Enlisted soldiers were segregated into training battalions that trained a single skill – driver, gunner or loader – which meant that they were not cross-trained in other tasks, as German tankers were.

Driver skills and manoeuvreing training over typical cross-country terrain were extremely basic, but gunnery training remained deficient throughout the war. Indeed, given the amount of effort put into increasing tank production, it is an amazing oversight that the NKO put so little effort into training Soviet tankers to execute their main tasks of manoeuvreing and shooting. Gunnery training was particularly deficient and handed a major advantage to German tankers. Bryukhov noted that after he graduated from the Kurgan Tank School he was assigned to a reserve tank regiment where 'we received a tank, drove it fifty kilometers to a firing range and fired three rounds from the main gun and one machine-gun ammo drum, after which the tank was considered officially ready for shipment to the front.'[44] Soviet tank gunners and commanders were taught to engage targets within 10 seconds, which was an eternity on the battlefield; the German standard was five seconds for the first round on the way. In combat, German tankers noted how slowly Soviet tankers fired – which was how they were trained. Nor was any effort made to teach Soviet tankers how to lead a moving target or use boresighting techniques, so Soviet optical sights were not properly aligned with the gun barrel, greatly reducing the accuracy of the main gun. Given these standards, it is truly amazing that Soviet tankers managed to hit as many German tanks as they actually did. The only saving grace for Soviet tankers was that as more tankers survived their first action in 1943–44, the veterans gradually learned essential skills that they should have been taught in training. In 1944, several tank training centres were established for Guards Tank units and crews at these sites received more firing and manoeuvre training, but still only a fraction of what most German tankers received.

Nevertheless, the annual output of tens of thousands of even partly-trained tankers was one of the great wartime miracles of the Soviet Union and helps to explain why the Red Army gradually gained the upper hand. Yet it was a frightfully wasteful method of replacing personnel losses, and had the Red Army built even a single modern gunnery training facility like Putlos and a manoeuvre training area like Grafenwöhr, Soviet tank losses would have dropped significantly and greater losses would have been inflicted on the Germans. Indeed, lack of attention to quality training constituted a self-inflicted wound for the Red Army, which was not resolved during the war. The Soviet Communist approach to warfare was driven by industrial imperatives, not concern for the well being of the 'little cogs' at the front.

Soviet Tank Production and Lend-Lease
Initially, Stalin had selected Vyacheslav Malyshev, an engineer with great experience expanding Soviet heavy industry in the Five Year Plans, as his People's Commissar of the Tank Industry (NKTP). Malyshev had worked

wonders during the industrial evacuations of 1941 and jump-starting tank production at Chelyabinsk and Nizhniy Tagil. However, Malyshev was more of an industrial manager and had no direct experience with designing armoured vehicles. In July 1942, Stalin had decided to replace Malyshev as NKTP with Isaac M. Salzman, the former director of the Kirov plant in Leningrad. Salzman was certainly more knowledgeable about tanks, but he was also involved in the rivalries between the three primary Soviet tank design bureaux and he tended to favour engineers and designs that originated from the Kirov group. During Salzman's tenure, T-34 production hit its highest mark in December 1942, with 1,568 units built. However, Salzman was directed by the NKO not to effect any major changes in existing tank designs that could reduce production output, and the same went for trying to develop new tanks. Consequently, a certain inertia and stagnation settled into the Soviet tank industry on Salzman's watch, even though he was discouraged from taking proactive steps to match advances in German tank technology.

Thanks to the efforts of both Malyshev and Salzman, Soviet industry was able to expand tank production to outstrip Germany's industrial output. Automatic welding techniques were introduced to speed up assembly-line procedures. Additionally, constant efforts to cut corners resulted in reducing the man hours required to manufacture a single T-34 tank from 5,300–9,000 hours in early 1942 to 3,700–7,200 hours by January 1943.[45] The Nizhniy Tagil factory (renamed the Stalin Ural Tank Factory183) achieved the greatest efficiencies in tank production and was building nearly half of all T-34s. However, the emphasis upon reducing labour input for tank production – although statistically pleasing to Soviet labor officials – resulted in a serious decline in the quality of tanks being built. The new cast turret, introduced in late 1942, was plagued with fractures and the hulls produced at Nizhniy Tagil and Sverdlovsk also had a high rate of cracks. Even the heretofore reliable V2 diesel engine suffered an increased rate of failures and tests in 1942 indicated that the mean-time-between-failure for the engine was 200–300km instead of the design specification of 1,000km.[46] Consequently, the Soviet tanks that were used in the early campaigns of 1943 tended to be less mechanically reliable, particularly with crews that were ignorant about preventative maintenance.

It is important to note that while Soviet industry was able to consistently out-produce the German tank industry, the Soviet Union only had one front to worry about and its tank factories were not being bombed. Nor did the Soviet Union have to divert steel to naval production, while Germany expended considerable industrial resources in 1942–44 in building up its U-Boat fleet. Furthermore, in order to boost tank production in 1941–42, the Soviets had to convert one of their primary truck factories, GAZ, to manufacturing light tanks. Consequently, Soviet domestic production of trucks was significantly less than that of Germany and the difference was only made up by Lend-Lease. The situation was even worse in terms of armoured halftracks (see Table 1), which were essential for employing mechanized infantry in fast-moving armoured formations. The Soviet Union never developed a vehicle that was analogous to the German SPW and relied entirely upon a small number of U.S.-built M2 halftracks and M3A1 scout cars to outfit the mechanized infantry in a few chosen Guards units. None of the Soviet mechanized infantry units in 1943 were fully motorized and were forced to use the expedient of *Desant* (landing), whereby at least one battalion in each brigade rode atop tanks. Thus while outnumbered in terms of tanks, German mechanized units retained a significant edge in motorization over the Red Army until mid-1944, when the balance finally shifted in favour of the Soviets.

Type	Germany		USSR		Lend-Lease	
	1943	1944	1943	1944	1943	1944
Armoured Halftracks (SPW)	7,153	9,486	0	0	c.1,330	c.1,770
Trucks	94,963	75,474	41,600	57,400	80,900	122,100

Table 1: Comparison of Halftrack and Truck Production, 1943–44

Lend-Lease also continued to provide important augmentation to the Red Army's tank strength in 1943–44. During 1943, the Soviet Union received another 2,995 Lend-Lease tanks from the Western Allies: 2,102 from the British (1,776 Valentine, 179 Churchill and 147 Matilda) and 893 from the United States (469 M4A2 Sherman, 260 M3/M5 Stuart and 164 M3 Lee).[47] In addition, the Soviets received 41 M31s, an armoured recovery vehicle based on the Lee tank, for which they had no equivalent. Although the Soviets often complained about the quality of Lend-Lease tanks, the Shermans and Valentines both proved reliable and were retained in service to the end of the war.

Although Soviet armoured fighting vehicle production exceeded that of Germany, few realize that it essentially hit its ceiling in late 1942–early 1943. Afterwards, the introduction of any new design such as the T-34/85 and IS-2 significantly impacted production. The NKO was considering an upgraded version of the T-34 tank and was interested in a new heavy tank to replace the KV-1, but was unwilling to divert resources to these efforts while the Germans were still reeling from the Stalingrad debacle. The one area where the NKO gave Salzman some leeway was on the SU programme, since it wanted to replace the T-70 light tank with a better-armed vehicle. Salzman put one of his engineers from the old OKMO design bureau, Semyon A. Ginzburg, in charge of developing the SU-76 self-propelled gun. General-polkovnik Nikolai D. Yakovlev's Main Artillery Directorate provided the 76.2mm ZIS-3 gun for the new vehicle. Using a lengthened T-70 chassis, Ginzburg designed a lightly-armoured housing for the ZIS-3 gun atop the hull and had a prototype ready in December 1942. Salzman approved the prototype for limited production without trials and the first SU-76 were built before the end of 1942. In January 1943, a few of these SU-76 were sent to the Volkhov Front, where they proved to be a complete failure. The T-70's two GAZ-202 truck engines had been adequate to move the T-70 light tank, but the addition of an extra ton of weight was too much and the SU-76 was difficult to steer and its transmission was inadequate. A clear sign that the vehicle was underpowered was the high number of final drive failures. Salzmann and Ginzburg tried to fix the design problems of the SU-76, but this caused production to cease in April 1943.

Unlike Hitler, Stalin did not tolerate engineering failure and after six months of Ginzburg's fumbling with the SU-76 project, Stalin issued GKO Decree 3530ss on 7 June 1943, which stated that:

The State Committee of Defence [GKO] decrees that the SU-76 self-propelled guns, designed by comrade Ginzburg of the People's Commissariat of Tank Production [NKTP], and accepted by GOKO decree No.2559 on December 2, 1942, turned out to be of unsatisfactory quality. Furthermore, the NKTP (comrade Saltzman) and GAU KA (comrade Yakovlev) did not carry out trials with due diligence before accepting the SU-76 for production. The modifications proposed by the NKTP (comrade Saltzman) and GAU KA (comrade Yakovlev), confirmed by GOKO decree #3184ss on April 14, 1943, did not result in serious improvements and did not increase the quality of the SU-76 to satisfactory levels, which also suggests that the NKTP and GAU KA trials were executed poorly.

The State Committee of Defence decrees that:

Production of SU-76 SPGs at factory #38 must cease immediately.
The People's Commissar of Tank Production, comrade Saltzman, must be made aware of his mistakes regarding production of SU-76 SPGs at factory #38. The designer of the SU-76 SPG, comrade Ginzburg, must be removed from work at the NKTP, and not allowed to participate in NKTP projects further. He is to be transferred to the NKO for assignment to less critical work in the Acting Army. The NKTP (comrade Saltzman) and GAU KA (comrade Yakovlev) must find and punish guilty workers in the NKTP and GAU KA, which carelessly performed trials of the SU-76 SPG.

Ginzburg was removed from his position and sent to the front as deputy commander of the 32nd Tank Brigade, where he was killed in action two months later. Salzmann was forced to resign, but was reassigned as a director at Chelyabinsk. Malyshev was brought back to head the NKTP, which he remained in charge of until the end of the war. First, he resolved the problems with the SU-76, which was reissued as the SU-76M. Although still a problematic design, Malyshev ensured that it was built in great quantities and that its main faults were corrected. Next, he began lobbying Stalin and the NKO to approve an up-gunned version of the T-34 as well as a new heavy tank. The whole experience of the SU-76 program ably demonstrates the level of stress and micro-management that Soviet tank industry operated under; engineers and program managers who made mistakes would not remain in their positions. Stalin's bullying tactics were cruel but effective in getting the desired results within the Soviet industrial system.

Chapter 2

Armoured Operations in 1943

Retreat from the Caucasus, 1 January–2 February 1943

Operation *Edelweiss*, the German attempt to seize the Caucasus oil fields with Heeresgruppe A, culminated in October 1942 after having only seized the sabotaged oilfields around Maikop. When Generalfeldmarschall Ewald von Kleist's 1. Panzerarmee (PzAOK 1) entered the Caucasus in July 1942, it had over 600 tanks and assault guns and it was initially able to route the ill-equipped Soviet North Caucasus Front. However, the Soviets managed to hastily improvise a strong defensive line along the Terek River with the 9th Army, which brought von Kleist's pursuit to a halt. Although von Kleist succeeded in conducting an assault crossing of the Terek on 2 September, Soviet reinforcements and German fuel shortages brought his panzers to a halt 85km short of the Grozny oil fields. In early November, von Kleist made one last desperate effort to achieve a breakthrough, but the 13.Panzer-Division was encircled and nearly destroyed near Ordzhonikidze.[1] Thereafter, the 1.Panzerarmee settled into a positional defence along a nearly 200km-wide front, with the III Panzerkorps in the west, three infantry divisions of the LII Armeekorps in the centre and the XXXX Panzerkorps in the east. The Kalmyk Steppe between Heeresgruppe A's flank in the Caucasus and Heeresgruppe B's flank along the Don was screened by small detachments. Von Kleist moved up to take command of Heeresgruppe A and General der Kavallerie Eberhard von Mackensen took over PzAOK 1.

General-leytenant Ivan A. Maslennikov, an NKVD officer, commanded the Northern Group of the North Caucasus Front, which consisted of the 9th, 37th and 44th Armies. As soon as Maslennikov realized that von Kleist had shifted to the defensive, he began probing actions to find weak spots in the German line and the most dangerous area for the Germans was the area north of the Terek River held by General der Panzertruppen Sigfrid Henrici's XXXX Panzerkorps. Here, Generalmajor Franz Westhoven's 3.Panzer-Division held an extended 30km-wide front from Stoderevskaya on the Terek River to Aga Batyr on the Kalmyk Steppe.[2] On Westhoven's left flank, Korps z.b.V. Felmy, an improvised brigade-size formation led by Luftwaffe General der Flieger Hellmuth Felmy screened PzAOK 1's open northern flank. By doctrine, Panzer-Divisionen were offensive formations and unsuited for protracted defence, but von Kleist had no alternative and the situation grew even worse after the Soviet offensive at Stalingrad threatened Heeresgruppe B. On 21 November 1942 the *Oberkommando des Heeres* (OKH) ordered von Kleist to transfer his strongest formation, the 23.Panzer-Division, to Heeresgruppe Don in order

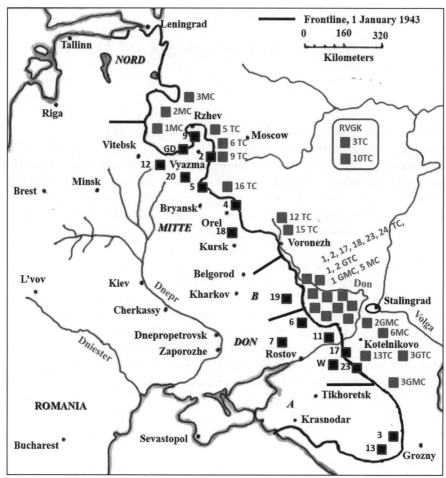

Disposition of German Panzer-Division and Soviet Tank/Mechanized Corps on 1 January 1943. Most of the major armoured formations are deployed on the Rostov–Stalingrad axis and around the Rzhev salient.

to participate in Operation *Wintergewitter*, the attempt to relieve the trapped 6.Armee at Stalingrad.[3] In mid-December, the SS-Panzergrenadier-Division *Wiking* was also transferred to Heeresgruppe Don, leaving PzAOK 1 badly outnumbered by Maslennikov's northern group.

Beginning in early December 1942, General-major Vasiliy A. Khomenko's 44th Army began mounting regular attacks with infantry and tanks all across the front of the 3.Panzer-Division. Khomenko was another NKVD officer with limited field experience and he had only a few small tank units, but the Soviet attacks were relentless and began to wear down the German defences. In three weeks of heavy defensive combat, the 3.Panzer-Division's Panzer-Regiment 6 lost a battalion commander and two veteran company commanders, while the commander of the SPW-equipped I./Panzergrenadier-Regiment 3 was also killed. Overall, PzAOK 1 suffered more than 5,000 casualties in December 1942. Khomenko's 44th Army also paid a heavy price for its aggressiveness, including 8,037 troops captured and 68 tanks lost, but its combat capabilities were actually increasing. Although Hitler was reluctant to cede territory since he believed that he could restart his Caucasus offensive in 1943, he finally agreed to let von Kleist pull back the XXXX Panzerkorps' most exposed positions and to create a straighter front line.

Nevertheless, by the end of December 1942 Westhoven's 3.Panzer-Division was in very poor condition. Due to the shortage of spare parts, the division only had about 30 operational tanks and a similar number of SPWs. Worn-out track and engines could not be replaced. Repeated enemy artillery bombardments damaged the rubber jacket on tank road wheels, which then led to 'chunking' when the vehicle moved, often resulting in track pins becoming bent or broken. However, there were no replacement road wheels or track pins en route. Thus, even the tanks that were declared operational had numerous mechanical faults, which degraded their performance. Panzer-Regiment 6 had started the campaign with three Panzer-Abteilungen, but was now forced to consolidate all of its remaining tanks into Panzer-Abteilung Stockmann. The surplus crews of the III./Pz.Regt. 6 were put into the line as infantrymen. Ammunition was in very short supply, as were radio batteries, which forced the Germans to limit their use of tactical radios. However, the worst deficiency was the crippling lack of fuel; the OKH gave priority of fuel to Generalfeldmarschall's Erich von Manstein's Heeresgruppe Don and Heeresgruppe A was told in late November to expect no more fuel deliveries for the time being. The supply situation became so critical that 3.Panzer-Division's logistic troops shifted entirely to Russian *Panje* carts for resupply of forward areas.[4] Consequently, the 3.Panzer-Division could not conduct a mobile defence and was forced to disperse its combat power into company- and battalion-size *stützpunkt* (strongpoints). By Christmas, it was obvious even to Hitler that PzAOK 1 could not remain in place and had to pull back or face gradual destruction. On 30 December, Hitler authorized PzAOK 1 to withdraw 100km to a line from Pyatigorsk to the Kuma River, to begin at dusk on 2 January 1943.

On the Soviet side, the Stavka wanted to follow up its success at Stalingrad by trapping Heeresgruppe A in the Caucasus. The Soviet South and Southwest Fronts were about to begin an offensive against Heeresgruppe Don with the objective of taking Rostov, which would sever von Kleist's line of communications. The Northern Group's mission was to push back von Kleist's PzAOK 1 and herd them toward destruction around Rostov. Meanwhile, the Black Sea Group, which had only a single tank brigade and a few OTBs, would mount supporting attacks against the 17.Armee around Tuapse and Novorossiysk, with the end goal of clearing the Kuban. The Stavka anticipated a 'second Stalingrad' in the Caucasus, with the bulk of Heeresgruppe A becoming isolated and eventually destroyed. However, in this case the Germans were aware of the danger and less inclined to be caught like fish in a barrel.

In order to carry out his part of the Stavka's grand design, Maslennikov prepared an even larger offensive to strike the left flank of the XXXX Panzerkorps. Khomenko's 9th Army was reinforced with the 4th and 5th Guards Cavalry Corps and additional tanks. Up to this point, Maslennikov had used his armour in company-size detachments and the North Caucasus Front had no tank corps. Yet it was clear that in order to penetrate the German defensive line and achieve a decisive breakthrough, the Soviets would have to mass their available armour at one point. In order to provide the 44th Army with an armoured shock force, General-major Georgy P. Lobanov formed a composite tank group from five separate tank units. Altogether, Tank Group Lobanov had 106 tanks (of which 46 were T-34s, 18 Valentines , 6 M3 Lees and 36 T-60/70) and 24 BA64 armoured cars, but no attached infantry or artillery. Maslennikov's intent was to attack north of the 3.Panzer-Division's *stützpunkt* at Aga-batyr, held by Kampfgruppe Hoffman (II./Panzergrenadier-Bataillon 3) and overwhelm the Kosaken-Regiment von Jungschultz (a German-led unit consisting of Caucasian volunteers); the 9th Rifle Corps would attack first and then Lobanov's tanks would pour through the gap.

Dawn on New Year's Day 1943 was cloaked in heavy fog, but the 44th Army began its artillery preparation on schedule. There was a light snowfall on the hardened ground and temperatures were just above freezing. Although the indirect fire was inaccurate in the fog, it was heavy enough to disrupt the defence and at 0900 hours Lobanov's tankers rolled forward behind the infantrymen of the 9th Rifle Corps. The Cossack cavalrymen gave way, exposing the flank of the German 3.Panzer-Division to envelopment. During the afternoon, Major Stockmann led 20 tanks from his battalion northward to try and block Lobanov's tanks, engaging in several skirmishes. The German tankers popped in and out of the fog, sniping at the flanks of the Soviet breakthrough corridor. Lobanov's group suffered a total loss of 17 tanks on the first day of the offensive but still made good progress. Westhoven realized that his flank was being turned and decided on his own to move up the time to begin the withdrawal by 24 hours. Stockmann's panzers were ordered to conduct a delaying action – despite the severe shortage of fuel – while the rest of the division began retreating westward to the Kuma River. For the next three days, Stockmann managed to delay Lobanov's armour and the 5th Guards Cavalry Corps while the bulk of 3.Panzer-Division slipped away. Numerous immobilized vehicles that could not be withdrawn were destroyed. On 3 January, Stockmann was forced to fight a large-scale tank battle near Piev, where Lobanov brought his T-34s into action. On the same day, the Soviet 9th and 37th Armies also began attacking the front of PzAOK 1 and the German retreat accelerated. However, Khomenko's 44th Army botched the pursuit operation and its tanks and cavalry had lost contact with the retreating XXXX Panzerkorps, allowing it to retreat to the Kuma River unhindered.

In order to re-energize the Soviet pursuit, Maslennikov formed a second tank group under Podpolkovnik Vladimir I. Filippov. Tank Group Filippov consisted of 123 tanks (including 31 T-34s) from seven different tank units that belonged to either the 9th Army or the front. Once the 9th Army was firmly across the Terek River, Filippov's armour was sent directly up the Prokhladnyy-Georgiyevsk road on 7 January to seize Mineralnye Vody. In this sector, the German 50.Infanterie-Division was retreating in very strung-out columns and made the mistake of assuming that it was fairly safe after crossing the Kura River, oblivious to the fact that the frozen river was not a serious obstacle to enemy tanks. Filippov's lead brigade came out of the early morning fog on 8 January and struck the I. and II./Grenadier-Regiment 122 near the village of Kommayak, 20km east of Georgiyevsk. In a four-hour action, the Soviet tankers destroyed two companies of German infantry and killed the battalion commander of I./GR 122, creating a hole in the centre of the new German defensive line. The next morning, Filippov tried to expand this breakthrough, but had almost no infantry or artillery support. Von Mackensen dispatched Kampfgruppe Hake from the 13.Panzer-Division and panzerjägers to deal with Filippov's incursion and a lively tank battle occurred on the morning of 9 January; the 140th Tank Brigade was defeated and lost 12 M3 Lees and two Valentines.

Nevertheless, by 10 January Maslennikov's 9th and 44th Armies were beginning to get across the frozen Kuma River in force, because the German frontline was merely a string of strongpoints with gaps in between. Both Lobanov's and Filippov's tank groups were across the river, along with cavalry and a few infantry brigades, which threatened to collapse the thin German main line of resistance (HKL). The 13.Panzer-Division, which was in even worse shape than the 3.Panzer-Division, made a brief stand in front of Mineralnye Vody to delay the Soviet tanks, then fell back toward Armavir. Westhoven's 3.Panzer-Division continued to fend off Lobanov's tanks, fighting another action on 11 January, before also retiring westward. Von Kleist was now aware that the Soviet Southern Front was aiming to close his retreat route through Rostov and opted to fall back toward Armavir, but this was only a waypoint along the path of evacuating the entire Caucasus. Hitler only grudgingly gave approval of tactical withdrawals as long as von Kleist promised to move PzAOK 1 toward the Kuban to hold a bridgehead in Caucasus, but he still refused to accede to von Manstein's and von Kleist's requests to transfer any part of PzAOK 1 to assist Heeresgruppe Don in the defence of Rostov.

Once PzAOK 1 pulled back from the Kuma River, Maslennikov's armour-cavalry pursuit forces lost contact with the retreating Germans again. The Soviet tank groups were not configured for pursuit operations since they lacked proper support units, which meant that the tankers were dependent upon refuelling from the 9th and 44th Armies, which lagged well to the rear. Only the Soviet cavalry corps, operating on the Kalmyk steppe, was able to maintain pressure on PzAOK 1's left flank. Yet rather than pursuing Soviet tanks and cavalry, the real problem for the retreating Germans was the icy roads and insufficient fuel. Hundreds of trucks and prime movers that ran out of fuel were blown up during the retreat. By ruthless economizing, PzAOK 1 was able to keep some of its vehicles running by abandoning others. Many disabled tanks were towed by Sd. Kfz. 9 (FAMO) recovery vehicles.[5] As SS-*Wiking*'s last tanks retreated to the bridge over the Don at Bataisk, they carried their frozen dead with them:

> We followed the oil pipeline back to Bataisk. Our dead comrades, whom we could no longer bury, accompanied us to Rostov. In one of the tanks lay Ustuf. Buscher, behind Flugel, the commander of the 2. Kompanie. He was shot in his tank, killed immediately. After a short time he was frozen stiff and it was impossible to extract him from the tank. We had to break his arm before we could remove him, but we did not want to leave him behind.[6]

Von Kleist steadily fell back, occasionally sparring with pursuing Soviet tanks, but also pausing here and there to repair vehicles. On 22 January, Hitler finally agreed to allow part of PzAOK 1 to retreat to Rostov and two days later he changed this to the entire army. Instead, the 17.Armee would retreat into and hold the Kuban bridgehead; this decision, although belated, enabled PzAOK 1 to contribute to shoring up the crumbling German front in the Donbas region instead of becoming isolated in the Kuban. On the night of 7–8 February, the last tank from the 16.Infanterie-Division (mot.) crossed the pontoon bridge over the Don at Bataisk into Rostov; then German pioneers blew up the bridge. Von Kleist had successfully completed a difficult 610km-long winter withdrawal under extremely unfavourable conditions and saved over 150,000 of his troops to fight again another day. Although PzAOK 1 had only suffered 1,455 casualties in January 1943 (including 398 dead or missing), it had been gutted in material terms. The PzAOK 1 had abandoned something like 600 vehicles in the retreat and had fewer than 40 tanks left by the time it reached Rostov; thus von Kleist's withdrawal was a moral victory for the Germans but a material victory for the Soviets.

The Soviet tank groups did about as well as could be expected of improvised formations, performing well against German infantry units, but much less well whenever German panzers appeared on the battlefield. Lobanov's group lost 70 tanks (incl. 31 T-34, 15 M3 Lee, 10 Valentines and 14 light tanks) in the month-long pursuit operation and suffered 471 casualties. Filippov's group lost 30 tanks to enemy action and 29 more to mechanical faults. Both tank groups had accomplished their immediate tactical purposes and were disbanded after the Germans evacuated the Caucasus, with remaining units returned to infantry support duties. The Stavka had realized its goal of recovering all of the Caucasus except for the Kuban, and reduced PzAOK 1 to a decimated horde of refugees.

The End at Stalingrad, 1 January–2 February 1943
After the failure of Operation *Wintergewitter* on 19 December 1942, Generaloberst Friedrich Paulus knew that the fate of his encircled 6.Armee at Stalingrad was sealed. While he still had 201,000 troops in 6.Armee, the Luftwaffe's failure to meet expectations with its airlift meant that Paulus' troops were not receiving even one-third of the food, fuel and ammunition required to sustain combat capability. Instead, the 6.Armee was consigned to a slow death by cold and starvation, which sapped the troops' will to fight. Amazingly, Paulus' armoured units still had 94 operational tanks and 31 assault guns at the beginning of January, although many of these vehicles were damaged. Since no spare parts were coming in by air, tanks and assault guns could only be kept functional by cannibalizing damaged vehicles; this stop-gap method kept some armour in the fight but gradually reduced much of the armour in the pocket to spare parts bins. Fuel was in very short supply, but 6.Armee was still able to issue 6 cbm (30,000 litres) of petrol on 30 December 1942, which was enough to provide limited mobility to its armoured vehicles.[7] Ammunition was also in short supply, but by taking ammunition from inoperative AFVs, the remaining tanks and assault guns likely still had 30–40 rounds each. Yet as the Red Army began to overrun one Luftwaffe airfield involved in the airlift after another – and the daily supply tonnage dropped to miniscule levels – the 6.Armee had to depend more upon the 300-odd anti-tank guns and 8.8cm flak guns still in the pocket, which were less dependent upon fuel but equally short of ammunition.

On 1 January 1943, the 6.Armee held a perimeter which was 53km long from east-west and 35km wide from north to south. Except for the urban terrain in Stalingrad, most of the 6.Armee's units were deployed on flat, treeless terrain that offered little cover. Daily temperatures hovered around 15–20 degrees F, but at night they dropped well below 0 degrees F, which caused plenty of frostbite casualties among infantrymen and tankers. Deep snow cover restricted mobility within the pocket. The key terrain within the pocket was the Pitomnik and Gumrak airfields, both near the centre. Even though Heeresgruppe Don's forces were in full retreat away from Stalingrad, Paulus kept 6.Armee deployed as if relief was still coming, with General der Panzertruppe Hans-Valentin Hube's XIV Panzerkorps holding the vulnerable Marinovka salient jutting out to the southwest. Hube placed two of his motorized infantry divisions in the salient with 46 panzers.[8] Paulus kept the 14.Panzer-Division in reserve, supporting the VIII Armeekorps' defence of the western side of the pocket. The rest of 6.Armee's armour was deployed on the northern side of the pocket, with General der Infanterie Karl Strecker's XI Armeekorps; the Soviets had been continuously attacking here in the Kotluban sector since September. Paulus reorganized his army for defence, dug-in and waited for the inevitable.

The Stavka had assigned General-polkovnik Konstantin K. Rokossovsky's Don Front the honour of destroying the trapped 6.Armee in Stalingrad, while the South and Southwest Fronts dealt with von Manstein's Heeresgruppe Don. Rokossovsky's ramshackle command included seven different-numbered armies whose subordinate units included 281,000 troops in 35 rifle divisions and 13 rifle brigades. Rokossovsky's infantry was worn out after months of fighting in Stalingrad, with most units reduced to 40–60 strength. Likewise, the Don Front's armoured strength was modest, since most of the available armour had gone to support the flanking attacks against the Romanians in November, then to stop the German relief effort in December. Rokossovsky had just four tank brigades, four tank regiments and one OTB, with barely 100 operational tanks spread across seven armies. In addition, the Don Front's logistic situation was only slightly better than that of the trapped 6.Armee, with infantrymen and tankers in forward areas subsisting on minimal rations. Consequently, the Don Front did not have a significant numerical superiority over the 6.Armee and the depleted condition of Rokossovsky's forces suggested a protracted battle of attrition to finish off Paulus' army.

Marshal of Artillery Nikolai N. Voronov, the commander of the Red Army's artillery, was sent as Stavka representative to the Don Front to help plan Operation *Koltso* (Ring), intended to begin on 10 January 1943. In order to reinforce Rokossovsky's Don Front for Operation *Koltso*, Voronov brought in about 30,000 infantry replacements as well as a large number of artillery units as reinforcements. The 11th Artillery Division was assigned to the Don Front, adding over 300 guns/heavy mortars and 16 multiple rocket launchers to Rokossovsky's arsenal. In addition, the Stavka sent 10 independent guards breakthrough tank regiments with 110 KV-1S heavy tanks and 21 Lend-Lease Churchill tanks to the Don Front to participate in Operation *Koltso*. However, Voronov planned Operation *Koltso* primarily as an artillery offensive, with infantry-armour shock groups only attacking once the German defences were thoroughly smashed. Don Front's main effort would be made against the western side of the pocket with the 21st, 24th and 65th Armies, while the 57th and 65th Armies made a supporting attack against the southern side of the pocket. Voronov confidently expected that *Koltso* would collapse the pocket in just four days. Yet it is clear that the Stavka greatly underestimated the residual combat power of the 6.Armee and failed to provide Rokossovsky with enough resources to achieve a quick victory.

While building up to Operation *Koltso*, Rokossovsky's Don Front limited themselves to mostly reconnaissance and raiding activity on 1–5 January, but on 6 January they began mounting a series of local attacks on the northern and western sides of the pocket. On 7 January, the Soviet 65th Army mounted a two rifle division attack against the German 44.Infanterie-Division on the western side of the pocket and succeeded in penetrating its defensive line (HKL) and inflicting significant casualties. In response, the VIII Armeekorps committed 24 tanks and a number of assault guns to contain the Soviet breakthrough, which exposed these units to concentrated Soviet artillery fire. Not only did the commitment of German armour fail to restore the former frontline in this sector, but it consumed fuel and ammunition for no gain. One of the cardinal rules of defence is not to commit one's reserves prematurely, and Paulus had allowed a substantial part of his armour in the western sector of the pocket to be committed before the main Soviet offensive had even begun. The simple fact was that 6.Armee was trying to hold too much terrain with too few troops and the only logical solution was to withdraw into a tighter perimeter, but Hitler would not accept even modest tactical adjustments at this point of a losing battle.

At 0805 hours (local time) on 10 January 1943, Operation *Koltso* began with a massive 55-minute artillery barrage. Despite some cloud cover, visibility was fairly good and the Soviet artillery fire hammered the German frontline positions. In the 65th Army sector on the western side of the pocket Voronov was able to mass over 500 guns/howitzers and 450 multiple rocket launchers across a 12km-wide attack sector – the highest Soviet artillery density yet of the war. Once the artillery fire lifted, Soviet ground attack aircraft from the 16th Air Army (16 VA) strafed and bombed German positions to the rear of the HKL. Around 0900 hours, the shock groups of the 65th Army, comprised of five rifle divisions supported by the 91st Tank Brigade and six tank regiments (a total of 111 tanks) advanced against the still-smoking positions of the 44.Infanterie-Division. A squad of Soviet infantrymen was mounted on the back deck of each tank. The 65th Army had almost half of Rokossovsky's armour, including about 60–70 KV-1S heavy tanks and 21 Churchill (Mk-IV) tanks in the 10th Guards Tank Regiment (10 GTR). The British-built Churchills were slower than the KV-1S but had slightly better armoured protection. On the flanks of the 65th Army, the 21st and 24th Armies launched smaller supporting attacks with a total of five rifle divisions and 27 tanks, intended to prevent the Germans from transferring units from these sectors to help the 44.Infanterie-Division. Clearly, the Red Army was learning how to mass combat power in a critical sector.

Although the front of the 44.Infanterie-Division was smashed in fairly quickly and four depleted infantry battalions were overrun, the remaining Sturmgeschütz and anti-tank guns inflicted a fearsome toll on the attacking Soviet armour.[9] At the tactical level, the Red Army's coordination between tanks and infantry was still fairly primitive and a platoon of three ex-Soviet 7.62cm PaK 36 (r) anti-tank guns from Panzerjäger-Abteilung 46 was able to pick off a number of the KV-1S tanks before the unit was overrun.[10] The other Soviet supporting attacks went fairly well. In the south, the 57th Army routed the Romanian 20th Infantry Division, causing the IV Armeekorps to recoil inward, abandoning 26 of its precious PaK guns.[11] In the Marinovka salient, Hauptmann Rudolf Haen's 1./Pz.Abt. 103 from the 3.Infanterie-Division (mot.), supported by some 8.8cm flak guns, managed to shoot up virtually all of the 21st Army's 18 tanks. However, by the end of the second day of the offensive, the XIV Panzerkorps' 3. and 29.Infanterie-Division (mot.) were increasingly exposed in the Marinovka salient and Haen's Panzer-Kompanie was isolated. Overall, Hube's corps lost 30 of its 46 tanks and 11 of 18 PaK guns in the first 48 hours of the Soviet offensive.[12] In the northwest, the 24th Army's attack forced Strecker's XI Armeekorps to commit the last four assault guns from Sturmgeschütz-Abteilung 177 at the Kotluban rail station. These four assault guns knocked out four Soviet tanks before two of the StuG IIIs were destroyed by direct hits and a third suffered a mobility kill when struck on its final drive. Likewise, the 6.Armee succeeded in limiting the Soviet advance by committing its remaining AFVs and PaK guns, but this only prevented a complete collapse. Due to ferocious German resistance, the Don Front suffered 26,000 casualties in the first three days of Operation *Koltso* and 135 out of 264 tanks were knocked out.[13] The KV-1S heavy tanks performed particularly poorly, with nearly three-quarters disabled – a very disappointing combat debut. Nevertheless, the western side of the pocket was nearly smashed in and the decimated German units from the IV and VIII Armeekorps and XIV Panzerkorps were forced to retreat toward Stalingrad. While Soviet armour losses were heavy, the Germans had also lost over 60 tanks and assault guns in the opening phase of Operation *Koltso*.

By 15 January, the 6.Armee had contracted into a much tighter perimeter closer to Stalingrad, but was forced to hold the outlying areas around Pitomnik and Gumrak airfields. Yet since Hube's XIV Panzerkorps was combat ineffective after five days of fighting, Paulus no longer had the means to defend the airfields. Almost all of the German tanks and assault guns were either knocked out or immobilized by lack of fuel, although Sturmgeschütz-Abteilung 243 still had two StuG IIIs defending Pitomnik and Sturmgeschütz-Abteilung 245 had a few at Gumrak. Hauptmann Haen from Panzer-Abteilung 103 had been badly wounded in action on 13 January but he was fortunate enough to be flown out on 15 January; those panzer crewmen still on their feet were turned into infantrymen.* Nearly one-third of 6.Armee's personnel had become casualties in five days of fighting, leaving fewer than 20,000 combat troops to hold the shrinking perimeter. Rokossovsky had hoped to split the German pocket into several easily-digestible sub-groups, but instead the 65th Army's attacks from the west and the 57th Army's attacks from south merely herded the 6.Armee in closer to Stalingrad. With only about 100 tanks still in operation, Rokossovsky used his armour in small groups to help his infantry mop up various German *Stützpunkte*. In some sectors, Soviet infantry was advancing with only 2–3 tanks in support, but German defensive capabilities were sharply decreased due to starvation, frostbite and limited ammunition. German Pak guns continued to destroy Soviet tanks, but now they were literally down to their last few rounds.

---

* Haen recovered and became the battalion commander of the rebuilt Panzer-Abteilung 103, which he led in the Italian Campaign. Remarkably, he survived the war but was shot in US captivity on the day after Germany's surrender in 1945.

On 16 January, infantrymen from the 51st Army overran Pitomnik airfield. After this, the battle began to slow down as Rokossovsky shifted toward more deliberate tactics, relying upon his superior artillery to decide the issue. The Don Front's remaining 110 tanks were reduced to a secondary role by this point and the German armour was essentially out of the battle. From 18–21 January, Rokossovsky paused his offensive in order to bring up his artillery and replenish his combat units, knowing that he could afford this luxury since Paulus could not replace any of his losses. The Luftwaffe's aerial resupply effort was reduced to a pitiful average of 86 tons per day; German soldiers were already starving to death and the last few German tanks were now immobilized by lack of fuel. On the morning of 22 January, Rokossovsky resumed his offensive and Gumrak fell the next day, which forced the Luftwaffe to resort to parachuting in a token amount of supplies each day. After that, the Don Front slowly pummelled the 6.Armee into submission, with Paulus surrendering on 31 January. The last German troops in Stalingrad surrendered on 2 February.

Stalingrad was a debacle for the German Panzertruppe and Sturmartillerie, removing three Panzer-Divisionen and three motorized infantry divisions with a total of 12 Panzer-Abteilungen, as well as four Sturmgeschütz-Abteilungen from the Heer order of battle. Although the loss of hundreds of tanks and assault guns was serious, they could be replaced. However, the loss of more than 5,000 veteran tankers and Sturmartillerie crewmen was grievous. Some panzer crewmen, mostly wounded like Haen and Oberst Hyazinth Graf Strachwitz, had been flown out. Major Willy Langkeit, commander of the II./Panzer-Regiment 36, was one of the few able-bodied tankers flown out of the pocket and he would be instrumental in rebuilding Panzer-Regiment 36. Hitler also intervened to save a few select senior officers, such as General der Panzertruppe Hube and four infantry division commanders. However, Hitler did not order the evacuation of any of the three Panzer-Divisionen commanders; Lattman from 14.Panzer-Division and von Lenski from 24.Panzer-Division both went into Soviet captivity and later collaborated with the anti-Nazi League of German Officers (BDO). Generalleutnant Günther von Angern, commander of the 16.Panzer-Division, committed suicide on 2 February 1943.

Hoth's Stand on the Manych River, 1–31 January 1943
At the start of January 1943, Generalfeldmarschall Erich von Manstein's Heeresgruppe Don was in retreat and barely able to hold a coherent front. Manstein's strongest formation was Generaloberst Hermann Hoth's 4.Panzerarmee (PzAOK 4), which consisted merely of the LVII Panzerkorps, part of a Luftwaffe field division and the remnants of the Romanian 4th Army. Nevertheless, General der Panzertruppe Friedrich Kirchner's LVII Panzerkorps possessed the 17. and 23.Panzer-Divisionen, the 16.Infanterie-Division (mot.) and Sturmgeschütz-Abteilung 203 and SS-Panzergrenadier-Division *Wiking* was just arriving from the Terek River front; altogether Kirchner's corps had

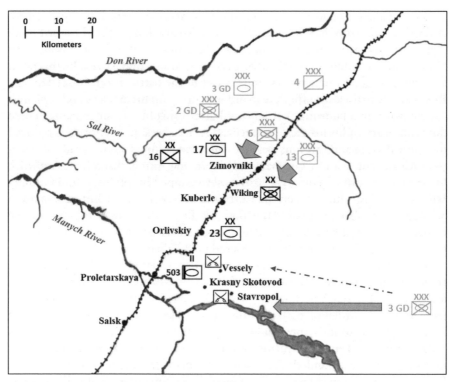

LVII Panzerkorps stand north of the Manych River, 5–11 January 1943.

fewer than 100 tanks and assault guns still operational. Having abandoned the Stalingrad relief effort, Hoth's Panzerarmee had retreated more than 100km down the Tikhoretsk-Stalingrad rail line toward the Manych River in the last half of December, pursued by General-polkovnik Andrei I. Eremenko's Southern Front. Manstein's other major formation was Gruppe Hollidt, which consisted of General der Panzertruppe Otto von Knobelsdorff's XXXXVIII Panzerkorps, the XVII and XXIX Armeekorps and Korps Mieth. General der Infanterie Karl A. Hollidt's ramshackle command had the 6., 11. and 22.Panzer-Divisionen assigned, with roughly 90 operational tanks and assault guns, as well parts of four infantry and two Luftwaffe field divisions. Hollidt's forces were in the process of retreating from the Chir River, pursued by General-polkovnik Nikolai F. Vatutin's Southwest Front.

Manstein's situation was grim, but he was about to receive some significant reinforcements in the shape of the rebuilt 7.Panzer-Division (156 tanks) just arriving from France and 2./s. Panzer-Abteilung 502 and 1., 2./s. Panzer-Abteilung 503 inbound with a total of 29 Tiger tanks and 35 Pz III Ausf N tanks. Obviously, German doctrine dictated that committing all these reinforcements in one sector would yield the most decisive results, but von Manstein was in a dilemma since he was facing crises in both Hollidt's and Hoth's sectors. He decided to split the reinforcements, sending all the Tigers to assist Hoth and 7.Panzer-Division to assist Hollidt.

By New Year's day, the first Tiger tanks were unloading at the rail station at Proletarskaya, just north of the Manych River. At that point, Kirchner's LVII Panzerkorps had established a thin screen with 17. and 23.Panzer-Divisionen and a Kampfgruppe from 16.Infanterie-Division (mot.) 75km to the northeast near Zimovniki, where 4.Panzerarmee quartermasters had established a supply dump. Although the rail line to Zimovniki was not really secure, some trains with replacement tanks and vehicles for Kirchner's corps were allowed to proceed there. The SS-*Wiking* Division was also detraining at Proletarskaya after its transfer from Heeresgruppe A; a single motorized battalion from SS-Panzergrenadier-Regiment *Westland* was moving rapidly up the road to Zimovniki, but the rest of the division was lagging well to the rear. Kirchner's forces were spread very thinly and their eastern flank was relatively open due to the disintegration of the Romanian 4th Army. Amazingly, only rear area troops were actually in Zimovniki when Soviet tanks appeared on the morning of 1 January.

Eremenko was advancing toward Proletarskaya with General-leytenant Rodion Ia. Malinovsky's powerful 2nd Guards Army and General-major Nikolai I. Trufanov's 51st Army, which altogether had two tank and three mechanized corps. Although Eremenko's armour was depleted after the heavy fighting since the beginning of Operation *Uranus* on 19 November 1942, he likely still had at least 300–400 operational tanks. Out in front was General-major Trofim I. Tanaschishin's 13th Tank Corps, approaching Zimovniki from the northeast. Tanaschishin was a veteran tanker who had been commanding armour units since the 1930s and he recognized that Hoth's frontline was fluid, so he decided to launch an immediate assault upon Zimovniki. Around 0830 hours, six tanks and a battalion of motorized infantry pushed into the northeastern corner of the town, catching the Germans completely by surprise. In panic, staff officers believed this handful of tanks to be the vanguard of Eremenko's host and ordered all stores and equipment at the rail station destroyed, including 47,000 winter uniforms and new tanks that had just arrived. All damaged vehicles in the repair units were also set on fire.[14] However, the Soviet incursion was just a raid and SS-Panzergrenadier-Regiment *Westland* arrived in time to prevent the fall of the entire town and evicted Tanaschishin's raiding force. The SS panzergrenadiers quickly established a coherent defensive hedgehog in the town, but their tanks were well to the rear and 17.Panzer-Division was covering their western flank out to the Sal River. It is important to note that the German panzer units were forced to spread their tanks around to cover a large sector, depriving them of mass and violating their accepted doctrine of concentration.

It took Eremenko a few days to bring up the rest of his two armies, but on 3 January he sent the 2nd Guards Mechanized Corps and 3rd Guards Tank

Corps against the 17. Panzer-Division, while the 6th Mechanized Corps reinforced Tanaschishin for an assault upon Zimovniki. General-major Aleksei P. Sharagin's 3rd Guards Mechanized Corps was sent to envelop *Wiking's* eastern flank, forcing them to extend their front. Although the 17. Panzer-Division managed to destroy about 17 Soviet tanks, Kirchner was forced to refuse both his left and right flanks to prevent from being encircled. Reinforced by part of the SS-Panzergrenadier-Regiment *Germania*, the *Wiking* managed to hold Zimovniki until 7 January when mounting pressure on both flanks forced Kirchner to retreat 25-km south to Kuberle. It was at Kuberle that SS-Sturmbannführer Johannes-Rudolf Mühlenkamp's SS-Panzer-Abteilung 5 finally arrived. Yet no sooner had Mühlenkamp's panzers driven into Kuberle than the SS-*Wiking* Division received a report that Soviet infantry had cut the rail line behind them at Orlivskiy. Although the 23. Panzer-Division was supposed to be screening the area east of the rail line to Proletarskaya, its positions were so thinly spread that they had failed to detect a battalion of Sharagin's 3rd Guards Mechanized Corps getting around behind the SS-*Wiking* Division. When the Soviet infantry entered Orlivskiy on the morning of 8 January there were only rear-echelon troops there and they quickly retreated, leaving the Soviets in control of half the town. Mühlenkamp's panzers were immediately ordered back to Orlivskiy to clear the Soviet raiding party but by the time that they arrived, a local counter-attack by an engineer unit had chased off the Soviets; the SS tankers were then ordered to drive back to Kuberle – an exhausting back-and-forth effort that exhausted both men and tanks. On the icy roads in the dark, the panzers were only capable of making 3–4km/hour, which meant that Mühlenkamp's panzers spent over 24 hours driving to and fro to no purpose.

Meanwhile, the main body of Sharagin's 3rd Guards Mechanized Corps (3GMC) advanced westward along the north side of the Manych, heading for Proletarskaya. Sharagin's corps had only been in action for two weeks and was close to full strength, although it did not have sufficient trucks for its nine infantry battalions. Despite frequent snow showers, Luftwaffe reconnaissance spotted Sharagin's forces 40km east of Proletarskaya and alerted Generalmajor Nikolaus von Vormann, who had just taken command of the 23. Panzer-Division. This Panzer-Division was in exceedingly poor condition, having just 19 operational tanks in Panzer-Regiment 201 and 4 SPW in the I./Panzergrenadier-Regiment 128.[15] Indeed, the division was so short of infantry that it had been forced to create two ad hoc infantry companies from dismounted tankers. Ammunition and fuel stocks were extremely low. Nevertheless, von Vormann realized that his forces were too weak to defend against a full-strength Soviet mechanized corps, so he opted to attack instead. Both Tiger companies from s. Panzer-Abteilung 503 were attached to von Vormann's division. The other Tiger company, 2./s. Pz.-Abt. 502 was sent north to Kuberle to assist the 17. Panzer-Division's rearguard. [16]

On 5 January, both Kampfgruppe Bachmann (Pz. Regt. 201) and Kampfgruppe Post (17 Tigers and 20 Pz III from s. Pz.-Abt. 503) conducted probing attacks eastward and encountered strong resistance from the vanguard of Sharagin's corps near the village of Stavropol.[17] The next day, von Vormann mounted a deliberate assault upon the Soviet mechanized brigade in Stavropol, with the Tigers mounting a frontal assault while Kampfgruppe Bachmann enveloped the town. The Luftwaffe managed to provide a few Stukas to support the attack, but the Tigers received only limited infantry and artillery support. The attack on Stavropol was noteworthy as the first major combat experience of the Tiger tank on the Eastern Front and the first time that the Germans encountered the new-style Soviet mechanized corps on the defence. In between snow squalls, the Tigers moved across the flat terrain toward the town in several wedge formations, with a thin screen of dismounted infantrymen following. The Soviet mechanized brigade in Stavropol had about 20–25 tanks in support, as well as a battalion of 76.2mm cannons and 12 45mm anti-tank guns. The Soviet 76.2mm guns succeeded in destroying one of the Pz IIIs and inflicted heavy losses on the German infantry, but could not stop the Tigers. Instead, the Tigers knocked out 13 Soviet tanks and several artillery pieces. However, it was the outflanking manoeuvre by the Pz IIIs and Pz IVs of Kampfgruppe Bachmann that forced the Soviet mechanized brigade to retreat. The next day, Kampfgruppe Bachmann continued to pursue the defeated Soviet brigade eastward but by 8 January it had nearly exhausted its supplies; Panzer-Regiment 201 was reduced to just 3–4 Panzergranate rounds and 300 machinegun rounds per tank and about 140 litres of fuel – just enough to make it back to Proletarskaya.[18]

While von Vormann was pushing one of Sharagin's brigades back, the others were pushing into the centre of 23. Panzer-Division's sector near the village of Vessely. Without Bachmann's panzers, von Vormann's command post was nearly overrun and Sharagin's infantry and tanks threatened to split the LVII Panzerkorps' defence. Von Vormann ordered an immediate attack against the Soviet force in Vessely, including the Tigers from Kampfgruppe Post and the exhausted Kampfgruppe Bachmann. At 0930 hours on 9 January, the German counter-attack began with 11 Tigers and 12 Pz III Ausf N lumbering across the open steppe toward Vessely. Indeed, the Tigers were moving across the snowy terrain at just 10km per hour – little more than the British Mark V tank in the First World War. However, in the 24 hours since taking the village, Sharagin had reinforced the mechanized brigade here with additional tanks, artillery and anti-tank guns, which gave the Germans a warm welcome. Amazingly, the first German assault was repulsed and the accompanying German infantry suffered crippling losses. Undeterred, von von Vormann personally ordered a second assault and a third – both of which were repulsed. While the Tigers managed to destroy eight T-34s over the course of the 6-hour battle, two Tigers were knocked out by 76.2mm fire and all the rest suffered considerable damage.

In addition, 2 Pz III Ausf N were destroyed and seven more damaged. [19] One Tiger was hit 11 times by 76.2mm fire and 14 times by 57mm; although the fighting compartment was not penetrated, the tank was reduced to a wreck. Bachmann's panzers also suffered heavy losses and were reduced to just seven operational tanks.[20] The German panzer counter-attack at Vessely was a costly fiasco that reduced both the 23. Panzer-Division and s. Pz.-Abt. 503 to combat ineffectiveness. Sharagin's mechanized troops had won an impressive defensive victory which did not go unnoticed by the Stavka.

Von Vormann wasn't willing to accept defeat and when a trainload of replacement tanks arrived in Salsk, he used them and the last two Tigers to form a new armoured spearhead, Kampfgruppe von Winning. On 11 January, Kampfgruppe von Winning succeeded in eliminating most of a Soviet artillery battalion west of Vessely, but at the same time Sharagin's corps was overrunning the 23. Panzer-Division's SPW battalion to the south, at Krasny Skotovod. Kampfgruppe von Winning re-oriented southward and the next day launched a major counter-attack against the Soviet mechanized brigade at Krasny Skotovod. Despite receiving fire support from 23. Panzer-Division's entire artillery regiment and two Stukas, the attack was a failure. Not only did the Soviet mechanized brigade retain the town, but it was now apparent that Kirchner's LVII Panzerkorps could no longer remain north of the Manych River much longer. Over the next few days, the panzers, assault guns and remaining infantry conducted a delaying action back to Proletarskaya. The 2./s. Panzer-Abteilung 502, supporting the 17. Panzer-Division, knocked out 11 Soviet tanks but was reduced to just 3 operational Tigers. On 14 January the 17. Panzer-Division pulled south of the Manych, followed by the 23. Panzer-Division on 16 January. During the retreat, Kirchner's LVII Panzerkorps destroyed hundreds of vehicles that could not be repaired or were immobilized by lack of fuel. In the harsh winter weather, the retreat was hazardous and Mühlenkamp's SS-Panzer-Abteilung 5 lost three Pz IIIs that slid off the road into ditches and had to be abandoned.[21] Once the rest of Kirchner's corps had crossed the 1,000-meter wide Manych, the SS-*Wiking* Division, reinforced with the last 2 operational Tigers, deployed into a hedgehog to defend the bridgehead at Proletarskaya as long as possible.

In no time, Sharagin's 3GMC, reinforced with additional infantry and artillery from the 28th Army, was pressing against SS-*Wiking*'s perimeter. Furthermore, Malinovsky's 2nd Guards Army had shifted its line of march westward and was threatening to cross the Manych in a sector that was screened by the 16. Infanterie-Division (mot.), which only had a few Pz IIIs left. Mühlenkamp's battalion succeeded in repulsing several Soviet infantry probes into Proletarskaya but he had just 10 tanks still operational and Soviet artillery fire was gradually pulverizing the town.[22] The SS-*Wiking* managed to hold Proletarskaya until dusk on 19 January, giving additional time for Kirchner's LVII Panzerkorps and Panzerarmee 1 to retreat toward Rostov. Then the SS troops broke contact, blew up the bridge over the Manych and joined the retreat to Rostov. Although Sharagin's 3 GMC, joined by the 4th Guards Mechanized Corps. did an excellent job hounding Hoth's retreat, Malinovsky was shifting his armour westward along the northern side of the Manych, looking for a crossing site to cut off their escape route to Rostov. Malinovsky formed an armoured group consisting of General-mayor Karp V. Svirodov's 2nd Guards Mechanized Corps (2GMC), General-leytenant Pavel A. Rotmistrov's 3rd Guards Tank Corps (3 GTC) and General-major Semen I. Bogdanov's 5th Guards Mechanized Corps (5 GMC) and tasked them to cross over the Manych near its confluence with the Don at Manychskaya and head toward Bataisk, only 40km away. If Rotmistrov's armour reached the bridge over the Don at Bataisk, Heeresgruppe A's primary escape route from the Caucasus would be severed. Although running short on fuel and ammunition after their long advance across the steppe, Rotmistrov put one of his ablest subordinates, Polkovnik Ivan A. Vovchenko in the lead with the 3rd Guards Tank Brigade (3 GTB) and they succeeded in crossing at Manychskaya on 22–23 January. Since Rotmistrov's advance threatened to get behind PzAOK 4, Hoth shifted the 17.Panzer-Division to guard his escape route and asked von Manstein to temporarily transfer part of Generalleutnant Herman Balck's 11. Panzer-Division south of the Don to meet this threat.

After some preliminary skirmishes with Vovchenko's brigade on 24 January, Balck's 11.Panzer-Division spearheaded a counter-attack on 25 January against the Manychskaya bridgehead. By means of a clever feint attack, Balck was able to defeat Vovchenko's 3 GTB and knocked out 20 Soviet tanks.[23] In his memoirs, Rotmistrov claimed that Vovchenko's brigade was attacked by 120–150 enemy tanks and three to four regiments of infantry, but Balck's force was about 30–40 tanks and two motorized infantry battalions. Rotmistrov also claimed that Vovchenko's brigade knocked out 20 German tanks, but admitted in his memoirs that, 'we suffered great losses in manpower and material' and asked Malinovsky permission to shift to the defence in this sector.[24] Malinovsky agreed, not realizing how small the German blocking force was in this sector. Thus Balck's armoured Kampfgruppe stalled the advance of the Soviet 2nd Guards Army for the better part of a week and held the corridor open long enough for Hoth's battered panzer units to conduct a fighting retreat to Rostov. Here and there, the remaining German panzers turned and inflicted some losses on their pursuers, but by the time that Hoth reached Rostov's outskirts on 31 January, his 'panzer army' was reduced to fewer than 50 operational tanks and assault guns.

While Hoth's month-long delaying action served to save Heeresgruppe A from isolation in the Caucasus, it came at a high price in men (almost 4,000 casualties) and equipment. The commitment of Tiger tanks in this sector had only provided Hoth with a temporary tactical advantage and while the three Tiger companies managed to knock out a total of at least 39 Soviet tanks, only five of 29 Tigers were still operational after just two weeks of combat. In contrast, the ability of units such as Balck's 11.Panzer-Division, equipped with just a handful of Pz III and Pz IV medium tanks, to conduct a mobile delay and inflict reverses upon much larger pursuing Soviet mechanized forces offered far more cost–effective value to the Ostheer. On the other side of the hill, the performance of Sharagin's 3 GMC on the offensive, the tactical defence and pursuit had been exemplary – indicating a steady improvement in the Soviet practice of mechanized warfare. Yet it was also clear that the Red Army had not mastered the art of logistical sustainment in mobile warfare, which caused its spearhead units to run out of fuel and ammunition at the worst possible moment. Even elite guards mechanized units were forced to use Panje carts in their support units and at least half the infantrymen in the mechanized brigades rode atop tanks as *desantniki*, all due to the scarcity of trucks.

The Crisis of Heeresgruppe Don: Gruppe Hollidt, 1 January–14 February 1943

While Hoth's panzers were delaying Eremenko's drive to cut off Heeresgruppe A, Gruppe Hollidt was struggling protect the eastern approaches to Rostov from Vatutin's Southwest Front. Rostov was the anchor for the entire German position in southern Russia and the supply lines for both von Manstein's Heeresgruppe Don and von Kleist's Heeresgruppe A ran through the city. Throughout December, Gruppe Hollidt's primary mission had been to defend the airfields at Morozovskaya and Tatsinskaya, from which the Luftwaffe was conducting the airlift missions to the encircled AOK 6 at Stalingrad. However, after Vatutin's 'Little Saturn' offensive began and the Tatsinskaya airfield was overrun by a Soviet mechanized raid on 24 December 1942, the Luftwaffe airlift was disrupted and Hollidt's mission rationale began to erode.[25] Even though Tatsinskaya was reoccupied, both it and Morozovskaya were now too close to the front line and the Luftwaffe relocated the airlift mission to Salsk. By early January, Gruppe Hollidt had already fallen back from the Chir River under heavy pressure and was slowly drifting back to the Donetsk River.

On Hollidt's left flank, another ad hoc formation – Armee-Abteilung Fretter Pico under General der Artillerie Maximillian Fretter-Pico – attempted to hold the area between the Don and Millerovo with a single complete infantry division, the 304. Infanterie-Division just arrived from Belgium, part of the Italian Ravenna Division and some flak units. Gruppe Kreysing, consisting of 6,000 German troops from the 3.Gebirgsjäger-Division was encircled inside Millerovo by the Soviet 17th and 18th Tank Corps from the 1st Guards Army. Kreysing was being supplied by air and had established a hedgehog defence supported by two artillery battalions, so the Soviet tankers unwisely decided to besiege the town until the 6th Guards Rifle Corps arrived. Fretter-Pico's situation was even worse than Hollidt's, but the Soviet fumbling around Millerovo for three vital weeks enabled him to cobble together a defence. In December, the OKH had created an independent tank unit – Panzer-Abteilung

138 – from two panzer replacement units in Germany and this battalion was provided with 30 brand-new Pz IV Ausf G and 8 Pz III Ausf L/M, then sent east by rail. On 4 January, Panzer-Abteilung 138 arrived at Kamenka and quickly deployed to provide a vital counter to the two Soviet tank corps in this sector. The sudden appearance of a fresh panzer unit in this sector was a tonic for German morale and helped to slow down the advance of the 1st Guards Army.

Although Hitler was opposed to unnecessary retreats, von Manstein recognized that the hidden benefit of retreating toward the Donets and Rostov was that German supply lines were shortening and it was becoming easier to bring reinforcements into battle by rail, whereas Vatutin's supply lines were stretched to the breaking point and getting worse as they moved westward. Nevertheless, von Manstein's Heeresgruppe Don was under great pressure in the centre and on both flanks and one mistaken command decision could lead to a disastrous encirclement; the only factor that blocked Vatutin from swiping the bedraggled units of Gruppe Hollidt out of his way was a handful of battle-worn Panzer-Divisionen and a single Panzer-Abteilung.

At the start of January, Gruppe Hollidt had established a porous HKL along the Taymbiya River, with von Knobelsdorff's XXXXVIII Panzerkorps holding the northern shoulder, Generalmajor Dietrich von Choltitz's XVII Armeekorps in the centre and Armeekorps Mieth holding the right flank on the Don. The German front suffered from a lack of quality infantrymen and two Luftwaffe Feld-Divisionen were committed into the centre. Flak units were also inserted into the frontline, using 2cm, 3.7cm and 8.8cm guns in the direct-fire role. A few surviving Romanian battle groups were still at the front, but their combat value was minimal. Hollidt's three Panzer-Divisionen were a mixed bag; General-major Erhard Raus' 6.Panzer-Division was down to about 40 tanks, including 4–5 Pz IVs with long 7.5cm guns, but was still full of fight. Hollidt used Raus' division as the core of XXXXVIII Panzerkorps. Oberst Eberhard Rodt's 22. Panzer-Division, which was attached to the XVII Armeekorps, had been virtually demolished during Operation Uranus and von Manstein described it as 'a complete wreck'; by January, the division had been reduced to a regimental-size Kampfgruppen with no more than a dozen tanks.[26] Hollidt kept Balck's still effective 11.Panzer-Division in reserve to deal with any Soviet breakthroughs; this division had 32 tanks, including three Pz IV with long 7.5cm guns.[27] It is noteworthy that the Pz III with long 5cm gun remained the principal German battle tank in the winter battles and how only token numbers of Pz IVs participated in these crucial battles.

Flushed with success from Operation 'Little Saturn,' Vatutin's Southwest Front was presented with a multitude of options because the enemy was weak in so many sectors. Although Vatutin concentrated General-leytenant Markian M. Popov's 5th Tank Army and the General-leytenant Dmitri D. Lelyushenko's 3rd Guards Army (3 GA) against Gruppe Hollidt, he directed General-major Vasily I. Kuznetsov's 1st Guards Army (1 GA) to crush Armee-Abteilung

Fretter-Pico. Vatutin was one of the Red Army's best front commanders but he was attempting to mount two simultaneous major parallel operations, which strained Soviet C^2 and logistic capabilities. Furthermore, most of Vatutin's mechanized units were in poor condition after six weeks of continuing combat and had less than half their tanks still operational. The two tank corps that had conducted the raids against Tatsinskaya and Morozovskaya airfields on 17–28 December 1942 – Badanov's 24th Tank Corps and Popov's 25th Tank Corps – were reduced to wrecks. Rather than pull them out to rebuild in the RVGK as was standard, the Stavka ordered them to remain with Lelyushenko's 3 GA and they were combined with the equally mangled 1st Guards Mechanized Corps. Vasiliy M. Badanov, who had angered Stalin by his unauthorized withdrawal from Tatsinskaya, was put in charge of this agglomeration of wrecked units; in his memoirs, Badanov noted that these three corps had barely 50 tanks left between them and very few trucks or infantry.[28] Consequently, Vatutin's best field commander – Lelyushenko – was left with very few tanks to support the advance of 3 GA. Popov's 5th Tank Army (5 TA) still had two tank and mechanized corps with roughly 200 tanks left and it was supposed to be Vatutin's spearhead, but its performance had been disappointing since the fighting on the Chir River. A large part of the problem was Popov himself, who was a drunk and frequently negligent commander. Eventually, he would be relieved of command for his failings, but in an army that was quick to punish officers, Popov was tolerated for far too long. Even when sober, he was the wrong sort to command a tank army, since he had a linear, set-piece approach to warfare that was not unlike Bernard Montgomery's. Popov was content to use his superiority to gradually shove Gruppe Hollidt rearward, rather than conduct anything too daring. The recent fate of the 24th and 25th Tank Corps' Deep Operations likely also dissuaded Popov from trying to go deep, even though Hollidt's right flank was little more than a screen.

In order to achieve decisive success in war, particularly mobile warfare, one must be willing to take risks, but it takes a combination of experience – and luck – to know when the risks become unacceptably dangerous. German panzer commanders had figured this dynamic out in 1941–42 and often managed to made it work for them; in the post-Stalingrad hubris Vatutin believed that he could accomplish this feat as well, although the tools and subordinates available were not up to the task.

Gruppe Hollidt's main position was near the airfield at Morozovskaya, on the main rail line to Stalingrad, which was held by the remnants of the 22.Panzer-Division and the 7. and 8.Luftwaffe Feld-Divisionen. Vatutin attempted a pincer operation against this strongpoint, attacking from the north with Badanov's ad hoc armoured group and from the east with General-major Mikhail D. Borisov's 8th Cavalry Corps and some of Popov's armour. Considering the poor quality of the defence, Popov's 5th Tank Army should have simply rolled over the two inexperienced Luftwaffe divisions, but instead it merely pushed them back and the 22.Panzer-Division abandoned Morozovskaya on 4 January. South of Morozovskaya, Eremenko had sent the 1st Guards Rifle Corps from 2 GA across the Don to push in Hollidt's right flank near Tsimlyansk and Hollidt was obliged to commit Balck's 11.Panzer-Division to prevent this flank from collapsing. Meanwhile, Lelyushenko's 3rd Guards Army was gradually overcoming the XXXXVIII Panzerkorps and the commitment of General-major Efim G. Pushkin's refitted 23rd Tank Corps from front reserve threatened to break Hollidt's left wing, so von Manstein decided to send the fresh 7.Panzer-Division to reinforce von Knobelsdorff's sector.

Generalleutnant Hans Freiherr von Funck's 7.Panzer-Division began detraining near Kamensk on 5 January and brought 91 Pz III Ausf L/M, 14 Pz III Ausf N and 18 Pz IV Ausf G, as well as a company of Marder III Panzerjäger. In addition to the welcome addition of the full-strength Panzer-Regiment 25 with two battalions, von Funck's 7.Panzer-Division brought four fresh Panzergrenadier-Bataillonen into the fight, including one equipped with SPWs. Less than 48 hours after detraining, the lead Kampfgruppe from 7.Panzer-Division marched eastward to confront Pushkin's 23rd Tank Corps, which was shoving its way past the depleted 6.Panzer-Division's left flank. Like the proverbial cavalry arriving in the nick of time, von Funck's veteran panzers halted the Soviet armoured advance in a series of tank battles fought on the steppes amid swirling snow showers. Lelyushenko's 3rd Guards Army was brought to a screeching halt. However, Hollidt had to commit all his available armour to hold both his left and right flanks, leaving only the threadbare 22.Panzer-Division to hold the centre. After halting Vatutin's offensive for a week, Hollidt finally gained permission to withdraw behind the Donetsk River on 15 January and by the night of 16–17 January all his forces had established a more compact and solid HKL on the western bank.

At the same time, von Manstein ordered Gruppe Kreysing to break out of Millerovo. Amazingly, the German Gebirgsjägers succeeded in escaping past the 18th Tank Corps and reached German lines near Voroshilovgrad. By 18 January, Armee-Abteilung Fretter-Pico was tucked in behind the Donetsk, protecting Hollidt's left flank.

Amazingly, Gruppe Hollidt and Armee-Abteilung Fretter-Pico were able to halt Vatutin's advance on the Donetsk and hold this line until 9 February. Although Vatutin managed to gain a bridgehead across the Donetsk in Fretter-Pico's sector, he was stymied against Hollidt and forced to shift to the defence in this sector. Indeed, Soviet offensive pressure slacked off so much by late January that Hollidt was able to hold his sector on the Donetsk with just six depleted infantry divisions, enabling the 6.Panzer-Division to briefly pull back and refit. By 30 January, Raus' Panzer-Division was back up to 64 operational tanks. Likewise, much of Popov's 5TA was pulled back to refit, contributing to an operational pause for both sides in this sector. Yet Vatutin was ready to gamble that von Manstein had no further reserves and he had decided to shift his offensive toward von Manstein's weak left flank on the northern Donets around Starobelsk. On 29 January, the Southwest Front began Operation *Skachok* (Gallop) with the intent of crossing the Donets and then swinging south into the rear of Heeresgruppe Don. It was a very bold plan, but Vatutin failed to maintain fixing attacks against Gruppe Hollidt, which allowed Hollidt to transfer the 7.Panzer-Division to deal with the crisis on his left flank. Soon thereafter, von Manstein pulled the remnants of Hoth's PzAOK 4 back to reinforce Gruppe Hollidt, while he hurriedly transferred Mackensen's PzAOK 1 to the northwest to counter Operation Gallop. As the situation in the west grew more critical, Hollidt was finally allowed to retreat from the Donets on 9 February and Rostov was abandoned on 13–14 February. Gruppe Hollidt then fell back to the Mius River, where it established a solid front for the rest of the winter.

The delaying actions fought by Gruppe Hollidt and Armee-Abteilung Fretter-Pico in January 1943 contributed greatly to the stabilization of the German southern front along the Donets after the disaster at Stalingrad and prevented 4.Panzerarmee and Heeresgruppe A from being isolated south of the Don. As von Manstein noted in his memoirs, Gruppe Hollidt's defence 'could never have been maintained had not our Panzer-Divisionen time and again shown up at danger spots at just the right moment.'[29] Nevertheless, the German defensive victory did not come cheaply. During January, Gruppe Hollidt suffered 14,909 casualties, including 4,808 dead or missing. During this period, the 6. and 11.Panzer-Divisionen lost a total of 89 tanks '*totalausfalle*' (destroyed) and received 92 replacement tanks. At least nine of these replacement tanks were not new-build models but older, short-barrelled Pz III or Pz IV models from repair shops. On the Soviet side, Vatutin kept Popov's 5 TA at the front too long and his armour reserves were spent, which led to the culmination of his offensive before reaching Rostov or cutting off Heeresgruppe A's retreat. However, von Manstein opted to abandon Rostov in order to transfer armour to save his crumbling left flank, providing a consolation prize for Vatutin.

Destruction of the 2nd Hungarian Army, 12–29 January 1943

Before Vatutin could crush Heeresgruppe Don with Operation Gallop, the Stavka wanted to deal a fatal blow to Heeresgruppe B in the Voronezh sector in order to open the doorway to Kharkov. If both the Donbas and Kharkov could be liberated before the end of winter, the Red Army would have greatly weakened the Wehrmacht's hold on the eastern Ukraine. Following the winning formula employed during Operation Uranus against the Romanians, the Stavka decided to make a maximum effort against the Hungarian 2nd Army and the remnants of the Italian 8th Army.

General Gustav Jány's Hungarian 2nd Army held a 186km-wide sector along the Don, south of Voronezh. Jány commanded the III, IV and VII Army Corps, with a total of eight light infantry divisions. Although General-polkovnik Filipp I. Golikov's Voronezh Front held a bridgehead across the Don in the Hungarian sector at Uryv, the Hungarian troops had occupied this sector for five months and were fairly well dug in. In open terrain, the Hungarian infantry divisions would have been at a major disadvantage against Soviet armour, since they were still equipped with 37mm and 47mm anti-tank guns and their division-level artillery was obsolescent. Nevertheless, Generaloberst Maximilian Freiherr von Weichs, commander of Heeresgruppe B, believed that with proper support the Hungarian 2nd Army could hold its own; he assigned two Luftwaffe Flak battalions to support the Hungarian IV Corps in the critical Uryv sector. Von Weichs also placed Generalkommando z.b.V. Cramer in Jany's sector to act as a reserve, but under German command. Cramer's force included two German infantry divisions and the Hungarian 1st Armoured Division. Altogether, the Hungarian 2nd Army was supported by about 100 Axis tanks and 40 assault guns, in the following units:

- The Hungarian 1st Armoured Division, under Brigadier General Ferenc Horváth, had the 30th Armoured Regiment with two tank battalions consisting of 50–60 operational Pz 38(t) light tanks and up to 20 older Pz IV medium tanks with short 7.5cm howitzers. In addition, Horváth's division had a company of Toldi light tanks, a company of Csaba armoured cars and a battalion of Nimrod 40mm self-propelled AA guns that could also serve in the anti-tank role. By East Front 1943 standards, the Hungarian 1st Armoured Division was fragile, but it did have the structure of a combined arms team in its attached motorized artillery, infantry, engineers and AA which increased its overall combat value.
- In autumn 1942, Panzer-Verband 700 had been formed from a Panzer-Abteilung staff from 14.Panzer-Division and three Panzer-Kompanien from the 22.Panzer-Division, consisting of a total of 27 rather worn-out Pz 38(t) light tanks.[30]
- Sturmgeschütz-Abteilung 190, commanded by Major Gerhard Peitz, was attached to Gruppe Cramer.
- Sturmgeschütz-Abteilung 242 had just been organized in Germany in November 1942, but one Batterie was sent to Tunisia and the other two went to Heeresgruppe B. The two assault gun batteries were just unloading at Ostrogoshsk on 12 January when Soviet offensive was beginning and the battalion was hurriedly dispatched to support the Hungarian IV Corps.

South of the Hungarian 2nd Army, the remnants of the Italian 8th Army continued to hold a sector along the Don. The three-division Italian Alpine Corps was still relatively intact, plus one other division, but the 8th Army had no organic armour and negligible artillery and anti-tank capabilities. Von Weichs positioned General der Artillerie Martin Wendel's XXIV Panzerkorps to protect the Italians' right flank, even though this formation consisted of just the incomplete 27.Panzer-Division (this Panzer-Division had never fully formed and now consisted of just eight operational Pz III/Pz IV medium tanks and a regimental-size mixed arms Kampfgruppe) and a single German infantry division. In addition, the 19.Panzer-Division and Sturmgeschutz-Abteilungen 201 and 209 were deployed in the Italian sector, with 30–40 tanks and 50 or more assault guns. The area between Kantemirovka and Starobelsk was the most dangerous, since the Red Army was across the Don here in force and the seam between the Italian 8th Army and Armee-Abteilung Fretter-Pico was full of gaps.

Under these conditions, Heeresgruppe B needed to have a clear idea of what Golikov's Voronezh Front intended, but German operational intelligence failed miserably during the winter of 1942–43. In fact, General-leytenant Kirill S. Moskalenko's 40th Army opposite the 2nd Hungarian Army was reinforced with four tank brigades and the 10th Artillery Division. Moskalenko was a veteran commander who had led the 1st Tank Army in July–August 1942 and now he was provided with plenty of veteran infantry and supporting troops. Even more significant, General-leytenant Pavel S. Rybalko's 3rd Tank Army was transferred from the RVGK to Golikov's front, where it moved by rail from Tula to Kantemirovka in early January. Soviet *Maskirovka* (deception) was so effective that Heeresgruppe B was unaware that a Soviet tank army had moved into this sector until it was too late. Amazingly, Rybalko had held no operational commands in the first two years of the war and had been an instructor at the Kazan Tank School in 1941–42, but he was intelligent and a quick learner. Unlike other Soviet commanders, Rybalko was a very hands-on leader and he taught himself to drive a T-34 tank and spent many hours with his front-line tankers.[31] Rybalko's army was not fully equipped since it had only the 12th and 15th Tank Corps and 122 of its 493 tanks were non-operational due to mechanical problems. To make up the shortfall, General-major Sergei V. Sokolov's 7th Cavalry Corps was attached to Rybalko's army. Soviet logistic preparations for the offensive were rushed, which made it difficult for Rybalko's tank army to go into battle ready for a protracted operation.

In early January, General Georgy K. Zhukov and General-Polkovnik Aleksandr M. Vasilevsky arrived from the Stavka in Moscow to 'help' Golikov develop his plan for the upcoming offensive.* The plan was fairly complex, with three different shock groups attacking across a wide front to smash both the Hungarian and Italian armies.[32] Golikov's north shock group, Moskalenko's 40th Army, would punch out of the Uryv bridgehead while von Weich's vulnerable right flank was hit by the southern shock group – Rybalko's tank army. An independent formation, General-major Petr M. Zykov's 18th Rifle

---

* On 18 January 1943 Zhukov was promoted to Marshal of the Soviet Union and Vasilevsky was promoted to General of the Army.

Corps, would form a shock group to cross the Don on the Hungarians' right flank. On 12 January, Moskalenko conducted a preliminary attack from the Uryv bridgehead with two rifle divisions supported by the 86th Tank Brigade and succeeded in advancing 5km and mauling a regiment from the Hungarian 7th Light Infantry Division. Having gained some elbow room, Moskalenko's 40th Army conducted a massive artillery preparation the next morning and then hit the Hungarian 7th Division with four rifle divisions and more tanks. In a matter of hours, the Hungarian Division had crumbled under the onslaught and Moskalenko had achieved a breakthrough in the IV Corps sector. The only German reaction was to belatedly move Panzer-Verband 700 to attempt to seal off the Soviet breakthrough, which resulted in a sharp tank action with the Soviet 150th Tank Brigade; the Pz 38(t) light tanks were no match for Soviet T-34s and after losing 14 tanks the German unit retreated northward. Moskalenko began committing his second-echelon forces into the bridgehead, including General-major Andrei G. Kravchenko's 4th Tank Corps and the 25th Guards Rifle Division. By the end of 14 January, Moskalenko had carved out a larger bridgehead and destabilized the Hungarian centre. Further east, Zykov's 18th Rifle Corps attacked across the Don after a massive artillery barrage against the Hungarian VII Corps near Shchuchye. In this sector, the Hungarian 12th Light Infantry Division was crushed by nightfall, but Gruppe Cramer committed two German infantry regiments to prevent a breakout.

While Moskalenko was getting across the Don, Rybalko's 3rd Tank Army also swung into action on the morning of 14 January, after a powerful artillery preparation from the 8th Artillery Division. General-major Vasily A. Koptsov led his 15th Tank Corps northwestward into the fog and struck the XXIV Panzerkorps near Zhilino. Not expecting Soviet armour, the German front in this area was only held by the *Führerbegleitabteilung* and Waffen-SS Kampfgruppe *Fegelein.** Koptsov was a very experienced armour officer who had commanded tanks at the battalion, brigade and division level – he knew his job well – and his armour slashed through the German frontline and quickly routed or encircled these small units. The German 387.Infanterie-Division was the only solid unit in this sector, but Rybalkov's armour blew past its right flank without stopping; once they realized Soviet armour was behind them, the German infantry began retreating. Koptsov's tankers advanced nearly 20km on the first day and overran the XXIV Panzerkorps command post in Zhilino, where General Wandel was killed in action; 68 of his headquarters staff were captured and later executed in the town square. The 12th Tank Corps and 7th

---

* The first unit was a battalion-size motorized infantry unit that was used to guard Hitler's forward headquarters but had been sent to the Eastern Front and attached to the *Großdeutschland* Division. The Fegelein Brigade was also motorized infantry. Neither unit had much artillery or anti-tank support.

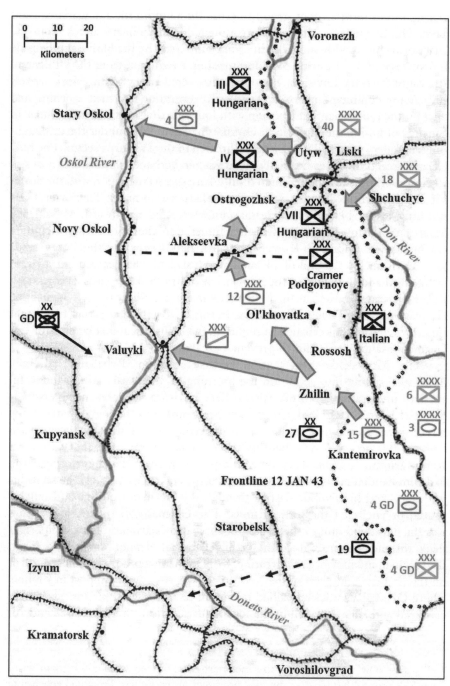

The Ostrogozhsk-Rossosh Operation, 13–31 January 1943.

Cavalry Corps covered Koptsov's flanks while he continued to march north, despite deep snow.

By 15 January, von Weichs was finally starting to react to the Soviet offensive by ordering Cramer to commit more of his German units and the Hungarian 1st Armoured Division to support the crumbling VII Corps. Hungarian morale cracked quickly once Golikov's troops were across the Don in force and Soviet tanks began to batter at their thin defences. The Hungarian Armoured Division made some spirited counter-attacks against Zykov's 18th Rifle Corps' Shchuchye bridgehead, but suffered heavy losses. Cramer's 26.Infanterie-Division bought valuable time, but was gutted by the Soviet avalanche coming across the Don and Cramer began a fighting retreat to the town of Ostrogozhsk. By 16 January it was clear that local counter-attacks had failed and that the Hungarian centre and right was on the verge of collapse. Rather than sending the two Sturmgeschütz Abteilung to support the Hungarians, Cramer kept both with his group and they managed to knock out seven Soviet tanks. Cramer's withdrawal also left the Italian Alpine Corps exposed. In the south, Rybalko's armour mopped up the remnants of the XXIV Panzerkorps and pushed toward Rossosh to cut off the Italian retreat. The only area that was holding was the German VII Armeekorps (from 2.Armee) at Voronezh, where remnants of the Hungarian III Corps were consolidating; Moskalenko pivoted Kravchenko's 4th Tank Corps to threaten the 2.Armee's left flank and to discourage von Weichs from attempting any counterstrokes from this direction.

Between 16–17 January, Heeresgruppe B's front became unglued and all the Axis forces in this sector were in retreat. Gruppe Cramer was briefly surrounded at Ostrogozhsk but he fought his way through Soviet lines with his Sturmgeschütz blasting a path clear; both battalions suffered heavy losses and would have to be sent back to Germany for rebuilding. On 17 January, Koptsov's 15th Tank Corps linked up with some of 40th Army's advance units near Alekseevka, cutting off the Italian Alpine Corps and thousands of retreating German and Hungarian troops. A Soviet tank battalion from 12th Tank Corps rushed into Rossosh and caught the Italians by surprise, but two German Marder IIIs arrived and knocked out a number of Soviet tanks, causing them to withdraw. Nevertheless, Rybalko's 3rd Tank Army had virtually closed the door behind the Italians and he focused his attention westward toward the rail junction at Valuyki, which he sent Sokolov's cavalry to capture. Meanwhile, Hitler ordered von Weichs to stand fast – he promised help was on the way – and Heeresgruppe B ordered the Italian Alpine Corps to maintain its positions on the Don. Realizing that they were already isolated by Rybalko's advance, the Italians ignored these nonsensical orders and began marching westward across the snow.

The rest of the campaign from 18–27 January was essentially an Axis retreat and a slow Soviet pursuit. The remnants of Gruppe Cramer and the Hungarians fell back to the Oskol River where they managed to stop the 40th

Army's advance for a while. Hitler did indeed transfer the *Großdeutschland* Division from Heeresgruppe Mitte to reinforce the line on the Oskol, but this was still a drop in the ocean. Amazingly, the Italian Alpine Corps fought its way out of encirclement by 29 January but all three of its divisions were ruined and it suffered over 30,000 casualties. In the south, the collapse of XXIV Panzerkorps forced the Axis forces to abandon Starobelsk and retreat behind the Donets River; this unfortunate formation lost two more commanders between 20–21 January.* The XXIV Panzerkorps was reduced to about 2,500 troops and both the 27.Panzer-Division and 385.Infanterie-Division were disbanded soon afterwards. Altogether, the Hungarians had suffered about 100,000 casualties and the Italians 30–40,000. Rybalko's army had won a significant operational victory, in conjunction with the 40th Army, which knocked both the Italian 8th Army and the Hungarian 2nd Army out of action and thereby created a 190km-wide gap in Heeresgruppe B's front; von Weichs could not plug all the gaps and his new line on the Oskol River was little more than a speed bump.

Rybalko's 3rd Tank Army was worn down by the rapid advance and its forward brigades were short on fuel and ammunition, but it was flush with victory. Every German armoured unit involved in opposing the Soviet offensive was either destroyed, dispersed or otherwise rendered combat ineffective – Heeresgruppe B was virtually stripped of armour. Although the two-week long Soviet Ostrogozhsk–Rossosh Offensive is not well known today, it represents a clear indicator that Operation Uranus was not a fluke in November 1942 and that the Red Army was learning how to conduct effective combined arms warfare. The Soviet use of *Maskirovka* in order to achieve operational surprise, as well as massing fires and using manoeuvre to exploit a breakthrough, were professionally executed. However, the operation also indicated lingering Soviet problems with logistical sustainment in mobile operations and Rybalko's tank army was unable to maintain its combat power for long due to shortages.

Heeresgruppe Mitte's trials at Rzhev and Velikiye Luki, 1 January–1 March 1943

For the period January–February 1943, most histories of the Eastern Front tend to focus on the Soviet offensives across the Don and the German counter-offensive at Kharkov, while ignoring the rest of the Eastern Front. In fact, the Soviet Winter Offensive of 1942–43 was across the board and inflicted significant damage on the Ostheer in both Heeresgruppe Mitte and Heeresgruppe Nord. More than half of the Ostheer's casualties in January 1943 occurred in the

---

* Generalleutnant Arno Jahr committed suicide on 20 January 1943 when his unit was surrounded and General der Infanterie Karl Eibl was killed in action during the retreat on 21 January.

northern and central sectors of the front, not the south.* Indeed, had the Red Army allowed these other sectors to remain relatively quiet, von Manstein and von Weichs would have received considerably more reinforcements from these commands. Despite the defeat of Zhukov's Operation Mars in November–December 1942, both the Western and Kalinin Fronts continued to pound on Generaloberst Walter Model's 9.Armee in the Rzhev salient during January 1943, which necessitated Heeresgruppe Mitte keeping five Panzer-Divisionen and three Sturmgeschütz-Abteilungen in this hard-pressed sector. Only the *Großdeutschland* Division was transferred south. Eventually, Model was able to convince Hitler that it was no longer worth the sacrifice to hold the Rzhev salient and that the resources required to hold the salient could be better used in the south. On 6 February, Hitler finally authorized Model to evacuate the Rzhev salient, although the operation would not begin until 1 March. Consequently, the mass of Heeresgruppe Mitte's panzers and assault guns remained in the Rzhev sector throughout the winter campaign.

Another crisis for Heeresgruppe Mitte was unfolding around the city of Velikiye Luki, near the boundary with Heeresgruppe Nord. General-major Kuzma N. Galitski's 3rd Shock Army from the Kalinin Front had encircled the city on 27 November 1942, trapping 8,000 German troops from the 83.Infanterie-Division and other units. The city was heavily fortified and the Luftwaffe could provide aerial supplies to this small force for a time, but it was clear that a relief operation needed to be mounted. Generalleutnant Erich Brandenger's 8.Panzer-Division was equipped with only 32 tanks, mostly obsolete Pz 38 (t) light tanks, but it was assigned to Gruppe Chevallerie to mount a relief operation.† Hauptmann Horst Krafft's Sturmgeschütz-Abteilung 185 was also provided to the relief operation; as an experiment, the 3.Batterie in this battalion was entirely equipped with the StuH 42 armed with the 10.5cm howitzer.[33] However, two hastily-assembled relief attempts in late November and mid-December 1942 failed with heavy losses, including all the StuH 42 assault guns and many of the Pz 38(t) tanks. Galitski's 3rd Shock Army was supported by vastly more and better armour, including General-major Ivan P. Korchagin's 2nd Mechanized Corps, the 13th Guards Tank Regiment equipped with KV-1 heavy tanks and two other tank brigades and five other tank

---

* In January 1943, the Ostheer reported a total of 82,110 casualties, of which 17,183 occurred in Heeresgruppe Mitte (21 per cent of the total) and 29,023 occurred in Heeresgruppe Nord (35 per cent of the total). While some of AOK 6's casualties at Stalingrad were not reported until February, the fact that Heeresgruppe Nord and Mitte together suffered over 12,000 dead or missing in January 1943 indicates the ferocity of combat occurring elsewhere on the Eastern Front.

† General der Infanterie Kurt von Chevallerie, commander of the LIX Armeekorps, was in charge of the overall relief effort. The 20.Infanterie-Division (mot) was also attached to this operation, but had no tanks.

regiments. Korchagin was a veteran tank officer and his corps was equipped with over 100 T-34 tanks and 70 T-70 light tanks – in itself more than a match for Brandenberger's scrap-heap Panzer-Division. Consequently, it came as no surprise that the German relief efforts failed and Galitski's infantry and artillery proceeded to reduce the encircled garrison in Velikiye Luki. However, Soviet efforts to send tanks into the city proved costly, due to the effectiveness of the German Panzerjägers in the wrecked city streets.

By New Year, Velikiye Luki had been surrounded for five weeks and pounded into rubble; it was clear that the garrison could not hold out much longer. Von Chevallerie was resolved to make one more relief attempt and was provided a handful of additional units, including the I./Panzer-Regiment 15 with 37 tanks (including 28 Pz III Ausf L/M and 3 Pz IV Ausf G). This battalion belonged to the 11.Panzer-Division and had been designated to return to Germany to re-equip with the new Panther tank at Grafenwöhr but had been diverted to Heeresgruppe Mitte to save the Velikiye Luki garrison. On 4 January, von Chevallerie launched Operation *Totila* and was able to batter his way to within 9–10km of the city, before the effort bogged down in the face of determined Soviet resistance. One German panzer platoon leader, Oberfeldwebel Gerhard Brehme, distinguished himself during the relief attempt by knocking out eight Soviet tanks; like a number of veteran German panzer NCOs, Brehme already had about 40 'kills' over the past two years of combat. Nevertheless, the effort failed and Galitski's troops overran the eastern part of the city.

On 9 January, Major Günther Tribukait, commander of Jäger-Bataillon 5, proposed one last desperate attempt to reach the remaining defenders in Velikiye Luki's citadel: mounting his Jägers on the remaining panzers and SPWs and making a full-speed dash through the Soviet lines to reach the citadel. Unwilling to write the garrison off, von Chevallerie agreed even though it seemed a futile gesture. By afternoon, Tribukait assembled nine tanks from I./Pz. Regt. 15, 8 SPWs and 1 Sd. Kfz. 10/4 with a 2cm flak in a wooded area near the front. All the German vehicles were white-washed to blend in with the snow. Some infantrymen mounted on the tanks and others rode in the SPWs. At 1330 hours, Tribukait ordered the armour to advance in a wedge at high speed across the snow-covered terrain, followed by the halftracks. There was no artillery preparation and the Soviets were caught by surprise – these were not standard German panzer tactics. By the time the Soviets eventually began to react, the bulk of Tribukait's formation had blitzed its way through the outer defences, losing some vehicles to anti-tank guns. In just an hour, the panzers reached the citadel, to the joy of the defenders. However, there was to be no rescue. A Soviet 76.2mm ZIS-3 anti-tank gun destroyed the trailing Pz III tank just as it entered the citadel gateway, trapping the other German tanks in the courtyard area. Soviet artillery then pounded the citadel, reducing the German panzers and SPWs to junk. Tribukait and the survivors joined the defenders. With no hope left, the German garrison attempted a breakout on the night of 15–16 January, but fewer than 200 troops succeeded in reaching German lines.[34]

The battles of Heeresgruppe Mitte against the Western and Kalinin Fronts in early 1943 have not made much of an impression on Eastern Front historiography to date, but these actions did impact the availability of armour on other fronts and influenced the coming summer campaigns. As if to highlight this point, on 1 March Model's 9.Armee began Operation *Büffel* (Buffalo), the evacuation of the Rzhev salient. Within three weeks the evacuation was completed and had reduced the German front line by over 300km. Operation *Büffel* freed three Panzer-Divisionen to deploy elsewhere and provided Hitler with a sizeable operational reserve to use for either offensive or defensive purposes.

Relief of Leningrad: Operation Spark (*Iskra*), 12 January–19 March 1943
At the northern end of the line, the continuing siege of Leningrad dominated events. Heeresgruppe Nord's 18.Armee (AOK 18) had the city under siege since September 1941. Inside the city, General-leytenant Leonid A. Govorov's Leningrad Front was no longer starving and had recovered some of its combat capability. Outside the city, General Kirill A. Meretskov's Volkhov Front made two attempts during 1942 to break through the German siege lines, but failed. The main area being fought over was the Siniavino corridor east of the Neva River, a swampy and heavily-wooded region measuring 15 x 15km that had no real roads. Although the two Soviet fronts were separated by less than 14km, the German XXVI Armeekorps had heavily fortified the Siniavino Corridor and the terrain greatly favored the defence. Hitler was determined that the Red Army not raise the siege of Leningrad and in order to reinforce the German defence in the Siniavino corridor, he had ordered that the very first Tiger tanks sent to the Eastern Front go to this sector. In September 1942, the 1./s. Pz. Abt. 502 had arrived by train and its Tigers were the first to see combat. By early January 1943, this single company – which still had seven Tigers and 16 Pz III tanks operational – was the main operational reserve for the XXVI Armeekorps.[35] In addition, the Sturmgeschütz-Abteilung 226 was stationed in the Siniavino corridor.

Meretskov's plan for Operation *Iskra* (Spark) was similar to previous attempts: the Volkhov Front's 2nd Shock Army would attack the Siniavino corridor from the east while simultaneously, the Leningrad Front's 67th Army would cross the Neva River and attack the western side of the corridor. If the plan succeeded, the two Soviet fronts would link up somewhere in the corridor and a ground route opened to encircled Leningrad. The main weight of the attack came from the 2nd Shock Army in the east, which would attack with five rifle divisions and plenty of artillery. Although the 2nd Shock Army had 217 tanks (including 83 T-34 and about 20 KV-1) in its four tank brigades, one guards tank regiment and four OTBs, it could only employ company-size detachments of armour due to the marshy, restricted terrain. The 67th Army committed three tank brigades and two OTBs to the offensive, totalling another 222 tanks; altogether the Red Army committed 439 tanks to the offensive against no more than 50 German tanks and assault guns.[36]

At 0700 hours on 12 January 1943, Operation *Iskra* began with two hours and 20 minutes of artillery preparation on the German positions along the east bank of the Neva. Govorov's Leningrad Front massed 144 guns and mortars per kilometre of front and fired three basic loads of ammunition – an almost unprecedented amount of artillery preparation for the Eastern Front so far. The temperature had fallen to -9 degrees F and the Neva was covered with snow and frozen solid, although artillery impacts broke the ice in places. Around 1150 hours, four Soviet rifle divisions from the 67th Army attempted to cross the 500-metre-wide frozen river, but the German defences were still intact and repulsed two division-size attacks with heavy losses. However, the other two Soviet rifle divisions, supported by 61 T-60 light tanks and 28 BA-10 armoured cars from Podpolkovnik Vladislav V. Khrustitsky's 61st Tank Brigade, managed to seize a small bridgehead near Marino and they began to push eastward. The Soviet T-60 was not much of a tank but in this terrain, it was worth more than a road-bound Tiger since it could manoeuvre across the frozen marshland without bogging down. By dusk, Khrustitsky's T-60s had penetrated 4km into the German positions and threatened to outflank the 96.Infanterie-Division. Meanwhile, Soviet engineers hastily prepared the crossing site near Marino – which had steep banks on the eastern side – enabling 25 T-34 medium tanks to cross before dusk. This was the first time that the Leningrad Front had managed to get a significant number of tanks across the Neva. In the east, the 2nd Shock Army attacked with four rifle divisions and small numbers of tanks after an even larger artillery preparation, but achieved only modest success.

The German XXVI Armeekorps regarded the 67th Army's crossing of the Neva as the primary threat and reacted by committing most of the available armour to support a counter-attack by the 96.Infanterie-Division at 1615 hours on 13 January. Four Tigers under Oberleutnant Bodo von Gerdtell and 8 Pz III tanks moved up to support an attack by Grenadier-Regiment 284 against the Soviet 268th Rifle Division near Gorodok. The Tigers were camouflaged with whitewash, but were noisy enough to be heard at a distance. The Soviet infantrymen were nor expecting to see enemy tanks, much less Tigers, and many took to their heels, causing the Soviet division to reel back 2km. Govorov committed about 20 T-34s from the 152nd Tank Brigade into this sector to support his infantry, precipitating a close-quarter tank battle. Von Gerdtell's Tigers did well, shooting up 12 T-34s but six or seven Pz IIIs were knocked out and their crews suffered 17 killed. Furthermore, the infantry battalions from the 96.Infanterie-Division were badly depleted, leaving the Tigers with minimal infantry support. While trying to defend this sector, von Gerdtell was killed the next day and 1./s. Pz. Abt. 502 was ground down under constant artillery fire.

Meanwhile Khrustitsky's T-60 tanks and infantry from the 67th Army continued to press eastward, across terrain that the Tigers could not traverse, toward a link-up with the slowly advancing 2nd Shock Army. For reasons that defy military logic, the German XXVI Armeekorps commander moved a Kampfgruppe Hühner with five Tigers, four Pz III and five StuG III to the town of Shlissel'burg on 16 January, just as the jaws of the two Soviet armies were closing in from both side of the Siniavino corridor. The Germans were desperate to hold a work settlement known as WS-5 that was on a key trail intersection in the middle of the corridor and for two days Kampfgruppe Hühner fended off one attack after another. However, the terrain was perfect for infantry infiltration and the Germans were road-bound, so Kampfgruppe Hühner was gradually isolated and cut off. On the morning of 18 January, the Soviets finally stormed WS-5 and troops from the two fronts linked up at 0930 hours. Khrustitsky's tiny T-60 tanks were in at the kill; while its 20mm cannon was normally not useful in tank-v-tank combat, it was very effective in destroying the wooden buildings in WS-5. The loss of WS-5 completely cut off the 8,000 troops in Kampfgruppe Hühner, who were now determined to break out to the south before it was too late.

Putting the tanks in the lead, Kampfgruppe Hühner moved south along a trail, through an area consisting of peat bogs and scrub forest. Soviet anti-tank gunners were waiting and they hammered the German armoured column, which could barely move off the road; four Pz IIIs were knocked out and even a Tiger was knocked out by 76.2mm fire. The German column tried to fight its way through the ambush, but the Tigers were hit repeatedly and disabled one by one. Two Tigers were blown up by their crews and another was burning. The last Tiger accidentally drove off the trail into a peat bog and became hopelessly mired. The Germans tried to retrieve this tank or destroy it, but were driven off by Soviet fire. Five of Khrustitsky's T-60 tanks managed to hook tow cables to the abandoned Tiger and pull it free of the bog – the first intact Tiger captured. Although all five Tigers were lost, most of the troops of Kampfgruppe Hühner were able to escape to the south. By the end of 18 January, Operation *Iskra* had accomplished its main objective of opening up a land corridor to Leningrad, officially ending the siege.

Unfortunately for the front-line soldiers on both sides, Marshal Zhukov regarded Operation *Iskra* as an incomplete victory and ordered both the Leningrad and Volkhov Fronts to continue the battle until the high ground around Siniavino was captured. The result was another 10 days of tough fighting with heavy losses on both sides, but the German defences held. The 1./s. Pz. Abt. 502 played a major role in stopping the Soviets from capturing the Siniavino Heights by knocking out 55 enemy tanks, but one Tiger was destroyed in action as well as 12 Pz III tanks. By the time that the battle ended in mutual exhaustion on 31 January, the company had only one operational Pz III and two non-operational Tigers left.[37] Soviet armour losses were also very heavy, with about 200 of 400 tanks knocked out or inoperative. Overall, the battle was a bitter disappointment for the Germans, who lost most of their armour, and 1./s. Pz. Abt. 502 was hors de combat. Furthermore, the captured Tiger would be intensely studied by the Soviets, leading to a decision by the GKO to finally upgrade the firepower of the T-34 and to develop a new heavy tank. Despite their success, the Red Army was not entirely satisfied with the performance of its tank units and the Leningrad Front issued a harsh criticism to the 67th Army on 27 January 1943:

> Combat experience from the 67th Army shows that the employment of tank units had major deficiencies that resulted in unjustifiable heavy losses of tanks. Combined-arms commanders introduced tanks into battle too quickly, without taking the necessary time to prepare tanks for battle, or for reconnaissance or for coordination, nor did they use engineers to prepare the routes for tanks. The commanders of [rifle] divisions and regiments did not coordinate their actions with tanks on the battlefield… Tanks rushed at the enemy defences without adequate artillery support and tank units were usually not on the artillery radio net… [38]

Nor was Zhukov done with Heeresgruppe Nord, since he had been working on a plan known as 'Polar Star' that was intended as a follow-on to Operation *Iskra*. His grand plan was that Marshal Semyon Timoshenko's Northwestern Front would crush the German-held Demyansk salient then coordinate with the Leningrad and Volkhov Fronts to envelope and crush the right flank of Heeresgruppe Nord between them. A new 1st Tank Army, led by one of the most experienced senior Soviet tankers – General-leytenant Mikhail E. Katukov – was formed in the Northwest Front at the end of January 1943. Katukov was given the 3rd Mechanized Corps and 6th Tank Corps and other units for a total of 631 tanks.[39] Zhukov wanted to drop a large force of parachutists behind German lines then have Katukov's armour punch through the front to relieve them and split open Heeresgruppe Nord's defences. As often happened with Zhukov's bold, grand plans, it was more than the Red Army could accomplish and it failed to anticipate enemy actions. Timoshenko's 1st Shock Army had mounted a powerful but clumsy attack against the Demyansk Salient in early January that had cost it 423 tanks in six weeks and failed to break through. As this offensive was dying down, Zhukov ordered Meretskov's Volkhov Front to mount a strong fixing attack toward Tosno to prevent Heeresgruppe Nord from shifting reserves to Demyansk. Anticipating this attack, Heeresgruppe Nord moved 1./s. Pz. Abt. 502, which had received three new Tigers, to the Krasny Bor sector on 7 February.

Three days after the Tigers moved by rail, the Soviet 55th Army launched a major attack against the Spanish Blue Division (250.Infanterie-Division) at Krasny Bor. After a massive artillery barrage, the Soviets blasted through the centre of the Spanish division with the 63rd Guards Rifle Division, supported by 21 KV-1 tanks from the 31st Guards Tank Regiment. Although the Spanish defenders managed to knock out four KV-1 tanks, their centre was shattered within two hours and they lost Krasny Bor by the end of the day. It was a significant Soviet victory and the Spanish Division was badly hurt, but the Soviets failed to anticipate that the loss of terrain always provoked a German counter-attack. The 1./s. Pz. Abt. 502 (three Tigers and three Pz III), led by Leutnant Gert Meyer, was attached to a Kampfgruppe from the SS-Polizei Division and ordered to contain the Soviet breakthrough. Unlike the Siniavino sector, the area around Krasny Bor and Mishkino was better suited to the use of heavy tanks since the ground was more solid and flat, with few trees. Attacking into the left flank of the Soviet salient on 11 February, Meyer's Tigers had a field day and knocked out 32 Soviet tanks. The next day, they knocked out 10 more. Bloodied, the Soviet 55th Army paused its offensive in order to bring up its own armour, then attacked at Mishkino again on 17 February; Leutnant Meyer's Tigers were occupying hull-down positions and they calmly picked off 10 KV-1 tanks in a matter of minutes. German Panzerjägers also contributed to the slaughter, since they had just received a large shipment of HEAT ammunition (High Explosive Anti-Tank). A Dutch Panzerjäger Kompanie in the SS-Legion Nederland, equipped with 7.5cm Pak 97/38 anti-tank guns, repulsed an attack by the Soviet 124th Tank Brigade and knocked out 19 tanks.

Following the success of Operation *Iskra*, the Red Army continued to pound on Heeresgruppe Nord throughout the rest of the winter, but without success. Zhukov transferred the 1st Tank Army to Timoshenko's Northwest Front to use for another offensive against the Demyansk salient – a swampy area that had already proven totally unsuitable for tanks – but the Germans began evacuating the salient on 17 February and completed the operation by early March. Timoshenko was surprised by this German operation and failed to strike them as they were withdrawing; the Stavka decided to transfer Katukov's 1st Tank Army to the Voronezh Front. Running out of options, Zhukov pressured Meretskov to make one last effort against the Siniavino Heights before the winter ended – a truly futile effort.

On 19 March, the Soviet 8th and 55th Armies attacked, hoping to capture the rail junction at Mga. The 1./s. Pz. Abt. 502, now with four Tigers and three Pz III, was committed to stop the 55th Army's push to Krasny Bor. In three tense days of action, the Tigers knocked out 40 Soviet tanks and helped to shut down the Soviet offensive. Although the Tiger's 8.8cm gun proved itself to be highly lethal when given a good field of fire, the tank's weight and lack of mobility was a definite liability in this kind of terrain. The Tigers were continually bogging down in the soft soil and frequently required major recovery efforts. In contrast, the T-34 was somewhat inhibited in this terrain, but the light T-60s and T-70s were quite handy in marshy areas. While the Leningrad sector was far from ideal tank country, the operations in the winter of 1942–43 demonstrated that light tanks could still operate in areas that would generally be considered 'no-go terrain.'

Operation Gallop (*Skachok*), 29 January–18 February 1943

Vatutin's Southwest Front was still recovering from Operation Little Saturn and the advance to the Donets, when the Stavka directed it to begin planning for a follow-on operation to crush Heeresgruppe Don and liberate the Donbas region. Most of Vatutin's units were at 50 per cent strength or less and his supply lines had not caught up with his forward combat units. Nevertheless, he believed that he still had enough strength to deal von Manstein a decisive defeat. Vatutin's plan was characteristically bold, using the 6th Army and the 1st Guards Army to smash through a thin screen of German infantry divisions northwest of Voroshilovgrad and then pivot southward to seize a crossing over the Donets. Once these armies had secured a crossing over the Donets, an armoured group led by Popov would be committed to push south to seize Mariupol on the Sea of Azov, thereby cutting off Heeresgruppe Don. It was a vision of mobile warfare influenced by the pre-war concept of Deep Operations (*glubokaya operatsiya*), which had theorized armoured penetrations of up to 200km. Thus far in the Second World War, Deep Operations had only been attempted once before, during the armoured raids against the Tatsinskaya and Morozovskaya airfields in late December 1942, with mixed results.

Mobile Group Popov consisted of the 3rd, 10th and 18th Tank Corps and the 4th Guards Tank Corps, with a total of just 212 tanks. All these units were reduced to one-third of their authorized strength in tanks and manpower; for example, General-major Pavel P. Poluboyarov's 4th Guards Tank Corps started Operation Gallop with just 40 tanks.[40] Vatutin had transferred much of the assets of the 5th Tank Army into this ad hoc group, leaving the 'tank army' with just three rifle divisions and no tanks. This reconfiguration of his remaining armour was done in large part in an effort to deceive von Manstein about his intentions, since the rump 5 TA remained in place opposite Gruppe Hollidt on the lower Donets. However, the mobile group was an ad hoc formation that lacked the support units to conduct a protracted mobile operation. Vatutin expected Mobile Group Popov to traverse 270km in one lunge, whereas full-strength Soviet armour units in Operation Uranus and Little Saturn had only been able to advance 100–120km in one lunge, which corresponded with how far a T-34 could be expected to go cross-country on one load of fuel. Nor was the lacklustre Popov the man to lead a daring armoured advance deep behind German lines, and he had demonstrated an inability to defeat Gruppe Hollidt when he had far stronger resources.

Yet beyond the understrength units and questionable leadership, the greatest threat to the viability of Operation Gallop was the woeful state of the Southwest Front's logistical support, which was still dependent upon railheads on the far side of the Don. Simply put, the Red Army at this point still lacked the support infrastructure to sustain mechanized Deep Operations. Vatutin's front was extremely short of trucks and thus he had been unable to build up any forward logistic depots to support the offensive. Even with the trucks available, they had great difficulty moving on roads that were often covered with a metre of snow. There were limited numbers of ZIS-42 halftracks based upon the ZIS-5 truck, but their lack of front-wheel drive severely reduced their mobility in snow or mud. Nor could the VVS help much with transport aircraft – in stark contrast to the Luftwaffe's Ju-52 transports that routinely provided aerial resupply – since the 17 VA supporting the Southwest Front had only a single transport regiment with 20 Li-2 transports (based upon the American-built DC-3). Furthermore, the VVS preferred to use its Li-2s as night bombers instead of bringing up fuel for tank units at the front. Thus, when Popov's armour drove off into the white snowy wilderness beyond the Donets, they would essentially be out of supply for an extended period.

Nevertheless, Vatutin believed that Operation Gallop, with the Voronezh Front's Operation Star occurring on its northern flank, would carry the day despite a host of problems. Indeed, Soviet operational planning was driven by post-Stalingrad hubris and an almost French-style attitude that they would muddle through somehow. In the process, any potential German responses were ignored. This style of planning, which omits terrain, weather, logistics and the enemy, begs for disaster.

On the morning of 29 January, General-leytenant Fedor M. Kharitonov's 6th Army attacked on Vatutin's right flank with four rifle divisions while General-major Vasiliy I. Kuznetsov's 1st Guards Army (1 GA) attacked on the left flank with three rifle divisions. In this sector that was over 100km wide, von Manstein had Armee-Abteilung Lanz with the 298. and 320.Infanterie-Divisionen and the 19.Panzer-Division, which only had a small number of operational tanks. The Germans were hopelessly outnumbered in this sector and they elected to conduct a fighting withdrawal which upset Vatutin's timetable. Vatutin relied on his rifle divisions to conduct the pursuit, enabling his armour to enjoy a few more days of rest, and committed only the 4th Guards Tank Corps to assist the infantry. Although mauled, both German infantry divisions eventually succeeded in retreating across the Donets at Izyum and Zmiyev. The 19.Panzer-Division pulled into a hedgehog north of the Middle Donets at Kremennaya and put up stiff resistance for two days before pulling back across the river. Consequently, the 4th Guards Rifle Corps (4 GRC) of Kuznetsov's 1GA did not begin crossing the Donets until 1 February. The 6th Guards Rifle Corps, with the 18th Tank Corps in support, crossed the Donets further east near Lysychansk and mounted a fixing attack against the 19.Panzer-Division. Meanwhile, Kharitonov's 6th Army slowly moved westward against light resistance, but did not capture Izyum until 5 February and did not reach Zmiyev until 10 February.

Ominously, the first elements of the SS-Panzerkorps were already beginning to arrive in the vicinity of Kharkov just as Operations Gallop and Star were commencing and had been detected on the Northern Donets by Soviet scouts. Yet more immediately serious was von Manstein's successful effort to transfer the bulk of the 1.Panzerarmee from the Rostov area on his right flank to Slavyansk on his left flank, a move he described in chess terms as 'castling'. Von Funck's 7.Panzer-Division, with 35 tanks, was the first to arrive at Slavyansk, just as the 4GRC was crossing the Donets to the northwest. Generalleutnant Hermann Breith's III.Panzerkorps headquarters also established itself in Artemovsk and selected positions for the 3. and 11.Panzer-Divisionen, which were still enroute. Vatutin waited until Kuznetsov's infantry had moved three rifle divisions across the Middle Donets and established viable bridgeheads before committing Popov's armour. Poluboyarov's 4th Guards Tank Corps (4GTC), with 37 tanks, was the first across on 1 February and while 4GRC went to secure Slavyansk, 4GTC brushed past the city and went on to occupy Kramatorsk. However, by the time that the vanguard of 4GRC arrived outside Slavyansk, Panzer-Grenadier-Regiment 7 was firmly established in the town, along with artillery.

Kuznetsov elected to mount a set-piece attack on the German defence in Slavyansk on the morning of 2 February, but only had the 195th Rifle Division nearby. Not only were the initial attacks by this division repelled by von Funck's Panzergrenadiers, but the 7.Panzer-Division mounted a counter-attack with tanks on 3 February that threw the Soviet infantrymen out of the city suburbs. Kuznetsov thought he could pry the 7.Panzer-Division out of Slavyansk with a little extra firepower, so he requested Popov to bring up the 3rd Tank Corps while 1GA brought up the 57th Guards Rifle Division. Poluboyarov's 4GTC formed a defensive hedgehog at Kramatorsk, but took no active role. By 5 February, von Funck's 7.Panzer-Division was nearly encircled in Slavyansk and it looked grim for Heeresgruppe Don, since there was now a huge gap between Armee-Abteilung Lanz and Breith's III.Panzerkorps. There was literally nothing to block the 6th Army or Popov's armour from pushing west and south to sever von Manstein's lines of communication. However, like the Chateau de Hougoumont at Waterloo in 1815, capturing Slavyansk became an object in itself and Vatutin, Kuznetsov and Popov lost sight of the real objective at a critical moment. Rather than simply bypassing Slavyansk, Vatutin decided to commit the bulk of Popov's armour to reducing the German hedgehog in the city.

Popov was able to attack the 7.Panzer-Division's hedgehog with three of his tank corps, along with the infantry of 4GRC, from three different directions and almost completely encircle the division, but the city did not fall and fighting went on for more than a week. Given the fact that Breith had relatively few tanks and only modest amounts of infantry and artillery, the stand at Slavyansk against the bulk of 1GA and Popov's armour seems improbable. The answer lies in logistics – Vatutin's frontline units were running out of fuel and ammunition and could not afford a protracted battle. German logistics were somewhat better, since Breith's panzers were operating close to friendly rail lines. Furthermore, Breith was able to bring up the 3.Panzer-Division to the east of Slavyansk, which engaged the 10th Tank Corps from 3–11 February. The 11.Panzer-Division, with 16 tanks, was brought up from Rostov and sent against the 4GTC at Kramatorsk but was badly ambushed, losing 10 SPWs and many anti-tank guns.[41] Popov sent the 3rd Tank Corps to Kramatorsk to reinforce Poluboyarov, which temporarily halted the German counter-attack. Once the Germans brought up the 333.Infanterie-Division and some artillery, the two Soviet tank corps began to suffer heavy losses. Unsupported tank units tend to perform poorly in an extended defence, particularly in an urban environment. By this point in Operation Gallop, Popov's armour was not being used as an exploitation force for Deep Operations, nor was it massed against a single objective. Instead, Popov's four tank corps were dispersed between Kramatorsk, Slavyansk and Lysychansk and half his armour had actually shifted to the defence.

In contrast, the German Panzer-Divisionen were depleted but well-coordinated. Many of the German Pz III, Pz IV tanks and StuG III assault guns involved in the counter-attack mounted *winterketten* (winter tracked extenders), which improved their mobility in snow. By the second winter of the War in the East, German tankers were somewhat better adapted to winter operations, compared to the first winter in which virtually all of their tanks became non-operational. Freezing cold weather still caused problems, particularly with routine maintenance; grease turned nearly solid at temperatures hovering near or below 0 degrees F and road wheels or support rollers without proper lubrication quickly burned out. Although operational readiness rates were poor during the winter battles, by early 1943 the Panzer-Divisionen had learned to keep a portion of their armour running even under the worst weather conditions. Indeed, the ability of the German Panzer-Divisionen to adapt and operate in winter weather conditions in 1943 enabled von Manstein's mechanized units to slowly regain the initiative. Furthermore, the combined arms nature of the Panzer-Divisionen – in contrast to Soviet tank units – enabled them to substitute mobile Flak guns, Panzerjägers and Pioniers to make up for the shortage of tanks.

Amazingly, the biggest Soviet success in Operation Gallop was achieved by infantry, not tanks. While Popov's armour and 1GA were tangled up trying to overcome III Panzerkorps' defence, a handful of rifle divisions from 4GRC marched southwest toward the Dnepr. On 11 February, the 35th Guard Rifle Division captured the important rail junction at Lozovaya. The way to the Dnepr River was open. The 6th Army also had infantry near Zmiyev within 35km of Kharkov. Suddenly, Vatutin realized that a decisive victory was possible and that he needed to extract Popov's armour from the useless slugfests at Kramatorsk-Slavyansk. He ordered Kuznetsov to shift his axis of attack westward, bypassing

Slavyansk for now. Bypassing enemy armour units can be perilous since its leaves a mobile threat on one's flanks, but Vatutin was buoyed by the Stavka's overly-optimistic assessment that Heeresgruppe Don was withdrawing westward and the desperate stand at Slavyansk was merely a rearguard action.[42]

For their part, 1.Panzerarmee believed that Group Popov could not get around their open left flank south of Kramatorsk because of the numerous *Balkas* (ravines) filled with deep snow; the Germans regarded this area as impossible for their tanks.[43] However, the Soviet tankers did not share this view. Late on the night of 10–11 February, Poluboyarov pulled his 4GTC out of Kramatorsk, bypassed the 11.Panzer-Division's left flank and boldly conducted an 85km night march through the bleak and snowy wasteland. At 0900 hours the next morning, his tanks seized the rail junction at Krasnoarmeyskoye and cut Heeresgruppe Don's primary line of communication.* Although there was a secondary route to the south through the Zaporozhe to Mariupol line, the loss of Krasnoarmeyskoye was a serious threat to von Manstein's forces because it immediately delayed the timely arrival of fuel and ammunition. In order to reinforce success, Vatutin sent Poluboyarov the 9th Guards Tank Brigade and ski troops and told him to hang on, employing 4GTC as a blocking force. Von Manstein reacted at once, ordering the III and XXXX Panzerkorps to launch immediate counter-attacks to defeat Popov's enveloping manoeuvre. The SS-Panzergrenadier-Division *Wiking*, fresh from the Caucasus, was sent to destroy 4GTC, while the 7. and 11.Panzer-Divisionen went after the 10th Tank Corps, still near Slavyansk. Initially, the German attacks achieved little, due to the difficulty of manoeuvreing through deep snow and inadequate support. Poluboyarov had deployed anti-tank guns and anti-aircraft guns firing in direct fire mode to slow the German advance. On 12 February, one Kampfgruppe from *Wiking* fought its way into Krasnoarmeyskoye, but the action devolved into a week-long battle of attrition, rather than one of rapid manoeuvre.[44] On 15 February, Gruppe Hollidt was finally forced to abandon Voroshilovgrad as part of the retreat to the Mius River and Slavyansk was ceded two days later, but the German defence along the Donets had wrecked Vatutin's timetable for Gallop.

On 17 February, the stalwart 35th Guards Rifle Division captured the town of Pavlograd, only 55km from the Dnepr River. Shortly afterwards, Vatutin committed his last front reserves – General-major Petr P. Pavlov's 25th Tank Corps and the 1st Guards Cavalry Corps – to reinforce the 6th Army's push to the Dnepr. By 18 February, Pavlov's tankers captured Sinel'nikovo, just 32km from the Dnepr. Apparently on the verge of a major victory, Vatutin did not realize that his offensive had already culminated and that the Germans were

---

* Heeresgruppe Don was redesignated as Heeresgruppe Süd on 13 February 1943 when Heeresgruppe B was dissolved. However, Heeresgruppe A remained as a separate command in the Kuban.

gaining the advantage. Popov's four tank corps were all virtually immobilized, very low on fuel, food and ammunition, and no longer capable of offensive action.

As a tanker, running out of fuel is a traumatic event. I recall when winter weather played havoc with my battalion's fuel supply and our tank company was forced to make an extended march without much fuel remaining. One after another, tanks began running out of fuel and we had to abandon them and their crews; I remember tossing a box of rations to my sergeant as we passed his immobilized tank, telling him to keep his men warm and that we would come back for them in a few days. Once the column was gone, his tankers chopped down small trees and made a fire, spending the next three days huddled under blankets near the fire. Their tank was frozen and silent inside and, later, proved most difficult to start again even when refuelled. The main gun breach was covered in frost and, had a round been placed in it, it would have become stuck. I imagine that Popov's immobilized tankers did much the same, trying to stay warm and waiting for resupply, but in just a few days of this cold and hungry misery, their ability to fight must have been severely degraded.

Operation Star (*Zvezda*), 1–16 February 1943
In late January, the Stavka began directing Golikov's Voronezh Front to prepare for a follow-on offensive toward Kharkov as soon as it was across the Oskol River in force. Golikov's forces were depleted after weeks of heavy combat, but he still had Rybalko's relatively intact 3rd Tank Army (3TA), which the Stavka wanted to use to secure an important objective before the spring mud arrived. Marshal Zhukov inserted himself into the planning process for the offensive designated as Operation Star (*Zvezda*) and unilaterally decided that Golikov's Front had the ability to capture Kursk and Belgorod as well. Consequently, rather than a focused offensive to seize Kharkov, from the outset the Stavka-dictated plan for Operation Star forced Golikov to disperse his forces against multiple objectives on diverging axes. Rybalko's 3TA and General-leytenant Mikhail I. Kazakov's 69th Army were expected to advance 200–250km and encircle Kharkov within five days – a very tall order. As with Vatutin's Operation Gallop, Golikov's supply situation at the start of the offensive was poor, his units were tired and well under strength and there were no significant reserves immediately available.

Opposing Golikov, Heeresgruppe B had managed to erect a thin screen line along the west side of the Oskol River, to cover the gap left by the destruction of the Hungarian 2nd Army. Armee-Abteilung Lanz blocked the southeastern approaches to Kharkov with two infantry divisions and had fortified Kupyansk. Generalkommando z.b.V. Cramer, another ad hoc formation, had received the *Großdeutschland* Division to protect the northern approaches to Kharkov and had deployed the 168.Infanterie-Division to protect Belgorod.* After heavy

---

* On 12 February Generalleutnant Erhard Raus took command of this formation and it was renamed Generalkommando z.b.V. Raus.

fighting at Rzhev, the *Großdeutschland* Division was worn down, but this elite formation still had an under-strength Panzer-Abteilung with 14 operational tanks on 11 February (including three Pz III and six Pz IV) as well as a few assault guns.[45] In the north, the battered 2.Armee protected the approaches to Kursk from the rest of Golikov's armies. However, Heeresgruppe B did not have a continuous front east of Kharkov and significant gaps existed between blocking positions. The German covering forces were extremely weak and incapable of sustained defence; if faced with Soviet armour, the best that they could hope to achieve was delay.

Just before Operation Star began, the first elements of General der Waffen-SS Paul Hausser's SS-Panzerkorps arrived in Kharkov from the west.* This powerful formation consisted of the SS-Panzergrenadier-Divisionen *Leibstandarte Adolf Hitler* (*LSSAH*), *Das Reich* and *Totenkopf.* Except for *Totenkopf*, which had to be rebuilt after its protracted blood-letting at Demyansk, the other two Waffen-SS Divisionen had spent the bulk of 1942 in France and were well-rested and nearly fully re-equipped with the best weaponry Germany had to offer. Altogether, the SS-Panzerkorps had over 50,000 troops in its ranks, as well as six SS-Panzer-Abteilungen with 317 tanks (including 28 Tiger, 95 Pz IV Ausf G, 162 Pz III Ausf L, 10 Pz III Ausf J and 22 Pz II Ausf F), three Sturmgeschütz-Abteilungen with 63 StuG III Ausf F/8 assault guns and three Panzerjäger-Abteilungen with 45 Marder II/ III tank destroyers. In addition, each division was provided with 7.5cm Pak 40 and 8.8cm Flak guns which significantly improved their anti-tank capabilities. However, this large formation with hundreds of AFVs took almost two weeks to arrive by rail and would require time to assemble. Hitler was adamant that the SS-Panzerkorps would not be committed into battle piecemeal and ordered that it would remain under OKH control until ready for battle. Nevertheless, von Weichs was able to make a case that some of the earliest arriving Waffen SS units would need to screen the assembly area in Kharkov since there were no other Heeresgruppe B combat units in the area that could accomplish this task. Once the OKH conceded on this point, Heeresgruppe B liberally interpreted this to dispatch the *Das Reich*'s SS-Panzergrenadier-Regiment *Deutschland* and a reinforced reconnaissance battalion (SS-Aufklärungs-Abteilung *Das Reich*) as a covering force forward of the Donets near Velikiy Burluk, while the rest of the SS-Panzerkorps assembled in Kharkov. By the afternoon of 31 January, SS-Panzergrenadier-Regiment *Deutschland* had two battalions screening far to the east of the Donets.

---

* This formation had been established in July 1942 as SS-Panzer-Generalkommando and during the Third Battle of Kharkov in February–March 1943 it was known as the 'SS-Panzerkorps'. In June 1943 it was redesignated as the II. SS-Panzerkorps and retained this designation for the rest of the war.

Rybalko kicked off Operation Star on 1 February by moving his 3TA across the Oskol River. He started the offensive with 165 tanks in his 12th and 15th Tank Corps, but used his four attached rifle divisions and General-major Sergei V. Sokolov's 6th Guards Cavalry Corps (6GCC) on 2 February to push back the German blocking detachments, rather than committing his armour too soon. Rybalko also wisely decided to bypass the German *Stützpunkt* at Kupyansk and make straight for the Donets River at Pechenegi, where he intended to cross. Kazakov's infantry advance on Rybalko's right flank, while the 6th Army from the Southwest Front covered his left flank. Outflanked by Rybalko's 3TA, the German 298.Infanterie-Division was forced to abandon Kupyansk – demonstrating once again that it is best for armour to bypass enemy strongpoints rather than hit them head-on. The infantry division was forced to abandon much of its artillery in the retreat and fell back in columns toward the Donets, hounded by Rybalko's tanks. However, Rybalko's advance units quickly noted the presence of the *Das Reich* blocking units, which led him to believe that the SS-Panzerkorps could arrive in force to defend the Donets crossings at any moment. Based upon this assessment, Rybalko decided to commit both his tank corps into battle ahead of schedule on 3 February in order to accelerate the advance to the Donets. While Rybalko's two tank corps made good progress toward the Donets, SS-Panzergrenadier-Regiment *Deutschland* at Velikiy Burluk put up very stiff resistance, which halted some of Rybalko's infantry and forced him to divert a brigade from General-major Vasiliy A. Koptsov's 15th Tank Corps to deal with his unexpected obstacle. Although the Waffen-SS troops eventually ceded the town of Velikiy Burluk, they maintained a salient that interfered with the advance of both Rybalko's 3TA and Kazakov's 69th Army. The *Großdeutschland* Division also put up very stiff resistance, which delayed Kazakov's 69th Army for several critical days.

Nevertheless, the rest of Koptsov's 15th Tank Corps reached Pechenegi on 4 February and was shocked to find that elements of the SS-Panzergrenadier-Division *Leibstandarte Adolf Hitler* (*LSSAH*) were already defending the heights on the far side of the Northern Donets. The *LSSAH* detachments were small, but included SS-Sturmbannführer Kurt Meyer's reconnaissance battalion, some Panzerjägers and a few assault guns. The Germans emplaced a few 8.8cm Flak guns on the heights and they were able to engage Koptsov's tanks at distances up to 6,000 meters and succeeded in setting nine tanks on fire. Afterward, Koptsov kept his tanks under cover in Balkas (ravines) and sent his infantry forward.[46]

Rybalko's attached infantry units made three separate attempts on 4–6 February to cross the river, which was less than 50 metres wide at this spot, but each attempt was repulsed by intense German fire. Nor were Waffen-SS junior leaders like Meyer content to fight a static defensive battle, and instead he crossed the Donets and ambushed a Soviet column, inflicting an estimated 250 casualties before returning to the German-held side of the river.[47] Similarly, the *Das Reich* also opted for an active defence. Once the SS-Panzergrenadier-Regiment *Der Führer* and the I./SS-Panzer-Regiment 2 arrived at the front, they were committed to a major counter-attack into the right flank of Rybalko's 3TA on the morning of 5 February.[48] The Luftwaffe even managed to provide a few Stuka sorties to support the attack. Just after dawn, a Kampfgruppe from *Der Führer* and at least two companies of tanks attacked southward into the Soviet 48th Guards Rifle Division near Velikiy Burluk and caught it by surprise, advancing 10km. Rybalko was forced to detach the 179th Tank Brigade to deal with this enemy action, which distracted him from crossing the Donets. A second SS-Kampfgruppe, supported by 2./SS-Panzer-Regiment 2, pushed eastward toward the village of Olkhovatka. Rottenführer Ernst Barkmann, commanding a Pz III tank, was involved in the attack. Here, the *Das Reich*'s lack of recent mechanized combat experience was evident in the lack of reconnaissance prior to contact with the enemy. The overconfident SS-tankers rolled toward the town in a frontal assault, straight into a well-prepared anti-tank defence that shot them to pieces; about 13–14 tanks were knocked out. Barkmann's Pz III was one of three that made it into the village and they encountered close-quarter combat:

> At full speed the Panzer raced toward the village. 'Watch out! Molotov Cocktails! Bottles filled with gasoline burst on the nose of the Panzer. Burning gasoline ran downward…Then the commander saw the flash from a muzzle and recognized a Pak behind a house corner. Opposite, the enemy Pak commander spotted the Panzer, which had closed in to about 30 meters. He brought the Pak around to destroy it. Barkmann saw the blank ring of the muzzle swing toward him. They were still some ten meters apart. 'Run over the Pak!' The engine howled. At the moment when the Panzer rammed the gun and pushed its barrel down, the shot roared. Two seconds too late! The shell hit the ground below the Panzer without effect.[49]

After securing the village, Barkmann's Panzer was sent back to the assembly area to escort recovery vehicles to come and retrieve the damaged tanks, but was not able to return until after sunset. Driving back in the dark, through deep snow and with limited visibility, Barkmann's Panzer became stuck in a drift. By the time that two FAMO recovery tracks found Barkmann's tank at sunrise, Soviet infantrymen were closing in on his position and a 76.2mm anti-tank had been brought up to engage the immobilized tank. The Soviet anti-tank gunners were quite good, first destroying one FAMO and then shooting up Barkmann's tank; he managed to escape on foot.

Frustrated by his inability to just push across the Northern Donets, on 7 February Rybalko sent Sokolov's 6th Guards Cavalry Corps (6GCC), reinforced with the 201st Tank Brigade, to cross the Donets River further down at Andreyevka where the 6th Army had already secured a bridgehead and to sweep around to the south to cut the main German rail line heading into Kharkov. However, this cavalry raid was spotted and the Germans dispatched a Kampfgruppe from *Das Reich* that drove it off. Rybalko's 3TA was effectively blocked and his timetable for taking Kharkov ruined. Instead, Rybalko began preparing for a deliberate assault crossing of the Donets and had to hope that Golikov's other armies were doing better in their sectors. To the north, Kazakov's 69th Army was slowly pushing back the *Großdeutschland* Division, but it was Moskalenko's 40th Army, bearing down on Belgorod, that provided the means to unhinge the German defence on the Northern Donets. Although Moskalenko did not have a lot of tanks, he used them well, forming small mobile strike groups based upon the 116th and 192nd Tank Brigades. Korps z.b.V. Cramer only had the 168.Infanterie-Division defending Belgorod, which was easily bypassed by Moskalenko's armour. Alarmed by the sudden appearance of Soviet armour near Belgorod, Cramer directed *Großdeutschland* to send its reconnaissance battalion and two motorized infantry battalions, along with five Pz IV tanks and two StuG IIIs,to reinforce the Belgorod sector, but it was too late. During the night of 7–8 February, Moskalenko's troops fought their way into Belgorod, which threatened to envelop the entire German front north of Kharkov.

Combined with the loss of Belgorod, Kazakov's 69th Army continued to push against *Großdeutschland* and *Das Reich*. On 8 February, *Das Reich* made another attack against Soviet forces near Velikiy Burluk, but once again failed to conduct adequate pre-battle reconnaissance and eight tanks were destroyed by anti-tank gun fire. For the first time, the *Das Reich* committed a few of its newly-arrived Tiger tanks, but the company commander SS-Hauptsturmführer Rolf Grader was killed in the opening action. After this, both *Großdeutschland* and *Das Reich* were obliged to withdraw across the Donets on 9 February.

By 10 February, the *Großdeutschland* was protecting the northern approaches to Kharkov, while *Das Reich* and *LSSAH* were defending the eastern approaches to the city. Hausser's SS-Panzerkorps was still incomplete, since *Totenkopf* had not yet arrived. On the night of 9–10 February, Rybalko's 3TA began its deliberate crossing of the Donets with infantry seizing small bridgeheads. On the morning of 10 February, elements of Koptsov's 15th Tank Corps crossed and seized Pechenegi while General-major Mitrofan I. Zinkovich's 12th Tank Corps did the same at Chuguyev. German resistance at the river's edge was light, since the bulk of *LSSAH* had pulled back into a tighter perimeter closer to the city. The original concept for Operation Star was that Rybalko's 3TA would envelop Kharkov by manoeuvre, rather than attempting to storm into the city with a frontal assault, but this was now abandoned. On 11 February, Rybalko's two tank corps, supported by four rifle divisions, began attacking westward straight toward the city. Slow, grinding progress was achieved, but Rybalko's tanks were being regularly picked off by Panzerjägers and StuG IIIs – this was not how a tank army was supposed to be employed. The *Das Reich* had established a strong defensive position at Rogan, east of the city, which could not easily be stormed without significant artillery preparation, but Rybalko's tankers only had limited air and artillery support.

Meanwhile, Sokolov's 6GCC continued to try and sweep around to the south of Kharkov and Hausser decided to conduct a major counter-attack to remove this threat to his line of communications. A covering force known as the *Deckungsgruppe* was left to hold off Rybalko, while an assault formation known as Angriffsgruppe Dietrich was assembled under the *LSSAH*'s commander SS-Obergruppenführer Sepp Dietrich consisting of three subordinate Kampfgruppen. Kampfgruppe Meyer had the *LSSAH*'s reconnaissance battalion, Sturmbannführer Max Wünsche's I./SS-Pz Rgt. 1; Kampfgruppe Kumm consisted of two battalions from the SS-Panzergrenadier-Regiment *Der Führer* and two companies from II./SS-Pz. Rgt. 1; Kampfgruppe Witt consisted of one infantry battalion from *LSSAH*, plus engineers, the Sturmgeschütz-Abteilung and artillery.[50] In addition, *LSSAH* committed five of its Tigers to the operation. This was a very large force, including half of Hausser's available armour and a good portion of his infantry and artillery, leaving the defence of Kharkov short-handed. However, Hausser figured that he would be able to crush Sokolov in a couple of days and then return his forces to defend Kharkov before Rybalko could overcome the blocking position at Rogan. In order to achieve decisive results in warfare one has to accept risk, but that decision has to be based upon sober analysis, which in this case was lacking. The Germans did not have a lot of respect for Soviet cavalry, which heretofore had not been equipped with heavy weapons. However, Sokolov's 6GCC was quite well equipped, since Rybalko had dispatched it to serve as a mobile group and in addition to its three cavalry divisions, had Polkovnik Ivan T. Afinogenovich's 201st Tank Brigade (equipped with 25–30 Matilda and Valentine tanks), a multiple rocket launcher battalion, an anti-tank regiment with 76.2mm ZiS-3 guns and an anti-tank battalion with 45mm guns.

At 0800 hours on 11 February, Angriffsgruppe Dietrich began its attack southward against Sokolov's 6GCC from assembly areas near the rail station at Merefa. The German plan was ambitious, anticipating Kampfgruppe Meyer and Kampfgruppe Witt to conduct enveloping manoeuvres against Sokolov's east and west flanks, while Kampfgruppe Kumm went up the middle. Straight up, the Waffen-SS found that off-road manoeuvre was practically impossible due to snow that was up to two metres deep; tanks that attempted to move through it would 'belly out' with snow compacted against their hull and tracks to the point that they just skidded in place. The Tigers proved particularly useless and one caught fire near Merefa and had to be abandoned.[51] Consequently, the German attackers were road-bound and despite the support of some Ju-87 Stukas from StG 77, they could not conduct proper manoeuvre warfare. In the centre, Sturmbannführer Martin Groß led his II./SS-Pz. Rgt. 1 in an ill-advised frontal assault into the town of Birky, which was well-defended by anti-tank guns and the German Panzer attack was repulsed with heavy losses. Aside from this setback, the two German flanking movements went much slower than expected due to the snow and the lead elements were quickly running out of fuel. By the end of the second day of the counter-attack, the German pincers had still not closed around Sokolov and many of the villages were skillfully defended by Soviet rearguards which inflicted painful losses. Furthermore, the Soviet cavalry was not road-bound in the snow and easily slipped away from the slow-moving Panzer columns. Sokolov was soon alerted to the German pincer attack but, rather than withdraw, he fortified several towns included Okhoche, 50km south of Kharkov; he realized that the longer he could tie up the SS armour in these side-show actions would benefit Moskalenko's and Rybalko's assaults upon Kharkov.

On 14 February, the jaws of Angriffsgruppe Dietrich finally closed around the 6GCC at Okhoche. Wünsche's I./SS-Pz. Rgt. 1 and a battalion of SS-Panzergrenadiers confidently attacked the village across an open field – again without proper reconnaissance – and ran into a hailstorm of tank, anti-tank and mortar fire. One infantry company was virtually annihilated and Wünsche lost a number of his tankers before falling back.[52] Sokolov had skillfully deployed his anti-tank guns and concealed about 25 of Afinogenovich's tanks inside or next to buildings. After skirmishing with the Germans for the rest of the day, Sokolov ordered his forces to withdraw southward to avoid encirclement. Later, the Germans found five abandoned tanks in Okhoche (probably Matildas), but the rest of the Soviet armour had escaped with Sokolov's cavalry. At 1730 hours, Angriffsgruppe Dietrich received orders that it was to suspend its attack due to the deteriorating situation in Kharkov and return to Merefa. Although Sokolov's 6GCC had suffered significant losses, it had not been encircled or destroyed and the diversion of so much of Hausser's resources to this effort weakened the defence of Kharkov just as Moskalenko's 40th Army was enveloping Kharkov from the northwest.[53]

While Angriffsgruppe Dietrich was pushing southward away from Kharkov, Moskalenko's 40th Army ran roughshod over Armee-Lanz and kept forcing *Großdeutschland* to pull back to protect its open flanks. By 12 February, Moskalenko was sweeping down behind Kharkov with four rifle divisions and it accelerated when he committed General-major Andrei G. Kravchenko's 5th Guards Tank Corps into the battle.[*] Supported by a fresh infantry unit, the 25th Guards Rifle Division, Kravchenko's tanks smashed through Lanz's blocking detachments, cleaved Generalkommando z.b.V. Raus in two and reached the northern outskirts of Kharkov by the evening of 13 February. Furthermore, the *Deckungsgruppe* left to keep Rybalko out of eastern Kharkov was attacked repeatedly and forced to yield the blocking position at Rogan on 12 February.[54]

---

[*] The 4th Tank Corps was redesignated as 5th Guards Tank Corps (5GTC) on 7 February 1943.

The Soviet pincers were closing and only a narrow line of communications for the German units in Kharkov remained to the southwest. Suddenly, Hausser's SS-Panzerkorps was in serious trouble.

Moskalenko followed up Kravchenko's bold advance by pushing infantry units into the northern part of Kharkov on 14 February. On the same day, Hitler gave von Manstein command over both the SS-Panzerkorps and Armee-Abteilung Lanz. The first elements of the *Totenkopf* Division were just arriving in Kharkov as Kravchenko's tankers moved into the northern suburbs, but the division's tanks and heavy weapons were still en route. Von Manstein directed *Totenkopf* to assemble in Poltava, west of Kharkov, since he recognized that the unit could not immediately contribute much to the defence of the city.

Hitler ordered that Kharkov was to be held at all costs, but Hausser did not see it that way. Both of his divisions were fixed in place holding off Rybalko's constantly attacking 3TA and *Großdeutschland* was fending off the 69th Army's attacks, but there were no significant reserves left to stop Moskalenko's advance into the city. As the Soviets began to threaten to cut the German lines of communication into the city, by evening of 14 February Hausser requested permission to evacuate the city. Both von Manstein and Lanz refused this request. However, Hausser had no intention of dying in place and at 1645 hours he ordered his two divisions and the *Großdeutschland* to begin evacuating the city. At 1800 hours von Manstein ordered Hausser to stop the withdrawal, but Hausser refused to comply. Throughout 15 February, Hausser disengaged his units and conducted a tactical withdrawal through the city and to the southwest through Merefa. Soviet artillery bombarded the city, but otherwise the Soviets did not make a major effort to interfere with the evacuation. The final rearguard consisted of Major Otto-Ernst Remer's I./Grenadier-Regiment *Großdeutschland* (equipped with SPWs) and Hauptmann Peter Frantz's *Sturmgeschütz-Abteilung Großdeutschland.*[*] On 16 February, Rybalko's tankers met up with Kravchenko's tankers in the centre of the city, completing the liberation of Kharkov.

For a few days, Golikov's forces were tied up in the congested streets of Kharkov, but on the morning of 18 February Rybalko sent Koptsov's 15th Tank Corps probing to the west and encountered *Großdeutschland*'s blocking positions. About 20 Soviet tanks, including T-34s, overran two German infantry companies, then knocked out two German tanks. At the same time, Zinkovich's 12th Tank Corps attacked the 320.Infanterie-Division at Merefa and captured the town. Generalkommando z.b.V. Raus, which controlled these two divisions, was strained on 19–20 February to prevent Rybalko from attacking into the rear of the SS-Panzerkorps, which had pivoted to the southeast and was assembling for a counter-attack. Hausser was forced to detach both the SS-Schützen-Regiment *Thule* and the SS-*Totenkopf*-Sturmgeschütz-Abteilung to

---

[*] Remer would later gain considerable notoriety for crushing the July 20th Plot against Hitler.

reinforce Raus's faltering command. Nevertheless, Rybalko attacked again on 19 February and forced *Großdeutschland* and the SS-Regiment *Thule* to retreat.

The Backhand Blow, 19 February–16 March 1943

Once Kharkov was lost, von Manstein's situation actually improved because the SS-Panzerkorps was no longer tied to the defence of the city and at least part of it could be employed where it would cause the most trouble to the Red Army. Although both the *Das Reich* and *LSSAH* had suffered substantial losses in the defence of Kharkov, including at least 60–70 tanks lost or damaged, the fresh *Totenkopf* Division was detraining at Poltava and added considerable capability. On the night of 18–19 February, the SS-Panzerkorps was assigned to Hoth's 4. PzAOK, which had been moved westward to direct part of von Manstein's counter-offensive in coordination with von Mackensen's 1.PzAOK. On the other side of the hill, both Vatutin's and Golikov's forces were nearly spent and well beyond their supply lines, but still advancing. Rybalko's 3TA had lost about 60 tanks around Kharkov and had 100 or less still operational, and its supporting rifle divisions were at 30–50 per cent strength. Rybalko requested permission to rest and refit his armoured units for three days but was refused by Golikov, who wanted the armour to keep pushing westward against Generalkommando z.b.V. Raus. Popov's Armoured Group was in particularly poor shape, but Vatutin committed his last reserves – the 1st Guards Tank Corps (1GTC) and 1st Guards Cavalry Corps (1GCC) – to re-energize its efforts. On 19 February, the 111th Tank Brigade from Pavlov's 25th Tank Corps captured Slavograd, only 36km from Zaporozhe. Nevertheless, the only Soviet forces that were still able to achieve significant advances were the infantry-based 40th and 69th Armies, which were pushing westward against feeble opposition from Armeeabteilung Kempf and Generalkommando z.b.V. Raus, creating a salient between Heeresgruppe Süd and Heeresgruppe Mitte.

Von Manstein was astute enough to recognize that his opponents were over-extended and that there was an opportunity to regain the initiative. He also recognized that Popov's Armoured Group was the primary threat and should be dealt with first. On the other hand, he had to devote some of his best units, such as *Großdeutschland* and *LSSAH*, to defensive tasks to prevent his left flank from collapsing. As an opening move, von Manstein directed the 15.Infanterie-Division, which was arriving by rail from France, to detrain just outside the town of Sinel'nikovo on the evening of 19 February. Assisted by three Marder tank destroyers, the German infantrymen stealthily advanced into the town and caught Pavlov's 25th Tank Corps completely by surprise; since most of his armour was immobilized by lack of fuel there was little that he could do to stop the sudden German attack. His corps abandoned the town and a good deal of equipment.

Also on 19 February, the SS-*Wiking* Division finally finished off Poluboyarov's immobilized 4GTC at Krasnoarmeyskoye, which was virtually destroyed. Poluboyarov managed to escape with dismounted remnants and after 4GTC was rebuilt, he would command this formation for the duration of the war. The next day, the 11.Panzer-Division pushed westward from Konstantinovka across the supposedly impassible Krivoi Torpetz while the 7.Panzer-Division pushed north from Krasnoarmeyskoye; this manoeuvre began to close the jaws around the immobilized 10th Tank Corps and the 18th Tank Corps that Popov had just shifted from his other flank. Although Generaloberst Gotthard Heinrici's XXXX Panzerkorps had difficulty closing the ring due to the snow and limited forces available, by the night of 21–22 February three of Popov's tank corps had been effectively destroyed, although thousands of troops escaped. Given the limited number of tanks available and their unwillingness to close in on desperate encircled troops, the PzAOK 1 counter-offensive relied heavily on stand-off firepower, using artillery and 8.8cm Flak guns to pick off Soviet tanks and vehicles from a distance. For their part, the trapped Soviet tank corps tried to conceal their T-34s inside villages, protected by the remaining infantry, thereby forcing the Germans to fight their way into some towns. However, the real reason that the Soviet tank corps collapsed so quickly – aside from the obvious shortages of fuel, food and ammunition – was their lack of effective artillery support. By this point, Popov's tank corps had lost their attached multiple rocket launcher battalions and the only remaining artillery left to defend their hedgehogs were small numbers of 76.2mm field guns and 82mm mortars. By 24 February, PzAOK 1 had rolled up Group Popov and demolished it piecemeal. With their vehicles and tanks smashed, Popov's tankers began the long walk back through the snow to the Donets.

On 20 February, Hoth ordered the *Das Reich* and *Totenkopf* to begin attacking the flank of the 6th Army south of Krasnograd. *Das Reich* only had 41 operational tanks (33 Pz III, 7 Pz IV, 1 Tiger) and 15 StuG III, but *Totenkopf* was nearly full strength with about 100 tanks and 20 assault guns. The *LSSAH*, which had 73 operational tanks (10 Pz III, 45 Pz IV, 12 Pz II, 6 Tiger) and 22 StuG III and was sent to aid the hard-pressed Generalkommando z.b.V. Raus in its efforts to delay Rybalko's push westward from Kharkov. The attack began at 0500 hours, with columns of tanks and vehicles probing cautiously forward through thick, white fog. Initially, the SS-Panzerkorps was opposed by elements of two of 6th Army's rifle divisions, but very little armour. By noon, the sky had cleared enough for Ju-87 Stukas to provide close air support sorties, which helped to smash up Soviet positions in towns. The *Das Reich* was also fortunate to have some of the new Wespe 10.5cm self-propelled howitzers, which provided excellent mobile fire support. Only a single Tiger, from *Das Reich*, participated in the attack, but it enjoyed considerable success, destroying 11 anti-tank guns and four T-34s in the first two days. This Tiger spearheaded the attack into Pavlograd on 21–22 February, which put paid to the 25th Tank Corps. Due to ignorance about the impending German counter-offensive, Vatutin had never ordered these forces to shift to the defence and they were caught unprepared by the sudden arrival of German mechanized units. Elements of four Russian rifle divisions were isolated south of Pavlograd, which required considerable mop-up operations. The 6. and 17.Panzer-Divisionen, subordinate to the XXXXVIII Panzerkorps, arrived south of Pavlograd and assisted the SS-Panzerkorps in crushing one isolated Soviet unit after another. Here and there, a few T-34s and anti-tank guns put up a fight and cost the Germans some vehicles, but superior firepower and manoeuvre carried the day.

Although the Soviet spearheads nearest the Dnepr were relatively easy to dispose of, the 6th Army established a coherent defensive position at Lozovaya with General-major Aleksandr V. Kukushkin's 1st Guards Tank Corps and the 48th Guards Rifle Division. Hoth's basic plan was to conduct a frontal assault on Lozovaya with *Das Reich*, while *Totenkopf* manoeuvred around to isolate the town. As part of this effort, the II./SS-Pz. Regt. 3 sent one of its companies in a movement to contact west of Lozovaya on the night of 24–25 February; this was a tank-pure team with no infantry or artillery support. Even worse, the tanks were low on fuel and ammunition. Moving tanks in hostile territory at night without proper reconnaissance is very reckless and before long SS-Hauptscharführer Fritz Biermeier's 6 Kompanie was lost. However, the SS tankers continued to press on and just before dawn they blundered into a group of Kukushkin's T-34s. A short, sharp tank action ensued, with losses on both sides. While recovering from the action, Biermeier's company was next surprised by Soviet cavalry, who killed and captured some of his crews while they were outside working on their damaged tanks.[55]

Capping off this tactical fiasco, the *Das Reich* managed to lose one of its three operational Tigers on 25 February in a singular act of stupidity not uncommon among tankers. Tankers are often proud of their mounts and are prone to brag about them to outsiders. SS-Hauptsturmführer Friedrich Herzig, who like many SS tank leaders had no prior experience with tanks, had only been commander of *Das Reich*'s Tiger company (8./SS-Pz. Rgt. 2) for a week when he made a bet with some Luftwaffe officers that his 54-ton tank could cross a frozen river. Apparently, Herzig failed to notice that a thaw had begun the previous day and that the ice was thinning. After moving only a short distance on to the ice, the Tiger broke through and sank up to the top of its turret. It took three days of effort to recover this Tiger and then the water-logged vehicle, with its electrical system ruined, had to be sent back to Kassel for repair. The report on this embarrassing incident went all the way up to Hitler, who was not amused.*

The first part of von Manstein's counter-offensive culminated with the Battle of Lozovaya on 26–27 February. Since the *Das Reich* only had 19 operational tanks left, it relied heavily on its artillery, assault guns and Stuka attacks to reduce the Soviet defences. Kukushkin's tanks were well hidden in the town

---

* Herzig was not relieved of command for this lapse in judgment, but was quietly shifted to another assignment after a month. From January–May 1945 he commanded the King Tigers of the s.SS-PanzerAbt.503 in the final battles.

and put up a tough fight, supported by plenty of anti-tank guns. Kukushkin even managed a counter-attack with his T-34s, but six were quickly knocked out. By 27 February, the Germans had occupied Lozovaya and completed the destruction of Vatutin's spearheads. Recognizing defeat, Vatutin ordered the survivors to pull back toward the Donets. Von Mackensen's 1. PzAOK also kept up the pressure on 1st Guards Army, recovering much of the ground lost at the start of Operation Gallop.

Although Golikov's Voronezh Front was still advancing against Armeeabteilung Kempf with the 40th and 69th Armies, the Stavka recognized that Vatutin's Southwest Front had suffered a major reverse. Golikov used Vatutin's defeat to temporarily shift to the defence, allowing his exhausted forces a brief respite, but on 28 February the Stavka ordered him to send Rybalko's 3TA south from Kharkov to block Hoth's armour from approaching Kharkov. Given the lack of intelligence about the SS-Panzerkorps' dispositions, poor logistics and lack of air support, this was a foolish decision. Furthermore, Rybalko barely had 60 operational tanks left between his two tank corps, including at least five Matildas and 20–30 T-70 light tanks, but the Stavka had no replacements immediately available. Indeed, this inability of the Stavka to ensure a steady flow of tank replacements to the front in February–March 1943 illustrates a point that is often lost in macro-level assessments of the Eastern Front, namely that the Soviet Union was out-producing Germany in tanks, but could not always deploy this numerical superiority at the right time and place on the battlefield. At this point, the Stavka had no significant armoured reserves and was forced to transfer Katukov's 1st Tank Army (1TA) from the Northwest Front to the Voronezh Front to restore Golikov's armoured strength, but that would take weeks to accomplish.

While the Stavka and Front commanders were trying to determine what to do in the wake of Vatutin's defeat, von Manstein was quickly redeploying his forces against Kharkov before any new Soviet units could arrive. Golikov's decision to shift to the defence allowed Raus to pull the *Großdeutschland* out of the line to rest for a few days and, fortuitously, the II./Pz. Regt. *Großdeutschland* arrived from Germany at Poltava on 17–26 February with a welcome infusion of armour (95 tanks including nine Tigers, 10 Pz III, 42 Pz IV, 28 Flammpanzer IIIs and six command tanks). Oberst Hyazinth Graf Strachwitz, recovered from his wounds at Stalingrad, was given command of the new Panzer-Regiment *Großdeutschland*.

Rybalko's two tank corps headed due south on 1 March, straight at the SS-Panzerkorps, and bumped into their vanguards east of Krasnograd. In a rather inelegant action dubbed the 'Kegichevka *Kessel*', both the 12th and 15th Tank Corps were quickly surrounded by *LSSAH* and *Das Reich* and were destroyed as fighting units by 3 March. Parts of four Soviet rifle divisions were also destroyed. However, Zinkovich led a successful breakout with part of his 12th Corps, but Koptsov was killed. A good portion of Rybalko's men escaped northward, where they were reorganized and provided 24 repaired tanks, just enough to reconstitute a single brigade.

With Rybalko's 3TA effectively out of the fight, von Manstein now prepared to begin the second phase of his grand counter-offensive. All three divisions of the SS-Panzerkorps were assembled southwest of Merefa and for the first time they would be committed to battle together. The *LSSAH* was the strongest formation, with 74 operational tanks and 16 StuG IIIs, while *Totenkopf* had 64 operational tanks and 16 StuG IIIs. However, the *Das Reich* was battle-weary and had only eight Pz IIIs still operational. Altogether, Hausser's SS-Panzerkorps would advance upon Kharkov with fewer than 200 tanks and assault guns left. Hoth also brought in the XXXXVIII Panzerkorps and *Großdeutschland* to support the offensive; this was a vital lesson learned from Operation *Wintergewitter*, that a minimum of two Panzerkorps were needed to maintain operational momentum.

On 5 March, the *LSSAH* led the advance toward Kharkov, while Armee-Abteilung Kempf mounted fixing attacks against the 69th Army to prevent it from transferring troops to the threatened sector. Four Tigers from *LSSAH* were assigned to lead their division's attack in the direction of Valky, on the Mzha River, and fulfill the tank's intended breakthrough role. On the morning of 6 March, Sturmbannführer Max Wünsche's II./SS-Pz. Regt. 1 conducted an attack with two of his Panzer-Kompanien, supported by two Tigers and troops from Sturmbannführer Kurt Meyer's SS-Aufklärungs-Abteilung *LSSAH*, against the village of Sneschkov Kut (Snizhiv) 10km south of Valky. The battalion adjutant described the movement to contact:

We still had eighteen Panzers, with the two Tigers behind us, with the infantrymen [Meyer's men] ducked down hiding behind the turret. Shells! Halt! On the gently sloping hill and in front of it, fire suddenly sprang up across a broad front. It appeared to be an entire anti-tank front. The commander [Wünsche] ordered the two Kompanien: 'Faster, speed it up! Forward!' Ahead to the left, the crew of Beck's Panzer was bailing out… The rapid fire from our panzers had had its effect on the hill. The lead Panzers were still 800 meters from it. To the left and right of us, there were two tanks in flames. We were now in the phase of fighting in which most Panzer attacks become critical…We had gone about 150 meters when I saw the commander ahead to the right heading for a barn in order to get some cover from the enemy's view…In a fraction of a second I registered that it was humming all around us. From the hill, now clearly visible, flashes of light were coming with uncomfortable frequency. Apparently, by heading for the barn, we had managed to find a blind spot in their field of fire. When we reached the hill, with the commander 100 meters ahead…I could see the first houses about 200–300 meters away. Anti-tank fire started up from the first house and a shell landed right beside us. In the light of the gunfire,

I roared 'To the rear [to the driver]!' Seconds later there was a second shell. With my cry: 'Bail out!' we found ourselves in the snow beside the Panzer. The wires of our headphone sets were still hanging around our necks. The heat of the blast had given us some serious burns. Instinctively, we buried our heads in the snow.[56]

Huddled beside his burning tank, the adjutant detected a T-34 tank hidden behind one of the houses and watched as one of the Tigers entered the battle:

About 80 meters to one side of us, a Tiger crawled up the hill…The Tiger had hardly made it up the hill when there was a huge explosion, and light and debris flew all around us. When we looked up, we saw a gouge in the Tiger's turret a meter square in area. But at the same time we saw its 8.8cm gun move and point to the target like a finger. A stream of fire came out of it. Half of the house flew away, and we got a clear view of a burning enemy tank with its turret blown off…From the edge of the entire town, two dozen T-34s emerged from their hiding places.[57]

The Tiger, soon joined by its partner, picked off eight of the T-34s, causing the others to turn and flee. After the village was secured, the *LSSAH* troops found no less than 56 enemy anti-tank guns in the area – a startling indicator that Soviet defensive capabilities were steadily improving and that traditional Panzer attacks were becoming more costly to execute. Although the *LSSAH* managed to get across the Mzha River without too much difficulty, one Tiger broke through the ice and could not be recovered for several days.

On 7 March, the *LSSAH* closed in on the heavily-fortified town of Valkiy, held by 49th Guards Rifle Division, and was forced to conduct numerous small set-piece attacks against outlying villages. In one action, the *LSSAH* Sturmgeschütz-Abteilung attacked an anti-tank position in the village of Balki, where one StuG-III crew discovered the dangers of 'throwing track' while under fire:

Only down at the collective farm [Kolkhoz] headquarters, where there was evidently a commissar leading the resistance, was there even the weakest attempt at defence. Geschütz 234 moved out toward it, all its weapons firing away. It rolled right over the anti-tank gun, wound its way through the smoldering farm, dead Soviets lying everywhere, and suddenly got stuck in the meter-high snow, which had lifted the track off the drive wheel. The driver slammed it into reverse to pull up the track, which was still resting on the [return] rollers. Exactly the opposite happened. The track fell off the drive wheel completely, and the sticky snow, which had lodged itself between the rollers and the bogie wheels, began to push it off all along the way. Ivan spotted something now. An anti-tank gun began to fire, and the riflemen began to work their way forward in little groups, protected by the ruins of the town. Our men could still defend themselves with high-explosive shells and the on-board machinegun, but the ammunition supply was rapidly dwindling. In addition, those weapons only provided frontal support; once the enemy got into their dead space, the situation would get risky. Support could not be expected, for the radio equipment was out of order. On top of that, no one had noticed in the stormy advance that the Batterie had not followed. The only solution: jump out and try to get back to the Batterie.[58]

The StuG-III crewmen managed to run back to their unit and soon thereafter, successfully towed the immobilized assault gun under fire and brought it to a friendly assembly area. Well-trained crews can hook up tow cables in seconds, although if the final drive is not disconnected – which requires opening the back deck – the transmission will likely be damaged when the vehicle is towed.

Once the SS-Panzerkorps broke through the Soviet defences south of Kharkov, it swung to the west and began to envelop the city while von Knobelsdorff's XXXXVIII Panzerkorps advanced toward the eastern side of the city with the 6. and 11.Panzer-Divisionen. Hoth hoped to encircle the city and avoid sending his mechanized forces into urban combat, but Hausser and his troops were eager to avenge their earlier retreat from the city. Between 10–14 March, Hausser's SS-Panzerkorps fought its way into Kharkov and gradually overcame the uncoordinated Soviet resistance in vicious street fighting. On 14 March, the city was in German hands and Golikov's shattered Voronezh Front was in headlong retreat. Rybalko's 3TA was effectively destroyed.

After securing Kharkov, the third phase of von Manstein's counter-offensive began with the advance north toward Belgorod. The spring thaw was beginning, melting some snow and turning the roads into deep mud. Von Manstein wanted to seize as many follow-on objectives as possible before the weather and eventual Soviet reinforcements could halt his advance. It was *Großdeutschland* which made the most progress, smashing into Kazakov's battered 69th Army and rolling it up with a one-division mini-*Blitzkrieg*. On 13 March, the *Großdeutschland* captured Borisovka, east of Belgorod. Golikov brought Kravchenko's understrength 5GTC over to stop the *Großdeutschland*'s advance as well as the 3rd Guards Tank Corps. The Stavka even provided Golikov with Badanov's 2nd Guards Tank Corps (formerly the 24th Tank Corps), which had been virtually destroyed in the Tatsinskaya Raid in December 1942; although re-equipped, this formation was unready for combat. The Graf Strachwitz's well-trained panzer crews destroyed these ill-trained Soviet units piecemeal in a series of actions between 13–18 March that were reminiscent of the heady days of *Barbarossa*, except for the mud; the Panzer-Regiment *Großdeutschland* claimed 128 Soviet tanks destroyed in this period. In one action, the enemy simply abandoned their tanks and *Großdeutschland* captured 15 intact T-34s.

Although outnumbered 3–1 or worse, Strachwitz's panzers completely outclassed their opposition and, unlike the Waffen-SS tankers, knew how to keep their own losses down with proper battlefield reconnaissance. On the night of 14–15 March, the *Großdeutschland* detected an impending Soviet armoured counter-attack and Strachwitz deployed his panzers in ambush near Borisovka, as related by a German tank platoon leader:

> After a quick briefing of the tank commanders on the distribution of fire, radio silence was ordered. The platoon leader gave the order to open fire only on his command. Critical minutes now followed. Barely 1,000 meters away the diesel engines of enemy tanks suddenly roared to life. It wasn't just the sounds of two or five tanks – there had to be many more.
>
> The morning of 15 March 1943 dawned; the roar of engines slowly drew nearer. The tank commanders spotted the outlines of the first T-34s over on the road. The gunners at their sights were already restless, but in the twilight they could not yet see their targets clearly. They held their breath and sighed with relief when the first T-34 entered their field of view. All the while the loader crouched tensely by his gun, a shell in his hands, two more clamped between his legs; for every second counted…There were already five T-34s in the field of view. Unsuspectingly, the T-34s ground through the snow and mud. Seven were already visible, and their broadsides were too tempting for the gunners.
>
> The T-34s appeared to be uncertain, turning their barrels to the left and to the right; it was good that we were on parallel to them. Every gunner already knew which enemy tank to engage. The first two belonged to the man on the left wing, those behind it to the others echeloned to the right… For a moment, the calm developed after many engagements seemed to be shaken. Then, finally, the order: All tanks…guns up…fire! A loud bang! Then, in a matter of seconds, four – eight – twelve green tracer trails, between them brief radio messages. Then the firing settled down into a few individual rounds. On the enemy side huge jets of flame and smoke. The last T-34 tried to turn around and became bogged down in the process. The crew sprang like cats from the turret, but they were mowed down by our machinegun fire. Our tank drivers waved to each other joyfully.[59]

On 18 March, the SS-Panzerkorps exploded north from Kharkov and captured Belgorod that evening. Over the next several days, the SS-Panzerkorps and *Großdeutschland* mopped up Soviet remnants in the area, but von Manstein's offensive was finally brought to a halt by the spring thaw and increasing resistance. Katukov's 1st Tank Army (1TA) finally arrived north of Belgorod on 23–24 March, along with two other fresh armies from the RVGK, which created the front-line that stabilized for the next three months until the Battle of Kursk. While von Manstein's 'Backhand Blow' is rightly regarded as an operational masterpiece, it also indicated that the character of German mechanized offensives was changing as many of their traditional advantages began to wane. The German Panzertruppen still enjoyed a major edge in tactical skill, but Soviet anti-tank defences were becoming much more robust than in 1941–42 and the Red Army's tank units were also improved. Von Manstein did succeed in mauling eight of the 20 Soviet tank corps on the Eastern Front, which temporarily deprived the Red Army of the initiative and gave Heeresgruppe Süd a valuable breathing space.

Rokossovsky's Offensive, 25 February–28 March 1943
Although most of the action in early 1943 was occurring on the southern part of the Eastern Front, the Stavka was eager to put pressure on Generalfeldmarschall Günther von Kluge's Heeresgruppe Mitte as well in order to tie down German forces and to reclaim territory while the Germans were still hard-pressed. As planning for Operations Gallop and Star proceeded in late January 1943, the Stavka also began developing a plan for the Bryansk Front to attack Generaloberst Rudolf Schmidt's 2.Panzerarmee's (2.PzAOK) positions north of Orel and finish off General der Infanterie Walter Weiss' 2.Armee (2.AOK), which would disrupt Heeresgruppe Mitte's right flank and assist the advance of Golikov's Voronezh Front. Furthermore, the Stavka decided that once the Battle of Stalingrad ended, that Rokossovsky's five armies should redeploy by rail and form a new Central Front to supplement the Bryansk Front's offensive. Recognizing that Rokossovsky's armies were not equipped with a great deal of armour to spearhead a breakthrough operation, the Stavka decided to transfer General-leytenant Aleksei G. Rodin's 2nd Tank Army from the RVGK to Rokossovsky's new command, as well as the newly-formed 70th Army. Once Rokossovsky seized Orel, the Stavka intended to widen the offensive by including the Western Front. Zhukov optimistically hoped that the concurrent offensives of Vatutin, Golikov and Rokossovsky would prevent the Germans from forming a new front and force them to retreat to the Dnepr.

Heeresgruppe Mitte's right flank did appear ripe for the picking. There was a thinly-covered area between 2.AOK and 2.PzAOK near Sevsk, 140km southwest of Orel. Although the face of the burgeoning Orel salient was stoutly defended by the XXXXVI Panzerkorps with the 12., 18. and 20.Panzer-Divisionen, General der Panzertruppe Joachim Lemelsen's XXXXVII Panzerkorps was holding the extreme right flank of 2.PzAOK with just the 137. and 707.Infanterie-Divisionen; the 707.Infanterie-Division was a particularly weak formation that had only been employed in anti–partisan operations and possessed a single artillery battalion and no divisional anti-tank unit. Nor did the battered 2.Armee possess the resources to stop a concerted enemy push westward. Generalmajor Erich Schneider's 4.Panzer-Division was sent to hold Kursk, but its armoured strength was reduced to a single tank company, plus a few assault guns. As in the winter of 1941–42, the 4.Panzer-Division had so few

Panzergrenadiers left that it was forced to create an ad hoc infantry unit from dismounted tankers. The Stavka's plan was to have the Bryansk Front strike the face of the Orel salient and fix the XXXXVI Panzerkorps, then Rodin's 2TA and the 70th Army would crush Lemelsen's XXXXVII Panzerkorps and envelop Orel by driving for Bryansk.

Since the Stavka was in a rush to kick off the offensive before the spring thaw began or the Germans restored their frontline, Rokossovsky was given only six days to plan his offensive. Furthermore, transportation difficulties delayed the redeployment of his troops from Stalingrad to Voronezh; the Soviets were having difficulty repairing rail lines and Rokossovsky's armies only had one single-track line to support his new Central Front. Consequently, the Stavka decided to postpone Rokossovsky's offensive until late February, while beginning on schedule with those forces from the Bryansk and Voronezh Fronts already in place. This approach caught the Germans off guard. General-leytenant Nikolai P. Pukhov's 13th Army (Bryansk Front) attacked Schmidt's 2.PzAOK and captured the important town of Fatezh on 12 February, while General-leytenant Ivan D. Cherniakhovsky's 60th Army (Voronezh Front) pushed Schneider's 4.Panzer-Division out of Kursk.[60] During the fighting for Kursk, the 4.Panzer-Division lost a number of veteran panzer junior officers and NCOs, fighting on foot as infantry. By mid-February, a 60km-wide gap had been created between 2.PzAOK and 2.AOK by these limited offensives, thereby providing the perfect prequel to Rokossovsky's major offensive. Pukhov was particularly aggressive and continued attacking the XXXXVI Panzerkorps, seized Maloarkhangel'sk on 23 February and attracted German reserves to his sector.

However, the transportation difficulties severely impacted the deployment of Rokossovsky's Central Front and he was forced to begin his offensive on 25 February with only part of his forces in place. Pre-battle preparations were minimal and the weather turned rainy, just as the operation was beginning. Initially, Rokossovsky attacked Lemelsen's XXXXVII Panzerkorps with three rifle divisions from the 65th Army on his right flank and two rifle divisions attached to Rodin's 2TA on his left. Rodin's 11th and 16th Tank Corps, as well as the four cavalry divisions of General-major Vladimir V. Kriukov's 2nd Guards Cavalry Corps (2GCC), were kept in second echelon. Lemelsen could not hold off five Soviet rifle divisions with his two divisions and conducted a tactical delay, while calling for reinforcements. The 707.Infanterie-Division fell back a bit to occupy the fortified town of Dmitriyev-L'govsk, which was located behind the marshy Svapa River and proved to be a tough nut to crack. Rokossovsky decided to split Rodin's 2TA, sending the 11th Tank Corps and Kriukov's 2GCC to the west into the gap between the two German armies, but he sent General-major Aleksei G. Maslov's 16th Tank Corps to support the drive northward into the Orel salient. Rather than concentrate his armour, Rokossovsky dissipated it by sending it on two diverging axes.[61]

The 707.Infanterie-Division held Dmitriyev-L'govsk long enough for the 78.Infanterie-Division to arrive and slow the Soviet advance. Batov's 65th Army enjoyed success and was reinforced by General-major German F. Tarasov's 70th Army; together, these two infantry armies pushed back XXXXVI Panzerkorps and successfully tied down elements of three German Panzer-Divisionen. However, the 2.PzAOK's front south of Orel did not break and efforts by the Western Front to attack the 2.PzAOK's front north of Orel came to naught, so the Stavka's concept of crushing the Orel salient with a pincer attack proved unworkable at this time. Furthermore, the 16th Tank Corps was being misused in a positional battle as an infantry support unit, not as an exploitation force. Thus, the outcome of the offensive hinged on Rodin's advance westward toward the Desna.

By 1 March, Rodin was advancing westward with the 11th Tank Corps, the 2GCC and four supporting rifle brigades. There were virtually no enemy forces between his vanguard and the Desna River. The important city of Sevsk was held by only a single German infantry battalion, which was driven out by Soviet tanks and cavalry. Three intact Hungarian units – the 102, 105 and 108 Light Infantry Divisions – were deployed on the approaches to the Desna, but these formations were only trained and equipped to fight partisans in the forests, not to stop a tank army. Rodin's forces pushed into this void, against minimal resistance, but progress was slow due to rain, poor roads and limited logistical support. On 4 March, General-major Ivan G. Lazarev's 11th Tank Corps captured the important road junction of Seredina Buda from the hapless Hungarian 108th Light Infantry Division. On 7 March, Kriukov's cavalry reached the Desna River near Novgorod-Seversk. However, the impact of von Manstein's success against Vatutin's Southwest Front and the elimination of Rybalko's 3TA caused the Stavka to reconsider Rokossovsky's offensive just as it was on the verge of achieving a major success. Reserves and supplies that had been allocated to Rokossovsky's offensive were instead diverted to Golikov's tottering Voronezh Front and the Stavka directed the Central Front to change Rodin's axis of advance from west to north, pivoting 90 degrees. Rather than going deep for Bryansk, the Stavka opted to reduce the scale of Rokossovsky's offensive by simply chipping away at the Orel salient as much as possible.

Under the new guidance from Moscow, Lazarev's 11th Tank Corps turned northward while Kriukov's 2GCC screened the front along the Desna. However, von Kluge's Heeresgruppe Mitte was reacting to the Soviet offensive now, transferring two infantry divisions to stop the Soviet 65th and 70th Armies south of Orel and 4.Panzer-Division to counter Rodin's 2TA. Generalmajor Erich Schneider's 4.Panzer-Division had been reinforced with five new Pz IV Ausf G, 27 Marder IIs and some assault guns and then sent to Novgorod-Seversk, where 2.AOK still had a small bridgehead over the Desna.[62] Just after Lazarev's tank corps had left this sector, Schneider attacked with his Panzers on 8 March and began rolling up Kriukov's over-extended cavalry. One Soviet-held village after another was softened up by artillery, then stormed by tanks and infantry. Schnieder led his division up-front, from a Sd. Kfz. 251 command track. By mid-March, 2.AOK contributed two more infantry divisions to this counter-attack and Kriukov's corps was forced to retreat, thereby exposing Rodin's 2TA to envelopment. On 19 March, the 4. Panzer-Division had advanced 97km eastward and re-captured Sevsk. Although Schneider's Panzer-Division only captured 420 prisoners during the course of its counter-attack, parts of Kriukov's 2GCC were cut off and isolated in the forests along the Desna, south of Bryansk.[63] The loss of Sevsk forced Rokossovsky to call off his sputtering offensive, unable to break the German defences south of Orel or to deal with the counter-attack of a single Panzer-Division.

The poor performance of Rodin's 2TA in Rokossovsky's offensive was particularly evident. In three weeks of fighting, neither of his two tank corps advanced more than 45km, captured a significant objective or destroyed any Axis units. Given the large Soviet armoured superiority in this sector and the vulnerability of third-string German formations like the 707.Infanterie-Division, as well as the Hungarian light infantry divisions, this is remarkable. In this operation, numerical superiority did not equate to victory for Rokossovsky. While Rodin's 2TA survived the operation more or less intact, it also failed to accomplish anything worthy of a tank army.

The Soviet Offensive in the Kuban, 4 April–7 June 1943

Once the German 17.Armee (AOK 17) had retreated into the Kuban bridgehead in February 1943, General-polkovnik Ivan I. Maslennikov's Soviet North Caucasus Front wasted little time in planning an offensive to drive the Germans from their last toehold in the Caucasus. However, Maslennikov had counted on the amphibious landing south of Novorossiysk unhinging the German defence, but instead, an 8,000-man landing force was contained in the '*Malaia Zemlya*' ('Little Land') bridgehead and a battle of attrition ensued for seven months. By March, the AOK 17 was able to create a very strong defensive front known as the Blue Line (*Blau Stellung*), holding the approaches into the Kuban. The centrepiece of this defence was the Krymskaya sector, held by Generalleutnant Ernst Rupp's 97.Jäger-Division. In mobile reserve, AOK 17 relied upon Generalmajor Wilhelm Crisolli's 13.Panzer-Division and Hauptmann Alfred Müller's Sturmgeschütz-Abteilung 191 (21 StuG-IIIs) to counter-attack any Soviet breaches of the Blue Line. The Germans also had two batteries of Sturmgeschütz-Abteilung 249 providing direct support to Rupp's infantry and the adjoining 5.Luftwaffen-Feld-Division had its own attached battery of assault guns. Rupp's defence was situated behind a small stream and German pioneers had emplaced minefields and obstacles to their front – it was a strong position. Furthermore, since the Eastern Front was relatively quiet after the culmination of von Manstein's counter-offensive, the Luftwaffe was able to shift significant aircraft into the Crimea to support AOK 17 in the Kuban bridgehead. The Soviet VVS did likewise, committing almost 1,000 aircraft from the 4th and 5th Air armies (4VA, 5VA).[64]

General-leytenant Andrei A. Grechko's 56th Army was assigned the mission of breaking through Rupp's defences, seizing Krymskaya and then pushing westward to link up with the Soviet naval infantry in the *Malaia Zemlya* bridgehead. Grechko was provided with five rifle divisions to conduct his breakthrough, but relatively little armour and artillery. He had no large armoured units and his 150–200 tanks were spread across three tank brigades (63, 92, 151), one tank regiment (257) and six OTBs, with a very eclectic mix of tanks. The 151st Tank Brigade was entirely equipped with captured German tanks, abandoned during von Kleist's retreat from the Terek River. Grechko's armour also included a large amount of Lend-Lease M3 Lees and Mark III Valentines, but few T-34s. One unit, the 63rd Tank Brigade, had just received 12 M4A2 Sherman medium tanks and was one of the first armour units in the Red Army to employ this new American-built tank in combat on the Eastern Front.[65]

At 0900 hours on 4 April the 56th Army attacked Rupp's division, but the offensive failed to penetrate the German HKL. Maslennikov temporarily suspended the offensive and made preparations for the 9th and 37th Armies to launch supporting attacks on other parts of the Blue Line to assist Grechko in making a penetration. Additional armour, artillery and air support was also provided. On 14 April, Grechko committed three rifle divisions, each led by a tank battalion (OTB) against the 97.Jäger-Division and succeeded in making a 3km-deep penetration in Rupp's HKL. Crisolli's 13.Panzer-Division immediately committed Kampfgruppe Brux to seal the breach but this was not successful. Consequently, Rupp was forced to abandon his forward line and withdraw to his secondary positions. When Grechko's armour-infantry shock groups rolled forward to occupy the vacated German positions on 16 April, Rupp mounted a spirited counter-attack with a battery of assault guns, supported by Stukas; the Soviets had 48 tanks knocked out, which halted their advance.[66]

During the Kuban Campaign, the Luftwaffe made a concerted effort to improve its low-level anti-tank capabilities. In particular, the Luftwaffe experimented with arming both the Ju-87 Stuka and the Hs-129B-3 with the 3.7cm Flak gun. Hauptmann Hans-Ulrich Rudel was provided with a few prototypes of the Ju-87G and sent to the Kuban to test the new weapon against Soviet armour. The Ju-87G's two 3.7cm cannons, each with a six-round magazine, fired APCR rounds with tungsten carbide penetrators. The APCR rounds had a muzzle velocity of 1,170 m/sec and could penetrate up to 38mm of armour; the T-34's rear deck armour was limited to only 16–20mm of protection. Although Rudel was shot down by anti-aircraft on his first combat sortie in the Ju-87G, he quickly became a staunch advocate of the new method of destroying Soviet T-34s.[67] Based on his endorsement, limited production of the Ju-87G began in June 1943 and a small number would be available for Operation *Zitadelle*.

Meanwhile, Grechko continued attacking Rupp's defensive positions from 29 April–4 May and committed 60 tanks on one day, as well as massive air support. Luftflotte 4 made a major effort to gain air superiority over the Krymskaya sector, inflicting painful losses on the 4VA, but could not stop the incessant Soviet bombing and low-level attacks. Finally, Rupp was forced to abandon Krymskaya and pull his HKL back west of the city. However, the new German line was just as solid and Maslennikov had to pause to reinforce the 56th Army and prepare for a larger set-piece offensive. Disappointed by Maslennikov's failure to achieve a breakthrough, the Stavka decided to replace him with General Ivan E. Petrov, who had conducted the unsuccessful defence of Sevastopol in 1942. The Stavka also provided the 1448th and 1449th Self-Propelled Artillery Regiments (SAP), equipped with Su-76 and Su-122 guns, to spearhead a new offensive. Petrov decided to shift his attack axis northward, to make the main effort against the 101.Jäger-Division with the 37th Army this time, while Grechko made a supporting attack against Rupp. On 26 May, Petrov's Front began a 100-minute artillery preparation. However, the Soviet infantry was unable to penetrate the Blue Line and when the Soviet armour (a mix of T-34s, M3 Lees and Valentines) was committed, it became immobilized in the German minefields and was shot to pieces by assault guns, anti-tank guns and Rudel's Stukas; the Germans claimed 100 tanks destroyed on the first day of the new Soviet offensive. This number was likely exaggerated since many tanks immobilized by mines were subsequently recovered. On the positive side, Soviet air support for the attack was impressive and a new tactic was used, whereby Il-2 Sturmoviks dropped smoke bombs in front of advancing tank-infantry shock groups in order to reduce the effectiveness of the German defensive fire. Soviet air-ground cooperation was improving.

In order to prevent a breakthrough of the Blue Line, Crisolli's 13.Panzer-Division dispatched Kampfgruppe Polster (two understrength Panzer-Kompanie from Panzer-Regiment 4 with 12 Pz IV tanks and Müller's assault guns) and Kampfgruppe Gaza (the I./Panzergrenadier-Regiment 66, which had only a single company of SPWs and some artillery) to counter-attack the Soviet shock groups.[68] Over a period of several days, the Soviet offensive was blunted and then stopped. The Blue Line would hold for another three and a half months. Rupp did not live to see this, however, since he was killed by a Soviet air raid on his command post on 31 May. By early June, Petrov's offensive had been halted, although local attacks kept the pressure on AOK 17 in order to prevent the Germans from transferring units from the Kuban to reinforce Heeresgruppe Süd. Indeed, Crisolli's 13.Panzer-Division would remain in the Kuban until late August 1943 and two assault-gun battalions would remain there until AOK 17 evacuated the Taman Peninsula in September. While the Germans were able to achieve a defensive victory in the Kuban, the forces committed there would have been better employed in von Manstein's command.

For the Red Army, the Kuban proved a useful arena for learning how to crack open German defensive positions, as well as learning how to improve their combined arms tactics. The Soviet use of armour in the Kuban was limited to brigade-size infantry support attacks, which suffered heavy losses due to the density of German defences, but important lessons were learned in coordinating these attacks with artillery and close air support. The days of Soviet tank units attacking without adequate supporting fires was drawing to a close.

Building up for the Showdown, April–June 1943

By the end of March 1943, both sides were completely exhausted and incapable of further sustained offensive action until their depleted air and tank formations were refitted. The Germans had lost 2,152 tanks during January–March 1943 (many were non-operational tanks abandoned during the retreats or lost at Stalingrad) and only 53 per cent of their remaining 1,500 tanks were operational after von Manstein's counter-offensive concluded.[69] The Red Army had also suffered huge tank losses – 5,023 tanks lost in January–March.[70] However, the three months that followed brought a lull period that both sides used to refit their forces for the next test of strength.

How did the armoured units and tankers on both sides use this unusual three-month 'quiet' period in April–June 1943? As much as possible, tank units on both sides were pulled back from the front line in order to conduct maintenance and rest crews, but they were still within range of harassing artillery fire and occasional air attacks. Typically, armoured units dispersed, with each tank company being assigned a reconstitution area in or near a small village. Upon arrival, tanks were camouflaged and troops were given rest time after basic maintenance was completed. When possible, worn track blocks and road wheels were replaced and there were always air filters to clean. Unteroffizier Erich Hager, a Pz IV crewmen in the II./Pz. Rgt. 39 in 17.Panzer-Division, kept a detailed war diary and noted a variety of activities during the lull. Like many front-line soldiers, once the action stopped thoughts turned to alcohol, sex and rest, in that order. Hager noted on 25 April, that 'provisions arrive. We get thoroughly drunk. Otherwise nothing happens.' The unit lived in tents in the field near a village and had sufficient 'down time' to play soccer games on the steppe and go swimming in local streams. Later, Hager and his comrades were able to gain some R&R (rest and recreation) time in Kharkov and spent it skirt-chasing and bar-hopping. While some soldiers were granted home leave during this period, Hager was assigned to take driver training (earning his Class 1 licence) and radio operator training.[71] Surprisingly, the Germans conducted relatively little large-scale training, although company- and battalion-level training did occur. The spring rainy period lasted from 18–30 May, rendering large-scale training difficult. Soviet tankers had much less time for R&R and their brigade political officers filled most spare moments with field lectures.

While front-line tankers rested and hunted for diversions, the senior leadership on both sides planned their next major moves for the summer of 1943. Hitler had ordered the OKH to begin planning for a new summer offensive even before von Manstein had recovered Kharkov and Belgorod. On 13 March, he had the OKH issue a warning order to both Heeresgruppe Mitte and Heeresgruppe Süd to prepare for a pincer attack to eliminate the Kursk salient once the spring *rasputitsa* (mud) period had ended in late April.[72] On paper, the Soviet-held Kursk salient appeared a tempting target for an easy victory that could restore German morale after the Stalingrad debacle. Von Manstein was very much in favour of a large-scale offensive against the Kursk salient and pressed for this option. After rejecting the idea of limited offensives on other parts of the Eastern Front as unlikely to be decisive, Hitler settled on the Kursk salient as the primary operational objective for the summer of 1943. On 11 April, the OKH presented the first draft of a plan for mounting a double pincer attack on the Kursk salient, known as *Zitadelle*. In the operations order issued four days later, Hitler stated that he wanted the offensive to begin 'as soon as the weather permits' and that he wanted 'the best units, the best weapons, the best leaders and great quantities of munitions... to be focused at the *Schwerpunkt*.' Clearly, Hitler intended to repeat the methods of 1941–42 at Kursk and hoped to achieve the same kind of outcome as in previous *Blitzkrieg* offensives.

In order to mount a major attack on the scale of *Zitadelle*, the Panzer-Divisionen needed to be refitted with new equipment and personnel replacements. In particular, Hausser's SS-Panzerkorps had suffered over 11,000 casualties during von Manstein's counter-offensive and had barely one-third of its armour still operational.* The four other German Panzerkorps in the Kursk sector were in far worse shape. As noted earlier, Hitler assigned Generaloberst Heinz Guderian, in his new role as *Inspekteur der Panzertruppen*, the daunting task of rebuilding his depleted Panzertruppen on the Eastern Front in preparation for *Zitadelle*. Guderian was faced with both shepherding the introduction of multiple new types of AFVs (Panther, Ferdinand, Hornisse and Sturmpanzer), while also ensuring that significant numbers of existing models reached the front-line units. Guderian's preference was to get as many Pz IVs to the front as possible, since he did not believe that the Panther was ready for combat and he knew that the Tiger was only available in token numbers. The latest model, the Pz IV Ausf H, was just entering production at the end of May and its 7.5cm KwK 40 L/48 gun was greatly superior to the T-34's 76.2mm F-34 gun; the KwK 40 L/48 could penetrate the T-34's armour out to 2,000 metres, while the F-34 could only penetrate the Pz IV Ausf H's 80mm thick frontal armour from 500 metres. However, even the Ausf H had thinner side armour than the T-34 Model 1943 and was still inferior in terms of mobility and fuel economy.

---

* In June 1943 Hausser's SS-Panzerkorps was redesignated as II./SS-Panzerkorps.

In just three months, Guderian worked with the OKH to increase German tank strength on the Eastern Front by almost 900 tanks and 400 assault guns; by 1 July there were 2,398 tanks and 1,086 assault guns (including 862 Pz IV equipped with long 7.5cm guns). Guderian ensured that every Panzer-Division received at least some of the new Pz IV models in order to try and raise the capabilities of the entire Panzertruppen, not just a few elite units. Indeed, the influx of so many late-model Pz IV Ausf G and the new Ausf H models, brought great joy to the hard-pressed Panzertruppen. As one Gefreiter in the 4.Panzer-Division stated, 'Once we received the Panzer IV with the long main gun, the golden age of tanking started for us.'[73] A good number of the tanks were not new but repaired tanks, which the Panzer-Werkstatt (tank workshop) units at battalion and regiment level restored during the lengthy lull. One of the biggest benefits of the lull was the time that it provided for a large influx of spare parts and replacement track, engines and transmissions, which brought many inoperative tanks 'back to life.'[74] Furthermore, army-level maintenance units began installing *Schürzen* (side skirts) on Pz IIIs and Pz IVs in mid-March to protect them from Soviet anti-tank rifles and HEAT ammunition, although both were only modest threats.

When Hitler talked about using the 'best weapons' in *Zitadelle*, he was particularly thinking about the Tiger and Panther tanks. Hitler was mesmerized by both of these tanks and decided that *Zitadelle* would not begin until adequate numbers of both were at the front. On 1 April, there were just 31 operational Tiger tanks on the entire Eastern Front. By 1 July, this number had increased to 153 operational Tigers, of which 117 were committed to *Zitadelle* (the rest were at Leningrad). It is also important to note that while a total of 156 Tigers were built during this three-month lull, only 113 were delivered; the rest were provided to new heavy tank battalions being formed. Furthermore, the Tigers were not distributed as fairly as the Pz III and Pz IV medium tanks; von Manstein's Heeresgruppe Süd was given 90 Tigers whereas Model's 9.Armee received only the s. Pz.-Abt. 505 with 27 Tigers. In compensation, Model was given schwere Panzerjäger Regiment 656 with all 90 Ferdinand tank destroyers.

Of course, everyone wanted the new Panther medium tank, but June ended and not one had yet arrived. Where were they? After three prototypes were delivered on 11 January, limited production of the Panther Ausf D model began at MAN in Nurnberg, Daimler-Benz in Berlin and MNH in Hannover. Once preparations for *Zitadelle* began, Hitler ordered that at least 250 Panthers would be combat-ready by 12 May. However, the first prototype Panthers had barely begun testing at Grafenwöhr when it became clear that the design was riddled with serious defects. The main problem with the Panther design was caused by Hitler's decision in 1942 to increase its armour protection to 80mm, which raised the tank's weight from 36 to 45 tons. MAN had not designed the transmission and final drives for a 45-ton vehicle and the rush to production had not left time to correct this defect; the early production models proved sluggish and tended to sheer teeth off the drive sprocket. Nor could the Panther move in reverse with its under-powered final drive. Nevertheless, two battalions – Panzer-Abteilungen 51 and 52 – began converting to the Panther at Erlangen, near Grafenwöhr.* Speer came to watch the Panzer-Abteilung 51 in manoeuvre training at Grafenwöhr on 22 February and was stunned when six of the 13 Panthers involved suffered mechanical break-downs. German tankers quickly noticed significant faults in the Panther's turret and fuel pumps, as well as the engine's tendency to overheat and then catch fire. Speer concluded that the poorly-engineered Panther needed significant redesign and in April the initial production batch of 250 Ausf D models went back to the MAN factory for reconstruction. Speer's decision ultimately saved the Panther project, but the two battalions at Erlangen were left with no Panthers to train on for some time. Prior to *Zitadelle*, neither battalion conducted collective training with the Panther above the platoon level, nor had most crews progressed beyond familiarization before they were sent to the Eastern Front. Nor were any training materials, like the famous Panther-Fibel, yet available. With the pressure building from Hitler and the OKH to get the Panthers to the front as soon as possible, the technical fixes were rushed and the crews were only partly trained. When the rebuilt Panthers were issued in June, Guderian inspected them and found that, 'the track suspension and drive were not right, and the optics were also not yet satisfactory.'[75] Guderian informed Hitler on 16 June that the Panther was not ready for combat, but his sound technical analysis of the Panther's faults was rejected by Speer's assistant, Karl-Otto Saur. Many of the recommended improvements would go into the next version of the Panther, the Ausf A model, but that would not be available until well after *Zitadelle*. In the meantime, the Heer was stuck with the problematic Panther Ausf D. Both battalions were rail-loaded at Erlangen in late June and spent a week heading eastward, before arriving near Borisovka the day before *Zitadelle* began. Ominously, the two battalions suffered 10 per cent mechanical losses just in the short road march from the rail head to their tactical assembly areas, including two Panthers burnt out. Even worse, Major Karl von Sivers, an experienced tanker who was supposed to command Panzer-Abteilung 52, fell ill just before the unit went east, forcing a last-minute substitution.

Originally, the OKH had intended to give one Panther battalion each to Heeresgruppe Mitte and Heeresgruppe Süd, but in the end von Manstein received both. Indeed, the bulk of the new armour and personnel replacements went to von Manstein's Heeresgruppe Mitte (see Table 2). None of Model's six Panzer-Divisionen had more than a single Panzer-Abteilung, whereas five of von

---

* Panzer-Abteilung 51 was formed from the II./Pz. Regt. 33 (9.Panzer-Division) and Panzer-Abteilung 52 was formed from the I./Pz, Regt. 15 (11.Panzer-Division).

Manstein's divisions had two Panzer-Abteilungen each.* In Model's 9.Armee, only the 2. and 4.Panzer-Divisionen were brought back up to near authorized strength. Even after the three-month lull, many tanks were still inoperative awaiting spare parts, and the overall operational readiness rate for German tanks on the Eastern Front was 89 per cent. Of course, that meant 11 per cent, or 466 tanks, were still non-operational after months without combat.[76]

In addition to new tanks and tank destroyers, a total of 78 Wespe (10.5cm) and 54 Hummel (15cm) self-propelled howitzers were sent to reinforce the artillery regiments in the Panzer-Divisionen; this German move toward self-propelled artillery in their panzer units provided a major increase in tactical fire support. Both the Wespe and the Hummel would see their combat debut at Kursk. However, only the three Waffen-SS divisions and *Großdeutschland* received the full allocation of 12 Wespe and six Hummel each.[77] In AOK 9, only the 2. and 4.Panzer-Divisionen received their new howitzers. The situation was much the same with tracked and wheeled vehicles, which were essential for conducting mobile operations. The 15 mechanized divisions involved in *Zitadelle* had over 1,100 SPW halftracks to transport their Panzergrenadiers, but two-thirds of them belonged to von Manstein's forces. Only three of Model's six Panzer-Divisionen had a full Panzergrenadier Bataillon equipped with SPWs, the other three divisions either had one company or none. Losses of trucks and unarmoured halftracks during the retreats of January–March 1943 had been horrendous and not easily replaced. While the introduction of the highly-mobile *Raupenschlepper Ost* (RSO) tracked vehicles was a welcome addition, a number of Panzer-Divisionen were beginning to use Panje horses and carts for moving supplies; for example, the 18.Panzer-Division only had 68 per cent of its authorized motor vehicles, so it was given 1,900 horses to make up the transport deficit. The demotorization of the German forces in the East was beginning.

Von Manstein intended to mount his part of *Zitadelle* with Hoth's 4.PzAOK (II. SS-Panzerkorps and XXXXVIII. Panzerkorps) and Armeeabteilung Kempf (III. Panzerkorps), which were already in place near Belgorod. His concept was essentially to blast a path through the Voronezh Front with three broad panzer wedges, supported by copious amounts of artillery and air support; it was more Verdun 1916 than *Blitzkrieg* 1940–41. Conscious that the Red Army might launch a spoiling attack on the Mius River to distract him from *Zitadelle*, von Manstein decided to leave von Mackensen's 1.PzAOK to cover that sector with the XXIV. and XXXX. Panzerkorps, but he gave it an on-order mission to provide one of its Panzerkorps to support Hoth, if necessary. In the wake of Rokossovsky's failed February–March offensive, von Kluge had difficulty

---

* On 1 May 1943 the SS-Panzerkorps sent two of its six Panzer-Abteilungen (I./SS-Pz. Rgt. 1 from *LSSAH* and I./SS-Pz.Rgt. 2 from *Das Reich* back to Germany for conversion to Panthers.

Formation	Pz. and PzGr. Divisions	Pz-Abt.	StuG-Abt.	Tiger	Panther	Pz IV (long)	Pz III (long)	Ferdinand	StuGs	Total Tanks & StuGs
Model (Mitte)	6	6	7	27	0	274	82	90	228	747
Von Manstein (Süd)	9	14	7	90	204	358	339	0	266	1,508
TOTAL	15	20	14	117	204	632	421	90	494	2,255

Table 2: Allocation of German armour for *Zitadelle*

stitching together a new front between 2.PzAOK and 2.AOK and had no forces left to mount a major offensive toward Kursk. Consequently, the OKH directed Model's 9.AOK, which had just evacuated the Rzhev salient, to move to the southern side of the Orel salient and prepare to mount the northern pincer of *Zitadelle*. Model quickly recognized the difficulty of conducting a deliberate breakthrough offensive against Rokossovsky's Central Front with his depleted units and he only fielded one relatively full-strength Panzerkorps – Lemelsen's XXXXVII Panzerkorps. Instead, Model decided to rely heavily upon infantry and assault guns to break through Rokossovsky's front, while keeping most of his panzers in reserve. Consequently, von Manstein and Model intended to conduct *Zitadelle* with very different tactics, one relying upon an armour-heavy approach and the other upon an infantry-support approach.

Although *Zitadelle* was to be the first deliberate German offensive in a year, neither army group was able to assemble the logistical resources to maintain a protracted offensive as in 1941–42. According to the OKH *Zitadelle* plan, both AOK 9 and Hoth's PzAOK 4 were supposed to have enough supplies to enable 18 days of sustained operations. Yet even by 4 July, Model's AOK 9 never had more than 20 per cent of the required fuel and 40 per cent of the required ammunition, and PzAOK 4 was only moderately better supplied. Most panzer units had 2–3 basic loads of ammunition and 5 V.S. of fuel, essentially enough for one week of fighting. After that, both army groups would be unable to operate with more than a few mobile divisions at a time.

While the Germans were preparing for their offensive, the Red Army was also busy preparing a warm welcome for them in the Kursk salient. At the beginning of April, Rokossovsky had Rodin's 2TA with about 200 tanks left and a number of tank brigades, but his total armoured strength was no more than about 300–400 tanks. Despite the arrival of several tank corps from the RVGK to stop von Manstein's final push into Belgorod, General Nikolai F. Vatutin's Voronezh Front was in even worse shape with only a few hundred operational tanks.[*] Katukov's 1st Tank Army (1TA) arrived during the lull, raising strength

---

[*] Vatutin took command of the Voronezh Front on 28 March after Golikov was relieved by Stalin.

up to about 500 tanks. Initially, Stalin wanted to resume the offensive to recover Belgorod and Kharkov as soon as the weather improved, but the Stavka – chastened by von Manstein's 'Backhand Blow' – urged caution. Zhukov and Vasilevsky advised Stalin that the Germans were likely to attempt a pincer attack against the Kursk salient and they recommended that the best course of action was to create a very strong anti-tank defence in the salient to break the German Panzer-Divisionen, then follow up with major counter-offensives against Heeresgruppe Mitte and Heeresgruppe Süd. Intelligence from both the Lucy spy ring in Switzerland and Allied-provided signals intelligence reports supported the Stavka's assessment of German intentions for their summer 1943 offensive. For once, Stalin allowed himself to be persuaded and directed both the Voronezh and Central Fronts to create an impregnable defence around the Kursk salient, while a large operational reserve would be concentrated in the vicinity to conduct the counter-offensive once the German attacks had been defeated.

During the lull, the Red Army emplaced 503,663 anti-tank and 439,348 anti-personnel mines in the most likely sectors where the Germans would attack and dug three layers of entrenchments for their infantry.[78] For the first time in the war, the Red Army was able to emplace up to 1,600 mines per kilometre in the expected enemy armoured mobility corridors.[79] The Soviets also took the time to train their guards rifle units to withstand tank attacks through drills where T-34s ran over or near trenches filled with infantrymen; this time, the appearance of German tanks was not going to panic the front-line troops. Live-fire training was also conducted to improve tank-infantry cooperation.[80] In April 1943, NKO Order 0063 re-created Anti-Tank Brigades, each to be equipped with 20 45mm and 40 76.2mm anti-tank guns. These brigades provided the Red Army with the ability to mass anti-tank fire on a much larger scale than it had achieved in 1941–42.[81] Anti-tank gunners were trained to refrain from firing until approaching enemy tanks were very close, in order to improve the probability of a first-round hit and to increase penetration at point-blank range. The amount of anti-tank firepower deployed in the Kursk salient was intended to ensure that all obstacle belts were covered by fire and that wherever the German armour moved, it would be hit by flanking shots from hidden AT guns.

Another important structural change that the Red Army instituted during the lull was the reorganization of their tank armies into homogenous formations by excluding non-motorized elements. Heretofore, Soviet tank armies in 1942 had often included rifle divisions that could not keep up with armour in the attack. The first of the new-style tank armies was the 5th Guards Tank Army (5 GTA), established in late February 1943.[82] The Stavka's intent was to build the tank armies up into powerful manoeuvre formations, designed to exploit the operational success achieved by front-level forces.

The Stavka decided to employ an unprecedented amount of armour for the Kursk operation, including all five tank armies (which possessed a total of 3,474 tanks in 12 tank and four mechanized corps). In addition, six other independent tank corps were assigned as Front-level tactical reserves, two for Rokossovsky's Central Front and four for Vatutin's Voronezh Front. Each of the field armies defending the Kursk salient was also assigned tank brigades and tank regiments for direct infantry support, totalling eight tank brigades and 22 separate tank regiments. Trainloads of tanks were poured into the Kursk salient in April–June, refilling the depleted ranks of front-line tank units. In addition, seven self-propelled artillery regiments (SAP) were shipped into the Kursk salient, including three with the new SU-152 self-propelled guns. By July, Rokossovsky's Central Front had a total of 1,451 tanks and 115 self-propelled guns, including 447 in Rodin's 2TA. Vatutin's Voronezh Front had 1,613 tanks and 54 self-propelled guns, including 587 in Katukov's 1TA (see Table 3). Altogether, the two Soviet fronts that would have to defend against *Zitadelle* had 3,064 tanks and 158 self-propelled guns. This armour included 728 light tanks (23 per cent of the total) and 375 Lend-Lease tanks (12 per cent). However, this type of aggregation – which is used in many histories of the Battle of Kursk – is deceptive, since three of the 10 Soviet combined-arms armies in the Kursk salient (38, 60 and 65) were not actively involved in the battle and three others (40, 48, 70) were only partially engaged in the defensive phase; this means that at least 15 per cent of the deployed Soviet armour was not engaged during the defensive phase. Surprisingly, Vatutin and Rokossovsky left 329 tanks facing the 2.Armee on the face of the Kursk salient, even though this formation was not participating in *Zitadelle* and had only a single Sturmgeschütz-Abteilung in support. This deployment indicates that the Soviet Front commanders did not employ 'economy of force' with their armour assets as their German opposite numbers did.

Finally, the RVGK began assembling an operational reserve east of Kursk to spearhead the anticipated counter-offensive; this reserve initially consisted of General-leytenant Pavel A. Rotmistrov's 5th Guards Tank Army (5GTA), the 5th Guards Army (5GA) and 5th Air Army, but more formations were added once *Zitadelle* began. Rotmistrov was considered one of the Red Army's best senior-level armour leaders and he was given five corps and over 800 tanks; this formation was expected to achieve decisive results when committed. The Stavka kept 5GTA and 5GA under its control until the Battle of Kursk began,

Formation	Total Tanks	KV-1	T-34	T-60/T-70	M4A2 Sherman	M3 Grant	M3 Stuart	Matilda Valentine	Churchill
Central Front	1,451	75	851	135/239	38	85	9	19	0
Voronezh Front	1,613	23	1,012	46/308	0	65	68	49	42
Steppe Front	1,099	0	711	0/367	0	0	0	0	21
Total	4,163	98	2,574	181/914	38	150	77	68	63

Table 3: Allocation of Soviet armour for Kursk Defensive Operation.

then established the Steppe Front under General-polkovnik Ivan Konev to command them.

During the defence, Rokossovsky and Vatutin would also employ 169 self-propelled guns (SPGs), including 36 SU-152, 71 SU-122, 29 SU-76 and 33 SU-76i. The limited number of SU-76s deployed at Kursk and the inclusion of the Su-76i built on captured German Pz III hulls indicates the problems that the Red Army had in fielding an equivalent to the German Sturmgeschütz. All four types of Soviet SPGs employed at Kursk were built on different hulls and lacked any kind of standardization. Nor did the SPGs have a realistic tactical doctrine, blending between the infantry support, anti-tank and breakthrough roles. In terms of SPGs, the Red Army was still in the experimental phase.

Although Soviet tank production was going all-out by this point in the war and combat losses were light during the lull period, it is noticeable that the Red Army was still forced to use large numbers of T-60 and T-70 light tanks in their tank brigades, even in the elite Guards units. At Kursk, Soviet tank brigades comprised at least 20–30 per cent light tanks, even though the T-60 was clearly obsolete and the T-70 was inferior to the German medium tanks. The T-34/76 was the Red Army's main battle tank at Kursk, with 1,863 on hand at the start of *Zitadelle*, but it was still not available in the numbers required. On the other hand, the KV-1 heavy tank was a marginal player at Kursk, with a total of only 98 deployed in the Central and Voronezh Fronts – fewer than the American-built M3 Grant/Lee. Normally, the Lend-Lease tanks were employed only in the infantry support role, but the 2nd and 5th Guards Tank Corps each had 21 British-built Churchills, which were regarded as heavy tanks. Yet when actual deployments are taken into consideration, the Germans were going to attack with about 2,300 tanks and assault guns against roughly 2,700 Soviet tanks and self-propelled guns.

In the defensive phase at Kursk, the Red Army would enjoy a small numerical edge in armour but Vatutin and Rokossovsky were concerned about the enemy heavy tanks that had been encountered during von Manstein's counter-offensive. While Soviet tankers were probably not aware of the Tiger's mechanical reliability problems, they were aware that its 8.8cm gun and thick armoured protection put the T-34 at a grave disadvantage in a stand-up fight. The GABTU in Moscow, which directed Soviet armoured fighting programs,

Formation	Total SPGs	SU-152	Su-122	Su-76	Su-76i
Central Front	104	24	47	0	33
Voronezh Front	54	12	24	18	0
Steppe Front	70	12	36	22	0
Total	228	48	107	40	33

Table 4: Allocation of Soviet Self-Propelled Guns (SPGs) for Kursk Defensive Operation.

hoped that the new SU-152 could counter the Tiger's thick armour with its 152mm gun-howitzer. However, the SU-152 had been developed to defeat enemy fortifications and had not yet been tested in the anti-tank role prior to Kursk – it was untried in combat. Furthermore, there were only a token number of SU-152s at the front, which was inadequate against the growing numbers of enemy heavy tanks. Consequently, the Red Army decided to provide each Soviet tank corps in the Central and Voronezh Fronts with a battalion of 12 towed 85mm M1939 anti-aircraft guns to be used in the anti-tank role. Tests on the Tiger captured at Leningrad indicated that the 85mm AA gun could defeat its thick frontal armour at ranges out to 1,000 metres and further against its side armour. However, the 85mm AA gun was difficult to conceal and even more difficult to move around a battlefield, marking it as a stop-gap solution until the Red Army fielded a tank with a gun larger than 76.2mm. In order to improve the survivability of the T-34s during the defensive phase, Soviet sappers dug fighting positions for tanks so that they could fire from hull-down.

In addition to armour, the Red Army attempted to employ as many combat multipliers as possible to neutralize the German combined arms team. Rather than spending the lull period resting, Rokossovsky and Vatutin drove their troops hard to create three fortified lines of defence and protect them with tens of thousands of mines. Infantry underwent special training to prepare them to withstand an attack by panzers and to fight tanks in close-quarters combat. Elite Guards rifle units were placed in the expected German attack sectors, ensuring that there were solid units holding the key terrain. There were three additional measures taken that greatly reduced the ability of the German combined arms tactics to work at Kursk. First, each front was provided with a large anti-tank reserve to augment its battalion, regiment and division-level anti-tank strongpoints. Each of the seven front-level anti-tank brigades had 40 76.2mm ZIS-3 anti-tank guns, which could quickly redeploy to a sector threatened by German armour. Second, the Stavka expected the German Panzers to breach at least the first line of defence, so a new doctrinal feature was the creation of mobile obstacle detachments (*podvishnyi otriad zagrazhdenii* or POZ). The POZ were truck-mounted sapper teams that could create new minefields in front of approaching enemy armour. Finally, the Stavka authorized the fronts to use artillery corps to support their defensive operations, which enabled an unprecedented level of fire support. Unlike the old *Blitzkrieg* days of 1941–42, everywhere the German panzers turned, they would be confronted by mines, anti-tank guns and punishing artillery barrages.

Operation *Zitadelle*: The Northern Front 5–10 July 1943
Generaloberst Walter Model, commander of AOK 9, was not sanguine about *Zitadelle*'s chances for success, since he knew from aerial reconnaissance about the extent of enemy defences being prepared by Rokossovsky's Central Front. Indeed, Model presented this information to Hitler and tried to personally

dissuade him from launching the offensive. Instead, Model argued that the Germans should remain on the defensive and create a strong mobile reserve that would allow them to smash any Soviet offensives. Yet Hitler would not be diverted from this battle and Model accepted his role, but planned his part of the operation with particular attention to preserving his own armour. At best, Model would have 800 tanks and assault guns to commit to the offensive and he knew that losses in a breakthrough attack would be heavy. Instead of von Manstein's armour-heavy approach to *Zitadelle*, Model intended to rely more upon his infantry divisions, artillery and air support to crack the Soviet defences and only commit his armour when he saw an opening that could be exploited. Furthermore, Model also knew that the Soviet Bryansk and Western Fronts were planning to attack the Orel Salient as they had done in February–March, so he wanted to keep as much of his armour intact as possible to deal with this contingency. To Model, retaining Orel was more important than taking Kursk.

Opposite Model's AOK 9, Rokossovsky had placed General-leytenant Nikolai P. Pukhov's heavily-reinforced 13th Army in the Ponyri sector where he expected the Germans to attack. Pukhov's army held a 22km-wide sector and had four rifle divisions holding the first line of defence, two more holding the second line and six in the third line. The Soviet defences were built around entrenched rifle battalion strongpoints, enclosed by mines and protected by anti-tank guns. Each Soviet position incorporated all-around defences and was intended to hold out if surrounded – this type of reinforced hedgehog tactic was intended to function as a 'wave breaker' type defence. For infantry support, Pukhov had 178 tanks and 49 self-propelled guns, although most were kept back in the second or third lines of defence. The 13th Army's best armoured units were the 129th Tank Brigade with 49 tanks (incl. 10 KV-1 and 21 T-34) and the 27th and 30th Guards Tank Regiments (GTR) with a total of 44 KV-1s heavy tanks. In general support, Rodin's 2TA (consisting of the 3rd and 16th Tank Corps and 11th Guards Tank Brigade) was in reserve 25km south of the forward edge of the battle area. Rodin had a total of 305 T-34s and 142 light tanks. Rokossovsky also kept the 9th and 19th Tank Corps, which had a total of 232 T-34s and 148 other tanks, under front control.

During the night of 4–5 July, Model's army began its final preparations for the offensive by sending sapper teams forward to begin clearing lanes through the first layer of Soviet minefields. One team was ambushed and a prisoner revealed under interrogation that *Zitadelle* would begin at dawn. Zhukov, who was present in Rokossovsky's command post, pressured him into unleashing an artillery bombardment to disrupt the German offensive. However, the unplanned Soviet artillery barrages had limited effect on German front-line units and the German artillery preparation began at 0425 hours and continued until 0545 hours. Model launched supporting attacks with three infantry divisions from XXIII Armeekorps on his left flank and three infantry divisions from XXXXVI Panzerkorps on his right flank; despite support from three

Sturmgeschütz-Abteilungen, these efforts only advanced a few kilometres before being stopped by Soviet resistance and failed to achieve their objectives.

Model's main effort was made in the centre, with General der Panzertruppen Josef Harpe's XXXXI Panzerkorps and General der Panzertruppen Joachim Lemelsen's XXXXVII Panzerkorps. Harpe attacked along the Orel-Kursk rail line near Maloarkhangel'sk station, close to the boundary between Pukhov's 29th and 15th Rifle Corps. Oberstleutnant Baron Ernst von Jungenfeld's schwere Panzerjäger Regiment 656 was split up, providing a battalion of Ferdinands each in direct support of an infantry regiment from the 86.Infanterie-Division, while Sturmpanzer-Abteilung 216 followed in general support. Each battalion of Ferdinands was preceded by a Panzerkompanie (Fkl) with BIV demolition vehicles to clear a path through the enemy mines.* The Germans had not put a great deal of effort into developing armoured mine clearing tanks, unlike the British who fielded the Matilda flail tank (Scorpion) in October 1942 or the Red Army, which first used PT-34 mine roller tanks in the summer of 1942. Instead, the Germans opted for an ad hoc solution using vehicles intended to demolish bunkers, not mines, and the results were mediocre. Nor had the AOK 9 conducted realistic breaching drills with BIVs, tanks and infantry prior to *Zitadelle* – a major omission. As the BIV vehicles approached the Soviet defences around 0600 hours, they were met by a deluge of artillery fire that destroyed seven BIVs. Instead of clearing three lanes through the mines, the German pioniers only managed to clear a single narrow lane. The defending Soviet 410th Rifle Regiment, which had ample artillery and anti-tank support, kept this cleared lane under very heavy fire and prevented the pioniers from expanding it. Amazingly, the Germans did not use smoke to provide concealment for the breaching teams. All the while, the Ferdinands and StuG IIIs from Sturmgeschütz-Abteilung 177 provided fire support to the pioniers, but could not suppress the enemy defences.

With the main German attack on the verge of collapse, the Ferdinands were ordered to move through the cleared lane and overrun the enemy defences. The Ferdinand was designed as a long-range tank destroyer, not an assault vehicle. Its 200mm thick frontal armour was virtually impregnable to 76.2mm gunfire, but its tracks had no special immunity to mines and the 70-ton vehicle was very slow. Inside their buttoned-up Ferdinands, the German crewmen only had a vague idea where the cleared lane was through the smoke from burning

---

* Funklenk or Fkl were radio-controlled demolition vehicles. A team usually consisted of a Pz III control tank and several associated BIVs. The vehicles were driven into the edge of a minefield by a human driver and then detonated by radio command, intending to detonate nearby mines with blast over-pressure. The Germans estimated that at least four BIVs were needed to clear a 100-metre deep lane through a minefield and that this would take two hours to complete. However, a critical flaw was that the Panzerkompanie (Fkl) had no means of marking cleared lanes.

steppe grass and explosions, which caused many of them to roll over mines. Some suffered track damage and were immobilized, but one Ferdinand struck five mines and kept rolling. However, the shock of mine explosions damaged the batteries in many Ferdinands, for which no replacements were available in AOK 9. On the first day of the offensive, the Ferdinands had 30 batteries destroyed by mine damage, sidelining these vehicles for many days.[83] Eventually, a few Ferdinands and StuG IIIs made it through the lane and began to reduce the Soviet defences at point-blank range. The Soviet 15th Rifle Corps commander committed his armoured support, consisting of 34 KV-1 heavy tanks, 21 T-34s, 18 light tanks and 16 Su-122s.

Harpe also committed General-major Karl-Wilhelm von Schlieben's 18.Panzer-Division and the 292.Infanterie-Division to clear out the area west of the rail line. Von Schlieben's division was severely understrength, with only 72 tanks, most of which were older models or the Pz III Ausf N version with the short 7.5cm infantry support howitzer. The division's panzergrenadiers started *Zitadelle* with just 22 SPWs. Lacking firepower and mobility, Harpe used the 18. Panzer-Division as a mop-up force to clear bypassed Soviet strongpoints, rather than as an exploitation force. After hours of fighting, Harpe's corps finally managed to advance about 4km by nightfall, but it had not completely eliminated the enemy first line of defence in its sector.

On Harpe's right flank, Lemelsen's corps attacked the 15th Rifle Division (15RD) with the 6.Infanterie-Division, supported by the Tigers of Major Bernhard Sauvant's s. Pz.Abt. 505. Here, the BIVs also had difficulty clearing lanes and six of Sauvant's 31 Tigers were damaged by mines in the opening minutes. Army and Division boundary lines are acknowledged as tactically vulnerable areas since, if inter-unit coordination is not properly done, an enemy can sometimes find or create an opening. Pukhov's left flank was held by the 47th Rifle Regiment of 15RD, which had been badly disrupted by the German artillery preparation and had lost wire communications with its division command post. The German infantry from 6.Infanterie-Division were able to create a breach in this sector and after two hours, Lemelsen sent Generalmajor Mortimer von Kessel's 20.Panzer-Division forward to exploit the opening.* Kessel moved a mixed Kampfgruppe through the breach, which included his only company of SPWs and some medium tanks. Once through, the Kampfgruppe moved through dead space (i.e. not visible from the enemy positions) and managed to get through a small gap in the enemy defences and outflank one of the 47th Rifle Regiment's battalion strongpoints. A rapid Panzer assault, supported by Sauvant's Tigers, infantry and artillery, succeeded in overrunning this one position, which soon led to an unravelling of the 15 RD's

---

* Kessel was an odd choice to command a Panzer-Division in such a key battle since he had been head of the Heer's Personnel Department in 1939–42 and had no recent command experience. Nevertheless, he went on to command a Panzerkorps by late 1944.

forward line of defence and a panicked retreat by another battalion. One Soviet battalion strongpoint held out as ordered, but was bypassed and encircled by 6.Infanterie-Division. While mopping up continued, Sauvant was level-headed enough to take advantage of the disruption in the enemy defence and he pushed south with his Tigers and two small Kampfgruppen from 20.Panzer-Division. He succeeded in partially overrunning the 15 RD's second line of defence and surprised an anti-tank position in the town of Soborovka. The Soviets committed the T-34s of 237th Tank Regiment to block any further advance. By this point, Sauvant was low on fuel and ammunition and decided to halt, but he had a good day and his advance of 8km was AOK 9's furthest penetration on the first day of *Zitadelle*.

Model responded to the 20.Panzer-Division's success by moving up the 2. and 9.Panzer-Divisionen to assist with reducing the Soviet second line of defence on the next day. The AOK 9 had suffered very heavy personnel casualties on the first day of *Zitadelle*: 7,223 dead and wounded, particularly in the infantry and pioniers. While Pukhov's first line of defence had been severely reduced, no breakthrough had been achieved. Pukhov had already committed more than half his armour to contain the German advances, but with limited effect. Rokossovsky watched the partial collapse of Pukhov's first line of defence with dismay and with Zhukov hovering over him, he decided to commit Rodin's 2TA and the separate 19th Tank Corps to a major counter-attack on the next day to restore the previous frontline. Rokossovsky's hasty decision was a major departure from the Soviet battle plan (although Zhukov raised no objections), since the tank armies were supposed to stay out of the battle until the mines and anti-tank defences had reduced the Panzer-Divisionen, but this was not yet the case. Instead, Rokossovsky was playing straight into the German battle plan, provoking a major tank battle while the German heavy armour was still operational.

As dawn arrived on the second day of *Zitadelle*, the Germans were slow to resume their offensive and 2.Panzer-Division was still in its tactical assembly area. Suddenly, a group of 25 Soviet A-20 bombers came in low and bombed the assembly area, inflicting casualties and damage. Although Luftflotte 6 was winning the battle for air superiority over the northern battlefield, the VVS was still capable of conducting painful low-level raids. Meanwhile, Rokossovsky's armour was moving northward to engage the German armour near Pukhov's second line of defence. Rodin's two corps had to conduct a 'forward passage of lines' during the pre-dawn darkness, which is a tedious and problematic affair even for the best trained units. This passage entails tankers coordinating with the front-line infantry commanders to establish one or more lanes through their defensive positions, marking the lanes and posting guides, then moving through as quietly as possible in a long column that makes an excellent target for enemy artillery. At Kursk, particular attention had to be paid to not driving into friendly minefields in the dark. With luck, the combat elements of a large armoured unit like a tank corps might complete a forward passage of lines within a couple of hours, but this was not a strength of the Red Army's tankers. Instead of three tank corps hitting the Germans at dawn, only part of General-major Vasily E. Grigor'ev's 16th Tank Corps managed to complete its forward passage of lines by 1000 hours and then advanced northward to the village of Bobrik. In fact, Grigor'ev conducted his movement to contact with just his 107th and 164th Tank Brigades. This mass of about 90 Soviet tanks crawled forward without reconnaissance out in front or infantry or artillery support; it was just a wedge of steel.

Near the village of Bobrik, Major Sauvant's Tigers had finished a leisurely breakfast and re-supply while sitting in an overwatch position and awaiting orders to resume the attack. Sauvant was one of the most experienced junior Panzer commanders in the Heer, having risen from company commander in Poland in 1939 to battalion commander in 1942 and even being one of the lucky few from the old 14.Panzer-Division to survive Stalingrad. Now Sauvant was provided with the perfect killing machine in an optimal tactical position. Sauvant's crews spotted the approaching mass of Soviet armour and had plenty of time to ram Panzergranate rounds into their breaches and select targets. Polkovnik Nikolai M. Teliakov, a veteran tanker himself, led the lead 107th Tank Brigade. Sauvant's Tigers began the engagement at about 1,200 meters with the 8.8cm rounds ripping into the lead Soviet tank company. Although the Soviet tankers could clearly see the Tigers, return fire was completely ineffective at this range. Teliakov had difficulty controlling his brigade, which was being shot to pieces in just a few minutes, but finally managed to extract some survivors and beat a hasty retreat. In less than fifteen minutes, Teliakov's brigade lost 46 tanks for no loss to Sauvant's Tigers. Podpolkovnik Nikolai V. Kopylov's 164th Tank Brigade, trailing Teliakov, witnessed the destruction of his brigade and opted to steer away from the Tigers, but blundered straight into a Kampfgruppe from 2.Panzer-Division. This meeting action was more favourable for the Soviets; Kopylov lost 23 tanks but managed to knock out 10 German tanks before retreating. With Grigor'ev's 16th Tank Corps bloodied and the rest of his armour still unready to attack, Rodin was able to convince Rokossovsky to cancel the counter-attack and revert to a pure defence.

Model was in no hurry to resume the offensive. He decided to commit the 9.Panzer-Division in Harpe's sector and he ordered his two flank corps to continue limited objectives attacks. Then, he waited for Luftflotte 6 to gain air superiority over the sector, which they did. Soviet air losses over the northern battlefield on the first two days of *Zitadelle* were horrendous – 191 aircraft versus 36 for the Luftwaffe. With the skies cleared of enemy bombers, Model began to attack Pukhov's second line of defence around noon. There was no real *Schwerpunkt* on this second day of *Zitadelle*, just short-range jabs by 2.Panzer-Division and Sauvant's Tigers toward Ol'khovatka and by 9.Panzer-Division toward the Snova River valley. Harpe's XXXXI Panzerkorps mopped up the remnants of the 81st Rifle Division north of Ponyri, with the support of the remaining Ferdinands and 18.Panzer-Division. Polkovnik Nikolai V. Petrushin's 129th Tank Brigade (more than 40 tanks) tried to support the hard-pressed Soviet infantry but was driven off by the Ferdinand's long 8.8cm gun. However, a few SU-152s managed to get into good firing positions and engaged the Ferdinands; at least one Ferdinand was knocked out with a flank shot from 800 metres. Nevertheless, the Germans pressed on and with the added help of Generalleutnant Walter Scheller's 9.Panzer-Division approaching from the northwest, reached the outskirts of Ponyri by dusk. As the last of his first line of defence crumbled, Pukhov had time to move the 307th Rifle Division and the rest of Petrushin's 129th Tank Brigade to hold Ponyri. Pukhov placed General-major Mikhail A. Enshin, an NKVD officer, in charge of the defence of Ponyri.

Lemelsen's XXXXVII Panzerkorps pushed toward Ol'khovatka with Generalleutnant Vollrath Lübbe's 2. Panzer-Division in the lead. Lübbe's Panzers found the Soviet second line in this sector held by the 6th Guards Rifle Division (6 GRD), which was well supported by artillery and anti-tank guns. The German tanks blundered into a minefield and no less than 12 of Sauvant's Tigers suffered mine damage. Heavy artillery fire pounded the Germans while they were tangled out in the obstacle belt and high velocity 76.2mm rounds ripped into immobilized vehicles. Lübbe's Panzers managed to push through some weak spots in the 6 GRD's line, but then ran straight into elements of the 70th and 75th Guards Rifle Divisions. Soviet POZ detachments laid new mines in front of the approaching Panzers, just as they thought they had cleared the obstacle belt. As evening approached, General-major Ivan D. Vasil'ev's 19th Tank Corps mounted a sudden counter-attack into Lemelsen's right flank, but the 20.Panzer-Division was screening this area and knocked out 30 T-34s. The day was a disappointment for Model, with more heavy casualties and no breakthrough achieved. At best, his Panzers had advanced another 2–4km, but it was clear that Soviet resistance was getting tougher. Although not hopeful of achieving a real breakthrough and linking up with von Manstein's forces, Model decided to commit his remaining armour, the 4. and 12.Panzer-Divisionen on the next day.

By 7 July, Model decided to focus all his combat power in just the Ol'khovatka and Ponyri sectors, while essentially shifting to the defence on the rest of his front. At 0630 hours, Harpe's XXXXI Panzerkorps attacked Ponyri from the north with the 292.Infanterie-Division supported by Ferdinands and assault guns, while 18.Panzer-Division attacked from the west. Enshin's defence was rock solid and supported by over 300 artillery pieces, which repulsed four German attacks. It was not until 1100 hours that a fifth attack succeeded in gaining some ground and getting into the edge of Ponyri, but the rest of the day was consumed in Stalingrad-style urban combat that accomplished nothing. Nor did Scheller's 9.Panzer-Division achieve anything useful; it advanced 3km southwest in an effort to outflank Ponyri before running into mines and an impenetrable blocking position held by the 43rd Tank Regiment (30 T-34s) and the 1st Anti-Tank Brigade; Scheller lost nine tanks knocked out and 30

Left: T-34 tanks on the production line. By January 1943, Soviet industry was building over 1,000 T-34s per month against Germany's production of barely 200 medium tanks per month. Although German industry was able to increase production by late 1943, the Soviets continued to enjoy a 3-1 edge in tank production output throughout the critical phase of the war. Stalin's industrialization programs of the 1930s had prepared the Soviet Union for a war of production and its ability to out-produce Germany was the result of careful planning.

Left: Vyacheslav Malyshev was the Soviet engineer tasked by Stalin with running the Soviet Union's tank industry. Malyshev was ruthless, but competent, and he let plant managers know what would happen to officials that failed to meet production quotas. Here, he poses with a model of a new heavy tank design which eventually resulted in the JS-2. Malyshev was conservative and did not favour experimentation, but by 1943 he was forced to recognize that the Red Army needed a new tank to counter the German Panthers and Tigers.

Right: A Lend-Lease Matilda tank with a tank unit in the Central Front, January 1943. Although its 2-pounder (40-mm) gun lacked a high explosive shell, the Matilda continued to serve in the infantry support role in the Red Army throughout 1943. The Soviet tankers liked its thick armour, but by 1943 it was completely out-classed by German tanks armed with long 7.5-cm cannons.

Right: An Su-122 self-propelled gun negotiates its way down a very muddy trail. The Red Army was quick to note the value of the German assault guns in the infantry support role and decided to develop its own range of weapons mounted on tank chassis. The Su-122 was normally deployed in a self-propelled artillery regiment and attached to tank or rifle corps. The 122-mm howitzer provided Soviet assault groups with mobile firepower to reduce strongpoints – something that had been missing in 1941–42.

Left: German preparations for Operation Zitadelle were extensive. Here, brand-new Pz IIIs stand next to a mountain of new track, much of which would be used to restore older vehicles. Despite the association of Tigers and Panthers with Kursk, the obsolescent Pz III medium tank still played a very large role in the battle.

Right: A Soviet tank company commander briefs his platoon leaders on their next operation. By the summer of 1943, the Red Army had a leavening of veteran tank crews and commanders, which narrowed the qualitative gap between German and Soviet tank units.

Left: The turret of a Panther Ausf D after an internal explosion had shattered the interior. The Germans were forced to abandon large numbers of derelict Panthers during the retreat to the Dnepr and tried to destroy them when feasible. In 1943, the primary cause of loss of most Panthers was destruction by their own crews.

Right: A German StuG-III assault gun pauses by a burning T-34/76 Model 1942 in the summer of 1943. The StuG-III with the long 7.5-cm cannon was extremely lethal on the defence, but when pressed into offensive roles as at Kursk, it was unable to completely fill in for tanks. (Bundesarchiv, Bild 101I-688-0162-23)

Left: This is the same burning T-34 as in the previous photo. One of the assault gun crewmen is going through the pockets of a dead Soviet tanker. (Bundesarchiv, Bild 101I-688-0162-24)

Right: A Tiger positioned next to a knocked-out KV-1. It is interesting to note the tanks are roughly equivalent in size and both suffered from transmission problems. By mid-1943, the KV-1 was being phased out because of its poor mobility and insufficient firepower.

Left: Crewmen of a Panther loading 7.5-cm ammunition in a hurried, haphazard manner which begs for an accident. Most tank ammunition is base-activating and can be set off by static electricity, even from human hands. There are few records of non-combat casualties from the Eastern Front, but there must have been considerable losses due to lack of sleep and the strain of combat. As crews grew exhausted in protracted battles like Kursk, tank crewmen were increasingly vulnerable to making mistakes.

Right: A T-34 with its turret blown off after a massive explosion. The introduction of more powerful anti-tank weapons like the long 7.5-cm gun and the 8.8-cm gun transformed the firepower equation on the Eastern Front, which had heretofore favoured the Red Army. High-velocity APCR rounds proved highly lethal at Kursk and it was clear that the T-34's previous advantage in armoured protection had passed. (Bundesarchiv, Bild 101I-220-0630-04A)

Right: The crew of an SU-76M assault gun in action. This open-topped vehicle offered only minimal crew protection but the mobile firepower it offered helped greatly as the Red Army began advancing westward in 1943. Prior to this, the Red Army was generally dependent upon towed artillery and offensives petered out as advancing units out ran their fire support. Once the SU-76M reached the front in numbers, the tempo of the Soviet offensive became more aggressive.

Left: Soviet T-34s enroute to Zhitomir, November 1943. Rybalko's rapid breakout from the Lyutezh bridgehead and exploitation toward the southwest caught the Germans completely by surprise. Note that the T-34s carry desant infantry.

Left: A Soviet KV-85 tank captured during the German counter-attack near Radomyschyl in early December 1943. This tank was sent back to Germany for technical evaluation but there was little for the Germans to learn from it. The KV-85 was only produced in limited numbers as a way of getting an 85-mm equipped tank into the field in 1943, until the T-34/85 and JS-2 were fielded in 1944. (Bundesarchiv, Bild 101I-708-0270-13A)

Right: Soviet Lend-Lease Churchill tanks entering Kiev, November 1943. The heavily-armoured Churchill proved to be an excellent breakthrough tank and remained in Soviet service until the end of the war.

Left: T-34s advance with infantry across a frozen field, winter 1943/44. Note these latest-model T-34s are equipped with the cupola, but the tank commanders are still 'buttoned up'. This Soviet habit contributed to poor situational awareness and heavy casualties throughout much of the war. Despite ample evidence that tank commanders should keep their heads up as long as possible, the Red Army continued to teach this flawed habit long after the war.

Right: A German Pz IV advancing with an infantry section. Note that one of the grenadiers is carrying a magnetic hollow charge anti-tank mine. By the winter of 1943/44, German armour was increasingly employed in small counter-attacks against Soviet penetrations. Note the head of the German tank commander is just visible, giving him good situational awareness. (Bundesarchiv, Bild 101I-277-0835-29)

Right: The recapture of Zhitomir in late November 1943 was a minor tactical victory, but von Manstein's armoured counter-offensive failed to destroy Rybalko's 3 GTA or recover Kiev. The 4. Panzerarmee managed to temporarily halt the Soviet steamroller with its fresh Panzer-Divisionen, but could not stop Vatutin's massive offensive which began on 24 December 1943.

Above: A Kampfgruppe from 1.Panzer-Division advances during the effort to relieve the Korsun Pocket in February 1944. Initially, mobility was good over hard-packed snow, but a early thaw brought deep mud that greatly reduced German mobility. Like most of these rescue operations, the Germans were forced to operate under conditions that were poorly suited to the kind of mobile operations they favoured and they tended to degenerate into slugging matches to break through to trapped troops before they were annihilated.

Right: German infantry ride atop a Pz IV tank during the winter of 1944. During the breakout from Hube's pocket, 1.Panzerarmee had very few tanks, SPWs or trucks and had to conduct a mobile operation with very meagre resources. The fact that the breakout succeeded testifies to the determination and skill of the German Panzertruppen and Panzergrenadiers, even as the Third Reich slid inevitably toward defeat. (Bundesarchiv, Bild 101I-277-0835-04)

Left: A German grenadier with a Panzerfaust observes a burning T-34 in a village. The introduction of the cheap, easy-to-produce Panzerfaust anti-tank weapon in the autumn of 1943 was a potential game-changer since it finally provided the German infantryman with a reliable weapon to stop enemy tanks. However, by the time that it was introduced, the Heer was running out of trained infantrymen.

Right: A late-model Pz IV alongside a knocked-out late-model T-34/76 in the Ukraine, early 1944. The size comparison of these two medium tanks is interesting, as well as the effect of thick mud upon operations.

Right: A Panther from SS-*Wiking* in a wood line in Poland, September 1944. Note that trees have been cleared to create a clear field of fire in front of the Panther.

Left: A Lend-Lease Sherman in Red Army service. By mid-1944, the Red Army had a considerable number of Shermans and particularly liked the models with the 76-mm gun. Like the T-34, the Sherman was automotively reliable and was excellent in the exploitation role.

Right: A JS-2 lies disabled in the streets of an East Prussian town. The 122-mm gun on the JS-2 was a powerful weapon with the potential to destroy Tigers and Panthers at long-range, but like most heavy tanks, it was ill-suited for urban combat.

Left: Another JS-2 has come to grief in a German city street, which was far too narrow for armoured operations. In this type of urban environment, the Panzerfaust could knock out even heavy tanks with point-blank shots.

more immobilized by mechanical defects and damage. The fact that an entire German Panzerkorps could not capture a town held by a rifle division indicated the growing poverty of German resources.

Before Lemelsen could jump off on the morning of 7 July, Soviet A-20 bombers struck again and destroyed five Pz IV tanks in 2.Panzer-Division's tactical assembly area. Following that rude shock, Lübbe formed Kampfgruppe Burmeister (Sauvant's Tigers, Pz.Regt. 3, I./Pz. Gr. Regt. 304 (SPW), self-propelled artillery, Panzerjägers) under his most experienced armoured leader and ordered him to seize the corps objective – Ol'khovatka – while 20.Panzer-Division screened the extended right flank of XXXXVII Panzerkorps. Oberst Arnold Burmeister was one of the most experienced Panzer-Regiment commanders on the Eastern Front and German commanders were given wide tactical discretion under the mission–orders concept. Burmeister decided that before proceeding to Ol'khovatka that he needed to secure the Soviet-held village of Samodurovka, which was sniping at his Kampfgruppe with long-range anti-tank fire. His mass of armour struck units from the 140th Rifle Division holding this village and easily forced them to withdraw, while destroying a company of supporting T-34s in the process. However, Burmeister did not have sufficient infantry to hold this village so he left it vacant and turned eastward toward Ol'khovatka. Normally, moving parallel to the front of an alerted enemy is one of the worst tactical choices that a commander can make because it exposes them to enfilade fire. The Soviets had established a defence north of Ol'khovatka with the 75 GRD, supported by Grigor'ev's 16th Tank Corps and two batteries of 85mm anti-craft guns, with plenty of mines in front. As Burmeister presented his flank to the enemy, the Soviets unleashed volleys of 85mm armour-piercing rounds and barrages of heavy artillery on the armoured phalanx. One of Major Sauvant's Tigers was hit by an 85mm AP round in the side, which penetrated and destroyed it. The rest of Burmeister's Kampfgruppe was badly battered and Oberst Wilhelm von Goerne, commander of Panzer-Grenadier-Regiment 304, was killed. Rather than retire from a poor tactical situation, Burmeister elected to engage dug-in Soviet tanks in a long-range gunnery duel that lasted until nightfall. In order to have a reasonable probability of striking a dug-in T-34, with only its turret showing above ground, a Tiger had to close to within 500 metres, but mines made it difficult to close up on the target.[84] During the action between 2.Panzer-Division and 16th Tank Corps, which involved no more than 100 tanks on each side, Major Aleksei F. Sankovsky's 1541 SUP entered the battle with his SU-152s. Although Sankovsky claimed multiple Tigers and Ferdinands (which were not deployed in this sector) destroyed, it is more likely that he was aiming at Pz IVs. Soviet tankers tended to regard the Pz IVs with *Schürzen* as heavy tanks but in any case, Soviet propaganda dubbed Sankovsky's SU-152s as *Zvierboy* ('Animal Hunters'). In reality, it was the mines, 85mm AA guns and heavy artillery that defeated Burmeister's attack. At dusk, Burmeister withdrew after failing to accomplish his mission.

Model recognized that heavy losses and depleted supplies would soon force the culmination of his offensive, but he wanted to make one more try against both Ol'khovatka and Ponyri on 8 July. This time, Generalleutnant Dietrich von Saucken's fresh 4.Panzer-Division would spearhead Lemelsen's advance. At first light, Saucken's division was forced to retake Samodurovka, which the Soviets had reoccupied during the night. After that was accomplished, Saucken advanced toward Teploye, hoping this sector was not as heavily defended as the Ol'khovatka sector. It was. Teploye was held by the 140th Siberian Rifle Division, backed by the 3rd Anti-Tank Brigade and Polkovnik Fedor P. Vasetskaya's 79th Tank Brigade from 19 TC. Major Sauvant's last three Tigers led the advance to Teploye and they managed to overrun one Soviet rifle battalion and occupy part of the town before running into a wall of fire. Vasetskaya's T-34s were dug into hull-down firing positions, which made them difficult for the German tankers to hit. Another long-range gunnery duel developed, with at least three Pz IVs and four T-34s destroyed. Saucken called in Stukas, which pounded the Soviet hill-top positions, but could not get them to budge. The 4.Panzer-Division's attack faltered and ended without any success. Likewise, a renewed effort by Kampfgruppe Burmeister to push toward Ol'khovatka was stopped by mines, anti-tank fire, artillery and dug-in T-34s. Model had reached his high water mark and further advance was now impossible. There would be no victory parade through Kursk for AOK 9.

Harpe continued to grapple with Enshin's forces at Ponyri from 8–10 July and managed to capture half of the town at great cost. Four Ferdinands were destroyed in close-quarter fighting inside the town, which was the wrong place for them to be employed. Ponyri became an extended and pointless battle of attrition that exhausted Harpe's corps and played to Rokossovsky's objective of weakening AOK 9 as a precursor to the inevitable Soviet counter-offensive. Model recognized this as well and on 10 July he ordered his forces to suspend the offensive. He did not ask permission from the OKH or Hitler, he simply suspended his role in *Zitadelle*. When the OKH recommended that he shift his axis of attack, he ignored them. In six days of attacking, the northern German pincer had advanced barely 15km and captured no significant objectives and destroyed no major Soviet formations. Model's AOK 9 had suffered 22,201 casualties, including 4,691 dead or missing, which was the highest one-week loss for any single German army since *Barbarossa* two years earlier. Four of Model's infantry divisions were combat ineffective, but he did achieve his objective of conserving a viable armour reserve. The six Panzer-Divisionen fighting on the northern front lost only 29 tanks destroyed, including three of Sauvant's Tigers. The 3./s.Pz.Abt. 505 arrived in the final days of the battle, which meant that Sauvant's battalion still had 26 operational Tigers when Model called off the offensive. In addition, 19 Ferdinands and 17 assault guns were lost. Many vehicles suffered damage from mines and artillery fire, but could be repaired in a matter of days. Altogether, Model's AOK 9 lost 71 AFVs destroyed and

308 AFV damaged, but Model was left with at least 500 operational AFVs to counter the coming storm.

Rokossovsky's defence had held firmly, yielding very little ground, but had failed to inflict crippling losses on Model's armour. Post-war Soviet historians created tales of a four-day tank battle between Ponyri and Ol'khovatka, which they claimed destroyed hundreds of German tanks, but this was mostly fabricated to conceal Soviet frustrations. Instead of a great clash of armour, most of the tank combat in the northern front had been battalion, regiment and brigade-size actions. Rokossovsky's Central Front suffered 33,897 casualties and, like Model's AOK 9, the front-line infantry units got the worst of it. Soviet armour losses in the north are not exactly known, but were in the range of 200 tanks destroyed and 100–200 damaged. Rodin's 2TA lost 46 per cent of its armour, but was soon restored to combat effectiveness. The main point to be gleaned from Model's failed offensive was that neither side was able to seriously reduce the other's armoured reserves, which had considerable consequences for the events to follow.[85]

Operation *Zitadelle*: The Southern Front, 5–16 July 1943

Von Manstein had wanted to attack the Kursk Salient as an immediate follow up to his successful Backhand Blow counter-offensive, but was stymied first by the rainy spring weather, and then by Hitler's repeated delays of *Zitadelle* to await the arrival of the Panther medium tank and more Tigers. Although the point has often been made that an earlier German attack might have succeeded, this punditry disregards the weather, the logistic situation and the emaciated state of Hoth's 4.Panzerarmee. The simple fact is that the Red Army used the April–June lull better than the Wehrmacht did, fortifying the Kursk salient and forming a large mobile reserve for follow-on operations. Soviet intelligence about the *Zitadelle* plan was excellent, in part due to information forward from the Allied ULTRA signals intercept programme.[*] In contrast, the Germans knew about the Soviet defensive preparations in the Kursk salient due to regular photo reconnaissance, but they were unaware of the vast numbers of RVGK reserves that were being concentrated further to the rear. Von Manstein's hubris about slicing through the Soviet defences with his armoured battering ram was based on ignorance of the enemy's actual strength.

In planning *Zitadelle*, von Manstein displayed a certain inattention to details that would plague the operation from the start. Unlike Model, he failed to appreciate the depth of Soviet minefields and asked for no special engineering resources; Hoth's 4.Panzerarmee (PzAOK 4) received no Goliath or BIV demolition vehicles or other mine-clearing equipment. Von Manstein's operational plan was very basic, envisioning that Hoth's 4.Panzerarmee,

---

[*] TUNNY, a sub-set of ULTRA, was involved in intercepting copies of German operational orders. Both the April warning order for *Zitadelle* and the actual operational plan were passed on to the Soviets by the Soviet spy in Bletchley Park, John Cairncross.

consisting of General der Panzertruppe Otto von Knobelsdorff's XXXXVIII Panzerkorps (3., 11.Panzer-Divisionen and the *Großdeutschland*) and Hausser's II. SS-Panzerkorps (*LSSAH, Das Reich* and *Totenkopf*) would form the main effort, while Armee-Abteilung Kempf would conduct a supporting attack with General der Panzertruppe Hermann Breith's III Panzerkorps (6., 7. and 19.Panzer-Divisionen) and Generaloberst Erhard Raus' XI Armeekorps (two infantry divisions and Sturmgeschütz-Abteilung 905). Von Manstein believed that this mass of armour and troops, with over 1,500 AFVs and supported by Luftflotte 4, could blast its way through any defensive lines. Up front though, von Manstein violated the principle of unity of command by putting two Panzerkorps under Hoth and one under Kempf, when doctrine recommended that all three should have been under a single army commander. Consequently, Breith's III Panzerkorps contributed little to its primary mission of protecting the right flank of II. SS-Panzerkorps and essentially fought an isolated and operationally pointless battle. Nor did von Manstein ensure that his subordinates had conducted detailed tactical planning prior to execution, which became immediately obvious in both the III. and XXXXVIII Panzerkorps sectors. Finally, von Manstein's broad front implementation of *Zitadelle* left him with no operational-level reserves, other than General der Panzertruppe Walther Nehring's distant and under-resourced XXIV Panzerkorps. After the war, von Manstein would claim that Nehring's corps could have made a great impact upon the outcome of *Zitadelle*, but this formation had a total of only 171 tanks among its three mechanized divisions. Furthermore, Nehring's XXIV Panzerkorps was the only mobile reserve belonging to the 1. Panzerarmee and stripping this resource would seriously weaken Heeresgruppe Süd's right flank.

Facing Hoth's 4.Panzerarmee, Vatutin had arrayed his Voronezh Front forces in great depth. General-leytenant Ivan M. Chistiakov's 6th Guards Army (6 GA) was deployed in a two-up/one-back style echeloned defence across a 60km-wide front, with the 22nd Guards Rifle Corps (22 GRC) opposite XXXXVIII Panzerkorps and the 23rd Guards Rifle Corps (23 GRC) opposite the II. SS-Panzerkorps. In tactical reserve, Chistiakov had the 96th Tank Brigade (46 T-34s and 5 T-70) and the 230th and 245th separate tank regiments with a total of 34 M3 Grants and 44 M3 Stuarts. More importantly, Chistiakov had the 27th and 28th Anti-tank Brigades in general support, plus 10 separate anti-tank regiments which were attached to his rifle divisions, providing 6 GA with a total of 573 anti-tank guns.[86] However, Chistiakov's sector only had half the density of mines that Pukhov's 13th Army had on the northern front and, unlike Rokossovsky, Vatutin had not deployed an artillery corps to support the main defence. With fewer mines and less artillery support, Chistiakov's front was not as dense a defence as Model had confronted in the north.

Behind Chistiakov's 6 GA, Vatutin deployed the 69th Army in a third line of defence with five rifle divisions, the 35th Guards Rifle corps and General-leytenant Mikhail E. Katukov's 1st Tank Army, comprised of the 6th and 31st

Tank Corps and 3rd Mechanized Corps. Altogether, Katukov had 587 tanks of which 484 were T-34s – an unusually high proportion of medium tanks for the Red Army in mid-1943. Vatutin kept two more tank units, the 2nd and 5th Guards Tank Corps with a total of 410 tanks, under his control in front reserve. Vatutin's intent was to use Katukov's armour and the two separate tank corps to mount local counter-attacks to block any German breakthroughs, rather than as a *masse de manoeuvre*. General-leytenant Mikhail S. Shumilov's 7th Guards Army (7 GA) opposed Armee-Abteilung Kempf with the 25th Guards Rifle Corps in a 2-up/1-back defensive echelon, supported by two tank regiments with 33 T-34 and 22 KV-1s.

The long-awaited Panther tanks arrived by rail near Borisovka, beginning on 1 July, and the last trainload did not arrive until 4 July, the day before *Zitadelle* was to begin. All the technical problems aside, Hoth had made little effort to ensure that the two Panther-Abteilungen had proper command and control or were integrated into PzAOK 4's tactical plans. The 10.Panzer-Brigade was established in Berlin on 27 June under Oberst Karl Decker to command the Panthers, but the headquarters did not even begin moving to the Eastern Front until 3 July.* This mistake was another indicator that the efficiency of the German Panzertruppen was slipping by 1943. Realizing that someone had dropped the ball, Major Meinrad von Lauchert, who had been involved with training Panther crews at Grafenwöhr, formed the provisional Panzer-Regiment 39 to control the Panthers arriving at the Borisovka railhead. The Panthers were put under the operational control of *Großdeutschland*, which gave von Lauchert a radio command vehicle and enough resources to operate a small tactical command post. However, this ad hoc solution all occurred in the last evening before *Zitadelle* began, which meant that coordination and the tactical orders process were curtailed. One-third of the Panther crews had no combat experience and now they were being asked to go into battle attached to an unfamiliar unit and with vague tactical orders. Making matters significantly worse, there was no opportunity at the railhead to bore-sight the main guns (which after a long, bumpy train ride would definitely be out of alignment with the gunner's sights) or to set radios to correct frequencies. As soon as they left the railhead, Panthers began breaking down on the 35km road march to the assembly area near Tomarovka and by the time they reached it, only 166 out of 204 Panthers were still running.[87] Two Panthers were completely burnt-out by engine fires.†

---

* Decker and his brigade headquarters did not arrive until 11 July, by which point there were very few Panthers left to command.

† The engine fires were caused by excessive heat, caused by a rubber liner installed in the engine compartment intended to keep the compartment dry in river-crossings. However, the rubber lining also retained engine heat and resulted in the destruction of a number of Panthers.

While the Panthers were moving up to the front, Hoth's PzAOK 4 was already making its initial moves in *Zitadelle*. At 1450 hours on 4 July, Stukas from Luftflotte 4 conducted a massive airstrike against positions in the 6 GA's forward security zone, followed by an artillery bombardment from XXXXVIII Panzerkorps. Hard on the heels of the artillery barrage, infantrymen from both corps began an aggressive counter-reconnaissance probe to overrun Soviet units in their forward security sector. Most of the action involved battalion-size probes to eliminate Soviet artillery observation posts and to begin clearing the outer minefields. No tanks were involved in this effort, but assault guns and reconnaissance vehicles moved forward. In contrast to von Knobelsdorff's broad daylight approach, Hausser's II.SS-Panzerkorps did not begin its own counter-reconnaissance effort until after dusk. Hoth's troops succeeded in capturing a few villages and hilltops, but were shocked by the difficulty of clearing paths through the minefields and the heavy casualties. Nor were all the Soviet outpost positions or mines eliminated in the security zone.[88]

Unlike the northern front of Operation *Zitadelle*, the operations of von Manstein's southern pincer have been covered in great detail in a large body of literature and I do not intend to belabour this well-known side of the Battle of Kursk with a blow-by-blow description. In particular, this task has already been well accomplished by George M. Nipe's *Blood, Steel and Myth* (2011) and Valeriy Zamulin's *Demolishing the Myth*, which both provide great day-to-day detail on the fighting on the southern side of the Kursk salient. Instead, I intend to focus the remainder of my discussion of *Zitadelle* on the main implications for armoured warfare on the Eastern Front on three particular topics: (1) how von Manstein's armour penetrated the Soviet obstacle belts, (2) the poor performance of the Panther tank in its initial combat debut and (3) Rotmistrov's botched counter-attack at Prokhorovka. I also intend to avoid the simplistic pitfall of earlier analyses, which tend to base their assessment of *Zitadelle* upon numbers of operational tanks on either side and little else.

Hoth's main attack began at 0500 hours (local) after a 45-minute artillery preparation. On the left flank, von Knobelsdorff's XXXXVIII Panzerkorps attacked with the 3.Panzer-Division, *Großdeutschland* and 11.Panzer-Division advancing on line. The Panther-Abteilungen were still in their assembly area and did not move forward until about 0900 hours. There were still plenty of uncleared mines in the former security zone, which greatly complicated the forward movement of the German assault groups. Generalleutnant Franz Westhoven's 3.Panzer-Division attacked with four of its Panzergrenadier-Baitallonen, without the planned armoured support, against the Soviet 210th Guards Rifle Regiment. After clearing out the frontline positions, the German battalions were stopped for nearly five hours by a deep, muddy balka. While the German pioniers established a crossing, Soviet artillery pounded the stalled Germans, inflicting heavy casualties. When the balka was finally bridged around 1400 hours, Westhoven's infantry poured across, along with tanks from

II./Panzer-Regiment 6, and attacked the village of Korovino. The village was captured, but Oberst Gunther Pape, commander of Panzergrenadier-Regiment 394, was badly wounded. A minor counter-attack by Soviet tanks was repulsed by the German panzers. Westhoven's division had overrun a first-line rifle regiment and advanced a total of about 5km.

In the centre of the XXXXVIII Panzerkorps offensive, Generalleutnant Walter Hörnlein's *Großdeutschland* conducted a very mismanaged attack from the outset. As with 3.Panzer-Division, uncleared mines wrecked the *Großdeutschland*'s attack schedule. Oberst Hyazinth Graf Strachwitz's Panzer-Regiment *Großdeutschland* did not arrive in time to support the division's infantry in the attack. Oberst Erich Kahsnitz, commander of the Panzerfüsilier-Regiment *Großdeutschland*, was badly wounded in this unsupported attack and later died of his wounds. The III.Panzerfüsilier-Regiment suffered very heavy losses.[89] Finally clearing the mines, von Strachwitz pushed forward to catch up with the infantry, leading with his Tigers, then his two tank battalions. His objective was the village of Cherkasskoye, which was held by the 196th Guards Rifle Regiment and two anti-tank units. Visibility was hazy due to grassfires sparked by the artillery preparation. Only 30 minutes after crossing the line of departure, von Strachwitz was shocked to encounter a large flooded area, which was the 80-metre-wide Berezovyi ravine. The Soviets had placed barbed wire and mines on the enemy side of the ravine and recent heavy rains had turned the ravine into a mud bowl that ran laterally for about 3km across the front of *Großdeutschland*'s axis of attack. Although some of Kahsnitz's dismounted infantry made it across, no vehicle could cross until the pioniers had established a ford.

It is incomprehensible that Strachwitz and other senior commanders in the *Großdeutschland* were ignorant of this major obstacleafter having had three months to prepare for *Zitadelle*. In combat, even veteran commanders can make serious mistakes due to fatigue, but that was not the case here; Strachwitz and the leadership of *Großdeutschland* were well-rested after the long lull. It is a common theme in German memoirs that whenever some inexplicable mistake occurs, like Operation Typhoon in 1941 or the Berezovyi ravine in 1943, or the effort to relieve the Korsun Pocket in 1944, German tankers blame the Russian mud for their failures. In other words, circumstances were beyond their control. This was nonsense. Instead of executing a carefully planned deliberate attack, *Großdeutschland* conducted a movement to contact as if it was a training event. Adding to this failure, Strachwitz decided to try and send several tanks across, but they sank in the water-logged ground up to their fenders. Furthermore, he allowed the rest of his stationary regiment to bunch up south of the ravine, which invited a barrage of Soviet artillery and anti-tank fire. Even worse, Soviet Il-2 Sturmoviks arrived overhead and caught the Panzer-Regiment *Großdeutschland* flat-footed, dropping bombs that seriously wounded Oberstleutnant Graf

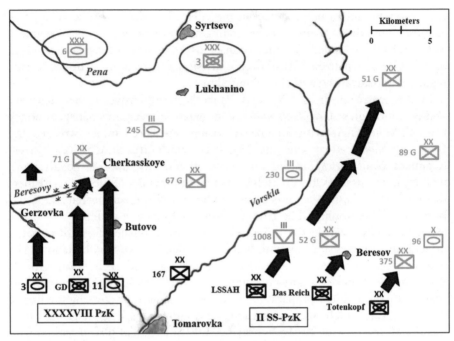

Advance of Hoth's Panzerarmee 4 on first day of Zitadelle, 5 July 1943.

Saurma, commander of II./Pz.Rgt. GD.* At least 20 of Strachwitz's tanks and perhaps five assault guns were knocked out by mines, stuck in the mud or damaged by enemy fire before he finally decided to pull back and try and cross the ravine 1,500 meters to the west.[90]

Compounding this mistake, Strachwitz did not bother to inform von Lauchert's Panzer-Regiment 39 about the obstacle. Von Lauchert managed to get a few hours to prepare the Panthers for combat in their assembly area before moving forward at about 0815 hours. Four more Panthers suffered engine fires before crossing the line of departure. Von Lauchert deployed both battalions in double row formation, with Hauptmann Heinrich Meyer's Panzer-Abteilung 51 in the lead and Major Gerhard Tebbe's Panzer-Abteilung 52 trailing. When Meyer's Panthers reached the ravine, a number of *Großdeutschland*'s immobilized tanks were still there and pioniers had attempted to create a crossing site with lumber. After a few minutes of confusion, Meyer tried to cross the ravine with his two lead companies, which resulted in a number of Panthers bogging down in the mud. Another company attempted to cross nearby and ran into a minefield, disabling the company commander's tank. Soviet fire pounded the

---

* Saurma was Strachwitz's brother-in-law. He was wounded by bomb fragments and later died of his injuries.

immobilized Panthers, damaging more tanks and creating complete confusion. A serious technical weakness in the Panther was also discovered: the Panther's final drive was too weak to move in reverse on a slippery slope and some tanks sat immobilized or sheered the teeth off their drive sprockets in frantic efforts to escape the kill zone. By the time von Lauchert received word that Strachwitz had found a better crossing site to the west, at least 25 Panthers had been put out of action. There is little doubt that the Panther's baptism of fire at Kursk was the worst combat debut for any major weapons system in the Second World War.

It took *Großdeutschland*'s pioniers hours to bridge the Berezovyi ravine and it is important to note that they suffered very heavy losses from Soviet artillery, which had the obstacle completely covered by fire. Furthermore, German pioniers were clearing the minefields by hand – as was the case with all Hoth's divisions – which was very slow and dangerous. It was not until 1600 hours that Strachwitz was able to cross the ravine with 30 Panthers, 15 Pz IVs and the SPWs of Major Otto Remer's I./Pz.Gr. Regt. GD and attack Cherkasskoye. Finally able to advance, the Panther's 80mm thick, sloped frontal armour easily shrugged off Soviet 45mm and 76.2mm anti-tank fire and enabled Remer's Panzergrenadiers to fight their way into the town and clear part of it. However, Soviet riflemen held onto part of the town and did not abandon it until nightfall. Nearby, the 1837th Anti-Tank Regiment opened fire against the Panthers with 85mm anti-aircraft guns, which posed a serious threat. Podpolkovnik Matvyey K. Akoponov's 245th Tank Regiment also made an appearance to support the retreating Soviet infantry, with its 27 M3 Grant and 12 M3 Stuart tanks. Von Lauchert's Panthers knocked out about six of Akoponov's American-built tanks before they retreated, but this was the culmination of the first day's attack for *Großdeutschland*. At great cost, the best equipped division in the Heer had advanced 7km but only dented the 22nd Guards Rifle Corps' first line of defence, not broken it. Mines had inflicted significant damage on the division, including nine of 12 Tigers immobilized. Indeed, *Großdeutschland*'s attack resembled the kind of poorly-planned/poorly-executed armoured attacks that the Red Army had often mounted in 1941–42.

In stark contrast to *Großdeutschland*'s poor performance, Generalmajor Johann Mickl's 11.Panzer-Division had done a thorough pre-battle study of the terrain and mission and requested additional pionier support. Although mines disabled at least eight of Panzer-Regiment 15's tanks, the rest were able to effectively support their infantry and pioniers in the attack against the fortified village of Butovo. Panzer-Regiment 15 also employed a company of attached Flammpanzers to burn out Soviet infantry positions. However, the Panzer-Regiment was caught in the open by Il-2 Sturmoviks twice, which bombed and strafed the formation, inflicting serious losses. Panzer-Regiment 15 assisted *Großdeutschland* in the capture of Cherkasskoye and also sparred with Akoponov's 245th Tank Regiment, claiming 10 tanks knocked out. By the end of the first day, 11.Panzer-Division had advanced 7km and had inflicted significant losses upon the 67th Guards Rifle Division's first line of defence. There is no doubt that the two front-line rifle divisions of the 22nd Guards Rifle Corps suffered crippling losses, but the survivors were falling back to the second line of defence held by the 90th Guards Rifle Division on the Pena River. Furthermore, Vatutin gave Chistiakov's 6 GA the fresh 27th Anti-Tank Brigade and the POZ detachments spent the night of 5–6 July laying more mines in the path of von Knobelsdorff's armour. Vatutin also alerted Katukov's 1TA to be prepared to fight a major action on the Pena.

Hausser's II./SS-Panzerkorps deployed *LSSAH* and *Das Reich* against the 151st and 155th Guards Rifle Regiments of the 52nd Guards Rifle Division near the village of Beresov. Hausser's divisions opted to open their attacks against the Soviet first line of defence primarily with their pioniers and Panzergrenadier-Regiments, supported by their Tigers and assault guns. Soviet mines inflicted considerable damage and, along with anti-tank ditches, caused the German armour to halt, while the pioniers cleared them by hand. SS-Untersturmführer Michael Wittmann's Tiger was one of two from *LSSAH* that was immobilized by mine damage. Podpolkovnik Ivan K. Kotenko's 1008th Anti-Tank Regiment, deployed with 24 76.2mm ZIS-3 anti-tank guns along the road to Bykovka, caused the *LSSAH* considerable trouble during the breaching operations; 8 StuG IIIs from the Sturmgeschütz-Abteilung were knocked out and the battalion commander was badly wounded. Another Tiger, which bypassed one of Kotenko's camouflaged guns, was hit in the rear and destroyed. However, the lavish firepower afforded to the Waffen-SS divisions and their gung-ho attitude finally prevailed. Kotenko's anti-tank guns were picked off one after another until three-quarters of them were destroyed, then two of the 52 GRD's frontline regiments were overrun.* Then the German assault groups overran the divisional artillery and command posts, completely disrupting the defence. Shocked by the rapid demise of the 52 GRD's first line of defence, Polkovnik Dmitri A. Shcherbakov's 230th Tank Regiment, equipped with a mix of M3 Grants and M3 Stuarts, was committed to try and slow the Germans and enable the remnants of the 52 GRD to retreat to the second line of defence. Committing obsolescent Grants and Lees against Tigers was suicidal and much of Shcherbakov's regiment was shot up within 30 minutes.[91] Hausser held most of his armour back on the first day, but the *LSSAH* still succeeded in advancing more than 12km through the 52 GRD's defences and was only stopped when it bumped into the 51st Guards Rifle Division in the second line of defence. Vatutin responded by deploying the 28th Anti-Tank Brigade to block *LSSAH*'s further advance. The *LSSAH*'s remarkable advance was achieved at a cost of 636 casualties.[92] *Das Reich* was less successful and advanced only 6–8km. On

---

* Kotenko survived the war and later recommended one of his battery commanders, who fought to the death, for the Hero of the Soviet Union (HSU) award.

Hausser's right flank, the *Totenkopf* chewed its way through the first line of the 375th Rifle Division, but five of its Tigers were immobilized by mines and three StuG IIIs were destroyed. After crossing a mined anti-tank ditch, *Totenkopf*'s assault troops encountered T-34s from Polkovnik Viktor G. Lebedev's 96th Tank Brigade and some Su-122s and Su-76s from the 1440th SAP, resulting in several platoon and company-size skirmishes.* By the end of 5 July, *Totenkopf* had advanced 5km. Altogether, the II. SS-Panzerkorps had suffered 44 tanks or assault guns disabled by mines, including 10 of its 35 Tigers, while personnel casualties were 1,081 (including 214 killed or missing).[93] Losses of pioniers were particularly heavy. On the other hand, the 6 GA had lost its first line of defence more quickly than expected. One of the primary reasons appears to have been the large amount of close air support provided to Hausser's II. SS-Panzerkorps, which the Soviets noted as inflicting greater damage than German armour.

Breith's III Panzerkorps, which was supposed to protect Hausser's right flank, had to cross the Donets River before it could even approach the first line of defence held by the 25th Guards Rifle Corps of Shumilov's 7 GA. Armee-Abteilung Kempf held a small bridgehead over the Donets at Michailovka, just south of Belgorod, with one bridge standing. Unlike Hoth's PzAOK 4, Kempf could not really conduct a counter-reconnaissance because of the river, so he opted to conduct counter-battery fire on the evening before *Zitadelle*; unfortunately, this consumed much of his ready artillery ammunition just prior to the assault. When dawn approached, the 6., 7. and 19.Panzer-Divisionen began crossing the Donets, first with infantry. There really is no subtle way for a large armoured force to cross a river under the gaze of an alert enemy, and in some ways Breith's III. Panzerkorps attack resembled the British VIII Corps' attack over the Orne River during Operation *Goodwood* in July 1944. Shumilov's artillery observers spotted the German crossings right away and pounded the far side with volleys of rockets and high explosive, which destroyed the Michailovka bridge and damaged some of the other assault bridges. Without the bridge, Breith's intent to use the Michailovka bridgehead became impossible and the attack in this sector was aborted. Breith had split up his Tiger battalion, s. Pz.Abt. 503, giving one company to each of his three Panzer-Divisionen – against the recommendation of Guderian to mass this key asset. Amazingly, Breith had put little thought into how these 58-ton heavy tanks were going to cross the Donets, since his pontoon bridges were only rated up to 24 tons. Consequently, the Tigers spent much of the first day sitting out the battle awaiting the pioniers to build a 60-ton bridge. Indeed, none of the

---

* Lebedev was a very experienced tanker who had fought in the Russo-Finnish War in 1940, the Luga River line in 1941, around Voronezh in 1942 and in the Ostrogozhsk–Rossosh Offensive in early 1943. He was part of the new breed of veteran Soviet tankers that would lead the drive to the west in 1943–45.

German armour was able to cross the Donets until 1030 hours, five hours after the beginning of *Zitadelle*.

The assault crossing of the 19.Panzer-Division was a near debacle and even once across the river, the pioniers had to clear minefields by hand in broad daylight under enemy fire. Soviet artillery pounded the hell out of the Germans attempting to breach the minefields, inflicting hundreds of casualties. When the Tigers of 2./s. Pz.Abt. 503 finally moved forward, first they ran into a friendly minefield that disabled two Tigers, then ran into uncleared enemy mines which disabled many more; by the end of the day the company had 13 out of its 14 Tigers disabled. The 7.Panzer-Division also suffered badly from enemy artillery, including losing the battalion commander of II./Pz.Rgt. 25. Eventually, the 7. and 19.Panzer-Divisionen were able to advance 3–6km, but 6.Panzer-Divisionen was unable to get its armour across until very late on the first day. Breith's III. Panzerkorps was hopelessly behind schedule from the start and it is hard to understand how either Kempf or von Manstein failed to appreciate the influence of terrain in this sector. Indeed, much of the German planning for *Zitadelle* appears to have been made with little regard for terrain or the enemy.

Hoth's PzAOK 4 and Kempf's forces overwhelmed Vatutin's first line of defence and pushed hard against his second line, but Soviet resistance was much tougher than expected. Hausser's II. SS-Panzerkorps enjoyed the most success, advancing to a depth of 28km by the third day of the offensive. In order to prevent the Germans from blitzing their way through the second line of defence, Vatutin was forced to deploy his reserves quicker than expected and he directed Katukov's 1 TA to assist in blocking XXXXVIII Panzerkorps on the Pena River with its 6th Tank Corps and 3rd Mechanized Corps. Katukov's armour was committed to the infantry support role – unusual for an entire tank army. Katukov was not happy about this since he wanted his armour kept massed rather than parcelled out to support various rifle divisions, but did as ordered. Vatutin and his subordinates were also shocked by the appearance of the Panther tank – of which Soviet intelligence had been unaware – as well as the unusually large number of Tiger tanks being used by Hoth's PzAOK 4.[94]

On 6 July, von Knobelsdorff's XXXXVIII Panzerkorps reached the 6 GA's second line of defence along the Pena River and was surprised to find that steep banks and swampy terrain made it impossible for tanks to cross.[95] Furthermore, Katukov's tanks and the remaining infantry from 6 GA were on the far side of the river, ready to counter-attack any crossing attempt. In modern terms, this ignorance of terrain would be termed a failure of intelligence preparation of the battlefield. Unable to cross the Pena, the XXXXVIII Panzerkorps was forced to shift its axis of attack eastward toward Dubrova in order to get around the Pena River obstacle and to protect the flank of II.SS-Panzerkorps. Katukov responded by positioning General-major Semen M. Krivoshein's 3rd Mechanized Corps (3 MC) in the vicinity of Dubrova, between Hoth's two

Panzerkorps, and shifting General-major Andrei L. Getman's 6th Tank Corps to protect the eastern end of the Pena line. Krivoshein was one of the most experienced tankers in the Red Army but he had been stuck in Moscow as head of training for GABTU for the past two years. Oddly, when Katukov visited Krivoshein's command post near Dubrova, he found that Krivoshein had his wife in the field with him.[96] In any case, when XXXXVIII Panzerkorps lunged toward Dubrova on 7 July, it ran straight into Krivoshein's 3 MC.

Hausser's II.SS-Panzerkorps had another very good day on 6 July, continuing its drive toward the northeast. As Valeriy Zmulin noted, 'the breakthrough on 6 July is especially impressive: in just eight hours of time, the SS divisions had managed to advance approximately 20km into the defences of a front that had several months in preparation.'[97] Stalin was sufficiently alarmed by Hausser's rapid advance that on the evening of 6 July he agreed to Vatutin's request to release Rotmistrov's 5 GTA from Steppe Front and move it up to support a major counter-attack against Hoth's armour. He also released the 10th Tank Corps from Steppe Front and transferred it to Katukov's 1 TA. In order to slow down Hausser, Vatutin tried mount a coordinated armoured counter-attack using General-leytenant Andrei G. Kravchenko's 5th Guards Tank Corps, Polkovnik Aleksei S. Burdeiny's 2nd Guards Tank Corps, plus the newly-arrived 2nd Tank Corps (General-major Aleksei F. Popov) and the 10th Tank Corps (General-major Vasily G. Burkov) against the eastern flank of Hausser's penetration. However, this proved far too difficult to execute since Vatutin allowed only eight hours for planning and two of the tank corps were just arriving in this sector.[98] Instead of a simultaneous effort, the Soviet tank attacks began early in the morning and continued until noon, in a series of piecemeal attacks. By sheer luck, Burkov's 10 TC attacked the tip of the German salient just when most of *LSSAH*'s and *Das Reich*'s armour was advancing westward to support XXXXVIII Panzerkorps, leaving the 29km-long eastern flank vulnerable. However, around 0920 hours the lead Soviet brigade ran into two damaged Tigers that had been left to watch the road to Prokhorovka. Although barely mobile due to mine damage, SS-Unterscharführer Franz Staudegger's Tiger could still shoot and he had a field day, picking off 22 Soviet tanks.[99] Burkov's attack fizzled out, even though Staudegger's Tiger had exhausted all its ammunition and the rest of *LSSAH*'s armour was not in a position to block this attack.

Most of the Soviet counter-attack on 8 July was focused against *Das Reich*'s extended flank. The *Das Reich* had temporarily shifted to the defensive here, holding the line with both its Panzergrenadier-Regiments and 12 StuG-IIIs, while the division's armour was pushing westward. Kravchenko's 5 GTC was the only attack that was preceded by an artillery preparation and some Il-2 Sturmovik sorties and it achieved the most success; around 1130 hours Soviet T-34s were able to overrun some of SS-Panzergrenadier-Regiment *Deutschland*'s positions. However, Kravchenko received no help from the Soviet corps, which were not yet ready to attack. SS-Panzerjägers shot up a number of tanks and the German artillery separated the Soviet tanks from their supporting infantry. After two attacks were repulsed, Kravchenko fell back to regroup after losing 31 of his tanks.[100] Officer casualties were particularly heavy in Kravchenko's 5 GTC, with two regimental commanders killed and another wounded, plus three-quarters of the battalion commanders. Popov's 2nd Tank Corps did not even begin to attack until after 1300 hours and then without artillery support. Popov's tankers not only had no information on the enemy's dispositions but they ran into Soviet minefields, causing casualties. Attacking with two tank brigades up front and the third in support, inadequate planning quickly caused Popov's attack to fall apart and part of one brigade managed to get lost and another fired on friendly troops. Popov's weak, uncoordinated armoured jabs were easily fended off by *Das Reich*. Burdeiny's 2 GTC was the most unfortunate, since it was detected by the Luftwaffe and Schlachtgeschwader 1 (Sch. G 1), equipped with the HS-129 tank-busters, was sent *en masse* to attack it. The HS-129B-1 was fitted with the 3cm MK 103 cannon, firing high-velocity APCR ammunition, which could penetrate a T-34's thin upper surface armour. Attacking at low-level, the HS-129 aircraft inflicted considerable damage upon 2 GTC, knocking out about 50 tanks against two planes shot down.[101] This was a historical moment in armoured warfare – the first time that aircraft had single-handedly broken up an enemy tank formation. However, some of Burdeiny's tanks did reach *Totenkopf*'s lines late in the day and enjoyed one singular success. SS-Sturmbannführer Eugen Kuntsmann, commander of SS-Panzer-Regiment 3, decided to conduct a personal reconnaissance in his Befehlpanzer (command tank) to determine where a group of Soviet tanks had appeared and he ran into a Soviet anti-tank ambush. His tank was hit twice and he was killed in action.[102]

Vatutin was responsible for the botched Soviet armoured counter-attack on 8 July, which missed an opportunity to knock II.SS-Panzerkorps off balance. On the other hand, Hausser's corps survived a major Soviet armoured counterstroke against its vulnerable eastern flank, but the threat remained and it was still devoting more effort to protecting its flanks than advancing toward Kursk. Furthermore, the diversion of much of the armour of the *LSSAH* and *Das Reich* to assist the XXXXVIII Panzerkorps' stalled advance against Katukov's 1 TA had achieved nothing useful. Increasingly, the German Panzerkorps were forced to divert more and more of their strength away from the *Schwerpunkt* in order to protect their flanks. Nor did Hoth have any reinforcements to give to Hausser, so the shortage of infantry was proving more inimical to the German advance than tank losses. Consequently, only parts of each Waffen-SS division were still capable of advancing and much of Hausser's corps had essentially shifted to a tactical defence. Hoth did provide two infantry divisions to assist in protecting Hausser's flanks – the 167. and 168.Infanterie-Divisionen – but both failed utterly. German infantry simply could no longer advance and hold ground when opposed by large Soviet armoured formations.

Nevertheless, von Manstein's forces continued to slowly advance, but Hausser needed to shift his axis of attack northward, instead of northeast to Prokhorovka. Soviet mines and anti-tank strength sapped Hausser's strength with each kilometre gained; on 9 July, *Das Reich* had 18 tanks knocked out making a 3km advance. Although most damaged tanks could be repaired, the number of operational tanks was quickly dwindling.[103] For their part, both Stalin and the Stavka were increasingly concerned about Vatutin's inability to completely halt von Manstein's advance. The Stavka had already directed Rotmistrov's 5 GTA and other elements of the Steppe Front to begin move toward assembly areas near Prokhorovka. On the morning of 7 July, Rotmistrov's tank army began moving westward and in three days the bulk of his forces had moved 350–400km and was reorganizing for combat. A total of 227 tanks and self-propelled guns, a total of 31.5 per cent of Rotmistrov's armour, fell out on the march, but 101 of these were repaired within 48 hours or less.[104] The movement of Rotmistrov's 5 GTA on its own tracks over such a distance was an amazing demonstration of the Red Army's growing operational mobility and the basic mechanical soundness of its armoured vehicles. In contrast, the German Panthers and Tigers had much less operational mobility and reliability and could not move so far and so fast without suffering crippling mechanical casualties.

On 10 July, *Totenkopf*'s Panzergrenadiers managed to establish a small bridgehead over the Psel near the hamlet of Kliuchi, at the cost of 374 casualties.[105] The river was only 30 metres wide, but the riverbanks were very marshy, so a 60-ton pontoon bridge would be required to get Tigers across. Once *Totenkopf*'s armour crossed into the bridgehead, Hausser expected to use this as a springboard to push northward and outflank Soviet defences at Prokhorovka. However, Hausser's II.SS-Panzerkorps stopped 8km short of Prokhorovka, since its right flank was exposed. The slow progress of Breith's III. Panzerkorps acted as a brake upon the progress of the Waffen-SS and the large gap between the two corps was a constant distraction during *Zitadelle*. Hoth and Kempf also found that they did not have adequate infantry to hold ground that had been captured, which forced them to use their limited number of Panzergrenadiers screening flanks instead of supporting the advanced toward Kursk. By 11 July, the German advance was slowing due to casualties and Soviet resistance, but the Stavka was increasingly concerned that nothing so far had actually halted the panzers. The decision to commit Rotmistrov's 5GTA from Steppe Front to smash Hausser's II.SS-Panzerkorps was intended to halt any further German advances.

Meanwhile, the Panthers in XXXXVIII Panzerkorps had not enjoyed much success in the drive toward Dubrova. By the second day of *Zitadelle*, von Lauchert only had about 70 of his original 204 Panthers still operational and his Panzer-Regiment 39 was wandering around lost. Strachwitz's Panzer-Regiment had pulled out of Cherkasskoye around 1000 hours, without providing any tactical instructions to the Panthers. Von Lauchert apparently missed the order to shift the axis of attack from due north to the Pena River instead due east toward Dubrova, so he advanced hoping to find Strachwitz's Kampfgruppe. Krivoshein's 3 MC had already emplaced the T-34s of the 14th and 16th Tank Regiments near Alekseyevka; the Soviet tanks were in hull-down positions behind an anti-tank ditch and minefield, with infantry and anti-tank guns in support. Strachwitz's panzers moved through the flat, grassy steppe and bumped unexpectedly into the anti-tank ditch and came under heavy fire. Meanwhile, von Lauchert decided to 'move to the sound of the guns', but had no idea of the situation. He put Major Gerhard Tebbe's Panzer-Abteilung 52 in the lead, with the first company in *Panzerkeil* (armoured wedge) formation, but the rest of the regiment in double columns. Without reconnaissance or support, the Panthers blundered straight into a minefield and came under heavy fire. Tebbe was an experienced combat veteran but he froze in the kill zone, allowing T-34s from the 14th Tank Regiment to engage the columns of Panthers with flank shots from 1,000–1,200 metres. The Panther's side armour was only 40mm on the hull and 45mm on the turret, which was insufficient to stop the Soviet 76.2mm BR-350A APHE round at that range (it could penetrate 60mm) and several Panthers were destroyed. Tebbe lost control and Oberleutnant Erdmann Gabriel, commander of the 8.Kompanie, took charge and ordered the Panthers to engage the hull-down T-34s. When the Panther's long 7.5cm KwK 42/L70 gun opened fire with their high-velocity Panzergranate 39/42 AP rounds, the Soviet tankers were stunned by the destruction inflicted and decided to break off the action. At least 19 Panthers were knocked out or disabled in their first real tank battle, in return for inflicting only a few casualties on their opponents. Von Lauchert finally caught up with Strachwitz's Panzers. Major Tebbe was relieved of command and replaced by Hauptmann Georg Baumunk, another experienced tanker.*

On 7 July, Strachwitz resumed the offensive toward Dubrova, but ran into another hornet's nest near Syrtsevo, where 20 T-34s from the 16th Tank Regiment and anti-tank guns were dug in behind mines. Apparently there was little reconnaissance or pionier support for this advance – another indicator that the German combined arms team was no longer fully functional – and Strachwitz ran right into mines placed in a ravine crossing site. More Panthers were immobilized, then shot up with flank shots. Oberleutnant Gabriel's Panther was hit:

I was severely hit by an anti-tank round that penetrated the munitions chamber at the left side, causing the later to explode immediately...I tore off the smoldering headset and microphone with my severely burnt hands,

---

* Tebbe had previously commander Panzer-Abteilung 116 in 1942–43. Despite being replaced for his failure of leadership during *Zitadelle*, Tebbe would command another Panther-Abteilung, I./Pz. Regt. 16, during the Battle of the Bulge in 1944.

which already had the fingernails popped off. By then the gunner was pushing out from below, but I had to push his head so as to get out of the turret myself. This all happened very fast…After me, the gunner was still able to rescue himself. He had suffered burns, mainly on his face.[106]

Eventually, von Lauchert and Baumunk were able to organize the remaining Panthers to lay down suppressive fired on the entrenched tanks and the T-34s were either picked off by the long 7.5cm guns or retreated. Strachwitz claimed that his Kampfgruppe had destroyed 62 enemy tanks, but this was likely exaggerated. However, 27 Panthers were knocked out and Walter Rahn from the Panzer-Abteilung 52 later noted that, 'we felt the day was a defeat and long thereafter referred to the Panther cemetery at Dubrova.' On 8 July, the XXXXVIII Panzerkorps made another major push past Dubrova, trying to advance along the road to Oboyan, but engaged in a fierce tank melee with Polkovnik Mikhail T. Leonov's 112th Tank Brigade and Polkovnik Nikolai V. Morgunov's 200th Tank Brigade, both from Getman's 6 TC, near Verkhopen'ye. However, only 10–20 Panthers were still operational and it was Major Peter Franz's StuG-IIIs from Sturmgeschütz-Abteilung *Großdeutschland* that won these tactical engagements for the Germans. Stung by the loss of about 50 tanks, Getman's 6 TC pulled back a bit and was reinforced with a fresh rifle division and the 29th Anti-Tank Brigade (as well as tank replacements), in order to block the Oboyan River.[107] During the period 9–11 July, the XXXXVIII Panzerkorps made only minor advances and the last operational Panthers fought a number of platoon and company-size actions against Getman's 6 TC, but failed to break through. Another 13 Panthers were lost in action against about 50 Soviet tanks, but the remaining Panthers were crippled by mechanical defects. Oberst Strachwitz was also a casualty, when he suffered a severe injury from breach recoil on 10 July.[*]

On 12 July, von Lauchert's Panzer-Regiment 39 was pulled out of the line to rest and refit. In one final action, the Panthers fought on the defensive near Verkhopen'ye on 14 July, against the Soviet 86th Tank Brigade; the Panthers destroyed 28 T-34s, but lost six more of their own. In ten days of combat, of the original 204 Panthers, 37 were destroyed and 148 were damaged or under repair. Unlike the Pz III and Pz IV series, it was extremely difficult for the Panzer-Werkstatt to repair damaged Panthers since spare engines, road wheels and fuel pumps for them were in extremely short supply. Later, von Lauchert claimed that the Panthers destroyed 263 enemy tanks during *Zitadelle*, but the actual number was likely half of that and compared to all the other models of German

---

[*] It is not uncommon inside a cramped tank turret to be in the wrong place at the wrong time, particularly when fatigued and stressed. Accidental injuries inside tank turrets are not uncommon and usually very serious. Strachwitz apparently suffered a crushed arm and shoulder.

tanks, the Panther had under-performed. Guderian had been right – the Panther was not ready for combat. On 10 July, Guderian visited the XXXXVIII Panzerkorps to observe the Panther and his after-action report emphasized the need for training crews properly before committing them to battle.

By 10–11 July, the German southern offensive was visibly approaching the culmination point due to personnel and equipment losses, and the lack of reserve forces to sustain further advances. It was clear that XXXXVIII Panzerkorps was unlikely to make it on the direct route to Oboyan. Nor was Breith's attack going well and his losses were very heavy. Originally intended as a supporting flank for II. SS-Panzerkorps, Breith's floundering advance was now a distraction that served to drain Luftwaffe support away from the main Prokhorovka axis. Although Hausser's II.SS-Panzerkorps was still capable of advancing, Hoth wanted Hausser to transfer one of his divisions to re-energize Breith's stalled offensive – a clear violation of the dictum that one should not reinforce failure. If anything, Breith and Knobelsdorff should have been provided Kampfgruppen to Hausser to sustain the one sector that was achieving significant success. Hausser ignored this order, just as he had ignored von Manstein's order not to abandon Kharkov five months before.

At 0500 hours on 11 July, Hausser resumed his advance toward Prokhorovka, with Kampfgruppe Peiper of *LSSAH*, but rainy weather deprived him of effective Luftwaffe close air support. Vatutin had rushed the 9th Guards Airborne Division to defend the final line of defence at Prokhorovka, supported by several tank and anti-tank units from 2 TC. SS-Hauptsturmführer's Heinz Kling's four Tigers led the attack, which quickly bumped into mines and an anti-tank ditch 5km southwest of Prokhorovka, covered by anti-tank guns and artillery. As the pioniers attempted to clear a path through the obstacles, platoon-size groups of T-34s from Popov's 2 TC suddenly appeared from cover and launched local counter-attacks. Twelve Churchill tanks from the 15th Separate Heavy Tank Regiment also joined the attack, striking the flank of the *LSSAH* formation.[108] A battery of 122mm howitzers engaged the German column with direct fire. Kling's Tigers provided fire support but were hit repeatedly; both Kling and his deputy were badly wounded, leaving Untersturmführer Michael Wittmann in command. Although the Tigers knocked out a large number of enemy tanks and anti-tank guns, it took the pioniers more than two hours to breach the obstacle. Once through, Peiper's Panzergrenadiers cleared the Soviet trench lines in close-quarter fighting around 1300 hours, but the rest of the day was spent repelling Soviet counter-attacks so the *LSSAH* vanguard stopped its advance 500 metres from the outskirts of Prokhorovka.[109] Nor had *Totenkopf*'s bridgehead over the Psel panned out, because the pioniers had not been able to complete a large pontoon bridge across the river until the afternoon of 11 July. By the time that *Totenkopf*'s armour began crossing into the bridgehead it was already under heavy attack by Soviet artillery and tanks. Indeed, the idea of pushing a mechanized division across a couple of pontoon bridges under constant artillery fire was rather reckless. At this point in the battle, Hoth intended to complete the link-up of the III.Panzerkorps and II.SS-Panzerkorps and then seize Prokhorovka station, but he knew that considerable mopping up remained. With Model's northern pincer already aborted, the most reasonable assessment for the southern pincer was to continue chewing up Soviet armoured reserves, rather than to extend its vulnerable flanks further. Hoth and Hausser both had indications that Vatutin had additional armoured reserves, but German intelligence failed to note the approach of Rotmistrov's 5 GTA.*

Hausser's II. SS-Panzerkorps had advanced into a narrow 4-km wide salient, with *LSSAH* at the tip near Prokhorovka station and *Totenkopf* holding the left flank on the Psel river valley. The terrain here was constrictive, due to the Psel River and numerous ravines and gulleys, which made it difficult to deploy large armoured units. With the 6 GA near collapse, Vatutin committed the infantry of the 69th Army to strengthen the front's third and final line of defence. Although Soviet losses had been heavy, particularly in terms of infantry and anti-tank, Vatutin and Marshal Vasilevsky (who was on site) believed that the commitment of the Steppe Front reserves would dramatically swing the battle in favour of the Red Army. Vatutin, with Vasilevsky's concurrence, had decided on 10 July to mount a major counter-attack against Hausser's II.SS-Panzerkorps, not only with Rotmistrov's 5 GTA, but also with Katukov's 1 TA and elements of the fresh 5th Guards Army. Although there was supposed to be plenty of infantry support, Vatutin conceived this counter-attack as a tank-heavy operation, with more than 800 tanks employed against a single objective. However, the devil was in the details and Vatutin's impatience to stop Hausser led to a very abbreviated planning process that undermined a combined arms approach. Very little effort was given to planning artillery fire support or close air support and Rotmistrov's tankers would go into battle with only 1.5 basic loads of ammunition and 1.5 loads of fuel.[110] In other words, Rotmistrov's carefully-assembled tank army was going to be thrown into the same kind of half-baked, ill-planned effort that had ruined so many Soviet armoured attacks in 1941–42. Vatutin and Vasilevsky were professionals, among the best in the Red Army, and they knew better than to conduct operations like this, but the problem was that when it came to key decisions they often were reduced to rubber stamps. It was Nikita Khrushchev, who inserted himself into the decision loop as senior commissar for the Voronezh Front and photos show him – not Vatutin – reporting to Stalin on the status of the 5 GTA, who realized that

---

* Both George Nipe and Valeriy Zamulin claim that Hoth was aware of 5 GTA's approach or at least that the Soviets were planning a major counterstroke. Perhaps, but the Lage Ost situation maps for 11 July 1943 do not indicate it and the general alarm noted in German accounts of Prokhorovka suggest genuine surprise that the Soviets were mounting such a large-scale armoured attack.

Hausser's continued advance threatened to break through Vatutin's third line of defence and reach open country, which was unacceptable. Stalin had been told by Zhukov and Vasilevsky months prior that the Voronezh Front could stop the German armour and Khrushchev intended to achieve that objective at any cost. Lacking any understanding of the complexities of modern warfare, Khrushchev pushed to use the 5 GTA as soon as possible and left it to the military professionals to smooth over the details.

Late in the process, Vatutin decided to assign both the 2nd Tank Corps and the 2nd Guards Tank Corps to 5 TA, although both units were still in contact with the enemy and this only added to the staff burden of integrating two new formations.[111] Rotmistrov was only able to issue his attack order at 1800 hours on 11 July, which gave very little time for corps and below units to develop and issue their own tactical instructions. Five hours later, Rotmistrov's tanks began moving into their assault positions, located less than 2,000 meters behind the front line. Rotmistrov developed his tactical plan without any substantive information about the enemy's dispositions, the terrain or mines. The RVGK provided substantial artillery to support Rotmistrov's attack, including 203mm howitzers and two regiments of BM-13 multiple rocket launchers, but poor communications and lack of observation posts ruined the artillery's contribution to the effort. Around 0830 hours, the Soviet artillery fired a largely ineffective 15-minute artillery preparation against *LSSAH* positions southwest of Prokhorovka. Soviet air support was negligible but Hausser immediately requested close air support. One of the first German air strikes struck the stationary 36th Heavy Tank Regiment (equipped with Churchills) and wounded its commander, Podpolkovnik Ivan S. Mitroshenko.[112] As is well known, the mythical clash of two great tank armies in 'the greatest tank battle in history' did not occur west of Prokhorovka that morning. Nor were the numbers of tanks involved particularly unusual by East Front standards. Rotmistrov's main effort was the simultaneous attack of the 18th and 29th Tank Corps, which committed six tank brigades with 339 tanks against *LSSAH*. The 2 TC and 2 GTC committed six depleted tank brigades with a total of 190 tanks against *Das Reich*, while the 5th Guards Mechanized Corps contributed two mechanized brigades with 66 tanks and the 1446 SAP added 20 self-propelled guns. Altogether, Rotmistrov attacked with 612 tanks and 30 SPGs.[113]

On the German side, *LSSAH* had six Panzergrenadier-Bataillonen and SS-Sturmbannführer Martin Gross's II./SS-Panzer-Regiment 1 (about 40 Pz IV and 5 Pz III) deployed just southwest of Prokhorovka, with the 13./SS-Panzer-Regiment 1 (four Tigers) deployed further behind the line. The SS-Panzerjäger-Abteilung 1 had at least one platoon of five Marder III tank destroyers deployed in direct support of the Panzergrenadiers. The *LSSAH* had good communications with its artillery and it had established a strong anti-tank defence to cover the open ground looking toward Prokhorovka. Around 0830 hours, the Soviet ground attack commenced as General-major Boris S.

Bakharov's 18th Tank Corps and General-major Ivan F. Kirichenko's 29th Tanks Corps attacked, advancing side-by-side across a narrow front. The two Soviet tank corps deployed four tank brigades with 234 tanks in the first echelon (with *desant* infantry riding on their decks), one tank and one mechanized brigade in the second echelon and one tank brigade in the third echelon. These two formations comprised more than half of Rotmistrov's attacking force on 12 July, advancing with 350 tanks and self-propelled guns. The Soviet tanks had to cross about 1,500 metres of open ground but due to black, grimy smoke hanging over the battlefield and the numerous gulleys, the Germans only caught glimpses of a mass of armour advancing. Obersturmführer Rudolf von Ribbentrop, commander of the 6.Kompanie, was the closest to the approaching Soviet armour and was first alerted when Panzergrenadiers began firing purple flares, indicating tank attack.[114]

Rotmistrov's armour came on quickly, surprising the Germans, but the Panzergrenadiers opened fire with all their anti-tank weapons and called in artillery (although it is extremely difficult to direct indirect fire onto moving vehicles). Ribbentrop's 7 Pz IVs knocked out a number of tanks from the 170th Tank Brigade but lost four of its own tanks as the Soviets assaulted through their position. Although wildly inaccurate, Soviet T-34s were firing on the move and did score some hits at a range of 200 metres. SS-Sturmbannführer Joachim Peiper's Panzergrenadiers were forced to fight a close-quarter battle with *Hafthohlladung* (magnetic hollow charge mines) as Soviet tanks and *desant* troops virtually landed on top of them. In just 30 minutes of fighting, the Soviet armour managed to overrun the *LSSAH*'s outer defences and a few tanks even managed to reach the supporting German howitzers. However, Rotmistrov's attack suddenly came to grief when it unexpectedly encountered the anti-tank ditch lost the previous day. Apparently, Rotmistrov's tankers were unaware of this obstacle and German accounts claim that some T-34s ran at full speed into the ditch. In any case, the lead four Soviet tank brigades came to a halt in the open, on the far side of the ditch. They had no engineer support. Gross counter-attacked the stalled Soviet armour with his 33 tanks, plus Ribbentrop's remaining 3 Pz IV and the 4 Tigers; at a distance of about 800 metres they shot two of the lead Soviet tank brigades to pieces, claiming over 60 kills. The Soviet 170th and 181st Tank Brigades tried to skirt around the flank of Gross' Panzers but were engaged by the four Tigers and methodically destroyed.[115] Meanwhile, part of Kirichenko's 29th Tanks Corps attacked SS-Obersturmführer Albert Frey's SS-Panzergrenadier-Regiment 2, located in the Storozhevoye woods. Frey's Panzergrenadiers were supported by five Marder III tank destroyers under the command of SS-Oberscharführer Kurt Sametreiter, which knocked out 24 tanks from the approaching 25th Tank Brigade. By 0900 hours, Rotmistrov's first echelon brigades had been badly defeated, but the second echelon advanced at 0920 hours to renew the attack. The 53rd Mechanized Brigade made a particularly deep penetration, getting past the anti-tank ditch, but suffered over 1,100 casualties in the process. After a bit of a lull, the third echelon attacked after noon, but was easily repulsed.

Further south, the *Das Reich* was screening an extended front, 13km wide. The SS-Panzer-Regiment 2 had no operational Tigers remaining, but its single Panzer-Abteilung had 18 Pz IV, 34 Pz III and several captured T-34s. The 2 TC and 2 GTC did not attack until 1140–1200 hours, by which point Rotmistrov's main attack had already failed. These two corps launched a number of armoured jabs but suffered moderate losses and failed to penetrate *Das Reich*'s lines. When heavy thunderstorms began in the late afternoon, both Soviet corps suspended their attacks. Altogether, Rotmistrov's four tank corps had 359 tanks and self-propelled guns knocked out (of which 152 were later repaired). Kirichenko's 29th TC was the hardest hit, having lost 153 of 199 AFVs. Rotmistrov's personnel losses were 3,563 (including over 1,500 dead or missing) including two brigade commanders.[116] German losses were modest, with *LSSAH* suffering 374 casualties and it had about 10–12 Pz IV and 1 Tiger knocked out.[117] *Das Reich*'s casualties were about 211 and it apparently suffered no tank losses.[118]

There were two important postscripts to the Battle of Prokhorovka. First, even as Rotmistrov's armour was attacking, the *Totenkopf* moved its two Panzer-Abteilungen (with 54 Pz III, 30 Pz IV and 10 Tigers) across the Psel River pontoon bridges and attacked northward against positions held by the 95th Guards Rifle Division. Concealed anti-tank guns inflicted significant losses upon SS-Sturmbannführer Georg Bochmann's SS-Panzer-Regiment 3, but Bochmann's panzers broke through the Soviet positions and pushed north. However, Bochmann advanced into a hornet's nest and the 33rd Guards Rifle Corps massed the fire of over 200 multiple rocket launchers and several howitzer regiments against the German spearhead, inflicting great damage to the accompanying SPWs and wheeled vehicles. Bochmann's panzers managed to advance 5–6km by 1730 hours – the deepest advance achieved by the Germans during *Zitadelle* – before he decided to halt. Nipe claims that 45 of Bochmann's tanks were knocked out or disabled, including all 10 Tigers and that *Totenkopf* suffered 316 casualties. The commander of the Tiger-Kompanie was killed in action. Interestingly, Zetterling's statistics claim that *Totenkopf* suffered only a single Pz III disabled on 12 July, but clearly that is out of synch with actual participants' accounts.[119] In addition to losses, the appearance of the fresh 24th Guards Tank Brigade and 10th Guards Mechanized Brigade from 5 GMC, with over 100 tanks, was also discouraging. At this point, Bochmann's panzers were low on fuel and ammunition and had limited infantry and artillery support to engage another strong enemy force. Bochmann halted his advance for the night.

The other major postscript involves the belated advance of Breith's III Panzerkorps to link up with II.SS-Panzerkorps at Prokhorovka. Breith's corps had suffered heavy casualties in trying to close up on Hausser's right flank and by 11 July, the III. SS-Panzerkorps only had about 105–110 tanks still operational, of which 31 were Pz IVs and about a dozen Tigers. In a desperation play, the 6.Panzer-Division mounted a night infiltration attack on the night of 11–12 July with Major Franz Bäke's II./Pz.Rgt. 11 (about 20 tanks) and the SPWs of II./Pz.Gren.Rgt. 114, moving in column with two captured T-34s at the front.* Amazingly, Bäke's panzers were able to approach the Soviet-held bridge over the Northern Donets at Rzhavets before being identified. After a wild mêlée in which a company of T-34s were knocked out at point-blank range, Bäke and the Panzergrenadiers captured the damaged bridge and created a bridgehead over the Northern Donets.[120] By early morning, Breith's remaining armour was pushing west across the river, threatening to cut off three Soviet rifle divisions and to link-up with *Das Reich*. However, nobody bothered to inform the Luftwaffe that Rzhavets had been captured and the Panzergruppe headquarters was bombed by several He-111s, which wounded the commander of 6.Panzer-Division and killed the commander of Panzergrenadier-Regiment 114.[121] In addition, Oberst Hermann von Oppeln Bronikowski, commander of Panzer-Regiment 11, was wounded and four battalion commanders were also casualties.[122] Although Bäke would lead a remarkable armoured assault northward on 13–14 July, it was essentially too late since Hitler had already decided to call off *Zitadelle*.

On the morning of 13 July, Hitler summoned both von Manstein and von Kluge to his *Wolfsschanze* headquarters in East Prussia to discuss *Zitadelle*. Von Kluge stated that Model's 9. AOK could no longer attack and had its hands full dealing with the Soviet counter-offensive. Von Manstein was more upbeat, claiming that 'victory on the southern front of the Kursk salient is within reach. The enemy has thrown in nearly his entire strategic reserves and is badly mauled. Breaking off action now would be throwing away victory!'[123] Hitler was nervous and pensive, as he often was in moments of crisis. Ignoring von Manstein's prediction of victory, Hitler spoke of the Allied landing in Sicily on 10 July and the danger to Italy, which he believed would require the transfer of some forces from the Eastern Front to prevent this situation from becoming worse. In essence, Hitler was unsettled by the heavy losses and the relative lack of success – as Guderian had predicted – and was unwilling to put any more resources into *Zitadelle*. Thus, he ordered *Zitadelle* halted, but granted von Manstein permission to temporarily continue local operations to finish off the fight around Prokhorovka.

---

* Franz Bäke (1898–1978) was a pre-war dentist and reserve officer, who rose very rapidly in the Panzertruppe. He served as a tank platoon leader in Pz 35s in Poland, a company commander in France in 1940, then a battalion commander in 1942. He led II./ Pz.Rgt. 11 in *Wintergewitter*, the Third Battle of Kharkov and *Zitadelle* in 1942–43. In November 1943, he was promoted to Oberstleutnant d. R. and given command of Panzer-Regiment 11.

On 13 July, Rotmistrov's 5 GTA remained on the defensive and was able to repulse a limited attempt by *LSSAH* to advance closer to Prokhorovka; the *LSSAH* suffered another 326 casualties for no gain. North of the Psel, the 5 GMC and the 5th Guards Army mounted a counter-attack that convinced Bochmann's Panzergruppe to withdraw to the bridgehead under heavy pressure. However, the main action on 13–14 July was the effort by II.SS-Panzerkorps and III.SS-Panzerkorps to encircle and eliminate the Soviet 48th Rifle Corps (48 RC). The capture of the Rzhavets bridgehead had made this Soviet formation vulnerable and Bäke led a fierce attack with III.Panzerkorps' remaining panzers against the 81st Guards Rifle Division while *Das Reich* struck the other side of the mini-salient. Although the 2 TC and 2 GTC fought to delay the German armoured pincers from closing behind the 48 RC, this effort failed and Vatutin ordered 48 RC to retreat. Around 0500 hours on 15 July, the II.SS-Panzerkorps and III.Panzerkorps belatedly achieved a link-up at the village of Shakhovo, but the 48 RC had already slipped out of the salient just before the pincers closed.

The Meaning of the Battle of Kursk
Kursk is a highly controversial battle. Right after the battle, Marshal Vasilevsky wrote an after-action report that attempted to conceal the truth about 5 GTA's losses, but Stalin soon found out and was enraged. Initially, Stalin wanted to have Rotmistrov tried and executed, but eventually Vasilevsky softened his response. Instead, Stalin put Politburo member Georgy M. Malenkov in charge of a commission to determine the reasons why the 5 GTA's counter-attack had failed; Malenkov's report was sealed, but it concluded that the 5 GTA's attack was a model of an unsuccessful operation.[124] Rotmistrov was allowed to remain in command of 5 GTA until mid-1944 but afterwards he was kicked upstairs into various high-level desk jobs.

In the 1960s, Kursk was not well known in the West. Initially, popular memoirs by Guderian and Friedrich Wilhelm von Mellenthin depicted *Zitadelle* as a decisive defeat, but this view was challenged by von Manstein's memoirs that complained about Hitler 'throwing away a victory' in his decision to cancel *Zitadelle*. Paul Carell echoed von Manstein's claims in his well-known books written in 1964–70 and he helped to shape the early historiography of Kursk with his contention that von Manstein had indeed been on the cusp of a great victory when Hitler pulled the rug out from under his feet.* Carell's histories also helped to create a heroic mythology around the Waffen-SS troops involved

---

* Carell, aka SS-Obersturmbannführer Paul Karl Schmidt, was the press spokesman for the Third Reich's Foreign Ministry and the creator of the highly-successful *Signal* magazine. He was a major component of the Third Reich's propaganda machine but was not indicted after the war and reinvented himself as 'Paul Carell.' His books are interesting and well-written, but also convey the German wartime propaganda line that the Soviets only won due to superior numbers.

in *Zitadelle*, which retains great credibility even today. The Soviet version of Kursk began appearing with the multi-volume *History of the Great Patriotic War* in 1958 and Rotmistrov's inaccurate memoirs in the 1960s. This white-washed version of Kursk was designed to conceal the Red Army's disproportionate losses in the battle and Nikita Khrushchev's (by then First Secretary of the CPSU) role in the disastrous commitment of Rotmistrov's 5 GTA. Soviet accounts created a highly mythic account of Prokhorovka as 'the greatest tank battle in history' and Grigoryi A. Koltunov claimed that, 'in one day the Germans lost more than 350 tanks and over 10,000 officers and men.'* Soviet historians regarded Kursk as determining the outcome of the war in the East, stating that, 'the Germans had been bled white' and had permanently lost the initiative.[125] This version of the battle was melded with Carell's and influenced popular as well as academic histories written about Kursk until the mid-1990s. Even seasoned authors such as Albert Seaton, John Erickson and David Glantz accepted embellished accounts of Kursk as historical fact. In 1995, Glantz's landmark one-volume account of the Eastern Front, *When Titans Clashed*, still claimed that the Germans lost 320 tanks and assault guns at Prokhorovka.[126] At that point, two things happened which reduced most previous historiography on Kursk to pulp: the records of II.SS-Panzerkorps became available, and the Soviet-era archives were partly opened after the collapse of the Soviet Union.

Books written based upon this new information by Zetterling, Nipe, Glantz and Zamulin have given a much more realistic interpretation of Kursk, but still suffer from biases. Zetterling took a materialistic approach and provided a great statistical analysis of the battle based upon better – but not perfect – numbers. He used *Totalausfalle* numbers of tanks to show that the German armour was not crippled at Kursk and still retained the ability to advance, particularly if Hitler had allowed Nehring's XXIV Panzerkorps to reinforce Hoth. However, Zetterling's numbers are somewhat disingenuous, in that he suggests that tanks that were not completely destroyed were still useful to the Germans since they could be repaired, but in fact tanks which had been repeatedly hit by anti-tank fire and mines were increasingly 'degraded' to the point that they had only marginal combat value. He also fails to put the heavy German personnel losses in perspective: by 13 July von Manstein's Panzer-Divisionen had lost a large number of tactical leaders, including three Panzer-Regiment commanders and multiple battalion and company commanders; the loss of these leaders negatively impacted unit morale and motivation. The Tiger tank units were particularly hard hit; for example, the s. Pz.Abt. 503 had suffered about 40 per cent personnel casualties and the Waffen-SS separate Tiger tank companies had lost multiple commanders. Personnel losses tend to hit armoured units particularly

---

* Interestingly, after the fall of the Soviet Union Koltunov admitted that he had exaggerated German losses and had been part of an official white-washing about Soviet losses at Kursk.

hard, since experienced leaders, gunners and drivers cannot be easily replaced by rear-echelon personnel or partly-trained replacements. What Zetterling missed was that while the Germans were able keep their *Totalausfalle* numbers low in relation to Soviet losses, the repaired tanks and remaining crews did not have anything near the same efficiency as the tanks and crews at the start of the offensive.

In 1996, amateur historian Georg Nipe wrote *Decision in the Ukraine*, which used some of the new numbers from German records, but fell into the trap of endorsing von Manstein's claims about *Zitadelle* as a 'lost victory.' Without reference to any Soviet records, Nipe claimed that Rotmistrov lost 600–650 tanks at Prokhorovka on 12 July and that the Germans had actually gained numerical superiority in tanks in this sector and that the commitment of Nehring's XXIV Panzerkorps may have been decisive.[127] In 1999, David. M. Glantz wrote the best available single-volume history of the Battle of Kursk, based upon a good mix of Soviet and German records. However, Glantz failed to offer much insight into why major Soviet armoured counter-attacks on 8 and 12 July failed so badly, or why the II.SS-Panzerkorps was able to penetrate Vatutin's defensive lines so quickly. Nipe returned to the fray in 2011 with *Blood, Steel and Myth*, which focused even more narrowly on II.SS-Panzerkorps. Although he does not use Soviet records, Nipe added great detail on the operations of the Waffen-SS and concluded that the number of tanks involved in Prokhorovka was far fewer than previously stated, particularly on the German side. Indeed, it is now clear that no more than 210 German and 642 Soviet tanks participated in the fighting on 12 July 1943, which is quantitatively smaller than some of the tank battles around Smolensk in 1941 and Voronezh in 1942. Distancing himself from earlier claims, Nipe also concluded that the capture of Prokhorovka would not have made any difference and the commitment of XXIV Panzerkorps would not have been decisive. Finally, Valeriy Zamulin's ground-breaking *Demolishing the Myth* (2011) has revealed a treasure-trove of Soviet records about the battle that provide a much more realistic interpretation.

While Hoth's 4. Panzerarmee had inflicted grievous armour losses on Rotmistrov's ill-timed 5 GTA counter-attack, the combination of mines, anti-tank guns, artillery and air attacks had in fact worn down the German combined arms team – just as the Stavka had intended. Hoth could still cobble together an armoured spearhead with his remaining tanks, but it was the loss of Panzergrenadiers and pioniers that made further advance problematic. By 15 July, von Manstein's forces had suffered over 28,000 casualties, including 5,600 dead or missing.[128] Altogether, the three Panzerkorps committed to *Zitadelle* by Heeresgruppe Süd still had 340 tanks (including 134 Pz IV and 33 Tigers) and 156 assault guns operational (about one-third of starting strength). According to Zetterling, Heeresgruppe Sud lost only 119 tanks and 10 assault guns during *Zitadelle*, but this means that over 800 AFVs were under repair.[129] Although Kursk was not a 'death ride' for the Panzerwaffe, a number of German Panzer units, such as all three Panzer-Divisionen in Breith's III.Panzerkorps and the Panther brigade, were rendered combat-ineffective due to losses. Indeed, half of von Manstein's remaining armoured combat power was concentrated in Hausser's II.SS-Panzerkorps, with the other two Panzerkorps were no longer capable of attacking. The suggestion that the II./SS-Panzerkorps could have made any significant advance northward after the action at Prokhorovka on 12 July is absurd on a number of levels, beginning with the reality that the factors that were still slowing the German armour – the mines, anti-tank guns and artillery, as well as the lack of infantry to cover the flanks – were still intact. Soviet airpower was also intact and causing frequent damage to Panzer units in the open.

Operation *Zitadelle* was not the 'death ride' of the Panzerwaffe, as Soviet historians tried to depict for years. Far from it. Yet neither was *Zitadelle* a 'lost victory' as von Manstein claimed, since the Soviets were already at the point where they could replace losses far more rapidly than the Germans. Rather, *Zitadelle* was the end of the road for the traditional German combined arms team, built upon the integration of mechanized manoeuvre forces and close air support. After Kursk, the Germans still had plenty of tanks and assault guns, but fewer and fewer supporting arms, air support or veteran leaders. It was the German infantry divisions that were disintegrating, which made it increasingly difficult for the panzers to hold or retake ground.

Furthermore, the Germans learned the wrong lessons about tank warfare at Kursk – that it was a tank gunnery contest and that the side that outgunned the other won. The Tigers had done very well during *Zitadelle*, inflicting greatly disproportionate losses on the enemy and absorbing enormous punishment. Only 11 of 117 Tigers were destroyed during *Zitadelle*, although their operational readiness rate was very low so it was rare for more than a few Tigers to be involved in any given action. Increasingly, the Germans placed their faith in long 7.5cm and 8.8cm guns, at the expense of manoeuvreability. The Pz III had generally been kept in the background during *Zitadelle* and the Pz IV was now regarded as second-rate. Despite its shabby performance, Hitler and the OKH believed that the Panther would eventually counter-balance the Soviet numerical superiority in tanks. New heavy tanks, like the 68-ton King Tiger under development, were regarded as the answer to Soviet numbers, not trying to build a better medium tank. Effectively, after Kursk the Wehrmacht abandoned its interest in building more or better 30-ton tanks and settled on the fantasy that smaller numbers of super-heavy tanks would alter the trajectory of a lost war.

Soviet losses at Kursk are more difficult to pin down, but the Voronezh and Steppe Fronts suffered approximately 148,000 casualties in stopping von Manstein's offensive and lost between 1,600–1,900 tanks and self-propelled guns. However, the Steppe Front continued to pour fresh reserves into the battle even as Hitler called off the offensive and Vatutin's armoured formations still had between 1,500–1,900 operational tanks and self-propelled guns. Painful losses suffered against Panther and Tiger tanks finally encouraged the GABTU to press for an upgraded main armament for the T-34 and a new heavy tank; these two initiatives would lead to the introduction of the T-34-85 and the IS-2 within six months. However, the Red Army still regarded the medium tank as its primary mobile combat system and heavy tanks were intended only to level the playing field when enemy heavy tanks appeared.

In contrast to the Wehrmacht, the Battle of Kursk helped the Red Army to recognize that armoured warfare was not just about tanks and they learned to use their anti-tank and artillery capabilities to balance the tactical shortcomings of their tanks. Failures at Kursk taught the Red Army that launching hasty, ill-planned operations was counter-productive and as a result, the Red Army tried to fight in more methodical fashion. In time, Soviet improvements in combined arms warfare proved more decisive than German skill in tank gunnery.

Another aspect of the Battle of Kursk which is rarely considered is its indecisiveness. Neither side achieved what it hoped to accomplish in this inordinate expenditure of resources. On the Soviet side, the Red Army wanted the German armour to literally 'impale' itself on mines and anti-tank gun barriers, but was risk-averse to allowing the Germans to achieve any kind of breakthrough. Every time German armour threatened to break through a Soviet defensive line, the Soviet commander committed most of his available armour to counter-attack it, resulting in head-in engagements with German assault groups. However, in order for the Red Army to achieve any kind of decisive success at Kursk, Soviet tactical commanders needed to allow German spearheads to advance into the depth of the defence, creating vulnerable flanks. Given the forces available for *Zitadelle*, there was no way that the German pincers could have reached Kursk and held a viable front with the limited number of divisions available. Von Manstein would have required a dozen extra divisions to hold the flanks of a penetration stretching to Kursk. Yet lacking these divisions, deeper German penetrations meant longer, weaker flanks. If Stalin had granted Rokossovsky and Vatutin the flexibility to allow some loss of ground, Soviet armoured counter-attacks against the extended German salient would have increased the possibility of surrounding and destroying some of the attacking Panzer-Divisionen.

On the German side, lack of operational flexibility robbed *Zitadelle* of any chance of achieving decisive results even before it started. The Germans knew very well that the Soviets had identified their likely attack sectors and were deploying strong forces to block them. Without surprise or a favourable correlation of forces, *Zitadelle* was limited to being a frontal assault. However, the Germans could have used the obvious tactic of a double pincer attack as a deception to fix large Soviet forces in place, while shifting the actual axis of attack to the face of the Kursk salient. If both Model and von Manstein had shifted part of their armour against the relatively weak 38th and 60th Armies, while mounting strong feints against the expected attack sectors, they likely would have achieved operational surprise and an overwhelming local superiority. Soviet operational reserves were poorly deployed to respond quickly to a threat to the face of the salient, which would have delayed any response. Furthermore, the face of the Kursk salient was defended by far fewer mines and anti-tank guns, which would have increased the chance of a rapid breakthrough. By smashing in the face of the Kursk salient – which likely would have been far less costly than trying to reach Kursk through three lines of defence, von Manstein might have reduced the size of the Kursk salient and thereby shortened his front line. By 'hitting them where they weren't' – a tactic favored by the Panzerwaffe in 1941–42 – the Germans might have achieved one or more nice tactical victories in the summer of 1943, as they had in the past. However, inflexibility was the downfall of *Zitadelle*, since rather than using manoeuvre, the German commanders opted for brute force.

Operation *Kutusov*, 12 July–18 August 1943

As soon as Rokossovsky noted that Model had suspended his offensive, he notified the Stavka, which ordered the Central, Bryansk and Western Fronts to prepare to begin Operation *Kutusov*, the pre-planned counter-offensive, as soon as possible. This operation had been planned in detail since the spring and it intended to crush the German forces in the Orel salient by means of a multi-front attack from three directions.[130] During the lull, the Stavka had deployed great resources in the Western and Bryansk fronts to support *Kutusov*. Both Rybalko's 3rd Guards Tank Army (3 GTA) and Badanov's 4th Guards Tank Army (4 GTA) were scheduled to reinforce the offensive once it got going. However, two vital prerequisites for *Kutusov*'s success had not been met: Model's armoured reserves were supposed to have been ground to pulp in Pukhov's killing fields, but they were not, and the VVS was supposed to have gained air superiority over the Orel salient, but it had not. Furthermore, all three Soviet fronts were supposed to attack simultaneously, but Rokossovsky's battered Central Front needed several days to recover. Consequently, Operation *Kutusov* was conducted in an uncoordinated style that allowed Model to shift his resources around to deal with one threat, then another.

Only one day after Model suspended his offensive, reconnaissance units from both the Western and Bryansk Front began probing aggressively against 2.Panzerarmee's (PzAOK 2) front on the northern and eastern sectors of the Orel salient. The PzAOK 2 was holding a 250km-long front with 12 infantry divisions in the XXXV, LIII and LV Armeekorps. The only mobile forces available to PzAOK 2 was the 5.Panzer-Division and the 25.Panzergrenadier-Division, both under-strength. Although PzAOK 2's troops had held most of their positions for over a year and were well-protected by mines and entrenchments, the army had received few replacements since priority had gone to AOK 9 to build it up for *Zitadelle* and thus, the German front on the northern side of the Orel salient was quite brittle.

At the last moment, just before *Kutusov* was set to begin, the Germans saw what was coming and Model began transferring anti-tank assets to PzAOK 2, including some of the remaining Ferdinands and the new Hornisse tank destroyers. General der Infanterie Lothar Rendulic, commander of the XXXV Armeekorps, created a particularly strong anti-tank defence on the eastern side of the salient. Despite his lacklustre performance during Operation *Gallop*, General-polkovnik Markian M. Popov had been given command of the Bryansk Front and was designated as the main effort of Operation *Kutusov*. However, the level of effort he put into planning and organizing his forces for battle was characteristically deficient. At 0330 hours on 12 July, both the Bryansk and Western Fronts commenced their offensives with a massive 150-minute artillery barrage, conducted by eight artillery divisions.[131] The German front-line positions were pounded like they had never been pounded before – this was the first of a new type of Soviet offensive that dwarfed everything previously attempted by the Red Army.

As the artillery fire shifted, the Soviet assault troops advanced. Popov committed seven rifle divisions from the 3rd and 63rd Armies against two of Rendulic's infantry divisions and succeeded in pushing 5km into the German defences before his attack ran out of steam. Soviet air cover from 15th Air Army (15 VA) over Popov's troops evaporated when Luftflotte 6 arrived over the battlefield and shot down 50 VVS aircraft. This was repeated on the second day of Popov's offensive, when Luftwaffe Fw-190 fighters destroyed nearly 50 Il-2 Sturmoviks from 15VA, depriving Popov of his close air support.[132] Nonplussed by this loss, Popov decided to commit his armour to create a breakthrough, sending in over 300 tanks, including three regiments of KV-1 heavy tanks. Back in 1939–40, the KV-1 had been designed as a breakthrough tank and this was the type of deliberate attack that it had been intended to shine in, but now in 1943 the KV-1 was just a large, slow target. Rendulic had created an effective killing zone near the village of Arkhangel'skoye, with nine Hornisse 8.8cm self-propelled guns from Panzerjäger-Kompanie 521 and some of the new towed 7.5cm Pak 41, which fired PzGr 41 *Hartkern* (hard-core) rounds with tungsten penetrators.* Advancing in broad daylight across open fields, the KV-1s from Podpolkovnik Yakov F. Dligach's 114th Tank Regiment were shot to pieces long before most got near the German lines and the attack collapsed. The Battle of Kursk was the swan song for the KV-1 heavy tank and afterwards it was phased out in favour of a new heavy tank. Nevertheless, Popov committed General-

---

* The Pak41 was Germany's best towed anti-tank gun, introduced in April 1942, but only 150 were built. It used the tapered-bore principle to produce an exceptional muzzle velocity of 1,125 m/second. Using *Hartkern* rounds, the Pak 41 could defeat the KV-1's thick frontal armour out to 2,000 metres.

major Mikhail F. Panov's 1GTC, which was intended to be his exploitation force, to reinforce the 3rd Army's attack and it was able to gain some ground, at great cost.

Rendulic committed his corps reserve, the 36.Infanterie-Division (mot.) to delay Panov's 1GTC and Model agreed to transfer the 2. and 8.Panzer-Division to this sector. However, this was not Model's only crisis. General Vasily D. Sokolovsky's Western Front had attacked the LIII Armeekorps near Ulyanovo with the heavily-reinforced 11th Guards Army (11 GA) under General-polkovnik Ivan Bagramyan. In this sector, everything went right for the Red Army. Bagramyan massed six of his rifle divisions and several guards tank brigades, supported by the 8th Artillery Corps, against a single German division – the 293.Infanterie-Division. This unit was hard-hit by the concentrated Soviet artillery preparation, then bombed by the 1st Air Army (1VA). Since Luftflotte 6 had committed all its resources to stop Popov's Bryansk Front, it had nothing left to prevent 1VA from achieving air superiority over this sector. When Bagramyan's infantry attacked with tank support, the 293.Infanterie-Division collapsed and the Soviets surged forward. The Germans had one chance to stop or delay Bagramyan's breakthrough, since Generalmajor Ernst Fäckenstedt's 5.Panzer-Division (with 100 tanks) was deployed only 30km away in a reserve assembly area. The LIII Armeekorps immediately requested Fäckenstedt to reinforce the endangered Ulyanovo sector, but instead he took his time assembling his division and then elected to move toward the right shoulder of the Soviet breakthrough, rather than meet it head-on. Fäckenstedt's feckless action was the result of his lack of command experience, since he was a career staff officer who was pressed into command of a Panzer-Division due to the lack of other qualified candidates. Germany's panzers in 1943 were no longer led by the likes of Rommel or Guderian, but oftentimes by mediocrities such as Fäckenstedt. Since Fäckenstedt did not immediately counter-attack Bamgramyan's breakthrough, the 11 GA was able to advance more than 10km on the first day of *Kutusov*. Adding to the crisis atmosphere, the 61st Army from the Bryansk Front staged a separate attack north of Bolkhov, which managed to cross the Oka River and create another small breach in PzAOK 2's front. Shortly thereafter, the Soviets inserted the 20th Tank Corps into this bridgehead.

Model began to redistribute his armour from the *Zitadelle* battlefields to stop the offensives of the Bryansk and Western Fronts, but it was not until 14 July that Hitler gave him authority over all German forces in the Orel salient. Assuming that Fäckenstedt's 5.Panzer-Division would delay 11 GA, Model decided to focus first on defeating Popov's Bryansk Front. He transferred 26 of the remaining Ferdinands to Rendulic's XXXV Armeekorps and requested all Luftwaffe air support to concentrate in this sector. He also sent the 12.Panzer-Division to contain the 61st Army's attack. The Ferdinands from Panzerjäger-Abteilung 653 were deployed in excellent defensive positions and when Popov's armour attacked again on 14 July, their long 8.8cm guns picked off 22 enemy tanks at long range.[133] Popov's advance was slowed to a crawl.

However, Fäckenstedt failed in his mission to contain 11 GA's breakthrough and Bagramyan's assault troops tore a wide gap in the LIII Armeekorps front near Ulyanovo on 13 July. Satisfied that he had achieved a tactical breakthrough (e.g. the enemy's front line was torn asunder, but no penetration in depth yet), Bagramyan committed his exploitation force into the gap: General-major Vasily V. Butkov's 1st Tank Corps (1TC) and General-major Mikhail G. Sakhno's 5th Tank Corps (5 TC). This mass of Soviet armour advanced southward, past the ineffectual 5.Panzer-Division, slaughtering rear-area units in their path. The only thing that saved the Germans from complete disaster was that the breakthrough occurred in a remote area that was heavily wooded and the only roads were forest trails. The terrain slowed Bagramyan's breakthrough just enough for Model to pivot his attention and dispatch the 12., 18. and 20.Panzer-Division toward Ulyanovo. Schlieben's 20.Panzer-Division was the first to encounter Bagramyan's advancing armour on 14 July, but opted to conduct a mobile delay against Sakhno's 5TC, rather than launch a hasty counter-attack. Like Fäckenstedt, Schlieben was no Rommel. Nor was the Luftwaffe able to help much initially, since Luftflotte 6 was now engaged against three Soviet air armies and was unable to maintain air superiority over multiple sectors. Fuel shortages also began to impact Luftwaffe operations at this critical moment. When Luftflotte 6 tried to slow Bagramyan's advance, Soviet fighters from 1VA shot down five Bf-110 fighter-bombers and 15 bombers – this was definitely not the kind of warfare that the Wehrmacht was accustomed to in Russia.[134]

As if Model did not already have his hands full fending off both the Western and Bryansk Front attacks, Rokossovsky's Central Front joined Operation *Kutusov* on the morning of 15 July by attacking AOK 9's salient near Teploye. Major Sauvant's Tigers occupied excellent overwatch positions on high ground and they proved a formidable obstacle to the Soviet 16th and 19th Tank Corps. Over the course of 15–17 July, Sauvant's 16–20 Tigers knocked out 54 Soviet tanks at the cost of only two Tigers destroyed.[135] Nevertheless, Model could not hold off three Soviet fronts indefinitely, even by shuffling his Panzer-Divisionen around the perimeter of the shrinking Orel salient. Instead, Model opted on 16 July to pull AOK 9 back to its original start line for *Zitadelle* and leave just 4.Panzer-Division and Sauvant's Tigers to hold off Rokossovsky, while he shifted the rest of his armour to deal with Popov and Bagramyan. Model sent Harpe to lead the effort to contain Bagramyan's breakthrough. Luftflotte 6 also received significant reinforcements, including Hans-Ulrich Rudel's anti-tank Stukas from III./StG 2 and Hauptmann Erich Hartmann's III./JG 52.[136] Harpe used the 18. and 20.Panzer-Division to block Sakhno's 5 TC while Luftflotte 6 tried to gain air superiority from 1 VA, but failed. Luftwaffe aircraft losses over the Orel salient mounted rapidly and Luftflotte 6 was unable to give Model the amount of air support needed to mount successful counter-attacks on the ground. Rudel was shot down (but survived) and even Erich Hartmann's elite Jagdgruppe had its hands full with 1 VA's more numerous fighters.[137] Bagramyan continued to advance, but Zhukov denied him further reinforcements for the moment and demanded that he push east toward Bolkhov rather than south to cut off the Orel salient. Zhukov was apparently worried about pushing too much armour off into a void when he knew that Model still had powerful mobile reserves and he decided to reign Bagramyan in and conduct *Kutusov* in an orthodox, set-piece style rather than as a bold battle of manoeuvre. Zhukov had been defeated by Model in the Rzhev salient only seven months prior and now decided to play it safe – which saved Model's two armies from encirclement.

In the past, the Soviets had been unable to get three Fronts to work simultaneously against a single German army, but now the operational-level efficiency of the Red Army had increased to the point where coordinated action was achieved and the Germans were being pounded from all directions. Soviet artillery was particularly dominant, gradually wearing down every German front-line position. Faced with a deteriorating situation, Model opted to conduct spoiling attacks with his panzers to knock the Soviets off balance. On 17 July, 2. and 8.Panzer-Divisionen mounted a sharp counter-attack against Panov's 1 GTC that knocked out 25 tanks. However, Rendulic's XXXV Armeekorps was gradually being worn down by continuous infantry and artillery attacks from Popov's 3rd and 63rd Armies, forcing it back toward Orel. Model authorized Rendulic to conduct tactical withdrawals as needed, without the permission of either Hitler or the OKH. By the time that Zhukov finally allowed Rybalko's rebuilt 3rd Guards Tank Army (3 GTA) to be committed on Popov's Front on 19 July, Rendulic had already pulled back to shorten his lines and the Soviet armoured fist hit empty positions.

By 20 July, Harpe had stabilized the situation in the north and reduced Bagramyan's advance to a crawl. The OKH transferred several infantry divisions to rebuild the gap where the LIII Armeekorps had been and Model successfully lobbied for the *Großdeutschland* to be transferred to him from von Manstein's front. Bagramyan's 11 GA had also outrun its supplies. However, Popov's Bryansk Front was still in good supply since it had two functioning railheads nearby and Popov decided to use Rybalko's 3 GTA to break open Rendulic's increasingly thin frontline. Yet instead of using the armour in mass, Popov made the mistake of ordering Rybalko to split his armour and advancing on two divergent axes: the 15th Tank Corps and 2nd Mechanized Corps would proceed northwest to cut the rail line at Otrada while the 12th Tank Corps would advance southwest to overrun one of Rendulic's infantry divisions. The result of this dispersal was that the Soviet armour gained ground and knocked the German front line back toward Orel, but 3 GTA failed to encircle or destroy any German units. Instead, the Germans hunkered down with 12.Panzer-Division blocking Rybalko's 3 GTA from entering Orel. In the north, Harpe conducted a strong defence around Bolkhov and the Western Front opted to fight an extended positional battle for this unimportant town rather than using its mobility to outflank Harpe's Panzers. For nearly a week, Model's hard-pressed troops fought all three Soviet fronts to a near standstill. However, the cost was high in terms of resources and the Ferdinands, which had proved themselves as excellent defensive weapons, were almost all non-operational now due to mechanical defects and lack of spare parts.[138]

It was not until 26 July that the Soviets were able to make any progress. Rybalko's 3 GTA shifted south and reinforced an attack by 63rd Army against the boundary between the XXXV Armeekorps and XXXXVI Panzerkorps. Although Rybalko's armour was unable to break through, when Rokossovsky committed his forces to this axis as well, the Germans gradually began pulling back. German anti-tank fire devastated Rybalko's armour, knocking out 669 of his tanks in a week of combat. In the north, Zhukov finally released Badanov's 4th Guards Tank Army (4 GTA) and Kriukov's 2nd Guards Cavalry Corps (2 GCC) to reinforce the Western Front's offensive, but achieved only modest results. The *Großdeutschland* arrived just in the nick of time to block Kriukov's cavalry from severing the Orel-Bryansk rail line and 4 GTA only managed to force Harpe to abandon Bolkhov.[139] Model did the best he could to delay the inevitable and inflict maximum damage on the enemy, while conserving his own forces, but on 31 July he requested and received permission from Hitler to abandon Orel and retreat to the Hagen Stellung. Unlike von Manstein, Model had developed a contingency plan and had carefully prepared a rearward defensive line along the Desna River.

The 12.Panzer-Division conducted the rearguard mission in Orel, delaying the Soviet entry into the city and ensuring that all bridges over the Oka River were destroyed. On the night of 4 August, 12.Panzer-Division evacuated the city and the Soviet 63rd Army marched in the next morning. Badanov's 4 GTA and Rodin's 2 TA mounted a pursuit against Model's forces as they withdrew to the Hagen Stellung, but Model used his Panzer-Divisionen as mobile rearguards, successfully fending off Soviet probing attacks. During these missions, German tank platoons were deployed in defilade positions with their main guns over the rear deck; when the lead Soviet tanks appeared they would be knocked out and the German tanks would fall back to the next position to repeat again. These delay tactics were costly for the Soviets and induced caution in the advance tank brigades. By 18 August, Model's AOK 9 and the remnants of PzAOK 2 were entrenched in the Hagen Stellung and the Stavka declared Operation *Kutusov* to be completed with the liquidation of the Orel Salient. The 38-day Operation *Kutusov* inflicted four times as many casualties upon Model's forces as Operation *Zitadelle* had, a total of 88,000, including 27,000 dead or missing. All eight Panzer-Divisionen under Model's command had suffered considerable losses, including 229 tanks and tank destroyers. Between *Zitadelle* and *Kutusov*, Heeresgruppe Mitte had lost one-third of its armour.

While *Kutusov* was an operational triumph for the Red Army, at the tactical level it was a frustrating and costly effort. The three Soviet fronts had suffered a total of 429,890 casualties during the operation and lost 2,586 tanks – enormous losses even by Red Army standards. Furthermore, the performance of all three Soviet tank armies was sub-par since they were used to fighting positional rather than manoeuvre battles. Instead of penetrating and encircling German units, Soviet armour pushed German units back to their next delay position. Although hard-pressed, the German tankers had great sport ambushing the Soviet vanguard battalions then falling back to the next position. The Soviets triumphed in *Kutusov* primarily because of their artillery and air support, plus plentiful infantry, not because of their tankers. Thus one of the lessons for the Red Army about *Kutusov* was that it needed to employ its tank armies more efficiently to achieve decisive, rather than local, results. Numbers had not won the battle for the Soviets, dogged persistence had. For the Germans, *Kutusov* was an ominous preview of coming attractions.

The Mius River Battles, 17 July–2 August 1943

Von Manstein had only been able to assemble a large enough force to conduct *Zitadelle* by prioritizing reinforcements and replacements to Hoth and Kempf, at the expense of his other two armies – Generaloberst Eberhard von Mackensen's 1.Panzerarmee (PzAOK 1) and General der Infanterie Karl Adolf Hollidt's 6.Armee (AOK 6). Although von Manstein fully expected that the Soviet Southwest and Southern Fronts could mount a major assault across either the Donets or the Mius rivers at any time, he took a calculated risk that PzAOK 1 and AOK 6 could fend off these attacks while he used his main armoured forces to crush the Voronezh Front. For their part, the Stavka directed these two fronts to build up their forces and wait for the right moment. Unlike the resource-starved Wehrmacht, the Red Army was able to deploy three mechanized corps, one tank corps and 20 other tank units with a total of about 1,300 tanks to support these two secondary fronts.

Hollidt's AOK 6 was holding an extended front along the Mius River with nine infantry divisions in three corps. Although the rebuilt AOK 6 had not been seriously attacked along the Mius since early March, Soviet artillery had still managed to inflict 1,000–2,000 casualties per month during the lull, so Hollidt's infantry units were well below authorized strength. Furthermore, the Mius was only a minor obstacle, averaging about 50 metres in width and not very deep; AOK 6 was dug in on the western side, behind mines and barbed wire obstacles. The German HKL (main line of resistance) was based upon company and battalion-size *Stützpunkte*. For anti-armour support, Hollidt had Sturmgeschütz-Abteilungen 209 and 243 with about 40–50 StuG-IIIs. German defensive doctrine at this point was based upon a well-defended HKL to slow the enemy advance and rapid counter-attacks to smash any breakthroughs. However, Hollidt's only mobile reserve was Generalleutnant Gerhard Graf von Schwerin's 16.Panzergrenadier-Division, equipped with 58 tanks (incl. 37 Pz III and 11 Pz IV).

General-polkovnik Fyodor I. Tolbukhin's Southern Front intended to cross the Mius River between Dmytrivka and Kuybyshevo and smash through the centre of Hollidt's line, held by the XVII Armeekorps. Tolbukhin massed the 2nd Guards Army and the 5th Shock Army in this sector with General-leytenant Karp V. Sviridov's 2nd Guards Mechanized Corps (2 GMC) and General-major Trofim I. Tanaschishin's 4th Guards Mechanized Corps (4 GMC) ready to exploit the expected breakthrough. In order to deceive von Manstein, Malinovsky's Southwest Front would make diversionary attacks against Hollidt's left flank along the Donets with 1st and 3rd Guards Armies. On the morning of 17 July, Tolbukhin attacked after a short, sharp artillery preparation. The 44th Army made a supporting attack against the XXIX Armeekorps to the south, but the main effort committed seven rifle divisions against the boundary of the 294. and 306.Infanterie-Divisionen of the XVII Armeekorps. The Soviet 8th Air Army had complete air superiority over this sector, providing effective close air support as Soviet infantry poured across the river. Both German divisions were hard hit by the Soviet artillery, suffering 2,100 casualties on the first day, and the Soviet rifle divisions quickly managed to seize a 4km-deep bridgehead across the Mius before local German counter-attacks began to slow the advance. The 44th Army's supporting attack managed to gain a small bridgehead as well.

Hollidt realized that he needed to counter-attack immediately, before Tolbukhin got his mechanized corps across the Mius and before the XVII Armeekorps was overwhelmed. He appealed to von Manstein and the OKH for assistance, but decided to commit von Schwerin's 16.Panzergrenadier-Division as soon as possible. Von Manstein had already committed part of Nehring's XXIV Panzerkorps to deal with Malinovsky's diversionary attacks around Izyum, but sent the 23.Panzer-Division on its way to Hollidt. Hitler ordered von Manstein to transfer two divisions from the II.SS-Panzerkorps and the 3.Panzer-Division to eliminate the Soviet bridgehead across the Mius front, but they would take time to disengage from the Belgorod sector.

On the morning of 18 July, von Schwerin's division attempted to attack the left side of the Soviet bridgehead, but soon ran straight into Sviridov's 2 GMC, which had crossed the Mius. Intense Soviet anti-tank and artillery fire broke up the German attack and von Schwerin retreated after losing 20 tanks. Once the German counter-attack had been repulsed, the 5th Shock Army continued to advance and captured the towns of Stepanovka and Marinovka. By the end of the second day, Tolbukhin's bridgehead across Mius had been enlarged to 30km deep and 45km wide. Upon learning of von Schwerin's defeat, Hollidt requested that Generalleutnant Nikolaus von Vormann's 23.Panzer-Division move up quickly and launch another counter-attack against the bridgehead on 19 July. Kampfgruppe Sander, which included I./Pz.Rgt.201, a company of Marder tank destroyers and a reconnaissance company, moved out on the evening of 18–19 July and conducted a 170km night road march, with the rest of the division following. Amazingly, von Vormann's division was able to begin an attack toward Stepanovka at 0700 hours on 19 July, but quickly ran into strong anti-tank defences, supported by tanks from 2 GMC and 4 GMC. The 16.Panzergrenadier-Division conducted a supporting attack with its 20 operational tanks. Despite some Stuka sorties and an artillery preparation, two attacks on Stepanovka were repulsed. The I./Pz.Rgt.201 lost 11 tanks destroyed and all four company commanders were killed or wounded. Altogether, 23.Panzer-Division suffered 369 casualties, including 112 dead or missing. Von Vorman claimed that his division had knocked out 14 enemy tanks and 20 anti-tank guns, but the Soviet line was barely dented.[140] Following this failed attack, both the 16.Panzergrenadier-Division and the 23.Panzer-Division shifted to the defence from 20–29 July, assisting the XVII Armeekorps' defence. Although Tolbukhin's infantry and armour pounded on the thin German line around the bridgehead on 20–21 July and even gained a little more ground, they could not break out. On the afternoon of 22 July, Tolbukhin committed Tanaschishin's 4 GMC against the 16.Panzergrenadier-Division sector southwest of Stepanovka. Tanaschishin advanced with more than 140 tanks in a large formation, while von Schwerin only had a few tanks left and the assault guns of Sturmgeschütz-Abteilung 236. Once again, it was Luftwaffe batteries of 8.8cm flak guns that saved the day, destroying much of Tanaschishin's armour before it could overrun von Schwerin's frontline positions – the 4 GMC attack collapsed.[141]

Following the repulse of 4 GMC's breakout attempt, a brief lull settled over the Mius Front, as Tolbukhin regrouped for another offensive. Nehring's XXIV Panzerkorps arrived in sector and took command over both 16.Panzergrenadier-Division and 23.Panzer-Division, as well as the attached Sturmgeschütz-Abteilungen. Nehring concentrated the remaining 33 tanks and 47 assault guns into mobile reserves to help hold the HKL, which was desperately short of infantrymen. Meanwhile, Hausser's II.SS-Panzerkorps and the 3.Panzer-Division were en route by rail to make an all-out counter-attack. Hitler decided that he wanted the *LSSAH* sent to Italy, so Hausser was left only with the *Das Reich* and *Totenkopf*. These forces did not arrive in Hollidt's AOK 6 area until 27–29 July, at which point Hollidt began preparing for his major counter-attack against the bridgehead, designated Operation *Roland*.

Hollidt's plan was essentially a broad-frontal attack against the entire perimeter of the Soviet bridgehead, with the main effort against the hills around Stepanovka by *Totenkopf, Das Reich* and 3.Panzer-Division. Hausser had a total of 119 operational tanks (including about 15 Tigers) and about 30 assault guns in his two divisions, but even after acquiring *LSSAH*'s remaining armour when it departed for Italy his formations were about 30 per cent below strength.[142] Generalleutnant Franz Westhoven's 3.Panzer-Division, which had lost half its armour during *Zitadelle*, was able to put 37 tanks in the field, mostly

Pz IIIs. Nehring's two divisions would attack from the southwest with a total of 55 tanks, 28 assault guns and 17 Marder tank destroyers. The German XVII and XXIX Armeekorps would each also contribute one infantry division and a few assault guns to make supporting attacks on the flanks. Altogether, AOK 6 was committing five mechanized divisions with almost 300 AFVs against the Mius bridgehead. However, these German divisions could not count upon their traditional help from the Luftwaffe, which had suffered heavy losses during *Zitadelle* and depleted its limited fuel reserves. Fliegerkorps VIII had lost over 300 aircraft, including more than 50 Ju-87 Stukas, so close air support assets were in particularly short supply. Indeed, *Zitadelle* cost the Stuka squadrons eight of their best pilots, all holders of the *Ritterkreuz des Eisernen Kreuzes*.[143]

Tolbukhin's two mechanized corps had lost a substantial part of their armour during the efforts to break out of the bridgehead, but likely still had about 40–50 tanks each. Some tank replacements were arriving as well. More importantly, the 2nd Guards Army's 1st Guards Rifle Corps (1 GRC) had thoroughly fortified the town of Stepanovka and created a dense, three-tiered layer of minefields, covered by multiple anti-tank positions. In addition, the 8 VA was able to provide both fighter cover and close air support to the Soviet defenders.

Operation *Roland* commenced at 0810 hours on 30 July. Apparently, Hausser's assault groups attacked with minimal artillery support and no air cover. *Totenkopf* was the main effort, committing 68 tanks in two columns driving along a ridgeline trail for Hill 213.9, just east of Stepanovka. Brigadeführer Hermann Priess, commander of *Totenkopf*, put his 10 Tigers in front, leading the advance, which proved to be a mistake on this occasion. About 1,000 metres after crossing their line of departure, the Tigers unexpectedly ran into a dense minefield and seven were quickly immobilized when their tracks were blown off. Intense anti-tank fire from 76.2mm ZIS-3 guns opened up, many from flank positions, and the German tanks were sky-lined on the ridge which made them wonderful targets.* Tanaschishin's remaining T-34s were dug in so that only their turrets could be seen, and most of the ZIS-3 batteries were virtually invisible. Soviet infantrymen, using the PTRD anti-tank rifle, peppered the enemy tanks and forced their commanders to 'button up' – which made it very difficult to spot the enemy anti-tank guns. The immobilized Tigers were hit repeatedly and all were soon put out of action (two were later destroyed by their own crews when they could not be recovered). The rest of the *Totenkopf*'s panzers and assault guns were also hammered, and despite efforts by the divisional pioniers to breach the minefields, *Totenkopf*'s advance was repulsed. Efforts to mass the fire

---

* Sky-lining is a common tactical mistake made by inexperienced (or incautious) tankers, which entails moving with the vehicles' outline clearly visible on high ground with a rising or setting sun behind it. Normally, tanks traverse high ground along the 'military crest of the hill' (i.e. 10 metres below the actual crest) in order to avoid this dangerous mistake.

of *Totenkopf*'s divisional artillery failed to suppress the Soviet defences, which were difficult to pinpoint. Nor did *Das Reich* achieve much success, running into dense minefields and anti-tank guns west of Stepanovka, which knocked out 25 of its tanks. Adding to Hausser's discomfort, Soviet IL-2 Sturmoviks repeatedly attacked German assault formations, with no interference from the Luftwaffe. By mid-afternoon, *Das Reich*'s Panzergrenadiers fought their way into the outskirts of Stepanovka, but were fought to a standstill. Similarly, Westhoven's 3.Panzer-Division lost 18 of its 37 tanks and accomplished little. Amazingly, Hausser's II.SS-Panzerkorps had lost 73 of its 119 tanks and 12 assault guns on the first day of the operation, as well as suffering 812 casualties – much heavier losses than it had incurred during a similar day of *Zitadelle*.[144]

Hollidt's counter-offensive might have collapsed against a wall of Soviet mines and anti-tank guns, had not Nehring's XXIV Panzerkorps supporting attack achieved some measure of success southwest of Stepanovka. Von Vormann's 23.Panzer-Division attacked with Kampfgruppe Schägger at 0810 hours. The composition of this Kampfgruppe demonstrates the growing poverty of German Panzer-Divisionen after *Zitadelle*: Major Peter Schägger's Panzer-Aufklärungs-Abteilung 23, Hauptmann Robert Alber's I./Pz.Rgt. 201, the II./Pz.Gren.Rgt. 126 and the Feld-Lehr-Bataillon 128 (the division's replacement battalion). Despite lacking Tigers like Hausser's Waffen-SS divisions, both Schägger and Alber were experienced reserve officers who knew how to handle their limited resources. Avoiding high ground, Alber manoeuvred his tanks through lightly-wooded, low-lying ground and managed to overrun the town of Saurivka (Saur-Mogilsky in 1943). Soviet mines and anti-tank guns were a problem in this sector as well, but the 315th Rifle Division's defences were not as well-prepared. After breaking through the crust, Alber's panzers boldly advanced cross-country and seized the village of Garany, behind the 315 RD's main positions. At 1000 hours, the 16.Panzergrenadier-Division joined the attack and sent Kampfgruppe Sander (Panzer-Aufklärungs-Abteilung 116 and III./Grenadier-Regiment 50 from 111.Infanterie-Division) to link-up with Alber's Panzers, which was achieved at 1145 hours. A force of just five battalions had surrounded the 315 RD and succeeded in taking over 3,000 Soviet prisoners on the first day of *Roland*, as well as destabilizing the left flank of the Mius bridgehead.[145]

During the night of 30–31 July, *Totenkopf*'s pioniers were able to remove about 2,000 mines and cleared a narrow lane through the outer minefields, but pionier casualties for this effort were excessive. On the second day of the offensive, Hausser's II.SS-Panzerkorps began their attack at 0915 hours with a 45-minute artillery preparation and received some Stuka close air support sorties, but their assault units were substantially weaker. *Totenkopf* attacked into the teeth of the Soviet defence with only 15 tanks (including two Tigers) and was again repulsed with heavy losses. Both Tigers were knocked out by anti-tank fire.[146] SS-Unterscharführer Rolf Stettner commanded one of *Totenkopf*'s advancing tanks:

> Before us was the Russian field position. We pushed the Russians out and took some of the enemy trenches. I moved forward. We're hit by an anti-tank round. Then we were hit again. Out tank caught fire. Nothing to do but get out! My gunner and loader were able to get out quickly. I received a couple of small burns. I heard my other two comrades, the driver and the radioman, who did not get out in time, as they burned to death in the blazing Panzer. The Pak shot must have penetrated the frontal plate. We then worked our way to the rear.[147]

Before *Das Reich* could renew its effort to clear Stepanovka, it was struck by a large-scale counter-attack from the south at 0330 hours. Waves of Soviet infantrymen, supported by 70 tanks, converged on the town and the attack stunned the Germans by its ruthlessness. *Das Reich*'s Panzergrenadiers managed to hold onto one corner of the town by their fingernails but the panzers were forced to retreat and the Soviets mounted 14 separate attacks against the town during the day. SS-Panzergrenadier-Regiment *Der Führer* held its ground, but suffered over 200 casualties. However, Soviet casualties were much heavier and *Das Reich* took 1,400 prisoners. In the afternoon, heavy rain put a damper on the fighting for a while, but it was obvious that II.SS-Panzerkorps had failed to gain any ground. By the end of the day, Hausser's II.SS-Panzerkorps only had a total of 38 tanks (2 Tigers, 15 Pz III and 21 Pz IV) and 34 assault guns still operational. Once again, Nehring's XXIV Panzerkorps had a better day than the Waffen-SS, beginning with the elimination of the pocket created the day before. Elements of four Soviet rifle divisions were wrecked in this mini-*Kessel* and 52 anti-tank guns were captured. During the fighting around the pocket, the 23.Panzer-Division managed to destroy an SU-152 self-propelled gun, allowing the first close inspection of this new enemy vehicle. However, 23.Panzer-Division was reduced in strength to just 15 tanks and one assault gun, while 16.Panzergrenadier-Division had 12 tanks and 22 assault guns.[148]

Von Manstein was incensed when he learned about the scale of tank losses in Operation *Roland* and he flew to Hollidt's headquarters in Stalino. In just two days, Hollidt's forces had lost 105 tanks, including 24 *Totalausfalle*, and gained very little ground. Von Manstein wanted to suspend the operation before II.SS-Panzerkorps was wrecked, but Hausser argued that he could accomplish his mission. In reality, the Waffen-SS was being built up by Nazi propaganda as an elite assault force and failure at the Mius River would have serious repercussions in the struggle for resources in the Third Reich. Himmler was in the process of establishing more Waffen-SS mechanized divisions and he could not afford for Hausser's II.SS-Panzerkorps to fail to accomplish its mission twice in one month. Hausser was probably not high in von Manstein's regard, given that he had openly disobeyed his orders twice before, but he agreed to let the operation continue for a few more days. Waffen-SS tactics on the first two days had been crude and costly and von Manstein urged a more methodical approach.

Hollidt assembled all available artillery and put it at Hausser's disposal for an all-out attack on 1 August. By this time, the Germans knew where most of the Soviet artillery and anti-tank guns were located and thus the artillery preparation that started before dawn was far more effective. Prior to the ground assault, Nebelwerfer batteries created a thick smoke screen to conceal the advancing German infantry and tanks, thereby reducing the effectiveness of Soviet defensive fire. After much heavy fighting, *Das Reich* finally captured Stepanovka and then its panzers swept eastward, overrunning some of the anti-tank units blocking *Totenkopf*'s path. By 1600 hours, the centre of the Soviet defensive line was near collapse. However, Tolbukhin's troops made one last desperate counter-attack with several thousand infantrymen that nearly overwhelmed Hausser's exhausted troops before they could consolidate on the objective. SS-Unterscharführer Rolf Stettner, in another tank, once again fought for control of Hill 213.9:

> ...With all our power we sped toward the Pakfront...I ran over a Pak. Under our wheels and treads the metal crunched. We halted behind the enemy gun and raked every movement with the turret [coaxial] machine gun....I saw three T-34s moving to our left. 'Turret! 11:00 o'clock, range 400 meters, Panzergranate 39, tank!' the gunner calls out. 'Ready! Fire!' The shell hit the first T-34 under the turret. The turret hatch flew open but no one jumped out as white smoke rolled out of the hatch. The next round was loaded and ready. The second T-34 literally exploded into pieces. The next shell hit and penetrated the motor of the third T-34. It also caught fire and a black column of smoke rose high into the air.[149]

In the south, the XXIV Panzerkorps achieved a major breakthrough and advanced toward the Mius. By evening, the Soviet defence crumbled and the remaining units began retreating across the Mius. On 2 August, Hollidt's forces advanced to the river and crushed the last resistance in the bridgehead. Tolbukhin's forces had suffered a major defeat, leaving behind 17,895 prisoners, but the remnants of 2 GMC and 4 GMC escaped across the river. Although a tactical success, the Mius River fighting was extremely costly for the Germans. Overall, AOK 6 suffered 21,369 casualties in the 17-day battle. Hausser's II.SS-Panzerkorps was virtually burnt-out: *Totenkopf* suffered 1,458 casualties in its four-day attack and was reduced to just 23 operational tanks, while *Das Reich* suffered nearly 1,000 casualties and was left with 22 tanks.[150] While many damaged tanks would be repaired in time, losses in Panzergrenadiers and pioniers were particularly crippling and not easy to replace. The 3. and 23.Panzer-Divisionen were also reduced to a very depleted condition and 16.Panzergrenadier-Division was wrecked (3,957 casualties between 17–31 July) by the Battle for the Mius Bridgehead. Tolbukhin's short-lived Mius bridgehead succeeded in causing von Manstein to disperse his armour after *Zitadelle* and then crippling his strongest formation, II.SS-Panzerkorps.

Operation Rumyantsev, 3–23 August 1943

After the failure of *Zitadelle*, von Manstein believed that the Soviets would eventually mount a major offensive to retake Kharkov, as this had consistently been an objective for them. Once Hoth's and Kempf's forces withdrew to their original start lines, this possibility became increasingly likely. However, von Manstein also believed that it would take Vatutin's Voronezh Front at least a month or more to recover its strength after the Battle of Kursk. In particular, he over-estimated the amount of damage that Vatutin's two tank armies had suffered and he underestimated the ability of Soviet field workshops to repair damaged tanks. In fact, it took Vatutin just two weeks to refit his armies and prepare his own offensive, which the Stavka had designated Operation *Rumyantsev.**

During the two weeks following the end of *Zitadelle*, the balance of forces had sharply changed in the Kharkov-Belgorod sector as von Manstein sent II.SS-Panzerkorps to the Mius and von Knobelsdorff's XXXXVIII Panzerkorps lost 3.Panzer-Division to Operation *Roland* as well. Soviet deception efforts (*Maskirovka*) by 38th Army near Sumy convinced von Manstein that Vatutin might try an attack against the boundary of Hoth's PzAOK 4 and 2.Armee, so he shifted the 7.Panzer-Division and part of 11.Panzer-Division west to that sector.[151] In addition, *Großdeutschland* was sent to reinforce Model's AOK 9 and Panzer-Regiment 39 was disbanded. By the end of July, Hoth's PzAOK 4 was a shadow of its former self, with only Generalleutnant Gustav Schmidt's 19.Panzer-Division and Major Karl von Siver's Panzer-Abteilung 52 in tactical reserve near Tomarovka. Schmidt's 19.Panzer-Division had 49 tanks and assault guns, including about 20 Pz IVs, while von Sivers only had 27 operational Panthers. Armee-Abteilung-Kempf's sole armoured reserve was Oberst Wilhelm Crisolli's 6.Panzer-Division, which had 28 tanks (mostly Pz III). Most of Hauptmann Clemens-Heinrich Graf von Kagenek's s.Pz.Abt. 503 was pulled back off the line to rest in Kharkov, but the six operational Tigers were left with XI Armeekorps to defend Belgorod; the handful of Tigers remaining in this critical sector demonstrates the weakness of Zetterling's *Totalausfalle*-based statistics to explain the results of Kursk. Despite the fact that the s.Pz.Abt. 503 had only lost seven of its 45 Tigers as *Totalausfalle* during July, it still had 32

---

* Named after Count Pyotr A. Rumyantsev-Zadonaisky (1725–96), one of Catherine the Great's generals. The Stavka named a number of large operations after heroes from Catherine's wars and the later Napoleonic Wars, including Rumyantsev, Kutusov, Suvorov and Bagration. The Communist ability to use the names of formerly-reviled aristocrats to add lustre to military operations was amazing, akin to Orwell's 'double-think'.

tanks awaiting repairs when the Soviet counter-offensive began. Similarly, 106 Panthers were also still under repair. Not only was the Wehrmacht not receiving enough new Panzers, but it was having greater difficulty repairing damaged ones. Altogether, Hoth and Kempf could barely scrape together 200 tanks and assault guns in the Kharkov-Belgorod sector at the beginning of August 1943.

Vatutin had begun preparations for *Rumyantsev* on 24 July, but the Stavka had been planning the summer counter-offensive for months. Zhukov arrived at Vatutin's headquarters as Stavka representative and to assist in coordination between the Voronezh, Steppe and Southwest Fronts. Although Stalin pressed hard for an immediate counter-offensive, Zhukov successfully argued for granting Vatutin 10 days to finalize preparations before commencing the operation. Even with replacements, most of the Voronezh Fronts infantry units were at 60 per cent strength, which was not enough to conduct a protracted operation. Although rushed, *Rumyantsev* was still much better planned and organized than previous Soviet offensives and the Stavka was generous with resources; three artillery divisions were transferred to Voronezh Front and enough tank replacements to restore all Vatutin's tank units to combat readiness. Both Katukov's 1 TA (6 TC, 31 TC, 3 MC) and Rotmistrov's 5 GTA (18 TC, 29 TC, 5 GMC) were brought back up nearly to authorized strength in terms of

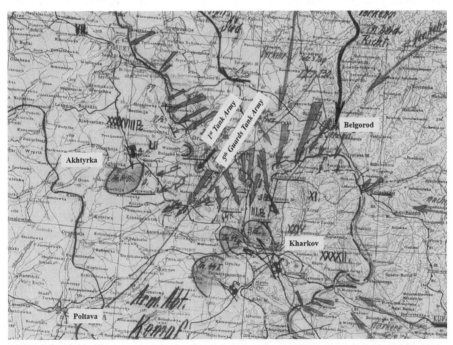

Operation Rumyantsev, the breakthrough of 1st Tank Army and 5th Guards Tank Army, 8 August 1943.

tanks and personnel, but at least one-third would be seeing combat for the first time. As Andrei L. Getman, commander of 6 TC noted:

> Of course, we did not have a complete set of personnel or equipment. We lacked artillery and some types of small arms. Our tank brigades only had 40–45 tanks, most of which were vehicles that had just been repaired. But it was a considerable force and we waited for the order to bring it down on the enemy.[152]

Rumyantsev was designed as a relatively simple, brute-force plan. Vatutin deployed the 5th and 6th Guards Armies (5 GA, 6 GA) northwest of Belgorod and intended to use them to blast a hole through two German infantry divisions of the LII Armeekorps. Once a breakthrough was achieved, Vatutin would commit 1 TA and 5 GTA as front-level mobile groups to exploit and envelop Kharkov from the west. Each combined arms army would also have an independent tank corps to act as army-level mobile groups, which would open a new chapter in the Red Army's operational use of tanks. The intermediate operational objective was Hoth's headquarters, near the rail junction at Bogodukhov, 56km northwest of Kharkov. Three other armies from the Voronezh Front would mount supporting attacks to widen the breach, while Konev's Steppe Front would use the infantry of 53rd and 69th Armies to mount a direct assault on Belgorod. Zhukov believed that Hoth's PzAOK 4 would be encircled and destroyed in or near Kharkov. *Rumyantsev* was not a hastily-thrown together operation like the counter-attack at Prokhorovka, but a carefully planned effort that tried to assemble everything that the Red Army had learned so far about combined arms warfare.

At 0500 hours on 3 August, the Voronezh Front began a 170-minute artillery preparation in its designated attack sectors. The density of the barrage was much larger than the Germans were accustomed to and the LII Armeekorps' forward positions were devastated. While the barrage was in progress, Soviet sappers moved forward and began clearing lanes through the German mines. Vatutin provided his two main assault armies, the 5 GA and 6 GA, with a special sapper brigade for obstacle removal. At 0750 hours, Vatutin's ground assault began. The 5 GA hit the boundary between the German 167. and 332. Infanterie-Divisionen with two corps-size shock groups, the 32nd and 33rd Guards Rifle Corps. Each of these shock groups had three rifle divisions, a tank brigade and self-propelled guns for close support and engineer battalions to clear mines – all indications that the Red Army was learning how to conduct offensives more efficiently. The correlation of forces in the assault sector was over-whelming and 5 GA rapidly broke through the LII Armeekorps first line of defence and smashed the 167.Infanterie-Division. Only three hours after the ground attack began, Vatutin committed the lead elements of 1 TA and 5 GTA into battle to hasten the German collapse in this sector. Each tank army was led by a reinforced tank brigade, which acted as an advance guard well ahead of the main body. In Katukov's 1 TA, it was Polkovnik Nikolai V. Morgunov's 200th Tank Brigade, from 6 TC, that was out in front. By nightfall, Vatutin's armour had achieved a penetration of 14km into Hoth's lines. In general, the supporting attacks also went well, although Zhukov brow-beat commanders into committing their tactical armoured reserves too quickly, before breakthroughs had been achieved.

There was little that Hoth, in his headquarters at Bogodukhov, could initially do to contain *Rumyantsev*. Both 1 TA and 5 GTA advanced southward, side-by-side, with nearly 1,000 tanks. Hoth positioned Schmidt's 19.Panzer-Division and its attached Panthers to create a *Stützpunkt* at Tomarovka on the west side of the Soviet breakthrough, but there was a growing gap in the LII Armeekorps sector that could not be closed. Assault guns from Sturmgeschütz-Abteilung 911 and Crisolli's 6.Panzer-Division tried to close the gap, but this proved impossible. A mobile delay with armoured forces is fought as a series of meeting engagements in reverse. Typically, the Germans would deploy a platoon of Pz IV medium tanks in concealed positions with their main guns slewed over the back deck; when the lead Soviet tanks appeared they would destroy the first few tanks and then race back to the next terrain feature to repeat the process. These ambush tactics usually resulted in tankers running up their 'kill tallies' without the risk of heavy losses. Mobile delay could be nerve-wracking, however, when crews were tired and inattentive; sometimes the pursuing Soviet tanks could approach from an unexpected direction.

Hoth ordered what was left of LII Armeekorps to establish hedgehog defences in towns but most of Katukov's 1 TA blew past the Tomarovka *Stützpunkt*. Instead, much of 6 GA's infantry and Kravchenko's 5 GTC (which was supposed to be an army-level mobile group) became focused on seizing this one town. Rotmistrov's 5 GTA lagged behind Katukov and 6.Panzer-Division conducted a mobile delay which slowed it even more. Meanwhile, the 53rd and 69th Armies eliminated the German defences north of Belgorod and closed in on the city. In order to envelope the city, Rotmistrov directed General-major Boris M. Skvortsov's 5 GMC to push in Crisolli's screen west of Belgorod. By 5 August, General der Panzertruppen Erhard Raus' XI Armeekorps was nearly surrounded in Belgorod and he was forced to evacuate the city.

Major Karl von Sivers, an educated former cavalry officer, commanded the remaining Panthers, deployed in blocking positions just outside Tomarovka. He had missed *Zitadelle* due to illness, but was now to able to lead Panthers into combat under more favourable circumstances. By 4 August, T-34s from Morgunov's 200th Tank Brigade were trying to skirt around Tomarovka to encircle the town, but von Siver's Panthers engaged them at long range and knocked out seven. When sitting in a defensive position, the Panther's long 7.5cm gun completely outclassed the opposition. However, by 5 August Tomarovka was nearly surrounded and von Sivers' Panthers and Schmidt's 19.Panzer-Division had to abandon the town and retreat southwest down the Vorskla River valley. Before evacuating the city, German pioniers blew up 72 damaged Panthers in the local Werkstatt; Hitler had ordered that no intact Panthers should fall into Soviet hands. Several long columns with thousands of German troops retreated westward, with the Panthers using their long-range gunnery to keep the wolves at bay. Over the course of 5–9 August, von Sivers' Kampfgruppe, which became separated from the main body, retreated 100km and fought their way through Soviet roadblocks. At one point, Kravchenko's 5 GTC manoeuvred a company-size force to block the road ahead of the retreating Germans, but von Sivers' Panthers knocked out eight T-34s and shoved the rest aside. On the road march, the Panthers would have run out of fuel, but von Sivers radioed the Luftwaffe to provide some via airdrop. Finally, von Sivers' Kampfgruppe linked-up with the *Großdeutschland* near Akhtyrka on 9 August. In five days of combat, the Panthers had destroyed 40 T-34s at no combat loss to themselves, but 16 Panthers broke down from mechanical faults on the retreat. Von Sivers' was left with only nine operational Panthers.[153]

Schmidt's 19.Panzer-Division and the LII Armeekorps fared poorly during the retreat and lacked the firepower of Siver's Panthers. They had to run a gauntlet with the 27th Army on one side and the 5 GA on the other, making it a shooting gallery for the Soviets. Schmidt's headquarters was ambushed on 7 August and he and his aid opted to commit suicide near Borisovka.[154] The remnants of the 19.Panzer-Division that reached Akhtyrka were so combat ineffective that they could not even contribute to the defence of the town. The 255.Infanterie-Division was so demolished in the retreat that it was disbanded and the 332.Infanterie-Division simply disappeared from German Lage Ost situation maps, with the survivors sent rearward to reorganize. German accounts tend to emphasize Soviet tank losses during this phase of *Rumyantsev*, while skimming over the fact that Heeresgruppe Süd's infantry was being eviscerated by one hammer blow after another.

Once the scale of the Soviet breakthrough became apparent, von Manstein immediately requested the return of *Großdeutschland* from Heeresgruppe Mitte and moved the 7. and 11.Panzer-Divisionen from the quiet Sumy sector to reinforce the battered LII Armeekorps. He also managed to get the 18.Panzer-Division from Heeresgruppe Mitte and placed it under Breith's III. Panzerkorps, which he intended to use to plug the growing gap between Hoth's PzAOK 4 and Kempf's forces. However, Katukov's and Rotmistrov's armour had already created a deep, 50km-wide penetration by the time that these additional forces began to arrive. Kravchenko's 5 GTC had advanced the furthest. German Panzer units were forced to move straight into combat from their rail unloading sites, with little knowledge of enemy strength or dispositions. In fact, enemy pressure was constantly increasing during *Rumyantsev* since Vatutin deliberately chose to commit his armies in echelon, meaning that additional formations kept joining the offensive to sustain operational momentum and keep the Germans off balance.

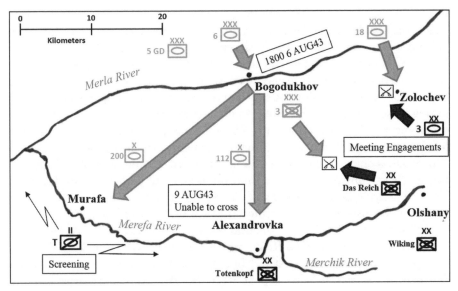

Battle of Bogodukhov, 13–16 August 1943, *Totenkopf* vs. the 1st Tank Army.

On the morning of 6 August, the 18th Tank Corps from 5 GTA fought its way into the town of Zolochev against negligible resistance.* Later that day, General-major Andrei L. Getman's 6th Tank Corps from 1 TA fought its way into Bogodukhov; the loss of 700 tons of fuel in the supply depot was a major blow for Breith's III.Panzerkorps. One of the first Soviet T-34s that fought its way into Bogodukhov was commanded by Leytenant Ivan M. Ivchenko, who had lived in this town before the war. When Ivchenko drove down the street, his wife recognized him and came running out of the house with his young son; Westerners often forget that this war was one of liberation for the Red Army, with troops having a personal stake in the outcome.[155] The loss of both these towns also threatened the German lines of communications to Kharkov. However, when Katukov and Rotmistrov began advancing south of the Merla River, they had unexpected meeting engagements with the first major reinforcements arriving for Hoth's PzAOK 4. The 18 TC ran into the 3.Panzer-Division south of Zolochev and General-major Semyon M. Krivoshein's 3rd Mechanized Corps ran into the lead elements of SS-Gruppenführer Walter Krüger's *Das Reich* (the reconnaissance battalion, two Panzergrenadier-Bataillonen and 20 assault guns). In both cases, the meeting engagements did not go well for the Soviet armoured units and the entire corps needed to deploy and prepare for a hasty attack.

---

* General-major Boris S. Bakharov was relieved of command after Prokhorovka – one of the few heads to roll for that disaster. Thereafter, the 18 TC was commanded by his deputy for a time.

Rotmistrov reinforced 18 TC with the Skvortsov's 5 GMC and launched several attacks against 3. Panzer-Division on 7–8 August; the Germans were forced to give up some ground, but inflicted significant losses on Rotmistrov's two corps. Likewise, Katukov sent General-major Dmitry Kh. Chernienko's 31st Tank Corps to reinforce Krivoshein and together they were able to push *Das Reich* back on 7–8 August. Neither side had much in the way of infantry or artillery support during these actions, which devolved into a series of company and battalion-size engagements. Hoth had no infantry in this sector and he was forced to use his precious motorized forces as blocking detachments, which was not the way that Panzer-Divisionen were supposed to be employed. On the other hand, Vatutin had to divert considerable forces from the 6 GA and 27th Army to deal with German hedgehogs at Borisovka and Grayvoron, which severely limited infantry support to Katukov during this critical moment of the exploitation phase.

On the night of 8–9 August, the lead elements of Katukov's 1 TA, Getman's 6 TC, reached the Merchyk River, which put them within striking distance of severing the main east-west rail line to Kharkov. There were virtually no German forces in this wide gap between Breith's III Panzerkorps and the remnants of the LII Armeekorps and XXXXVIII Panzerkorps concentrated near Akhtyrka. However, the lead elements of SS-Brigadeführer Hermann Priess' *Totenkopf* were rushing to establish blocking positions along the Merchyk. When Morgunov's 200th Tank Brigade attacked the town of Murafa on 9 August, he was able to seize the town and a crossing over the river without much trouble, but then ran into the SS-*Totenkopf*-Aufklärungs-Abteilung, which was screening on the other side. Polkovnik Mikhail T. Leonov's 112th Tank Brigade had an even ruder surprise when it tried to seize another crossing at Oleksandrivka and ran into two battalions from the SS-Panzergrenadier-Regiment 3. Leonov's initial attack on the town failed.

While Katukov and Rotmistrov was struggling to push south and envelop Kharkov, the 27th and 40th Armies were pushing westward toward Akhtyrka with the help of three tank corps (2 TC, 10 TC, 4 GTC) to expand the Voronezh Front's breakthrough. The LII Armeekorps and XXXXVIII Panzerkorps had established a thin line between Akhtyrka and Trostyanets with the *Großdeutschland*, 7. and 11.Panzer-Divisionen to try and prevent the Soviet advance from demolishing any link between Hoth's PzAOK 4 and 2.Armee. By the morning of 9 August, General-major Vasily M. Alekseev's 10th Tank Corps, acting as the mobile group for 40th Army, was threatening the rail junction at Trostyanets. Most of *Großdeutschland*'s armour was still en route, but a small Kampfgruppe with four Tigers from 13.Panzer-Regiment *Großdeutschland* and seven Panthers from 4.Panzer-Abteilung 51 were assembled and sent to stop Alekseev's tanks.* On paper, this small Kampfgruppe should have been a

---

* Panzer-Abteilung 51 had been sent to Bryansk to refit after *Zitadelle* and was in the process of receiving 96 factory-fresh Panthers. The battalion was attached to *Großdeutschland*.

formidable force, but it lacked any kind of support or information about enemy dispositions. En route to Trostyanets, one Panther's engine caught fire and burnt out. Approaching the town, the Kampfgruppe was engaged by numerous anti-tank guns and T-34s concealed in a wooded area; the Panther's long 7.5cm gun claimed several victims but when the tanks imprudently moved into the town, they were engaged at point-blank range. Here, Aleekseev's tankers were fighting as a combined arms team, with infantry, anti-tank guns and tanks working together, whereas the Germans were disadvantaged as an armour-pure force. Two Tigers and five Panthers were knocked out and abandoned, with the remaining three tanks beating a hasty retreat.[156]

On 10 August, General-major Pavel P. Poluboyarov's 4 GTC tried to rush Akhtyrka with two of his tank brigades before *Großdeutschland* arrived in strength, but the rest of Panzer-Abteilung 51's Panthers detrained in the town just before they arrived. A screen of Panthers met Poluboyarov's T-34s outside Akhtyrka and repelled their attack, but the lack of pre-battle preparation was costly for the Germans. A total of 11 Panthers were knocked out against 16 T-34s, which was not a very favorable exchange ratio. After this rebuff, Poluboyarov tried to envelop Akhtyrka, since there was a large gap with no German forces to the south of the town. Kravchenko's 5 GTC was sent into this gap, advancing against negligible opposition.

At the same time, Rotmistrov and Katukov were continuing to press Breith's III Panzerkorps hard and managed to drive an armoured wedge between *Das Reich* and 3.Panzer-Division on 10 August. Counter-attacks by both German divisions temporarily restored the situation and inflicted heavy losses on the 18 TC and 29 TC, but 3.Panzer-Division was nearly combat-ineffective. The loss of Panzergrenadiers in defending static positions in towns was particularly painful and once a Panzer-Division lost a good part of its infantry it could not maintain a coherent front. While Soviet tank losses were heavy, both tank armies continued to receive march companies with new tanks and crews which kept them in business. Furthermore, Katukov and Rotmistrov's units usually retained the battlefield now, improving the probability that their knocked out tanks would be recovered and repaired. However, the real problem was not shortage of tanks but the insufficient number of wheeled vehicles available to the Voronezh Front, which made it difficult to move artillery and supplies forward in a timely manner to support the advance of the tank armies.

On 11 August, Katukov fought his way across the Merchyk River despite desperate efforts by *Totenkopf's* Panzergrenadiers to stop him. Then he sent the lead elements of 6 TC and 3 MC south to Kovyagi, which was a station on the Polatva-Kharkov rail line. Getman's tankers, with some attached sapper squads, succeeded in blowing up several sections of rail track.[157] Priess committed Edwin Meiederdress' I.SS-Panzer-Regiment 3 to counter-attack Polkovnik Vladimir M. Gorelov's 1st Guards Tank Brigade, which had just stormed its way into Kovyagi. The result was another vicious meeting engagement and this one went very badly for *Totenkopf*; one company commander was killed in his tank and two others were badly wounded.[158] However, Meiderdress had better luck against the 22nd Tank Brigade, which only had seven tanks left and its commander, Major Aleksei A. Laptev, was killed in action.[159] Altogether, *Totenkopf* knocked out 18 Soviet tanks in its counter-attack. However, Polkovnik Aleksandr F. Burda's 49th Tank Brigade and the 17th Tank Regiment succeeded in slipping past *Totenkopf*'s reconnaissance battalion's screen and some tanks headed west along the rail line to Vysokopol'ye. Burda was one of the most experienced tankers in the Red Army and not afraid to plunge deep into the enemy's rear areas. Yet *Totenkopf*'s advance had isolated Burda's brigade and other forward elements of Katukov's 1 TA.

Breith's III.Panzerkorps had significantly slowed the advance of 1 TA and 5 GTA between 7–11 August, but it had not stopped them and Hoth was desperate to stabilize the front. He had been trading space for time while trying to bring up more reinforcements, but time was running out. Hoth wanted to launch a coordinated pincer attack by III.Panzerkorps and XXXXVIII Panzerkorps, but the later would not be ready for days, so he decided to launch it only with Breith's forces. The one bright spot for Hoth was the arrival of SS-Brigadeführer Herbert Otto Gille's *Wiking*, which would give Breith three Waffen-SS divisions.

Rotmistrov's 5 GTA actually kicked off 12 August by continuing its attack in the Zolochev-Olshany sector, which made it difficult for *Wiking* to deploy. Hoth began his counter-attack that morning, even though his divisions were not fully deployed. Altogether, Hoth had 130 tanks and 23 assault guns at his disposal: *Totenkopf* (36 tanks, including 3 Tigers), *Das Reich* (48 tanks, including 3 Tigers), *Wiking* (33 tanks) and s.Pz.Abt.503 with 13 Tigers. Katukov's 1 TA had 268 tanks still operational and 5 GTA had 115, giving Vatutin's forces a 2.4–1 local numerical superiority in armour.[160] *Totenkopf* began the attack by rolling up Katukov's units south of the Merchyk River and recapturing Vysokopol'ye, but this proved costly. The six Tigers in the lead bumped into a very strong anti-tank defence that knocked out one Tiger (possibly by an 85mm round from an AA gun) and damaged four more. Seven tankers in *Totenkopf*'s Tiger company were killed in the action.[161] A number of Soviet tanks, probably out of fuel, were knocked out or abandoned, but many of the tankers retreated to the river. When Katukov tried to rush reinforcements forward in the afternoon he was shocked to find that *Totenkopf* had already reached the river and blocked his crossing sites. *Das Reich* contributed to Katukov's problems by attacking Krivoshein's 3 MC near Gavrishi around 0930 hours, which threatened to split the boundary between 1 TA and 5 GTA. Rotmistrov sent a brigade from the 29 TC to stop this German armoured drive, resulting in a large tank battle. Honours were about even and *Das Reich* had over 20 tanks disabled, although 29 TC was badly hurt, as well. Hoth was able to get some Luftwaffe close air support to assist his counter-attack, but Vatutin managed to push two rifle divisions from 6 GA forward to stiffen Rotmistrov's vulnerable right flank.

On 13 August, *Totenkopf* deliberately chose a high-risk course of action, by deploying virtually all of the division north of the Merchyk River, but leaving only the *SS-Totenkopf*-Aufklärungs-Abteilung to screen south of the river. A major combined arms attack with tanks, infantry and artillery support at Nikitovka sent Krivoshein's 3 MC reeling and smashed in Katukov's left flank. However, Getman's 6 TC had launched a renewed attack south of the Merchyk River, reinforced by the 52nd and 90th Guards Rifle Divisions from 23 GRC. *Totenkopf*'s reconnaissance battalion could not stop this push and Getman's forces recaptured Vysokopol'ye and linked-up with Burda's brigade that had been left isolated in this area the day before. Fighting continued on 14 August and on 15 August *Totenkopf* and *Das Reich* made a renewed push that smashed in the flank of the 6 TC and recaptured Vysokopol'ye once again on 16 August. Breith believed that this attack destroyed Katukov's spearhead formations, as well as parts of two rifle divisions.

However, the commitment of virtually all available German armour to stop 1 TA and 5 GTA left only two Sturmgeschütz-Abteilungen to support Raus' XI Armeekorps in the effort to stop Konev's advance upon Kharkov. By 14 August, Konev had four armies pressing against the city's defences from the north and the east and Kempf was unwilling to see his command encircled in Kharkov; he made the mistake of openly complaining about Hitler's orders to hold the city. Unwilling to risk another commander making an unauthorized withdrawal – which would reflect badly on his authority – von Manstein relieved Kempf of command on 14 August. General der Infanterie Otto Wöhler was brought in to replace Kempf and his former command was soon redesignated as 8.Armee (AOK 8).

While III.Panzerkorps was continuing to spar with 1 TA and 5 GTA, *Großdeutschland* was delayed by difficulties in the rail transport of its armour to Akhtyrka. Four Tiger tanks and the maintenance section of one Panzer-Abteilungen were lost in the rail movement to Sumy.[162] The III.Panzer-Regiment *Großdeutschland* then had to conduct a 110km road march to its assembly area near Akhtyrka, which caused numerous mechanical failures in the Tigers. Rather than attacking with a well-organized, combined arms team, *Großdeutschland* hastily threw together Kampfgruppe von Natzmer from the I. and III.Panzer-Abteilungen (16 Tigers, about 15 Pz III/Pz IVs, 15 Panthers from Hauptmann Heinrich Meyer's Panzer-Abteilung 51, the divisional reconnaissance battalion and one battalion of self-propelled howitzers). The lack of infantry and pionier support was a severe deficiency. Nor was the Kampfgruppe given adequate time to plan its attack or conduct maintenance before the operation kicked off at 0630 hours on 15 August. With the Tigers in the lead, Kampfgruppe von Natzmer aimed to strike Katukov's flank south of Akhtyrka. Kravchenko's 5 GTC had pushed past Kotelva and its flanks appeared to be up in the air, although this was not in fact the case.

At 0630 hours on 15 August, Kampfgruppe von Natzmer advanced southward, with its Tigers in the lead. Approaching the town of Grun, the lead Tiger struck a mine and the rest of the battalion was engaged by enemy anti-tank guns, Su-122 assault guns and artillery hidden in a wooded area. In order to reach the town, the German tanks had to cross two deep ravines that were covered by fire. The Germans opted to have one Tiger company assault across the ravines while the other Tiger company provided overwatch fires. No smoke was used to conceal this effort, although the artillery battalion was within range. As soon as the Tigers entered the 'kill sac' the Soviets hit them with everything they had. The Tiger of Hauptmann Rene von Villebois, commander of 10.Kompanie, was hit on the turret by six 122mm rounds and another round penetrated the 60mm thick armour of the hull side; von Villebois was badly wounded and his Tiger was essentially wrecked. It is not clear if the Su-122s fired the new BP-460A HEAT round – although the hull penetration sounds like it – but the turret damage was likely from HE-FRAG rounds. In any event, after suffering heavy damage, the surviving Tigers fought their way into the town and destroyed the Su-122s.

Despite mines and a dense belt of anti-tank guns, the *Großdeutschland* overran the 166th Rifle Division and advanced over 12km within five hours to isolate the two Soviet tank corps near Kotelva. However, Zhukov worked with Vatutin in rapidly assembling a relief force from other elements of the 27th Army and 6 GA, which relentlessly attacked *Großdeutschland* and the German forces around Akhtyrka. Two rifle corps from the 47th Army, supported by General-major Viktor T. Obukhov's 3rd Guards Mechanized Corps, routed the German 57.Infanterie-Division north of Akhtyrka, which forced the XXXXVIII Panzerkorps to divert resources away from its own counter-attacks. Although a tenuous contact was made between *Totenkopf* and *Großdeutschland*, the XXXXVIII Panzerkorps lacked the strength to eliminate the two isolated Soviet tank corps. Furthermore, the Panthers continued to take a beating in combat; Meyer was killed on 19 August and most of his tanks were knocked out in just a few days.

The swirling tank mêlées continued south of Bogodukhov until 18 August, by which point the 1 TA and 5 GTA had been halted and severely damaged, but Breith's III.Panzerkorps was also in very poor shape. Over 35 German tanks had been knocked out or destroyed, including five of the 19 Tigers. The two Soviet tank armies had lost hundreds of tanks south of Bogodukhov and General-major Dmitry Chernienko, commander of 31 TC, was killed in action on 18 August. While the three Waffen-SS divisions still had some combat capability left, the 3.Panzer-Division only had 10 tanks left and 6.Panzer-Division had just four. All the German armour west of Kharkov barely amounted to 100 tanks and assault guns. Inside Kharkov, the Sturmgeschütz-Abteilungen 228 and 905 had a total of 22 assault guns left to defend the city. Since Rotmistrov's 5 GTA had failed to envelope Kharkov, Konev was forced to mount a costly frontal attack upon the city which ground up his forces and Raus' XI Armeekorps.

The final act of *Rumyantsev* occurred near Lyubotin, on the western road leading out of Kharkov. On Zhukov's orders, Vatutin transferred Rotmistrov's battered 5 GTA to Konev's control on 20 August for the final assault on the city. Within a remarkably short time, Rotmistrov was able to partly restore Yegorov's 18 TC and Skvortsov's 5 GMC and use them to support a major attack by 53rd Army against Lyubotin on 21 August. This sector was chosen because it was the left flank of Raus' XI Armeekorps and not as well defended, but the minor Udy River proved to be more of an obstacle than the German infantrymen. Rotmistrov's tanks tried to ford it, but became bogged down in its marshy banks. It took Konev's engineers half a day to build a pontoon bridge over the Udy, then Rotmistrov's two corps crossed. During the night, the bulk of *Das Reich* shifted eastward to block Rotmistrov's bridgehead. By coincidence, the first Waffen-SS Panthers arrived at the front and unexpectedly joined the defence; these were two companies of Hauptsturmführer Hans Weiss' I.SS-Panzer-Regiment 2 with 42 Panther Ausf D. At 0500 hours on 22 August, the 53rd Army fired a large artillery preparation against the German positions then Rotmistrov's two corps advanced with 111 tanks. A protracted tank battle ensued for three hours, with the Panthers knocking out about half of Rotmistrov's tanks but some Soviet tank-infantry teams fought their way into Korotych, in the western suburbs of Kharkov. Although Rotmistrov's depleted 5 GTA had failed to break through, by that evening von Manstein finally authorized Wöhler to begin evacuating the city. By 1100 hours on 23 August, Konev's forces fought their way into the city and liberated Kharkov.

Operation *Rumyantsev* had succeeded in taking Belgorod and Kharkov and it had effectively smashed Hoth's front line. However, the cost had been extremely high, even by Red Army standards. Altogether, Vatutin's Voronezh Front and Konev's Steppe Front suffered over 255,000 casualties (including 71,611 dead or missing) and lost 1,700 tanks. Since the Red Army controlled the battlefield, a good number of these tanks would be recovered and repaired. Hoth's and Kempf's forces had suffered over 32,000 casualties, including about 8,000 killed and 4,000 captured. German armoured losses were only a fraction of the Soviet losses – roughly 250 tanks and 50 assault guns – but they were enough. Virtually all of von Manstein's Panzer-Divisionen were combat-ineffective after *Rumyantsev* and the number of operational German tanks had dropped from 2,287 on 5 July to only 926 by 20 August.[163] Furthermore, the loss of territory during *Rumyantsev* cost the Panzerwaffe hundreds of damaged tanks that could not be moved in time; this was particularly true for the Panther and Tiger, both of which required multiple recovery vehicles to move.

It is also important to note that while Heersgruppe Süd was engaged in a protracted armoured battle of attrition around Kharkov, Hitler had decided to send four Panzer-Divisionen (16, 24, 26 and *Hermann Göring*) and five Panzergrenadier-Divisionen (*LSSAH*, 3, 15, 29, 90), which had a combined total of 572 tanks and 184 assault guns, to Italy to oppose the Anglo-American landings.[164] If Hitler had sent most of these forces to von Manstein and opted to abandon southern Italy to the Allies, Heeresgruppe Süd probably could have fought *Rumyantsev* to a standstill.

Rumyantsev contained a series of punishing, indecisive tank battles because both sides' armoured forces were approaching relative equality in terms of efficiency. The Germans often still enjoyed a small tactical edge, but this was being undermined by excessive losses of junior leaders. The tank battles around Bogodukhov were among the last occasions on which three Waffen-SS divisions attacked together, and although they inflicted great damage and showed a ruthless tenacity, they failed to accomplish their mission of destroying either 1 TA or 5 GTA. This time, there was no 'backhand blow'. The Red Army had demonstrated the ability to smash a German fortified line and exploit to 50–60km depth within a matter of days, which caught von Manstein completely by surprise. However, the failure to reinforce this success with more resources, and the tendency to try and reduce every German *Stützpunkt* rather than bypassing them, led to the main effort loosing too much combat power, too fast. In terms of C^2, Rotmistrov's handling of 5 GTA was clumsy and, coming on the heels of his humiliation at Prokhorovka, his days as a front-line leader were numbered. Katukov's forces had been tactically defeated, but demonstrated great pluck in staying in the fight. Even when units were isolated, they did not just dissolve into the woods as they had in the past.

Operation *Suvorov*: the Smolensk Offensive, 7 August–2 October 1943
In addition to *Kutusov* and *Rumyantsev*, the Stavka had also been planning to mount a major summer offensive toward Smolensk once Operation *Zitadelle* was defeated. General Vasily D. Sokolovsky's Western Front had already contributed its 11th Guards Army and a good portion of its armour to Operation *Kutusov* in mid-July, but the Stavka wanted to use the rest of this front's resources against the centre of Heeresgruppe Mitte's line. General-Polkovnik Andrei I. Eremenko's Kalinin Front would also make forces available for a push toward Smolensk. Stalin took great interest in the planning of the Smolensk offensive and it was named Operation *Suvorov* after one of Russia's greatest generals to indicate the importance of the task. Since Zhukov and Vasilevsky were supporting *Kutusov* and *Rumyantsev*, Marshal of Artillery Nikolai N. Voronov was sent as Stavka representative to coordinate *Suvorov*.

With his two tank corps committed to Operation *Kutusov*, Sokolovsky's only remaining large mechanized formation was General-leytenant Mikhail V. Volkhov's 5th Mechanized Corps (5 MC), but he also had five tank brigades and four tank regiments that could be allocated for *Suvorov*. Since many of these units were well under-strength from previous combat, Sokolovsky received

298 new tanks in July to replenish his armoured units. Eremenko contributed a heavily-reinforced 39th Army with three tank units to *Suvorov*, so he received only 70 tank replacements. Altogether, the Western Front committed about 1,280 tanks and 45 self-propelled guns to the offensive and Kalinin Front committed 110 tanks. Both fronts were still using considerable numbers of Lend-Lease tanks (Matildas and Valentines) as well as older tanks like the T-60. In order to clear enemy obstacles, the Western Front received four sapper brigades and two more went to the Kalinin Front. The only serious deficiency in the preparation for *Suvorov* was in logistics; although 3–5 basic loads of tank and artillery ammunition had been stockpiled, the amount of fuel available was only 1.3 loads, which was grossly inadequate for a breakthrough operation.[165] Given that the Western Front quartermasters had been primarily supporting positional warfare for the past 18 months, they do not appear to have been ready to shift to supporting mobile operations.

On the German side, Generalfeldmarschall Günther von Kluge's Heeresgruppe Mitte was very weak in armoured resources but had the advantage of well-prepared defences in depth. Generaloberst Gotthard Heinrici's 4.Armee (AOK 4), which was the main target of Operation *Suvorov*, had been holding the sector of the front between Yartsevo and Spas-Demensk since Operation *Typhoon* failed in 1941. Heinrici's troops had built multiple lines of fieldworks that represented a 12–15km deep defensive network that included anti-tank ditches, mines, barbed wire obstacles and reinforced wooden bunkers. Here, the German troops had sufficient time and resources to build very deep trenches that could survive all but the heaviest artillery bombardments and the obstacle belts were thick and covered by fire. The terrain also favoured the defence, with thickly wooded areas and swampy rivers that were difficult for tanks to cross. While not impregnable, Heinrici's defence was formidable. The only real problem facing Heeresgruppe Mitte was the lack of reserves. Heinrici's AOK 4 consisted of 12 infantry divisions that were well under-strength and most replacements were going to von Manstein's command. Since von Kluge had provided Model's AOK 9 with all his Panzer-Divisionen, the only mobile reserve left was Generalleutnant Werner von Erdmannsdorff's 18.Panzergrenadier-Division; this unit only had a combat strength of 3,000 troops and a few attached assault guns, which left it ill-equipped to seal off any Soviet breakthroughs, should they occur.[166] Von Kluge had retained some assault gun units and he provided Heinrici with elements of three Sturmgeschütz-Abteilungen, totalling about 60 StuG IIIs.

Sokolovsky decided to make his main attack against the Yelnya–Spas-Demensk sector of AOK 4, held by the 268. Infanterie-Division of IX Armeekorps and the 252. and 342.Infanterie-Divisionen of XII Armeekorps. A 16km-wide sector would be attacked by 17 rifle divisions and 300 tanks from the 5th Army (General-leytenant Vitaliy S. Polenov), the 10th Guards Army (General-leytenant Kuzma P. Trubnikov) and the 33rd Army (General-leytenant Vasily N.

Gordov). General-leytenant Evgeny P. Zhuralev's 68th Army stood in reserve, ready to reinforce the main effort with six more rifle divisions and 100 tanks. The attack would rely on firepower and sappers to breach the German tactical defensive zone, then commit Volkhov's 5 MC as a mobile group to exploit. The immediate objective of this attack was the city of Roslavl, whose capture was expected to unhinge Heinrici's right flank. Sokolovsky also intended to mount a supporting attack north of Yartsevo, along the Smolensk-Vyazma highway, which was held by the 113.Infanterie-Division of XXXIX Panzerkorps and 52. Infanterie-Division of XXVII Armeekorps. The supporting attack would be conducted by the Western Front's 31st Army and the Kalinin Front's 39th Army, with 14 rifle divisions and 160 tanks. Once a breakthrough was achieved in this sector, two mechanized brigades and a tank brigade would form a mobile group and push toward Smolensk.

Four days before the offensive began, Stalin arrived at the Western Front to inspect the preparations, which put considerable pressure on Sokolovsky. Everything appeared ready and Stalin left satisfied that success was imminent. Yet unlike other Soviet offensives, Sokolovsky had placed little emphasis upon *Maskirovka* (deception) and Heinrici knew that an attack was imminent and reinforced the threatened sectors. At 0630 hours on 7 August, *Suvorov* began with a massive 110-minute artillery preparation, which included the firepower of the 5th and 8th Artillery Corps. Although Voronov ensured a maximum artillery effort, the width of the attack sectors somewhat diluted his fire power but he achieved 175 guns and mortars per kilometre of front in Sokolovsky's sector and 100 in Eremenko's sector.[167] The 1st Air Army (1 VA) flew 1,200 sorties on the first day, striking German artillery positions. However, Heinrici's defences were barely scratched and when the Soviet shock groups moved forward they immediately ran into trouble. German mortars, machine-guns and anti-tank guns were still intact and inflicted heavy losses on the attackers. By the early afternoon, some Soviet tank-infantry teams did penetrate up to 4km into the German defensive lines, but they often became isolated. Polkovnik Oleg Losik's 119th Tank Regiment, which was supporting the 65th Guards Rifle Division, succeeded in digging its way through the outer layer of defences. Starshiy Leytenant Ivan S. Povoroznyuk, who commanded a company of T-34s in Losik's brigade, was at the tip of the spear and his tanks overran a German infantry platoon and some anti-tank guns. Povoroznyuk, was no rookie and he was one of the Red Army's new generation of tank leaders; he had first seen combat as a tank platoon leader in September 1941 and had already been wounded three times. He and his battalion fought for three days trying to break through the German lines but eventually his tank was destroyed by German Panzerjägers and he was killed in action; he was posthumously awarded the Hero of the Soviet Union (HSU).

In an effort to energize the offensive, Sokolovsky committed Zhuralev's 68th Army six hours after the beginning of the operation, but this only made the battlefield a more target-rich environment. In the north, the 31st and 39th Armies struck the XXXIX Panzerkorps near Yartsevo, but barely advanced 2km in the first two days. The 31st Army tried to commit an ad hoc mobile group comprised of Podpolkovnik Viktor F. Kotov's 42nd Guards Tank Brigade (22 T-34, 7 KV-1, 4 T-70 amd 18 T-60s), a motorcycle regiment and an anti-tank unit, even though no breakthrough had been achieved.[168] The German 113. Infanterie-Division, rebuilt from cadres that survived Stalingrad, had deployed 27 heavy anti-tank guns in its sector and was fortunate to be provided with the new RSO tractors; the German anti-tank defences knocked out 35 of Kotov's tanks.[169] Von Kluge reacted very quickly to the Soviet offensive, transferring a Kampfgruppe from 2.Panzer-Division and the entire 36.Infanterie-Division (mot.) to Spas-Demensk and sending the 18.Panzergrenadier-Division to reinforce the Yartsevo sector. Heinrici committed these units and Sturmgeschütz-Abteilungen 270 and 667 to local counter-attacks, which repeatedly repulsed the Soviet shock groups.

Even though Suvorov was making little progress, Sokolovsky ordered 10th Guards Army to commit Volkhov's 5 MC. On 12 August, Volkhov's corps conducted a 130km roadmarch to the front, under heavy attack by the Luftwaffe, but was ready to join the battle on the morning of 13 August. Leytenant Dmitry F. Loza commanded a company of Matilda tanks in the 233rd Tank Brigade of 5 MC and he recalled that the sudden appearance of Lend-Lease tanks in this sector caused a fratricide incident when his brigade launched a local attack against a German position, then returned to its start line, within sight of a Soviet artillery unit.

> The three lead Matildas appeared from behind a hillock and came straight across the field. A minute later we were staggered by what we saw: the muzzle flashes of artillery fire and two burning tanks. The guns were firing direct lay. Three men from my company rushed over to the artillery unit. While they were running in that direction, the artillery unit managed to fire off a second volley. A third Matilda was stopped in its tracks, the rounds having disabled its suspension. The crews of Knyazev's company reacted appropriately, firing high explosive rounds. Two artillery pieces were turned into twisted heaps of metal, their crews killed.[170]

Loza's brigade lost a platoon of tanks in this incident because Soviet artillerymen were unfamiliar with the Matilda and assumed them to be German tanks. Nevertheless, the commitment of 5 MC added impetus to the 10 GA attack and Spas-Demensk was liberated on the same day. Yet it was not the commitment of more armour that gradually weakened Heinrici's defence, but the relentlessly pounding of the Soviet artillery which ground up the German infantry. Between 7–21 August, AOK 4 suffered over 28,000 casualties, including 7,239 dead or missing. After the capture of Spas-Demensk, the Western Front continued to slowly grind its way through the German defences, but the offensive was temporarily suspended on 21 August in order to resupply and replenish depleted units. In 14 days of heavy combat between 7–21 August, the Western Front had advanced only 35–40km – roughly equivalent to what Hoth achieved during *Zitadelle*.

At this point, the Stavka realized that the Western Front could not hope to seize Smolensk in a single push and decided to restructure *Suvorov* as a multi-phase operation that would gradually slice up the German defences into digestible pieces. The next logical objective was Yelnya, in the centre of AOK 4's line. Despite the fact that the Yelnya sector was heavily wooded and marshy, Sokolovsky asked for – and received – additional armoured support. Polkovnik Aleksei S. Burdeiny's 2nd Guards Tank Corps (2 GTC) was transferred from Voronezh Front to reinforce Sokolovsky. After a week of refitting, the Western Front recommenced *Suvorov* on the morning of 28 August with a 90-minute artillery barrage, accompanied by airstrikes from 1 VA. Soviet artillery tactics were improving and the German front-line defences were badly chewed up. Attacking on a 25km-wide front, the 21 A, 33 A and 10 GA were able to penetrate 6km on the first day and extended the penetration to 12km on the second day. At that time, Burdeiny's 2 GTC was committed and his tanks advanced 30km in a single day. On 30 August, the battered German forces were forces to abandon Yelnya. Sokolovsky continued pushing until his troops reached the Dnepr River, then halted the offensive on 7 September for another week.

Hitler had grudgingly authorized the creation of the Panther Stellung (line) on 11 August, directing it to be a line of fortifications running behind the Dnepr and extending all the way up to the Baltic, intended as a bulwark against further Red Army advances westward. However, the Panther Stellung was primarily a propaganda soundbite at this point and in the Heeresgruppe Mitte sector engineers were only just beginning to lay out defences west of Smolensk, centred on the cities of Mogilev, Orsha and Vitebsk. Von Kluge needed to buy time for the engineers to actually begin work on the Panther Stellung, so he took measures to reinforce Heinrici's AOK 4. He ordered Model to transfer the s.Pz.Abt.505 from his AOK 9 to reinforce AOK 4 as soon as possible, although the battalion did not actually arrive until 17 September. However, before the Tigers could reach the front, Sokolovsky resumed the offensive. Having penetrated the outer defences of AOK 4, the Stavka now wanted Sokolovsky to push on to the main objectives – Smolensk and Roslavl. On 14 September, the Kalinin Front attacked first, followed by the Western Front on 15 September. This time, the Soviet shock groups made much better progress and it was clear that AOK 4 was no longer able to repulse large-scale Soviet attacks. Yartsevo was captured on 15 September, followed by Dukhovshchina on 17 September. On the same day, the Bryansk Front recaptured Bryansk from Model's AOK 9. By 19 September, Heeresgruppe Mitte's centre had been pierced and AOK 4 was in retreat. Von Kluge ordered

Heinrici to fall back to the Panther Stellung, even though construction had just begun. On 25 September, the Western Front's 5th Army fought its way into Smolensk and later in the day Roslavl was also liberated. It was only the fact that the Western Front's forces were severely depleted and that there was no large mobile exploitation force available that prevented *Suvorov* from leading to the collapse of Heeresgruppe Mitte in 1943. Instead, von Kluge's forces were able to withdraw to the putative Panther Stellung and established a new defensive line around Vitebsk, Orsha and Mogilev, which were heavily fortified during the winter of 1943/44.

Operation *Suvorov* accomplished its primary objectives of liberating Smolensk and pushing Heeresgruppe Mitte back over 150km. Sokolovsky's Western Front used armour primarily in an infantry support role and had only two large armoured units available for exploitation. Nevertheless, the Red Army had lost 863 tanks during Operation *Suvorov*, about 63 per cent of the total engaged.[171] Although Soviet progress through the Heeresgruppe Mitte defensive belts was slow and costly, it did teach them a number of valuable lessons that would improve tank-infantry-artillery coordination for the 1944 campaigns. On the German side, von Kluge and Heinrici only had limited amounts of armour available and they used it in small but powerful local counter-attacks to restore the AOK 4's deteriorating HKL. The problem was that there were fewer and fewer infantry to man the HKL, even if it could be restored.

Advance to the Dnepr, 24 August–6 November 1943

After the fall of Kharkov, any thoughts that the front might stabilize again vanished as the Soviets began a series of multi-front attacks against Heeresgruppe Süd from the Sea of Azov up to the Sumy sector. For two weeks, von Manstein tried to hold with his much-depleted forces but he was astonished by the Red Army's ability to quickly replenish its own combat units and resume the offensive, almost without let up. Mladshiy Leytenant Yuri M. Polyanovski, a tank platoon leader in the 24th Guards Tank Brigade of 5 GMC, was one of the Soviet junior tank officers at the tip of this spear. Polyanovski had already survived having his first T-34 knocked out by enemy fire at Kharkov and was provided with a replacement tank a few days after the city's liberation. Once outfitted with new tanks and crews, the 24 GTB moved out southward:

At dawn on 2 September, our three tanks were sent out to conduct a reconnaissance in force – that's the military term for it, but in reality to get killed. The Germans opened fire and we fired back...I had to look into the periscope and bend toward the gun sight, and it was when I was looking through the sight that we got hit. The round pierced the turret above my head. It didn't hit me, but slivers of armour struck my head, tore my helmet and damaged my skull. I fell on the tarpaulin covering the ammo. After that a fire started, since the next thing to get hit was the engine compartment. Much later I found out that the loader's head was smashed...[172]

Not only did Vatutin and Konev continue to push south and west from Kharkov with the intention of taking the German supply base at Poltava next, but the Southwest Front attacked PzAOK 1 in the Donbas and the Southern Front renewed its attacks on AOK 6 on the Mius. Malinovsky's Southwest Front had already gained a small bridgehead across the Northern Donets 8km south of Izyum between 17–27 July and on 16 August the 6th, 12th and 8th Guards Armies began to try and break out of the bridgehead. Von Mackensen's PzAOK 1 had deployed the 23.Panzer-Division, 16.Panzergrenadier-Division and Sturmgeschütz-Abteilungen 203 and 282 to seal off the bridgehead. Malinovsky initially committed six rifle divisions and three tank brigades to break the German ring, then eventually fed the 1 GMC and 23 TC into the fight. The Soviets mounted a series of powerful tank-infantry attacks but only succeeded in pushing the German cordon back a few kilometres. Between 17–23 August, von Vormann's 23.Panzer-Division claimed to have knocked out 302 enemy tanks, but suffered 1,817 casualties (including 482 dead or missing). In particular, PzAOK 1 was running out of infantry and von Vormann was forced to borrow infantry from other units to reinforce his badly-depleted Panzergrenadiers.[173]

Although Malinovsky's attacks were held, Hollidt's AOK 6 had much more difficulty in stopping Tolbukhin's second attack across the Mius. After the departure of the Waffen-SS divisions for Kharkov, Hollidt lacked the forces to rebuild a solid front or reserves to prevent an enemy breakthrough. On 19 August the 2nd Guards Army attacked across the Mius near the boundary of the XVII and XXIX Armeekorps and quickly gained ground. Hollidt only had Generalleutnant Hellmut von der Chevallerie's 13.Panzer-Division in reserve and it arrived piecemeal and too late to prevent a major breach in the front line. By 22 August, General-major Trofim I. Tanaschishin's 4 GMC was across the river and pushing west, while the Germans were unable to seal the breach. Von Manstein tried to shuffle his limited armoured reserves around to keep the front from breaking, but virtually every sector now faced crisis. In order to reduce the threat to Stalino, he sent the 9. and 17.Panzer-Divisionen, but again they arrived too late to save the front. The 2nd Guards Army completely broke open the German HKL east of Stalino with the 13th Guards Rifle Corps, then conducted a textbook exploitation with the 2 GMC, 4 GMC and 4th Guards Cavalry Corps; by 29 August the Soviet armour and cavalry was pivoting southward to envelope General der Artillerie Erich Brandenberger's XXIX Armeekorps (compromised of 13.Panzer-Division, the 17., 111. and 336.Infanterie-Divisionen, Luftwaffen Feld-Division 15 and Sturmgeschütz-Abteilung 243) at Taganrog. The next day, Soviet tanks reached the Sea of Azov, isolating the German corps. It was only due to the quick thinking of von der Chevallerie, who quickly organized a breakout effort spearheaded by his 13.

Panzer-Division, that the XXIX Armeekorps survived. After a day of fighting, the XXIX Armeekorps fought its way out of the Taganrog pocket to reach the rest of AOK 6. However, Brandenberger's XXIX Armeekorps had lost a great deal of personnel and equipment in the breakout and Hollidt was unable to restore his frontline.

Although von Manstein had been able to limit the advance of Vatutin's and Konev's forces, he had no real reserves left to save AOK 6's crumbling front and this situation quickly snowballed out of control. In an effort to create a new, shorter line, Hollidt pulled his XXX Armeekorps back and deployed the 17.Panzer-Division to hold Stalino on 2 September, but Tolbukhin increased the scale of his offensive and began attacking along the entire front of AOK 6. Within a few days, both the XXIX and XXX Armeekorps were forced to yield more ground and the dam burst on 6 September; Slavyansk and Kramatorsk were liberated by the 1st Guards Army and PzAOK 1's front was split wide open. Even worse, Tolbukhin's forces linked up with Malinovsky's bridgehead near Izyum, which now expanded rapidly. In order to prevent the loss of Stalino, von Manstein decided to commit one of his newly-arrived Panther battalions, Major Fritz Fechner's II./Pz.Rgt. 23, to restore the situation. Committed piecemeal as it arrived by train, Fechner's battalion managed to delay the loss of Stalino for a few days but once again, the Panther's experienced serious mechanical problems and at least half were non-operational within two days.[174] Despite the arrival of the Panthers, Stalino was liberated on 8 September.

During early September, von Manstein implored Hitler to authorize a retreat to the Dnepr, but the Führer still believed that Heeresgruppe Süd would stop the Soviet offensives, as they had in the past. Yet Tolbukhin had achieved a major breakthrough north of Stalino at Krasnoarmiis'k and General-leytenant Ivan N. Russiyanov's 1st Guard Mechanized Corps (1 GMC) and General-leytenant Efim G. Pushkin's 23rd Tank Corps were pushing rapidly west toward the Dnepr River at Dnepropetrovsk against negligible resistance. By 8 September, the vanguards of these two Soviet corps were approaching Pavlograd and were within 40km of the Dnepr. Von Manstein directed von Mackensen and Hollidt to make one last effort to cut off Tolbukhin's spearheads and seal the breach in their front by means of a pincer attack. Vormann's 23.Panzer-Division and the 16.Panzergrenadier-Division, which were subordinate to XXXX Panzerkorps, were reoriented to attack southward into Russiyanov's exposed flank, while Fechner's remaining Panthers (about 30 out of the original 96) were reinforced with some infantry and artillery into a combined-arms Kampfgruppe to attack Pushkin's flank. Vormann's division began the counter-attack on the morning of 9 September and slammed into the 266th Rifle Division at Slov'yanka; Tolbukhin had pushed some infantry units forward to hold open the breach, but they had yet to establish a strong defence. Vormann's panzers were able to overrun and destroy this isolated Soviet rifle division and then began pushing south. It took Kampfgruppe Fechner longer to reorient and they did not join the attack until

11 September, but Fechner's Panthers sliced into the flank of the 23 TC. On 12 September, Fechner's Panthers linked-up with the 16.Panzergrenadier-Division, thereby isolating the 1 GMC and 23 TC near Pavlograd. Fechner established a blocking position on the main road with three Panthers and a platoon of pioniers, which indicates the paucity of German combat power at this point. Eight Soviet tanks which approached the roadblock were knocked out. Hollidt and von Mackensen had succeeded in closing the breach in the front with a pincer attack and inflicting a sharp tactical defeat on Tolbukhin's advance guard, but the results were all for naught.

Despite the success in sealing the breach, it was obvious that AOK 6 was on the verge of collapse. Fechner's battalion was reduced to just five operational Panthers and the 9., 13., 17. and 23.Panzer-Divisionen were little more than battlegroups. Hollidt lacked the strength to eliminate the two isolated Soviet mechanized units near Pavlograd and it was obvious that the rest of Tolbukhin's forces would soon break through to them. Nor was Hoth's sector in any better shape, since the Voronezh Front had driven a wedge between 2.Armee and PzAOK 4 near Romny and Hoth's left flank was unravelling. Von Manstein met again with Hitler and stated that either Heeresgruppe Süd had to retreat to the Dnepr to avoid destruction, or the OKH had to immediately send 12 fresh divisions to reinforce it. Hitler was always reluctant to cede territory, but he had very few reinforcements to offer, so on 8 September he agreed to allow AOK 17 to finally abandon the Kuban in order for its troops to be sent to reinforce AOK 6. However, it took another week of heavy fighting and the realization that Hollidt's AOK 6 was in immediate danger of being encircled and destroyed to finally convince Hitler to change his mind. During the 10 weeks between the start of *Zitadelle* and the loss of Stalino, Heeresgruppe Süd had suffered over 185,000 casualties, including 51,000 dead or missing – the Third Reich simply could not afford to replace these losses in a timely manner. With Hitler's grudging approval, on 15 September von Manstein finally ordered his four armies to begin withdrawing to the Panther Stellung behind the Lower Dnepr River and the Wotan Stellung at Melitopol. The later city needed to be held, even though it was on the east side of the Dnepr, because it protected the land route to the Crimea, which Hitler wanted to hold. In his mind, the Panther-Wotan Stellungen were impregnable positions, even though he had only authorized construction four weeks before and no work had even begun on any fortifications.

Retreats are painful and even worse if the enemy is actively pursuing. Many of the German tanks that were damaged or awaiting repair had to be blown up, including 20 of Fechner's brand-new Panthers.[175] A total of 80 Panthers were lost in September, mostly due to mechanical defects that forced their crews to abandon them.[176] Discipline in some German units began to slip during the retreat as troops availed themselves of liquor from supply depots that were going to be abandoned. Other troops simply went missing. Von Manstein's forces had to retreat 150km or more to get behind the Dnepr and then cross at one of six bridges. The German infantry divisions relied on horses and carts to move their artillery and supplies, which meant that they could not outrun fast-moving armour units equipped with T-34s. This discrepancy in tactical mobility meant that most of the German Panzer-Divisionen would have to conduct rear guard actions in order to buy time for the slower-moving formations to retreat to the Dnepr. However, von Manstein also recognized that he needed to get some forces to the main crossing sites over the Dnepr – at Kiev, Kanev, Cherkassy, Kremenchug, Dnepropetrovsk and Zaporozhe – as soon as possible in order to prevent the Soviets from seizing any of these with a coup de main. Thus, von Manstein was on the horns of a dilemma about the best use of his armour during the retreat – to protect his infantry or to protect the crossing sites. Von Manstein decided to deploy all of the III. and XXXXVIII Panzerkorps to conduct a major delay operation at Poltava with four Panzer-Divisionen (3., 6., 7., 11.) and four Panzergrenadier-Divisionen (*Wiking, Das Reich, Totenkopf* and *Großdeutschland*) in order to give his slower-moving forces more time to withdraw. However, the 19.Panzer-Division was ordered to retreat straight to Kiev and then spread out to defend the far side of the river. Hoth was ordered to retreat toward Kiev, Kanev and Cherkassy, then spread out quickly to defend the various crossing sites. Wöhler's AOK 8 was to head for Kremenchug, but assist with the delay at Poltava. Von Mackensen's PzAOK 1 would head for Dnepropetrovsk and Zaporozhe, while Hollidt's AOK 6 would retreat to Melitopol. As the retreat began, it began to rain heavily, further slowing the Germans down.

The Stavka had been expecting von Manstein to retreat to the Dnepr at any time and once indications of withdrawal were detected by Soviet aerial reconnaissance, Stalin issued orders directly to the fronts for the advance to the Dnepr. Five fronts surged toward the Dnepr with over two million troops and 2,000 tanks. Vatutin would head for Kiev and the Dnepr Knee and was provided Rybalko's partly-refitted 3 GTA (7 GMC, 9 MC, 6 GTC, 7 GTC, 91 TB) to act as a mobile group (*podvizhnyi grupp*) in the drive toward the Dnepr from the Romny area. Although Rybalko only had about 50 per cent of his authorized tanks and one of his motorized brigades had no trucks, it was still a powerful force with over 300 tanks. Both Katukov's 1 TA and Rotmistrov's 5 GTA had been temporarily pulled back to refit after weeks of heavy combat, leaving Rybalko's half-strength tank army as the only large mechanized formation available for the time being. Konev was ordered to head for Kremenchug, Malinovsky for Dnepropetrovsk and Tolbukhin for Melitopol. While all these fronts received additional reinforcements from the RVGK, ammunition and fuel stockpiles at the front were very low after weeks of heavy combat and this impaired the ability of the Red Army to conduct high-tempo mobile operations for more than a few days.[177] Nor did the Red Army logisticians have the means of moving large amounts of supplies forward, due to shortages of trucks and the damage inflicted upon the rail lines by the retreating Germans. In terms of engineer support, the fronts moving toward the Dnepr had five pontoon bridging brigades and three heavy pontoon regiments, but the problem was that the 'scorched earth' tactics used by the Germans made it difficult to push these cumbersome support units forward to where they needed to be and the insufficient amount of fuel available was mostly going to combat units.[178]

Recognizing the difficulty of crossing the Dnepr, the Stavka began preparing several airborne brigades to support an assault crossing of the Dnepr. Vatutin was given operational control over a provisional airborne corps (1st, 3rd and 5th Guards Airborne Brigades) with 10,000 paratroopers and the authority to employ them. On the night of 19–20 September, Rybalko's 3 GTA began advancing toward the Dnepr, with Podpolkovnik Trofim F. Malik's 56th Guards Tank Brigade as the advance guard. The Stavka believed that the Germans would have all the major crossing sites well defended (a false assumption, as it turned out) so Rybalko was ordered to head for the so-called 'Dnepr Knee,' a great bend in the river south of Kiev and near the Kanev crossing site. Soviet partisans had reported that there were no German forces in this area and the Stavka hoped that Rybalko could 'bounce' this undefended section of the Dnepr before the Germans arrived.

Nehring's XXIV Panzerkorps retreated toward Kanev with the 10.Panzergrenadier-Division, Sturmgeschütz-Abteilung 239 and elements of three battered infantry divisions. Unknown to him, Rybalko's armour was coming up fast behind him, but Nehring did not opt to conduct any delaying actions. Oberst Hans Källner's 19.Panzer-Division crossed the Dnepr at Kiev on 20 September, the first of von Manstein's armoured units to regain the western bank. Even before Källner's division was assembled in Kiev, he was ordered to dispatch his reconnaissance battalion to the Dnepr Bend to look for any signs of Soviet crossing activity. Meanwhile, the III. and XXXXVIII Panzerkorps fought a bitter – and futile – delaying action at Poltava on 20–22 September against Konev's forces, before abandoning the city on 23 September.

Rybalko's armour advanced rapidly and covered 165km in a single day; by the evening of 21 September his lead units were approaching the Dnepr Bend. Then his tanks ran out of fuel, just short of the river. General-major Mitrofan I. Zin'kovich, commander of the 6 TC, frantically radioed Rotmistrov and requested an emergency fuel resupply of 20–30 tons of diesel.[179] Some of the Soviet infantry travelling as *desant* troops with Malik's brigade continued on foot to the river and the 95-man Submachinegun Company used a few small boats to cross near Grigorovka, north of Kanev, before dawn on 22 September. This tiny force was soon reinforced to battalion-size. Shortly thereafter, small numbers of infantry from General-polkovnik Kirill S. Moskalenko's 40th Army's 309th Rifle Division also crossed the Dnepr at Rzhyshchiv, 25km to the west. These initially non-contiguous lodgements of 3 GTA and 40 A were thereafter collectively known as the Bukrin bridgehead. The Bukrin area was heavily wooded and isolated. There were no German troops in the area, but

Rittmeister Helmut von Moltke's Panzer-Aufklärungs-Abteilung 19 had been assigned to conduct screening operations in this sector and was already en route. Rybalko's troops were the first to cross the Dnepr, but unless he could quickly get tanks and artillery across, the Germans would move against the tiny Bukrin bridgehead and crush it. At Grigorovka the Dnepr was 600–800 meters wide and 8 metres deep, so tanks could not cross without pontoon bridges or ferries, which would take days to prepare.

It took the Germans about 24 hours to realize that the Soviets had already gained a toehold across the Dnepr at Bukrin, but once this was confirmed by von Moltke's reconnaissance troops on the afternoon of 23 September, Källner was ordered to move a reinforced Kampfgruppe (two Panzergrenadier battalions, one artillery battalion, one tank company and a few Panzerjägers and pioniers) from his division to conduct a counter-attack. Nehring's XXIV Panzerkorps, still crossing at Kanev, was also ordered to send a Kampfgruppe from 57.Infanterie-Division to Kanev. On the night of 23–24 September, Rybalko and Moskalenko conducted a 'mass crossing' of the Dnepr with thousands of troops moving to the opposite shore on rafts and fishing boats or simply swimming. By 24 September, Moskalenko and Rybalko had enough troops on the west side of the Dnepr to expand their bridgehead to a depth of 3–4km and pushed back von Moltke's screening troops. General-major Zin'kovich personally decided to cross into the bridgehead with some of his infantry (an odd choice for a tank corps commander), but he was mortally wounded by a Luftwaffe air attack that struck the crossing site.[180]

However, the main Soviet play came that evening, when Vatutin decided to commit the airborne troops to reinforce and expand the bridgehead. The airborne operation was a three-star mess from the beginning, starting with a 24-hour delay due to weather and logistical problems, then shortages of transport aircraft. Instead of committing all three brigades (which would have delayed the operation further), Vatutin decided to go with two brigades and the last-minute planning changes led to chaos. At 1930 hours on 24 September, the Soviet transports began dropping paratroops from the 3 GAB and 5 GAB southwest of the Bukrin bridgehead. The drops were badly scattered and most of the 4,575 paratroops who jumped missed their drop zones; instead they landed on top of the Panzergrenadier-Regiment 73, which by the fortunes of war was just arriving in sector. With the sky full of white parachutes, the Panzergrenadiers had a field day and engaged the paratroopers with automatic weapons and light flak. In the first 24 hours, the Germans captured or killed 901 paratroopers and the airborne operation failed to reinforce the Bukrin bridgehead.[181]

Nehring tried to organize a counter-attack against the Bukrin bridgehead as quickly as possible, but he only had part of the 19.Panzer-Division and part of 57.Infanterie-Division, which he felt was insufficient to overrun the enemy position. In fact, the Soviets had not yet succeeded in bringing more than a few heavy weapons across the Dnepr and no tanks, so the Soviet position was still quite tenuous. However, the Germans were not sure exactly how many Soviet troops were in the bridgehead and Nehring decided to wait for further reinforcements. Von Manstein sent him Kampfgruppen from the 7.Panzer-Division and 20.Panzergrenadier-Division, but this delayed the counter-attack until 29 September. The Soviets used this week-long respite wisely, digging in their infantry and using a small number of pontoons to begin ferrying tanks and artillery across the river on 26 September. By the end of that day, Rybalko had 14 tanks and 18 120mm mortars on the western side of the river and Moskalenko was able to push 17 tanks, 27 76.2mm guns and 51 45mm anti-tank guns across on the first day.[182]

Just before the German counter-offensive began, von Knobelsdorff's XXXXVIII Panzerkorps assumed command over all German formations in the Kanev-Bukrin sector, which was not a very bright idea since all the preparations for the counter-attack had been done by Nehring's staff. The German counter-attack on 29–30 September inflicted over 2,800 casualties on the defenders and regained some ground, but was shocked to encounter dug in anti-tank guns and tanks. Air attacks by Fliegerkorps VIII succeeded in destroying one Soviet pontoon bridge, but this was soon rebuilt. Even worse, the Germans discovered that the Soviets had crammed elements of 19 rifle divisions into the Bukrin bridgehead.[183] Consequently, von Knobelsdorff decided to shift to the defensive and bombard the bridgehead with his artillery in order to conserve his own forces.

Meanwhile, the III.Panzerkorps succeeded in crossing the Dnepr in orderly fashion at Cherkassy and *Wiking* moved to the west bank on 27 September. However, the situation with XI Armeekorps and XXXXVII Panzerkorps at Kremenchug was much more chaotic, due to traffic jams at the bridges. Amazingly, the Soviet VVS failed to bomb these packed German formations awaiting to cross, which could have inflicted great slaughter. Yet even before all of the German forces had crossed, Konev's pursuing forces managed to seize toeholds across the Dnepr south of Kremenchug; on the night of 25–26 September at Uspenka and on 27–28 September at Deriyivka. Wöhler's AOK 8 had not yet had time to create a continuous front behind the Dnepr and were particularly thin in this sector: only the much-depleted 106. Infanterie-Division was nearby and it could do little to prevent the 7 GA from expanding its bridgeheads. Even worse, Konev's bridgeheads were near the boundary between Wöhler's AOK 8 and Mackensen's PzAOK 1. By the time that the Germans rushed the SS-Kavallerie-Division and Kampfgruppen from 23.Panzer-Division and *Großdeutschland* to this sector, the Soviets were already poised to break out and push southwest. German efforts to establish a viable defensive perimeter around the Soviet bridgeheads were hindered by the severe lack of infantry. Unit commanders were forced to start cannibalizing their rear area support troops and staff to refill depleted infantry units, which noticeably reduced the operational efficiency of the Wehrmacht.

Von Mackensen managed to conduct a fairly orderly crossing with PzAOK 1 at Dnepropetrovsk, but he was ordered to hold a bridgehead on the east side of the Dnepr at Zaporozhe with his XXXX Panzerkorps in order to protect the Dnepr dams. This dam provided hydroelectric power that was important for German war industries in the region, including tank repair facilities at Dnepropetrovsk amd Nikopol. Furthermore, Hitler did not want to completely abandon the east bank of the Dnepr and was still toying with fanciful ideas about future offensives to reconquer the Donbas. Consequently, von Mackensen was forced to keep six divisions of his PzAOK 1 on the east bank, including most of 9.Panzer-Division, where they could be relentlessly pounded into ruin by Malinovsky's 3rd and 8th Guards Armies. In order to stiffen the anti-tank capability of XXXX Panzerkorps, the Germans scraped together an ad hoc Kampfgruppe under Major Georg Baumunk from the remnants of schwere Panzerjäger-Regiment 656 and Sturmpanzer-Abteilung 216, consisting of 12 repaired Ferdinands and 13 Sturmpanzers. Major Gerhard Willing's s. Pz.Abt.506 also arrived from Germany with 45 new Tigers to reinforce the Zaporozhe bridgehead. Baumunk's Ferdinands and Willing's Tigers repulsed repeated Soviet attacks on the bridgehead for three weeks. Malinovsky committed the 23 TC and 1 GMC to overrun the bridgehead. On 10 October, Baumunk's Ferdinands repulsed a major Soviet armoured attack, claiming 48 enemy tanks destroyed. Yet despite the excellence of the Ferdinand and Tigers as defensive weapons, the Soviet artillery gradually pulverized the German infantry positions and PzAOK 1 was forced to evacuate the Zaporozhe bridgehead on 15 October.[184] Willing lost seven Tigers in the bridgehead battle and most of the remainder were damaged, leaving only seven out of the original 45 operational.

Similarly, Hollidt's AOK 6 (which was now subordinate to Heeresgruppe A), was forced to hold Melitopol in the vain hope of protecting the rail link to the Crimea. Hollidt's forces reached the illusory Wotan Stellung on 20 September and were shocked to find no prepared defences. All troops, including Panzertruppen, were ordered to dig in immediately. Unteroffizier Erich Hager, a Pz IV crewmen in the II.Pz. Rgt. 39 in 17.Panzer-Division, recounted digging in every night and fending off Soviet probing attacks every day. The weather was already turning cold due to frequent drenching rain and Hager wrote, 'we look like pigs'.[185] German front-line morale was increasingly brittle. Tolbukhin's forces soon arrived near Melitopol in strength and on 26 September, began a massive assault against AOK 6's left flank with the 5th Shock Army and 44th Army. This sector was held by the battered IV Armeekorps, which included two Luftwaffe Feld-Divisionen. Tolbukhin committed the 11 TC, 20 TC and 4 GMC against IV Armeekorps, along with a large amount of infantry and artillery. In order to prevent a breakthrough, Hollidt rushed the 17.Panzer-

Division to this sector and in five days of heavy fighting, the Germans claimed to have destroyed 181 enemy tanks.

The OKH dispatched forces to reinforce Hollidt, including the I./Pz.Rgt. 2, intended for the 13.Panzer-Division; this battalion was the first equipped with the Panther Ausf A model. The Panther Ausf A incorporated a number of minor product improvements that had been unable to include in the original Ausf D model, but it still possessed the same reliability issues. On 10 October, the new Panthers were committed to a counter-attack to repulse a local breakthrough by the 20 TC and 4 GMC, which resulted in the 'tank battle of Oktoberfeld.' As usual, the superior firepower of the Panthers inflicted punishing losses on the opposing T-34s – the Germans claimed about 60 knocked out – but numerous Panthers dropped out with mechanical defects. Despite heavy losses, the Soviets were often able to recover their damaged tanks and they kept pounding at AOK 6's front throughout October. Hollidt was finally forced to yield Melitopol on 23 October and Tolbukhin made a massive push that sent AOK 6 in pell-mell retreat for the Dnepr. While two German corps retreated toward Nikopol, the XXXXIV Armeekorps (Gruppe Becker) retreated toward Kherson with the 13.Panzer-Division, the Panther battalion and two infantry divisions. The Panthers were particularly useful during the retreat, keeping 4 GMC's armour at bay and preventing the Soviets from cutting off the escape of Gruppe Becker. Although Gruppe Becker succeeded in crossing safely at Kherson, very few Panthers of the I.Pz.Rgt. 2 were still operational. The IV and XXIX Armeekorps were less fortunate, in that rather than crossing at Nikopol, Hitler ordered them to remain on the eastern bank to protect the manganese ore mines near Nikopol; fighting for the Nikopol bridgehead would continue for nearly 100 days.*

In the north, the PzAOK 4 finally evacuated its Kiev bridgehead by 30 September and repulsed several efforts by Vatutin's forces to cross the Dnepr north of Kiev. On 5 October, the 38th Army managed to seize a small bridgehead at Lyutezh, 25km north of Kiev, which was reinforced with three rifle divisions in a week. For his part, von Manstein regarded the swampy terrain north of Kiev as unsuitable for armour and did not attach much importance to the Lyutezh bridgehead. Instead, he ordered the XIII Armeekorps to seal off the bridgehead with two infantry divisions and directed Hoth to position the 7. and 8.Panzer-Divisionen nearby as mobile reserves, just in case. By the beginning of October, von Manstein was focused on crushing the Bukrin bridgehead and containing Konev's lodgement south of Kremenchug. The Stavka was equally intent upon transforming these tactical successes into the springboard for a

---

* Manganese and molybdenum were added to steel in armour plate on tanks to improve hardening. Without these ores, German armour plate was significantly more susceptible to armour-piercing ammunition. The two primary manganese ore mines were located at Marganets and Ordzhonikidze on the northern/western bank of the Dnepr.

major operational victory and ordered Konev and Vatutin to attack as soon as they had sufficient forces across the Dnepr.

Vatutin moved an artillery division to support the Bukrin bridgehead and on 24 October he began a major effort to break through the XXXXVIII Panzerkorps' perimeter. The Soviets were able to gain a little ground, assisted by river crossings on both flanks, but the Germans moved up the *Das Reich* and the 11.Panzer-Division to reinforce the defence. In very heavy fighting, the Soviet offensive was stopped cold and the Germans claimed 140 enemy tanks knocked out. By late October, Vatutin realized that the German defences were too strong at Bukrin and he ordered his forces in the bridgehead to shift to the defence. On 20 October, the Stavka also decided to redesignate the Soviet fronts: Vatutin's Voronezh Front became the 1st Ukrainian Front, Konev's Steppe Front became the 2nd Ukrainian Front, Malinovsky's Southwestern Front became the 3rd Ukrainian Front and Tolbukhin's Southern Front became the 4th Ukrainian Front.

While Vatutin's front was stymied, Konev enjoyed the greatest success from his bridgeheads located between Kremenchug and Dnepropetrovsk. When looking at the German Lage Ost (Situation East) maps for 1 October 1943, it appears that von Manstein had succeeded in creating a continuous line behind the Dnepr and that the few small Soviet bridgeheads were highly vulnerable to the converging German Panzer-Divisionen. However, in order to create this continuous front, von Manstein had to spread his depleted armoured units out across an 800km-wide front – his only reserves were whatever unit was inbound on the next train from France or Germany. In the Uspenka-Deriyivka sector (which was soon known as the Myshuryn Rog bridgehead), the PzAOK 1's LII Armeekorps had the 23. Panzer-Division and *Großdeutschland* backing up two infantry divisions. While the presence of these units probably appeared sufficient to Hitler in Rastenburg, *Großdeutschland* only had 15 operational tanks (including five Tigers) and 23.Panzer-Division had seven tanks, nine SPWs and 1,100 infantry left.[186] Even worse, so many trucks had been lost in the retreat that panzer units were forced to borrow horses and wagons from nearby infantry units to conduct their resupply operations. Combat damage, worn-out equipment and mechanical defects had reduced almost all of von Manstein's armoured units to minimal combat effectiveness. Further diluting their combat power, the remaining panzers were spread out to reinforce the weakened infantry, meaning that in order to employ anything larger than a tank platoon in any sector, the Germans were forced to strip other sectors of armoured support. The Soviets were quick to notice this new German weakness and began attacking sectors that had been denuded of armour. On 2 October, Konev's infantry expanded their bridgehead and captured Myshuryn Rog; it took two days for 23.Panzer-Division to organize a counter-attack, which amounted only to a company of pioniers, some tanks and SPWs. By this time, Konev had a bridge built over the Dnepr near Borodaivka, on the eastern side of the Myshuryn Rog bridgehead, and was pushing tanks across. Furthermore, on 3 October, Konev received Rotmistrov's 5 GTA, which had spent three weeks refitting in the rear. Rotmistrov stealthily moved his tank army 200km forward to the Dnepr in night marches, to avoid Luftwaffe reconnaissance.

Through great effort by the *Instandsetzungsgrupe*, the 23.Panzer-Division was able to repair 15 tanks by 7 October, including some of Fechner's Panthers.[187] General der Panzertruppe Friedrich Kirchner, commander of LVII Panzerkorps, decided to commit both the 23.Panzer-Division and *Großdeutschland* to a joint counter-attack at Annovka and Borodaivka, in order to threaten the Soviet bridge site. On 8 October, Fechner's Panthers attacked Soviet infantry at Annovka and managed to knock out three T-34s and 11 anti-tank guns, without loss. However, *Großdeutschland*'s attack on 9 October was poorly organized and five Tigers advanced toward Borodaivka without close infantry support. On this occasion, the Tiger's powerful main gun and thick armour did not save them; all five tanks were surrounded and picked off at close range by concealed anti-tank guns and infantry tank destroyer teams. At least two crews were captured, the rest killed – a net loss of 25 Tiger crewmen.[188] Following this disaster, the German counter-attacks diminished somewhat, which allowed Konev a breathing space to begin moving the lead elements of Rotmistrov's 5 GTA into the Myshuryn Rog bridgehead on the night of 14–15 October.

On the morning of 15 October, the Soviet 37th Army and 7th Guards Army attacked the thinly-held German perimeter south of Myshuryn Rog with four guards airborne divisions and three rifle divisions, following a massive artillery preparation. Rotmistrov was only able to contribute the 7 MC and part of 18 TC on the afternoon of the first day of the offensive.[189] Vormann's 23.Panzer-Division was holding this sector with the depleted Panzergrenadier-Regiment 128 and divisional pioniers, but they were quickly overrun by this avalanche of men and tanks. Vormann committed his eight remaining tanks, but lost three Pz IVs when they encountered JSU-152 self-propelled guns and a wall of anti-tank guns. The remaining five German tanks retreated and Vormann's other Panzergrenadier-Regiment was nearly surrounded by Soviet armour, so the entire 23.Panzer-Division fell back. Although seven of Rotmistrov's T-34s were knocked out in the opening skirmishes, the German tankers noted that Soviet tanks had learned to use dead space to manoeuvre in order to reduce their vulnerability to anti-tank fire.[190] The Red Army was learning.

On 16 October, Rotmistrov brought the rest of 18 TC and 29 TC across the Dnepr and pressed the attack, quickly forcing the 23.Panzer-Division back, which created a 10km-wide gap in the German front. A Soviet tank brigade pressed into the gap, overrunning the 23.Panzer-Division's Flak-Bataillon, then pushing on to attack *Großdeutschland*'s divisional command post. Although Vormann managed to gather up three Panthers and three Pz IVs to conduct a mobile screen in the gap, they offered little serious resistance to Rotmistrov's mass of armour. By the third day of the offensive, Rotmistrov's armour had achieved a clear breakthrough and surged forward to overrun Vormann's command post and support units in Popel'naste. Although the Germans claimed to have knocked out many of Rotmistrov's tanks, the fact is that Soviet tanks were roaming in the rear areas, shooting up German support units. Both 23.Panzer-Division and *Großdeutschland* were forced to abandon many damaged tanks at workshops, leaving them with a combined total of about 12–15 operational tanks. Rotmistrov kept the pressure on, continuing to advance at night, in order to prevent the Germans from forming a new line. Soon, Kirchner's LVII Panzerkorps headquarters was threatened by Soviet tanks and had to flee, causing a disruption in German C^2 at a critical moment. Panic set in, as German support units fled rearward without orders – not unlike French troops in May 1940. It just got worse and worse for PzAOK 1, as Rotmistrov's armoured fist exploited rapidly to the south. In life, there are few experiences as exhilarating as an armoured pursuit of a broken enemy and this must have been a heady moment for Rotmistrov's tankers, as well as sweet revenge for Prokhorovka.

Vormann's 23.Panzer-Division tried to mount a defence of the rail station at P'yatykhatky, but this effort fell apart and Soviet tanks reached the virtually undefended town at 2030 hours on 18 October. At the train station, the Soviet *desant* troops on the T-34s discovered flatcars loaded with 10 brand-new Tiger tanks, destined for *Großdeutschland*.[191] Another train in the station was discovered loaded with wounded German troops, who were unceremoniously dispatched by the victorious Soviet *Desantniki* with grenades and small arms. Meanwhile, a massive column with over 3,000 German vehicles was fleeing from the as yet unoccupied southern side of the town. Spotting the escaping enemy, Soviet T-34s fired high explosive rounds into the column, inciting a panic.[192] Vormann's 23.Panzer-Division was wrecked, with only 10 tanks left, 30 men in Panzergrenadier-Regiment 126 and 29 in Panzergrenadier-Regiment 129. Having shattered the connection between PzAOK 1 and AOK 8, Konev was faced with the decision of whether to push west to Kirovograd to roll up AOK 8's right flank or south to Krivoi Rog, to threaten PzAOK 1's line of communications. He opted to split his forces and attempt to seize both objectives: Skvortsov's 5 GMC and the 53rd Army would push toward Kirovograd while the 18 TC and 29 TC advanced to Krivoi Rog. The Germans were literally reeling from the Soviet armoured breakthrough and resistance was patchy, which allowed the 5 GMC to reach Novo Starodub on the Inhulets River on 22 October and the rest of Rotmistrov's 5 GTA reached the outskirts of Krivoi Rog on 27 October. Mackensen's PzAOK 1 was threatened with envelopment by the Soviet advance, which forced him to abandon Dnepropetrovsk on 25 October. Malinovsky's 3rd Ukrainian Front swarmed across the Dnepr with three armies.

Time and again, the Germans proved themselves adept at recovering from tactical setbacks, just as the Soviets demonstrated great difficulty in logistically sustaining deep armoured penetrations. Fortuitously, Rotmistrov's fuel supplies in his forward tank brigades dwindled just as the Germans received powerful armoured reinforcements from the West. Both the 14. and 24.Panzer-Divisionen had been destroyed at Stalingrad in February, but now eight months later they reappeared on the Eastern Front. These units were the first of a new breed of watered-down Panzer-Divisionen, each equipped with 49 Pz IV tanks and 44 StuG III assault guns, configured primarily for mobile defensive operations. Von Manstein directed both fresh Panzer-Divisionen to assemble in Kirovograd. Major Willing's s.Pz.Abt.506 was sent from Zaporozhe to defend Krivoi Rog. The 11.Panzer-Division and *Totenkopf* were also moved to support this sector. General der Panzertruppe Sigfrid Henrici's XXXX Panzerkorps took control over the bulk of these forces and began planning a counter-attack to cut off Rotmistrov's spearheads. However, only a week before the German counter-offensive was to begin, Henrici was sent into the Fuhrer Reserve and the XXXX Panzerkorps was handed over to General der Gebirgstruppen Ferdinand Schörner, who was flown in from Finland. This was an amazing example of Hitler's interference in tactical matters. Not only did Schörner have no experience with mechanized operations, but he also had no experience with combat in the main war zone in Russia. Yet Hitler had not chosen Schörner randomly. He was selected because of his fanatical command style and devotion to the Nazi regime. When the chips were down, Hitler chose political reliability over professional skill.

Only days after taking command, Schörner ordered the counter-attack to begin immediately, even though only parts of the 14. and 24.Panzer-Divisionen had arrived. On 28 October, *Totenkopf* kicked off the attack against Skvortsov's 5 GMC with 5 Tigers and a handful of other tanks, while 11.Panzer-Division attacked Rotmistrov's spearhead near Krivoi Rog. The next day, those parts of the 14. and 24. Panzer-Divisionen that were available joined in. Rotmistrov was caught flat-footed, not expecting to be struck by fresh enemy armoured divisions and his 5 GTA recoiled from Krivoi Rog after suffering heavy losses. The German armoured counter-attack plugged the gap between PzAOK 1 and AOK 8, but a great opportunity had been squandered by Schörner, who unimaginatively opted to push the enemy salient back, rather than cut it off. Had these four Panzer-Divisionen been properly coordinated, the XXXX Panzerkorps might have cut off and destroyed at least two of Rotmistrov's three corps. Instead, Hitler and Schörner opted for an ordinary victory.

As October 1943 drew to a close, Konev and Malinovsky were across the Dnepr in strength, but Vatutin had been stymied for weeks. The Stavka recognized that the Germans had effectively contained the Bukrin bridgehead, but ordered Vatutin to instead shift his main effort to the tiny Lyutezh bridgehead north of Kiev. In order to provide an exploitation force, Vatutin ordered Rybalko on 25 October to shift his 3 GTA from the Bukrin bridgehead to Lyutezh. This was a very risky gambit and it would only work if von Manstein remained unaware that the mass of Vatutin's armour had shifted northward. Under Zhukov's

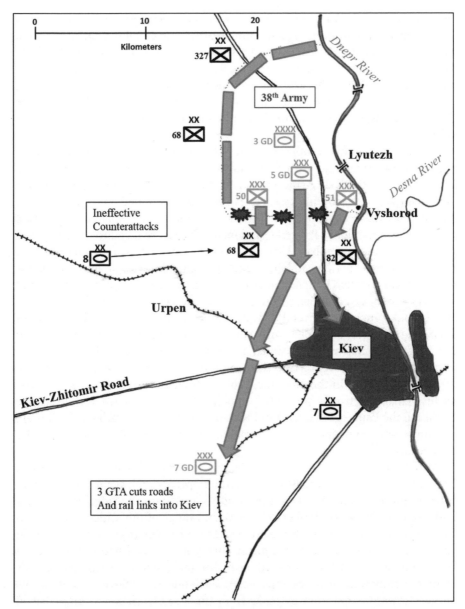

Soviet breakout from the Lyutezh Bridgehead and liberation of Kiev, 3–5 November 1943.

critical eye, Vatutin employed the full range of *Maskirovka* tactics to deceive the Germans and Rybalko's tanks were only allowed to move at night, under strict discipline. Rybalko used radio deception by leaving several rump command posts in the Bukrin bridgehead, pretending to represent the entire 3 GTA. Given that there were only three pontoon bridges over the Dnepr and a few ferries, it took Rybalko three nights to move the entire 3 GTA back to the east side of the river. However, fog and rainy weather prevented the Luftwaffe from noticing the transfer of Soviet armour. Rybalko's tank army still had about 400 tanks but it had lost a great deal of its trucks, so it took two days for his forces to move 150km and reach the crossing over the Desna at Letki, then begin crossing into the Lyutezh bridgehead. By the morning of 2 November, Rybalko's entire 3 GTA was assembled in the bridgehead and the Germans remained ignorant of this fact.

By early November, Hoth's PzAOK 4 had established a perimeter around the Lyutezh bridgehead with four badly-depleted infantry divisions (68, 82, 208, 327) from the XIII Armeekorps and the 88.Infanterie-Division from VII Armeekorps.[193] Nearby, in reserve, Hoth had positioned Oberst Gottfried Frölich's 8.Panzer-Division, which was a sad indication of what poor condition the Heer's once-mighty Panzer-Divisionen had been reduced to by three years of near-continuous combat. Although Frölich's division had a paper-strength of 13,665 troops on 1 November, he only had a total of 610 infantrymen in his four Panzergrenadier-Bataillonen and the pioniers, reconnaissance troops and Panzerjägers added another 545 troops. His sole tank battalion, I./Pz.Rgt.10, had 14 tanks, including seven Pz IV with long 7.5cm. The 8.Panzer-Division's Panzerjägers were equipped with seven 7.5cm Pak, two 5cm Pak 38 and five 3.7cm Pak 36, while divisional artillery support consisted of three self-propelled Wespe (10.5cm), two 10cm cannons, two 15cm howitzers and nine 10.5cm howitzers. On the plus side, Frölich still had 64 SPWs and 828 trucks, so his remaining troops were fairly mobile. Frölich deployed Kampfgruppe Neise (all the Panzergrenadiers) and Kampfgruppe von Mitzlaff (I./Pz.Rgt.10, reconnaissance and one artillery battalion) as tactical reserves for the XIII Armeekorps.[194]

At 0800 hours on 3 November, General-leytenant Kirill S. Moskalenko's 38th Army began a massive 40-minute artillery preparation against the German infantry positions around the southern side of the Lyutezh bridgehead. Vatutin had also moved the 7th Artillery Corps within range of the bridgehead, as well as numerous Katyusha rocket batteries. The German front-line infantry in this sector were not expecting a major enemy assault and had not built deep fieldworks in the marshy ground near Lyutezh; consequently, the Soviet artillery bombardment wreaked havoc. At 0840 hours, six Soviet rifle divisions surged forward, supported by tanks from the 5 GTC. Sappers proceeded in front to remove enemy mines. Although dazed, the German infantry put up a tough fight and limited the initial Soviet push to a 3km advance.[195] Frölich's 8.Panzer-Division was slow to react and then managed only a few local counter-attacks. As the 38th Army committed its second-echelon forces, including additional armour, the German 68. and 82.Infanterie-Divisionen began to collapse, yielding another 4km. In an unusual move, Rybalko's 3 GTA (6 GTC, 7 GTC, 9 MC) entered the battle at dusk and continued to advance forward during the night. On the second day of the offensive, drizzling rain deprived both sides of air support but also helped to conceal the fact that the Red Army had committed three tank and one mechanized corps to the breakout operation. Pounded relentlessly, the German XIII Armeekorps collapsed and the Soviet 51st Rifle Corps reached the outskirts of Kiev by the evening of 4 November. While 5 GTC followed Moskalenko's 38th Army into the city, Rybalko's 3 GTA swung to the southeast to cut the enemy road and rail links into the city. In order to conduct continuous operations, Rybalko ordered his tanks to drive through the night with headlights on, which enabled 7 GTC to cut the main road into Kiev before 8. Panzer-Division could block them.

By 5 November the 88.Infanterie-Division was virtually obliterated and the 8.Panzer-Division had been shoved rudely aside by Rybalko's armoured mass. Hoth quickly realized that defending Kiev was now a hopeless task and focused instead upon saving the rail station at Fastov, where the 25.Panzer-Division was just arriving. He deployed the 7.Panzer-Division to block the 6 GTC, but it arrived too late and the Soviet tankers occupied the station. During the early morning hours of 6 November, a motorized infantry company fought its way to the centre of Kiev and raised the Red flag. Once the Germans realized that Soviet units were in the centre of the city they brusquely retreated to the south. Vatutin's use of Rybalko's 3 GTA to liberate Kiev demonstrated a vast advance in the Red Army's practice of mechanized warfare and von Manstein was left chagrined at his failure to anticipate enemy actions. The fall of Kiev was the culmination of the Soviet Lower Dnepr offensive, which had seen Hitler's plan to transform the Dnepr River into an impregnable bulwark completely frustrated. In the process, Heeresgruppe Süd had suffered crippling losses, amounting to about 170,000 personnel (including over 48,000 dead or missing) and over 500 tanks. Furthermore, only 44 per cent of German tanks on the Eastern Front – about 600 vehicles – were still operational.[196] Nevertheless, this Soviet operational triumph did not come cheap, costing the Red Army at least 450,000 casualties and 1,800 tanks.

German counter-attacks near Kiev, 7 November–24 December 1943
Hitler was furious that Hoth had lost Kiev and he decided to replace him with General der Panzertruppe Erhard Raus. Von Manstein was also rapidly falling out of favour, but he argued with Hitler that it might be possible to conduct another 'Backhand Blow' counter-offensive against Rybalko's 3 GTA and retake Kiev. It was true that strong armoured reinforcements were arriving on the Eastern Front, including the refitted 1.Panzer-Division and the *LSSAH* (now redesignated as a Panzer-Division), which were very powerful formations, each equipped with one battalion of Panthers and one of Pz IVs. In addition, the newly-formed 25.Panzer-Division was arriving from Norway and the new s.Pz. Abt.509 from Germany with more Tigers. These formations were all at full-strength and totalled 558 tanks, including 172 Panthers and 72 Tigers. Von

Manstein also received *Das Reich*, which still had 33 tanks, including five Tigers. He decided to mass this incoming armour at Bila Tserkva and Berdichev under the control of XXXXVIII Panzerkorps and make a coordinated strike against Rybalko's left flank at Fastov. Always eager to approve offensives that might restore the situation, Hitler quickly agreed to von Manstein's recommendations. On the other hand, Hitler had issued Führer Directive 51 on the same day as the beginning of the Soviet breakout from the Lyutezh bridgehead; this edict shifted priority of replacements to the West in anticipation of an Allied amphibious invasion of France in 1944, which meant that von Manstein could not expect significant reinforcements beyond what was already en route.[197]

Von Clausewitz, the Prussian military writer, spoke of 'friction' in war – an often indiscernible sequence of small events and factors that can gradually undermine an operational plan. It was this friction – some of which was self-inflicted – which caused von Manstein's second attempted 'Backhand Blow' to fail. First, both Hitler and the OKH disrupted planning by shuffling commanders around, seemingly at random. General der Panzertruppen Heinrich Eberbach, commander of the XXXXVIII Panzerkorps, was replaced at the last moment by General der Panzertruppen Hermann Balck, who had been sent to command a corps at Salerno for a month then returned to the Eastern Front.* Second, Soviet partisans disrupted German rail traffic west of Fastov and many inbound units were arriving piecemeal and often unloaded at different rail stations, which seriously disrupted preparations to employ them in a coherent manner. Finally, enemy actions did not stop and PzAOK 4's left flank had virtually fallen apart, allowing the Soviets to advance toward Zhitomir and Korosten. Ideally, von Manstein would have waited until all his units were fully assembled and prepared, but Vatutin was not going to give him that time. Now, von Manstein was forced to conduct a major armoured counter-attack in the manner that the Red Army had employed in 1941 – with sloppy staff work, poor logistics and units committed as they arrived. The decision to begin a major counter-attack during a rainy period when deep mud seriously hampered tactical mobility further impaired German capabilities.

In order to prevent Ivanov's 7 GTC from over-running the German assembly areas, Raus committed the *Das Reich*, Kampfgruppe von Wechmar from the 25.Panzer-Division and s.Pz.Abt.509 to local counter-attacks south of Fastov on 9–13 November. Although the Germans claimed to have knocked out over 30 Soviet tanks in several days of tank skirmishing, the results were disappointing. In particular, s.Pz.Abt.509 lost seven Tigers destroyed and only had 14 operational by the time that von Manstein's counter-offensive was supposed to begin.[198] It was also obvious during the lead-up to the counter-offensive that

---

* Eberbach commanded three different Panzerkorps between 15 October and 15 November 1943. This was a ridiculous misuse of one of Germany's best senior panzer leaders. Balck was also being bounced around between commands.

the newly-arrived 25.Panzer-Division was a 'soft' unit that was not ready to be thrust into heavy combat; most of its personnel had been on occupation duty in Norway for years and its original commander, Generalleutnant Adolf von Schell, had no command experience and was in poor health. Guderian tried to stop him from going East with the division but he was overruled by the OKH; within a week, Schell was relieved of command. Indeed, Guderian tried to stop the entire division from being sent East since he believed that it was not combat-ready. In its first action, Kampfgruppe von Wechmar was sent to retake Fastov but panicked when attacked by T-34s and retreated in disorder, suffering heavy losses of men and vehicles.[199]

An even worse development than Rybalko's threat to the German assembly areas south of Fastov was that Vatutin achieved a major operational breakthrough west of Kiev and he sent General-leytenant Viktor K. Baranov's 1st Guards Cavalry Corps (1 GCC) as a mobile group east toward the main German supply base at Zhitomir, followed by General-leytenant Kirill S. Moskalenko's 38th Army. Moskalenko's army included the 7th Guards Heavy Tank Regiment equipped with 21 of the new KV-85 heavy tanks, which were intended as a stop-gap until the new IS-2 and T-34/85 tanks arrived in early 1944. Frölich's 8.Panzer-Division tried to block the Zhitomir-Kiev road, but they were forced to retreat by Baranov's cavalry, whose own armoured support greatly exceeded this threadbare Panzer-Division.* On 13 November, the 1 GCC and 23rd Rifle Corps captured Zhitomir.[200] The loss of Zhitomir was near-catastrophic since it was a vital rail junction and supply base; without it Heeresgruppe Süd's line of communications were reduced to single track rail lines. Von Manstein and Raus were forced to reorient their counter-offensive from a classic pincer attack into more of a head-on engagement to retake both Zhitomir and Fastov. Deploying the *LSSAH* as a covering force near Brusilov to prevent interference from Rybalko's 3 GTA, Raus sent the 1. and 7.Panzer-Divisionen to converge upon the 1 GCC at Zhitomir. Rybalko's tanks sparred with *LSSAH* and repulsed an attempt to capture Brusilov, but otherwise failed to support the isolated 1 GCC, so tanks and Panzergrenadiers stormed Zhitomir on 20 November.

Raus then brought up the 19.Panzer-Division from the south to conduct a double envelopment of Rybalko's armour at Brusilov, while *LSSAH* held their attention and 1.Panzer-Division shifted eastward to get around their northern flank. The terrain in the Brusilov area was heavily wooded and littered with ravines, which meant that most tank engagements occurred at ranges under 600 metres and rapid tactical movements were difficult. Once again, the Panther's

---

* The Soviet cavalry corps of late 1943 was vastly different from the earlier Red Army cavalry formations. The 1 GCC included three tank regiments with an authorized strength of 90 T-34s and 21 T-70s, as well as an SAP with 20 SU-76 self-propelled guns. The corps had an authorized strength of 21,000 men, 19,000 horses and several hundred trucks.

long 7.5cm gun easily defeated the T-34s, but mechanical defects sidelined over 50 of 1.Panzer-Division's Panthers in less than a week of combat. On the night of 23–24 November, 1.Panzer-Division linked up with 19.Panzer-Division, thereby creating a small *Kessel* at Brusilov. The Germans claimed 3,000 enemy troops killed and 153 tanks destroyed in the pocket, but most of Rybalko's forces slipped away before the pincers closed.[201] At that point, rainy weather and logistical problems caused von Manstein to temporarily suspend the XXXXVIII Panzerkorps counter-attack on 26 November. Although Zhitomir had been recaptured, the Germans had accomplished very little given the scale of effort expended.

After a brief pause, the XXXXVIII Panzerkorps resumed its counter-attack on 6 December. By this point, the ground had hardened and the first snow arrived, which improved German tactical mobility. This time, the 1. and 7.Panzer-Divisionen and *LSSAH* tried to outflank the Soviet 60th Army at Radomyschl from the west, while *Das Reich*, 8. and 19.Panzer-Divisionen tried to envelop it from the southeast. However, the *LSSAH*'s panzers ran out of fuel on the second day of the attack, and trying to surround infantry in forested areas with tanks proved rather difficult. Eventually, the German armoured pincers closed and von Manstein claimed three Soviet rifle divisions had been 'wiped out' in the four-day Battle of Radomyschl, but based upon the paltry haul of prisoners this was a bald lie.[202] Next, von Manstein decided to clear the area east of Korosten, where 38th Army had dug in around the town of Meleni. When Vatutin recognized that von Manstein was committing strong armoured reserves to a counter-offensive, he shifted his forces onto the tactical defensive, moving anti-tank and infantry units forward and pulling Rybalko's armour back. The Red Army was learning how to be flexible in order to absorb German counter-attacks, rather than rigidly carrying on with a preconceived operational plan, as Timoshenko had done at Kharkov in May 1942. On 18 December, the *LSSAH* and 1.Panzer-Division attacked Soviet positions near Meleni but quickly ran into a wall of anti-tank guns and mines. For six days the XXXXVIII Panzerkorps kept attacking, but it could not create a *Kessel* and von Manstein was forced to suspend the counter-offensive on 20 December. *Das Reich* was so burnt out by the end of this operation that the bulk of the division was sent to rebuild in France, but a brigade-size Kampfgruppe with two Panzergrenadier-Bataillonen, two Panzer-Kompanien (15 tanks), the reconnaissance battalion, two self-propelled artillery batteries and a Pionier-Kompanie remained on the Eastern Front until April 1944.

Von Manstein claimed a significant tactical victory in the tank battles around Fastov, Brusilov, Radomyschyl and Meleni. He declared that Vatutin had lost 700 tanks in these battles and that Rybalko's 3 GTA and the 38th and 60th Armies had been badly defeated. Again these were ridiculous exaggerations, intended to assuage Hitler's anger about the loss of Kiev. In order to buttress his claims, two KV-85 tanks captured during the December counter-attacks were sent back to Germany as trophies, although these provided an ominous indication that the Red Army would field new tanks in 1944. In fact, Vatutin's armour losses during this period were moderate because he did not allow Rybalko's 3 GTA to become decisively engaged, instead parrying XXXXVIII Panzerkorps' blows with his anti-tank units. Vatutin wanted to conserve 3 GTA for the exploitation role and instead relied upon the independent tank regiments attached to his infantry armies to support the defence. Von Manstein also ignored the fact that Soviet battlefield recovery techniques were improving, which meant that many tanks that were knocked out were salvaged and repaired. German recovery of damaged tanks was increasingly difficult due to the excessive amount of resources required to salvage 45-ton Panthers and 54-ton Tigers. During the counter-offensive, von Manstein failed to land any really solid blows upon Vatutin's armour, which meant that the results were indecisive. Even worse, by 20 December, only 46 per cent of PzAOK 4's armour was still operational (including 28 Panthers and 11 Tigers).[203]

While XXXXVIII Panzerkorps was futilely pounding away at Vatutin's infantry and anti-tank guns, Rybalko's 3 GTA was receiving an infusion of fresh tanks and crews to restore its fighting strength. In addition, Katutov's 1 TA (4 GTC, 11 GTC, 8 GMC) had been rebuilt to a strength of 42,000 troops and 546 tanks/self-propelled guns. Amazingly, the Red Army was able to restore the bridges and rail lines in Kiev in just three weeks and Katukov's 1 TA was brought across the Dnepr by rail, thereby sparing the tanks the wear and tear of a long road march. By 20 December, Katukov's 1 TA had been assembled behind Moskalenko's 38th Army near Fastov.[204] Vatutin intended to make his main effort against the German XXXXII Armeekorps near Brusilov, which was holding a 40km stretch of front with the 8., 19. and 25.Panzer-Divisionen; it was a mark of desperation that the Germans were holding a large chunk of front line with armoured units due to the limited amount of infantry available. Furthermore, PzAOK 4 was badly deployed, with the strongest formations, *LSSAH* and 1. Panzer-Division on the extreme left, near Korosten.

The morning of 24 December was overcast and it was raining. At 0600 hours, Moskalenko's 38th Army began a 60-minute artillery preparation against the XXXXII Armeekorps, then attacked with ten rifle divisions supported by 200 tanks. The main Soviet effort struck the boundary between the 19. and 25.Panzer-Divisionen and quickly gained ground. Generalmajor Hans Källner's 19.Panzer-Division had 16 operational tanks and eight self-propelled Panzerjagers, but only a few hundred Panzergrenadiers, so it was forced to fight a delaying action. The 25.Panzer-Division was considerably stronger, with 51 tanks and seven StuG IIIs, but its left flank was soon exposed and Källner fell back.[205] The same thing happened to the 8.Panzer-Division, as its right flank was exposed. By nightfall, the centre of XXXXII Armeekorps was collapsing under the hammer-blows of infantry and tanks and its three Panzer-Divisionen had to keep fighting their way out of encirclements. Once it was clear that

Moskalenko had achieved a tactical breakthrough, Vatutin committed both Katukov's 1 TA and Rybalko's 3 GTA to exploit – the first time that two tank armies had attacked simultaneously side-by-side. Caught by surprise, Raus tried to adjust his forces, but the Soviet armour moved much too quickly. By the third day of the Soviet offensive the XXXXII Armeekorps was falling apart and Raus had nothing to plug the gap. Raus focused on massing 1.Panzer-Division and *LSSAH* around Zhitomir, but Vatutin reoriented his tanks southward instead of westward, flowing around German strongpoints. By 30 December, the XXXXVIII Panzerkorps was nearly encircled in Zhitomir and PzAOK 4 had broken into three pieces, with large gaps in between. Raus abandoned both Korosten and Zhitomir and tried to mass his remaining forces around Berdichev. As the year ended, Vatutin had PzAOK 4 on the run and the German front was in complete chaos.

German accounts of this period of the war tend to emphasize tactical victories, where small numbers of German tanks knocked out much larger number of Soviet tanks. While there is some truth in these accounts, they are generally silent about German losses. These types of accounts also tend to miss the main point, that German armour was fighting delaying actions, not successful defensive operations, while the much-maligned T-34s were generally accomplishing their operational objectives. The fact is that by late 1943 the Panzer-Divisionen could no longer stop the Soviet 'steamroller', only delay it and increase the price of victories. Each retreat cost the Germans logistic resources that further degraded their ability to maintain combat-effective Panzer-Divisionen in the field and the breaking point was fast approaching. It is also important to note that the Panzer-Divisionen lost their freedom of manoeuvre in late 1943, due to being increasingly tied to the defence of critical sectors. Von Manstein no longer had a *masse de manoeuvre*.

There is no doubt that victory did not come cheaply for Vatutin's and Konev's fronts, which had suffered personnel casualties that exceeded 1 million (including 290,000 dead or missing) during July–December 1943, but they received a similar number of replacements. In the same period, the Red Army as a whole lost about 12,000 tanks, but 10,162 new tanks were built and about 7,000 damaged tanks repaired, which enabled the Soviets to maintain a 3–1 or better armoured numerical superiority over the Germans.[206] In contrast, the Germans lost a total of about 2,800 tanks and 850 assault guns in the East during July–December 1943, against 1,954 tanks and 1,328 assault guns received as replacements or reinforcements.[207] Indeed, only 60 per cent of German AFV production in this period went to the Eastern Front, the rest going to build up armoured units for the defence of Western Europe. Due to the loss of repair facilities in Dnepropetrovsk and Kiev, German support capabilities were severely disrupted: only half of the 2,053 German tanks on the Eastern Front on 31 December 1943 were operational.[208] The personnel situation was even worse for von Manstein, with Heeresgruppe Süd having suffered over

372,000 casualties (including 102,000 dead or missing) in the last half of 1943, but receiving fewer than 200,000 replacements.

Beyond the crushing quantitative imbalance, the failure of the much-anticipated Panther tank to deliver a qualitative solution to the Red Army's numerical advantage was a severe disappointment for the Panzer-Divisionen. Although the Panther's long 7.5cm KwK 42 gun had proven itself, the new tank's mechanical unreliability prevented it from making more than a local impression; at the critical moment in December 1943, only 28 of PzAOK 4's 139 Panthers were operational.[209]

Chapter 3

Armoured Operations in 1944

Heeresgruppe Nord retreats from Leningrad, 14 January–1 April 1944
For nearly three years, Heeresgruppe Nord had been holding its positions outside the city of Leningrad, with little change in the opposing lines. Although the Leningrad and Volkhov Fronts had opened a land corridor to Leningrad with Operation *Iskra* in January 1943, a year later the Germans were still within artillery range of the city. Generalfeldmarschall Georg Wilhelm von Küchler commanded Heeresgruppe Nord from his headquarters in Pskov and he had two armies: AOK 18 holding the lines around Leningrad and AOK 16 deployed between Novgorod and Velikiye Luki. Given the static nature of warfare on the Leningrad sector, the OKH had stripped Generaloberst Georg Lindemann's 18.Armee (AOK 18) down to the bone during 1943. Several Luftwaffe Feld-Divisionen were sent to this relatively quiet sector, which allowed Heer infantry divisions to be sent southward and AOK 18 received far fewer personnel replacements than other German armies. At the start of 1944, Lindemann had 20 divisions holding a 280km-long front. In terms of armour, AOK 18 had relied upon the Tigers from s. Pz.Abt. 502 to repel enemy attacks and this unit enjoyed a considerable amount of success outside Leningrad. Oberleutnant Otto Carius was one of the Tiger 'aces' who made a name for himself in this Stellungskrieg (positional warfare).

However, on 6 October 1943, the Soviet Kalinin Front launched a massive attack near the boundary of Heeresgruppe Nord and Heeresgruppe Mitte. The 3rd and 4th Shock Armies, with a total of 16 rifle divisions and 300 tanks, attacked the II.Luftwaffen-Feldkorps near Nevel and rapidly achieved a major breakthrough. Both AOK 16 and PzAOK 3 were compelled to commit all their reserves to this endangered sector, to prevent the Kalinin Front from driving a wedge between the two German army groups. Von Küchler had to send his only mobile reserve, the Tigers of s.Pz.Abt.502, to support a counter-attack intended to retake Nevel and crush the Soviet penetration. The fighting around Nevel dragged on indecisively for months, although the Germans claimed that 1,450 Soviet tanks were destroyed in this sector over the course of the battle.

Despite the distraction of the Nevel breakthrough, by late 1943 the OKH assessed that the Soviet Leningrad Front would eventually attack Heeresgruppe Nord's AOK 18 in force, so Obergruppenführer Felix Steiner's III.SS-Panzerkorps headquarters was sent to join Lindemann's command in ealy December 1943, along with 11.SS-Panzergrenadier-Division *Nordland* and 4.SS-Panzergrenadier-Brigade *Nederland*. Despite their grandiloquent titles, these recently-raised Waffen-SS formations were of mediocre quality, consisting primarily of Volksdeutsche, and poorly equipped. The *Nordland*'s SS-Panzer Battalion 11 was supposed to be equipped with Panther tanks, but most proved defective and the battalion was still unready for combat in January 1944.[1] A few of the immobilized Panthers were sent to the front and dug in as strongpoints. Instead, the *Nordland* had SS-*Sturmgeschutz* Battalion 11 with 42 StuG III and the *Nederland* brigade had a battery with 10 StuG III. In order to increase its anti-tank capabilities, AOK 18 had also formed Panzer-Zerstorer-Bataillone 477 and 478, each equipped with 20 of the new 8.8cm Panzerschreck rocket launchers. As a contingency plan, Heeresgruppe Nord began construction of the Panther Line on 7 September 1943; the line was intended to run from Narva, behind Lake Peipus to Pskov and Ostrov. By the end of December, some anti-tank ditches and fieldworks were in place, but the bulk of the fortification effort would not be completed until March 1944.[2]

The main problem for AOK 18 was the Oranienbaum salient, which the Red Army had held since late 1941. This heavily-fortified salient was supplied by sea and forced AOK 18 to maintain at least a corps-size formation to contain it. Steiner's corps was assigned to defend the southern side of the Oranienbaum salient, to prevent a link-up between the Soviet forces in Leningrad and the enclave. *Nordland* would serve as a mobile reserve for this critical sector. However, von Küchler and Lindemann were not particularly concerned about the Oranienbaum salient, which had been a quiet sector for two years. Instead, von Küchler and Lindemann focused on repelling a Soviet breakout from Leningrad toward the Pulkovo Heights. Once again, the Germans were let down by their poor intelligence support, which failed to note a shift in Soviet intentions. General-leytenant Leonid A. Govorov, commander of the Leningrad Front, was resolved to end the German threat to the city and to destroy AOK 18. Instead of attacking from the east, as he had tried in all previous offensives in 1941–43, this time Govorov decided to make his main effort from the Oranienbaum salient.

General-leytenant Ivan F. Fediuninskiy, a protégé of Zhukov, was put in command of the 2nd Shock Army, which consisted of seven rifle divisions, two tank brigades and three tank regiments. Fediuninskiy's strike force was quietly moved into the Oranienbaum salient in late December; not all of this could be concealed, but the Germans failed to appreciate this as the Soviet main effort. Instead, the Germans focused on General-polkovnik Ivan I. Maslennikov's 42nd Army, which was outfitted with nine rifle divisions, two tank brigades, six tank regiments and two artillery divisions. Golikov's preparations were meticulous, and for once the Red Army was allowed adequate time for preparation. On the morning of 14 January, Golikov attacked. Fediuninskiy's artillery commenced a massive artillery bombardment against the 9. and 10.Luftwaffe-Feld-Divisionen on the eastern side of the salient. Two Soviet battleships supported the attack, with 305mm naval gunfire. After smashing their positions with over 100,000 rounds in 65 minutes, Fediuninskiy then attacked with five rifle divisions and two tank brigades. Contrary to expectations, the Luftwaffe troops put up a stout defence that prevented an immediate breakthrough and enabled *Nordland* to send some reinforcements. At the same time, Maslennikov distracted the German L Armeekorps with a massive bombardment, which kept Lindemann from committing his limited reserves against Fediuninskiy's 2nd Shock Army. As night fell, Fediuninskiy committed a mobile group consisting of Polkovnik Aron Z. Oskotsky's 152nd Tank Brigade and two tank regiments to begin pushing toward the road junction at Ropsha.

On the morning of 15 January, Maslennikov's 42nd Army attacked the L Armeekorps after another lengthy artillery bombardment and quickly achieved a 4km-deep penetration on the Pulkovo Heights. The breakthrough was assisted by the 36th and 49th Guards Tank Regiments, each equipped with 21 Churchill tanks. Meanwhile, Fediuninskiy smashed the remnants of the two Luftwaffe divisions but mobile group Oskotsky was stopped by a counter-attack from *Nordland* before it could reach Ropsha. Lindemann was able to organize local counter-attacks on 16–17 January that temporarily slowed the two Soviet armies that were advancing toward each other. *Nordland* employed its assault guns and mobile artillery to strike at the flanks of the Soviet penetration, but could not seal it off. Maslennikov formed a mobile group with the 1st and 220th Tank Brigades, but these were stopped north of Krasnoye Selo. However after five days of battle, the German defence began to crumble and the Soviet armies surged toward Ropsha. On 19 January, the 2nd Shock Army and 42nd Army fought their way into Ropsha, which isolated a number of German units and forced Lindemann to retreat. Adding to von Küchler's problems, Meretskov's Volkhov Front launched an attack against AOK 16 which overran a Luftwaffe division at Novgorod and threatened to unhinge AOK 18's right flank, as well. Lindemann's centre was pierced and both flanks were in retreat.

Hitler ordered von Küchler and Lindemann to stand fast, as help was on the way. He promised the transfer of the 12.Panzer-Division from Heeresgruppe Mitte and Panzer-Grenadier-Division *Feldherrnhalle* from France to reinforce AOK 18, but neither would arrive soon enough to prevent Golikov from completing his breakout. Instead, the only immediate help came from s.Pz. Abt.502, which sent its 3.Kompanie under Leutnant Herbert Meyer with 15 Tigers by rail on 19 January. By the time Meyer's Tigers arrived at Gatchina on 20 January, the station was already under artillery fire and the lead elements of the 42nd Army were approaching. With the rest of the battalion still en route, Meyer's Tigers were scooped up by a local commander who ordered him to advance northwest to assist elements of the L Armeekorps, which were under pressure from Soviet armour. With a platoon of four Tigers, Meyer promptly advanced in a movement to contact, completely ignorant of both the friendly and enemy situation. Advancing to the sound of gunfire, Meyer unexpectedly bumped into an enemy tank battalion with 20–30 tanks. The terrain around Leningrad is heavily wooded and the ensuing action must have occurred at short range; three of Meyer's four Tigers were knocked out and abandoned. Meyer returned with his last Tiger to link up with the rest of his company north of Gatchina, assembling a blocking force on the main road to Leningrad. However, Meyer had no supporting infantry and when the 42nd Army came rolling down the highway the next morning, Kampfgruppe Meyer was quickly encircled. Although Meyer's Tigers knocked out eight enemy tanks and six anti-tank guns, the situation was hopeless since fuel and ammunition were low. In desperation, Meyer committed suicide and all 11 of his Tigers were destroyed or captured.[3] Without support, the Tiger was little more than a bunker.

With AOK 18's front broken and the Soviets rolling inexorably toward the Luga River, von Küchler's nerve cracked and he ordered both armies to retreat to the Panther Line, even though its fortifications were incomplete. Under heavy pressure, AOK 18 conducted a fighting retreat to the Luga River, while AOK 16 fell back about 30km. The remaining Tigers of s.Pz.Abt.502 assisted the AOK 18 in its withdrawal by turning to ambush the Soviet spearheads; on 25 January they claimed 41 Soviet tanks destroyed at Voyskovitsy, 5km southwest of Gatchina. However, German supply lines were disrupted by the retreat and resupply of fuel and ammunition became problematic. On 28 January, the Tigers made a brief stand at Volosovo while the infantry retreated to the Luga River. One lone Tiger was engaged by a battalion with 27 T-34s; despite having only three AP rounds and nine HE rounds, it managed to knock out seven T-34s and then fall back. Yet aside from the few remaining assault guns, Heeresgruppe Nord had almost no other armoured units to serve as a rearguard.

Von Küchler's retreat order was unauthorized and Hitler immediately sacked von Küchler and decided to replace him with Generaloberst Walter Model, who had already made a name for himself as a steadfast commander. However, by the time that Model arrived in Pskov on 31 January, Heeresgruppe Nord was already in full retreat and Fediuninskiy's 2nd Shock Army was on the outskirts of Kingisepp. Even worse, Model found that AOK 18 had barely 17,000 combat troops to hold the 115km-wide front on the Luga River, which was insufficient to repulse a determined offensive. Affecting a bold front, Model declared that Heeresgruppe Nord would employ *Schild und Schwert* (sword and shield) tactics to stop the Soviet steamroller. By this he meant limited tactical withdrawals to enable him to concentrate enough troops for local counter-attacks. Model ordered the establishment of large-scale *stützpunkte* at Narva and Luga, while combing out infantry replacements from Heeresgruppe Nord's rear-area troops. He personally went to inspect the defences at Narva and decided to commit the remaining Tigers to reinforce Steiner's III. SS-Panzerkorps' defence, since the loss of Narva would fatally compromise the Panther Line.

Yet despite Model's bravado, the Soviet steamroller kept right on coming, advancing up to 16km per day, overrunning Kingisepp on 1 February and then seizing bridgeheads over the Luga River. At Narva, Fediuninskiy's 2nd Shock Army managed to cross the Narva River south of the fortress city, but was stopped by a fanatical defence by Gruppe Sponheimer. Other Soviet elements crossed the frozen Lake Peipus, but were quickly destroyed. Generalleutnant Erpo von Bodenhausen's 12.Panzer-Division arrived by rail from Heeresgruppe Mitte and Model decided to use it in a *Schild und Schwert* effort to stop the 42nd Army on the Luga River. The 12.Panzer-Division had never been completely refitted from its losses in 1941 and could only field a single Panzer-Abteilung, equipped with a mix of Pz III and Pz IV tanks. In contrast, the Leningrad Front received additional armour for the breakout, included some of the new KV-85s and IS-1s. After a few failed counter-attacks, von Bodenhausen used his armour and Panzergrenadiers to slow the Soviet advance, but the 42nd Army still managed to capture Luga on 13 February. Any hope Model had for standing on the Luga were demolished when Popov's 2nd Baltic Front joined the Soviet offensive on 16 February and its 1st Shock Army overran the AOK 16 position at Staraya Russa. With Hitler's grudging acceptance, Model ordered all of Heeresgruppe Nord to retreat to the Panther Line. When the troops arrived at the designated positions, they were forced to dig fighting positions in the frozen, snow covered ground. One innovation that did help was the 'trench plow,' a large steel hoe that was towed behind a semi-track vehicle and used to rip open the ground.

Govorov focused most of his effort on Narva, hoping to capture the city and outflank the rest of the Panther Line. He decided to reinforce Fediuninskiy with the 8th and 47th Armies. General der Infanterie Otto Sponheimer commanded a mixed force of survivors at Narva, including the *Nordland* division, the *Nederland* brigade, four infantry divisions and s.Pz.Abt.502 (with 23 operational Tigers), as well as Estonian Waffen-SS troops and Luftwaffe troops. In early February, the Panzer-Grenadier-Division *Feldherrnhalle* arrived to bolster his command.* Narva was a formidable defensive position, located on a narrow isthmus between the Gulf of Finland and Lake Peipus, surrounded by marshes and forests. The city itself was located on the west side of the Narva River, which effectively served as a wide moat. While the *Nordland* division moved into the city, Oberleutnant Otto Carius and four Tigers were left as a rearguard on the east side of the river to gain time for the Waffen-SS troops to fortify their position. Model promptly arrived at this exposed position and personally told Carius, 'I am holding you personally responsible that no Russian tanks break through.'[4] Once the *Nordland* was dug in, Carius' Tigers were allowed to retreat across the river and the bridge was blown up.

Rather ambitiously, the Soviets attempted a double envelopment of Gruppe Sponheimer at Narva, with the 47th Army crossing the Narva River north of the city at Riigi and Siivertsi and the 8th Army crossing south of the city at Krivasso. In addition, on 13–14 February the Soviet Baltic Fleet landed a battalion of naval infantry behind German lines on the Gulf of Finland. Somehow, Sponheimer

---

* This division was formed from the remnants of the 60.Infanterie-Division (mot.) destroyed at Stalingrad. When it arrived at Narva, it had no attached tanks.

was able to scrape together just enough of a reserve to deal with each Soviet attack. Otto Carius' Tigers played a major role in defending Narva, first sending three Tigers to crush the amphibious attack on 14 February. Next, several Tigers assisted the *Nordland* in battering the northern Soviet bridgeheads on 18 February, then shifted to deal with the southern threat. While the Soviets came close to encircling Narva, the Tigers prevented the pincers from shutting and kept a narrow lifeline open. Soviet tanks crossed the river, but not in sufficient numbers to overcome s. Pz. Abt. 502, which was reinforced with 17 new Tigers in late February.

On 1 March, the Soviet 59th Army began a major offensive from the Krivasso bridgehead which created a substantial lodgement south of Narva. However, the *Nordland* division finally destroyed the small bridgeheads north of Narva, which allowed the Germans to shift the *Feldherrnhalle* division to block this southern threat. On 6 March, the Soviets heavily bombed Narva, turning it into a pile of rubble, then attacked across the river with 2nd Shock Army. On 17 March, the 59th Army attacked from the south to sever the main east-west rail line, but three Tigers under Carius managed to hold the thinly-manned HKL and destroyed 14 T-34s and 1 KV-1, which halted the attack.[5] Instead of overwhelming Carius' small force, the Soviets attacked piecemeal, with only company-size groups of tanks supporting a battalion of infantry. Despite heavy casualties, the German defence held and after two weeks of heavy fighting the Soviets ceased their attacks.

As the Soviet offensive ebbed, the OKH decided to mount a major counter-attack to try and eliminate the 59th Army's Krivasso bridgehead. It was a decidedly low-budget affair. Oberst Graf von Strachwitz was sent to Narva to lead a Panzerkampfgruppe formed from the remaining Tigers and a handful of Panthers and Pz IVs scraped up from repair depots. Elements of three infantry divisions were also committed to the effort. On 26 March, Strachwitz attacked and in six days he managed to demolish the western side of the Soviet bridgehead. The 59th Army had not expected a tank attack and failed to establish effective anti-tank defences. Strachwitz resumed the counter-offensive in early April and achieved more success until the spring thaw brought a halt to his mobile operations. The Soviets still maintained a toehold at Krivasso, but the threat to Narva was temporarily reduced. Strachwitz's counter-offensive inflicted about 12,000 casualties on the 59th Army and brought the Soviet steamroller to a halt.

By early April, the situation along the Panther Line had stabilized for Heeresgruppe Nord. The defence of Narva was difficult and resource-consuming, but the fanatical defence of the city brought Govorov's advance to a halt. The Soviets became too engrossed with taking Narva, rather than pressing hard at other sectors of the Heeresgruppe Nord front. Consequently, the rest of AOK 16 and AOK 18 were able to establish a new defensive line on the border of Estonia, although the army group lacked mobile reserves. As it was, the Leningrad Front came close to breaking Heeresgruppe Nord in

February and it was the lack of large armoured mobile groups that reduced the scale of the Soviet victory. With all the tank armies committed to the Ukraine, Govorov and Meretskov had to make due with combining various tank brigades and regiments into ad hoc groups, which was little better than the Red Army tactics of 1941–42. For the Germans, it was equally unnerving to realize how little armoured support they had when a positional campaign transitioned to mobile warfare.

The Evisceration of Heeresgruppe Süd, January–March 1944

There was no pause in Vatutin's offensive as January 1944 began and his troops succeeded in capturing Berdichev and Belaya Tserkov by 5 January. Vatutin had created a large gap between Heeresgruppe Süd and Heeresgruppe Mitte north of Korosten, into which Vatutin sent three infantry armies, but he had no tanks for exploitation in this sector. Rybalko's 3 GTA was reduced to only 59 operational tanks by 8 January and was soon pulled out of the line to refit, leaving Katukov's 1 TA to continue the advance.[6] During the first 10 days of January 1944, Vatutin lost 314 tanks and then another 294 in the next ten days. A steady stream of tank replacements kept Vatutin's armour advancing, but just barely. Meanwhile, Zhukov directed Vatutin and Konev toward a singular goal, which was a massive pincer effort to push back both PzAOK 1 and PzAOK 4 in order to encircle and destroy the German salient near Cherkassy. Recognizing that the front was collapsing, von Manstein pleaded with Hitler to allow him to pull back from the Dnepr in order to create a new front, but this was refused. Hitler regarded the propaganda value of holding part of the Dnepr line as more important than the military value of conserving his remaining forces. Unable to withdraw, von Manstein opted to quietly begin shifting parts of Hube's PzAOK 1 westward to shore up his broken left flank, held by the remnants of Raus' PzAOK 4. Von Manstein conducted these transfers without authorization from the OKH and knowing that Wöhler's AOK 8 would be hard-pressed to hold the right flank.

While Vatutin pushed Katukov's armour toward the main German supply base at Uman and von Manstein's headquarters at Vinnitsa, Konev began his own offensive against east of Kirovograd on the morning of 5 January. While the 5 GA and 53 Army achieved some success, Hube was able to prevent Konev's first-echelon forces from breaking through his front and deftly used 11.Panzer-Division to mount local counter-attacks. Easily frustrated, particularly when Zhukov was looking over his shoulder, Konev committed Rotmistrov's 5 GTA to the attack only two hours after the operation had begun.[7] Rotmistrov's armour ran straight into a still solid German defence and lost 139 tanks on the first day. Eventually, Konev shifted Rotmistrov's 5 GTA to a more favorable axis on the second day of the operation, but continued to misuse his armour. Hube was force to evacuate Kirovograd on 8 January, but managed to not only maintain a coherent front, but also to transfer some forces to reinforce

Raus' PzAOK 4. Indeed, Hube was so steadfast that he was given command authority over the VII and XXXXII Armeekorps holding the Korsun salient on the Dnepr. Like von Manstein, Hube pleaded to evacuate the salient, but was ignored. Throughout mid-January, Vatutin and Konev continued to grind forward, slowly overwhelming one German-held town after another. Katukov's 1 TA enjoyed the most success, threatening to overrun both Uman and Vinnitsa.

Although he was on the ropes, von Manstein recognized that the Soviet advance was slowing due to a combination of casualties and supply difficulties. He believed that if he could cut off and destroy Katukov's armoured spearheads, Vatutin's offensive would cease. With great difficulty, von Manstein managed to assemble a considerable counter-attack force consisting of the *LSSAH*, 16.Panzer-Division and 101.Jager-Division under von Vormann's XXXXVII Panzerkorps by 21 January. Brigadeführer Wilhelm Mohnke's *LSSAH* had 50 operational tanks and 27 assault guns left (including 1 Tiger, 22 Panthers, 25 Pz IV), but its two Panzergrendier Regiments had barely 30 per cent of their authorized strength. The 16.Panzer-Division was one of the strongest formations in PzAOK 4, with more than 60 operational tanks, including 38 Panthers and 24 Pz IV. As an experiment, von Manstein ordered the formation of Schwere Panzer-Regiment Bäke (34 Tigers and 46 Panthers), which was formed from s.Pz.Abt.503 and parts of 6.Panzer-Division; this was the first time that Tigers and Panthers had been integrated in the same unit. At 0600 hours on 24 January, von Vormann's strike force launched a slashing attack into Katukov's right flank east of Vinnitsa. Although Katukov was surprised by the appearance of over 200 German AFVs, he quickly shifted anti-tank guns into this sector and ordered his troops to emplace mines, which made German heavy tanks move cautiously. Due to the disruption of logistical bases, Schwere Panzer-Regiment Bäke ran out of ammunition on the second day of the operation and fuel shortages were also a recurring problem. Breith's III Panzerkorps (6. and 17.Panzer-Divisionen) was added to the counter-offensive, now dubbed Operation *Vatutin*, which culminated with several small encirclents on 30 January. Von Manstein claimed to have killed or captured 13,500 Soviet troops and knocked out 701 tanks and self-propelled guns.[8] Von Manstein's claims were slightly exaggerated; Soviet records indicate that Vatutin's entire front lost 513 tanks and 146 self-propelled guns during the last 10 days of January, suggesting that von Manstein's counter-attack probably accounted for 300–400 enemy AFVs.[9] Furthermore, none of Katukov's brigade commanders from either the 8 GMC or 11 GTC were casualties during this period, which one would expect if the bulk of 1 TA had been destroyed. Schwere Panzer-Regiment Bäke claimed to have knocked out 267 tanks in return for the loss of three Tigers and four Panthers, a purported 38–1 kill ratio. In fact, the German claims were nonsense. Operation *Vatutin* managed to temporarily force 1 TA onto the defensive and inflicted heavy material losses, but von Manstein's inflated claims were made in order to conceal the fact that his counter-stroke failed to alter the deteriorating situation.

While von Manstein was focused on Katukov, Vatutin was forming a new tank army for his next operation. On 20 January, General-leytenant Andrei G. Kravchenko took command of 6th Tank Army, comprised of Volkhov's 5 MC and Alekseev's 5 GTC; it was not a full-strength formation, totalling just 160 tanks and 50 self-propelled guns.[10] Volkhov's 5 MC had recently been reequipped with Lend-Lease M4A2 Sherman tanks.[11] On 26 January, Vatutin attacked the German VII Armeekorps with the 40th Army but his main effort failed to achieve a breakthrough. Surprisingly, a supporting attack against the over-extended XXXXII Armeekorps achieved a minor breakthrough and Kravchenko sent a mobile group under General-major Mikhail I. Savelev from 5 MC to exploit the gap. Savelev's mobile group consisted of the 233rd Tank Brigade (equipped with Sherman tanks), a regiment of Su-76, a motorized rifle battalion and an anti-tank battery.[12] However, Kravchenko was unable to send the rest of the 5 MC after Savelev, since Vatutin was concerned by Breith's counter-attack against 1 TA and ordered Kravchenko to send part of the corps to reinforce Katukov. Consequently, Kravchenko's 6 TA was reduced to barely 100 tanks just as it was achieving a major success.

Meanwhile, Konev renewed his offensive against Wöhler's AOK 8 on 25 January and overwhelmed the over-extended 389.Infanterie-Division, then quickly committed Rotmistrov's 5 GTA (20 TC, 29 TC) with 323 tanks. Rotmistrov's armoured wedge also forced the burnt-out 14.Panzer-Division to retreat. After 24 hours of fighting, Rotmistrov was able to squeeze the 20 TC and 29 TC through a gap in the German lines and they pushed west against negligible resistance. Wöhler mounted a quick counter-attack with the 11.Panzer-Division (15 tanks and 15 assault guns) which temporarily succeeded in severing the line of communications behind the two advancing Soviet tank corps, but lacked the strength to do any more.[13] By 27 January, Rotmistrov's armour was rapidly pushing west and close to linking up with Savelev's mobile group. The only hope to reverse this dangerous situation was Major Glässgen's I.Pz.Rgt.26 which had only arrived from Germany two weeks before, and it was quickly attached to XXXXVII Panzerkorps to cut off Rotmistrov's spearheads. Although the battalion had not yet seen combat, it already lost a dozen tanks disabled with mechanical problems and the 75km march to its assembly area cost it another Panther destroyed by engine fire and four broken down.[14] Clearly, the 'teething problems' associated with *Zitadelle* were still not resolved.

At 0600 hours on 28 January, the I.Pz.Rgt.26 attacked northward with 61 Panthers to Kapitanovka to link up with Major von Siver's Panthers from 11.Panzer-Division. In complete disregard for combined arms tactics, the attack was begun without infantry, artillery, air support or even reconnaissance, so Glässgen's inexperienced Panther crews moved blindly into a meeting engagement with an enemy of unknown strength. As it turned out, Konev had moved strong anti-tank units into this sector and General-major Vasily I. Polozkov's 18 TC was in the process of reopening the road. The German attack was a four-star fiasco, with the Panthers being engaged repeatedly in flank by anti-tank ambushes; Major Glässgen and two of his company commanders were killed, 10 Panthers were destroyed and 18 damaged. Another 16 Panthers broke-down from engine defects, leaving I.Pz.Rgt.26 with just 17 operational Panthers. While Polozkov's 18 TC lost 29 T-34s in the action, he succeeded in reopening the road to Rotmistrov's two tank corps that were driving west.[15]

On 28 January, Podpolkovnik Ivan I. Proshin was pushing his 155th Tank Brigade forward as fast as possible, as the advance guard of 20 TC. By the afternoon, his lead tanks had reached the town of Zvenigorodka, which was a German supply base. After scattering rear area troops, Proshin secured the town and around 1800 hours the lead Sherman tanks from Savelev's mobile group arrived, which created a link-up between 6 TA and 5 GTA.[16] A total of 59,000 German troops from the VII and XXXXII Armeekorps were now isolated in the Korsun pocket, comprising SS-*Wiking*, four infantry divisions (57, 72, 88 and 389) and two Sturmgeschütz-Abteilungen (228, 239). The German forces within the Korsun pocket were quickly redeployed for all-around defence and were redesignated as Gruppe Stemmerman, after General der Artillerie Wilhelm Stemmermann, commander of XXXXII Armeekorps. Amazingly, Hitler refused to allow Gruppe Stemmermann to conduct a breakout and ordered the Luftwaffe to begin an airlift and von Manstein to mount a ground rescue operation. It was Stalingrad all over again, on a somewhat smaller scale. Von Manstein was determined not to repeat the mistakes of Stalingrad, but it would take several days to organize a relief effort and, in the meantime, he had to create a new frontline in the vacuum south of the Soviet encirclement. Both Konev and Vatutin began pushing infantry units into the corridor to hold the ring around Gruppe Stemmermann, while the 29 TC advanced to expand the ring before the Germans could rush units to the new front.

Von Vormann's XXXXVII Panzerkorps was able to organize a small relief effort fairly quickly with 11.Panzer-Division, which had 22 Panthers, three Pz IV and 13 assault guns, but just 1,000 Panzergrenadiers. A small Kampfgruppe from 13.Panzer-Division could also participate. On the morning of 1 February, von Vormann attacked and his Panthers easily sliced through two Soviet rifle divisions which had not yet dug in. In six hours, 11.Panzer-Division advanced 31km over the frozen terrain and reached the Shpolka River at Iskrennoye, less than 20km from Gruppe Stemmermann. However, when the Panthers attempted to cross a bridge over the river it collapsed, bringing the advance to a halt. Von Vormann was able to bring up pioniers to build a bridge for his StuG-IIIs, but AOK 8 lacked material to build a 60-ton pontoon bridge for the Panthers. Hitler also intervened in von Vormann's relief operation, ordering him to wait since he was transferring the 24.Panzer-Division (which only had 17 tanks and 14 StuG IIIs) from the Nikopol bridgehead to reinforce him. Since this division was nearly 300km away and had to move via its own tracks, this was a remarkably stupid idea that helped to delay XXXXVII Panzerkorps when

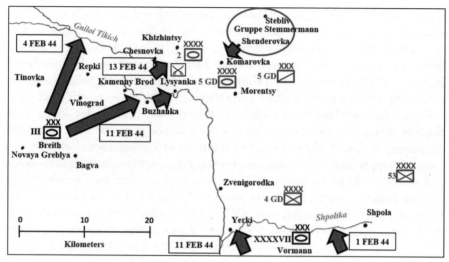

German effort to relieve the Korsun Pocket, 1–16 February 1944.

it had a brief window of opportunity. Instead, Hitler should have helped von Vormann to get bridging material forward, but the Führer was not interested in pontoon bridges. Instead, von Vormann paused at Iskrennoye, which allowed the Soviets to move the 29 TC and 49th Rifle Corps to block any further advance. Exacerbating von Vormann's problems, temperatures rose to 5 degrees C (41 degrees F) which caused the ground to thaw, reducing mobility. Although von Vormann would continue to try and advance toward Gruppe Stemmermann for the next two weeks, he achieved no further significant advances.

Meanwhile, von Manstein did not immediately cancel Operation *Vatutin* against Katukov's 1 TA, but by 30 January he ordered Hube to transfer Breith's III Panzerkorps to mount a second relief operation from the southwest, which was designated Operation *Wanda*. Due to the muddy roads caused by the thaw and the difficulty extracting armoured units from the ongoing battles, it took longer than expected to assemble Breith's III Panzerkorps for Operation *Wanda*. Breith's corps initially consisted of the 16. and 17.Panzer-Divisionen, Schwere Panzer-Regiment Bäke and s.Pz.Abt.506 with a total of 105 tanks (48 Panthers, 41 Pz IV and 16 Tigers) and 21 assault guns. On the morning of 4 February, both Panzer-Divisionen attacked side-by-side, with two infantry divisions in support. Although the Soviet 104th Rifle Corps put up tough resistance and mines hindered the German advance, Breith's two Panzer-Divisionen were able to advance nearly 19km on the first day. Vatutin committed Kravchenko's 6 TA and an anti-tank brigade to block Breith's panzers on the Gniloy Tikich, which was normally a minor obstacle but now widened by rain and melting snow. By the second day of *Wanda*, Breith's forces ran into Soviet armour and indecisive tank skirmishing cost both sides vehicles. Despite reinforcements from 1.Panzer-Division and *LSSAH*, Breith's advance was brought to a halt for a week. The Soviets had learned that the way to halt a German armoured drive was to constantly attack both flanks of a salient, which forced the Germans to divert troops to prevent from being cut off. Although this cost Kravchenko's 6 TA many of its tanks, Vatutin received regular replacements – unlike the Germans. Furthermore, the lack of engineer support made it difficult to get heavy tanks across the Gniloi Tikich and Bäke's panzers ran out of ammunition and fuel by the second day of the operation. Breith blamed the mud for reducing his mobility, but this tended to be a standard German excuse whenever a poorly-planned operation began to unravel. In Russia and the Ukraine, there was always mud.

By 6 February, both German relief efforts had been halted, 35–40km short of the Korsun pocket. Unlike Stalingrad, Gruppe Stemmermann was in no danger of starving to death, but Soviet pressure on the pocket was inexorably squeezing the defenders and forcing them to consume their ammunition. By 10 February, it was clear that Gruppe Stemmermann could not simply wait for relief and had to take some measures to increase the odds of a link-up with either Breith's or von Vormann's forces. Stemmermann decided to reposition his best division, *Wiking*, to be prepared to attack toward III Panzerkorps at the appropriate moment. SS-Brigadeführer Otto Gille's *Wiking* had about 20 operational tanks (Pz III/IV) and several assault guns, as well as 47 artillery pieces (including 9 Wespe and 3 Hummel).

Meanwhile, Breith's III Panzerkorps was stuck in the mud south of the Gniloi Tikich. Recognizing that Vatutin had blocked his current axis of advance, he decided to regroup and attack eastward, where enemy defences were thinner. By this point, Breith had 140 tanks (incl. 80 Panthers and 12 Tigers) and 14 assault guns. On the morning of 11 February, Breith attacked with Bäke's heavy tanks in the lead and advanced 8km in two hours. Within five hours, the Panthers had succeeded in capturing a bridge over the Gniloi Tikich at Frankovka. At this point, Breith decided to employ two *schwerpunkte* in his advance toward Gruppe Stemmermann: Kampfgruppe Bäke would advance northeast while Kampfgruppe Frank from 1. Panzer-Division (one battalion with 28 Panthers and one SPW battalion) would advance east to Lisyanka. With two spearheads advancing toward the pocket, Breith hoped to find weak spots in the Soviet defences. Frank succeeded in capturing Lisyanka in a night attack, before fuel shortages forced both him and Bäke to halt their advance. Both German spearheads were virtually out of fuel and had to waste the next day waiting for the supply units to catch up along the muddy roads.* One German supply column moving forward was shot up by Soviet units that had been

---

* Either von Manstein or Hube could have anticipated these supply problems and ensured that III Panzerkorps was provided with tracked RSO supply vehicles which could move through mud, or coordinate with the Luftwaffe to provide the panzer spearheads with air

bypassed in the rapid advance, indicating that Bäke's lines of communication were not secure.

Vatutin always seemed to have another card up his sleeve and now he introduced General-leytenant Semyon I. Bogdanov's 2nd Tank Army (3 TC, 16 TC, 11 GTB), which had been in the RVGK until a week before. Bogdanov moved four tank brigades directly into Breith's path on 12 February, while the German spearheads were immobilized by lack of fuel. The German two-wheel drive Opel Blitz used by the supply echelons were virtually immobilized by the Ukrainian mud and proved to be the Achilles' Heel of the relief effort. In addition, Kravchenko's remaining armour and infantry from the 40th Army continued to attack Breith's exposed flanks, which was a constant irritant. On 13 February, Breith finally had enough fuel to resume his advance and now von Manstein told him that it was 'now, or never' – he must reach Gruppe Stemmermann before it was crushed. Bäke advanced with 10 Tigers and 10 Panthers, followed by Kamfgruppe Frank from 1.Panzer-Division. Near the village of Dadushkovka, Bäke's panzers ran into T-34s from Polkovnik Roman A. Lieberman's 50th Tank Brigade (3 TC). One platoon of T-34s made the amateur mistake of trying to engage Tigers from a distance of 1,800 meters and paid for this ignorance in blood. However, the other T-34s were more cunning and remained in defilade positions near anti-tank guns, which forced the German panzers to get in much closer, where the T-34s could occasionally score. The tank battle lasted more than an hour, with the Germans claiming another Soviet tank brigade destroyed, but five Tigers and four Panthers were knocked out, leaving Bäke with just 10–11 functional tanks. Although Bäke managed to advance another 12km and reached Khizhintsy, he was still 10km from the pocket and once again out of fuel.

Konev's forces captured the Korsun airfield on 13 February, abruptly terminating the Luftwaffe airlift. It was clear that Gruppe Stemmermann could only last a few more days. On 14 February, as a desperate expedient, Luftwaffe Ju-52s flew low over his tanks and dropped drums of petrol in the mud, most of which burst. Bäke received just enough fuel to make a small advance, but he could not reach the pocket and he was stopped by intense enemy resistance on Hill 239. That day, the thaw ended and it began to snow again, which hardened the ground. Kampfgruppe Bäke and Kampfgruppe Frank sparred with Bogdanov's armour near Lisyanka, claiming another 19 T-34s from 5 GTC and some Shermans from 5 GMC, but four Tigers and three Panthers were damaged. With ammunition and fuel nearly exhausted and barely 20 tanks still operational, Breith's relief effort ground to a halt at Lisyanka on 15 February. Vatutin simply ordered Bogdanov to place more tanks and anti-tank guns to bar any further advance, while the remainder of his forces and Konev's reduced

---

drops, but they only made minimal efforts to ensure Breith got fuel and ammunition to his forward units. German operational planning during *Wanda* was sub-par.

the pocket. One of the units that arrived to reinforce the 16 TC was Polkovnik Nikolai S. Grishin's 13th Guards Heavy Tank Regiment, equipped with 21 IS-1 (IS-85) heavy tanks, equipped with the same 85mm D-5T as the KV-85. These heavy tanks were committed into action on 15 February and unwisely attacked Kampfgruppe Bäke instead of sitting on the defence; the Panthers and Tigers knocked virtually all of them out. Following this incident, the GABTU resolved to upgrade the new IS-series heavy tanks to the 122mm gun.

Finally recognizing that relief would not arrive in time, Stemmermann resolved to conduct a breakout operation on the night of 16–17 February to reach III Panzerkorps. In order to gain a springboard for the breakout, Stemmermann launched a series of night attacks from 11–13 February which captured the towns of Shanderovka and Nova Buda from the besieging 27th Army. Attacking at night wearing winter camouflage uniforms, the German infantry caught the Soviet trops by surprise and succeeded in getting a bit closer to III Panzerkorps at Lisyanka. During the day, Konev attempted to retake these towns, but *Wiking's* last tanks and assault guns, led by SS-Sturmbannführer Hans Köller, fought them off and defended the breakout assembly areas.[17]

Kampfgruppe Frank and Kampfgruppe Bäke made one last push to Oktaybr on 16 February, destroying part of another Soviet tank brigade but losing more Tigers and Panthers in the process. Frank's Panthers encountered KV-85s from the 13th Guards Heavy Tank Regiment, attached to the 16 TC, which was an unpleasant surprise.[18] Gruppe Stemmermann's lines were 7km away. Stemmermann's breakout began at 2300 hours on 16 February and initially went quiet well, as infantry from the 72.Infanterie-Division infiltrated through the Soviet cordon, which was held by elements of 5 GTA. However, the Soviets soon detected the breakout and all hell broke loose as the night sky was lit by flares and artillery fire. *Wiking* tried to break out with 11,500 troops, seven tanks and three assault guns, but was engaged by Soviet tanks and anti-tank guns. Although the combat troops maintained some semblance of discipline, many of the support troops panicked and scattered, or caused traffic jams with the vehicle columns. Stemmermann was killed in the stampede and Soviet cavalry appeared out of the woods to cut up the rear echelons. Thousands of German troops reached the Gniloi Tikich River on foot and were forced to cross this obstacle, which ended up with hundreds drowned or frozen to death. Soviet tanks fired into the horde at the river's edge, causing further panic. In the end, 35,199 Germans managed to flee the Korsun pocket and reach III Panzerkorps, but about 19,000 were killed or captured.[19] Gruppe Stemmermann abandoned all its artillery and vehicles in the pocket, including 20 tanks and 30 assault guns. *Wiking* lost over 3,000 men in the breakout and took six months to refit.

The relief effort cost the German Panzer-Divisionen involved dearly, with III. Panzerkorps and XXXXVII Panzerkorps suffering a total of over 4,000 casualties. Breith's III.Panzerkorps lost 156 tanks and assault guns during the relief effort and was left with only 60 tanks and six StuG IIIs operational. Approximately

56 per cent of the losses were due to mechanical defects, particularly with the problematic Panther (at least 15 of 37 lost in III Panzerkorps suffered engine problems and were destroyed). Indeed, on 29 February 171 of the 187 Panthers in PzAOK 1 were under repair. Von Vormann's XXXXVII Panzerkorps had lost about 80 tanks and assault guns and was left with 32 operational tanks and 27 assault guns. The combination of muddy roads and limited recovery vehicles meant that when the relief forces retreated to new defensive lines, many non-operational tanks were blown up rather than allowed to fall into enemy hands. In order to save part of five trapped divisions, von Manstein had expended his armoured reserves.

At one stroke, Vatutin and Konev had removed two corps from Heeresgrupe Süd's order of battle and incapacitated most of the German armour in the Ukraine, which made it virtually impossible for von Manstein to hold any kind of frontline. In the aftermath of Korsun, von Manstein was primarily focused on shoring up the left flank of Heeresgruppe Süd held by PzAOK 4, which was holding a 240km front with 12 depleted divisions. The gap between Heeresgruppe Süd's left flank and Heeresgruppe Mitte's right flank was only screened by the XIII Armeekorps, which failed to prevent Vatutin's 13th Army from seizing the cities of Rovno and Lutsk on 5 February. Indeed, there was little from preventing Vatutin from driving due west into Poland. However, von Manstein's right flank was also on the verge of collapse. The transfer of the 24.Panzer-Division to support the Korsun relief effort had weakened the German defence of the Nikopol bridgehead at a critical moment. On 2 February, Malinovsky's 3rd Ukrainian Front attacked the left flank of Hollidt's AOK 6 east of Krivoi Rog and quickly achieved a breakthrough that the Germans lacked the armoured reserves to block. Within 24 hours, the Soviets captured the vital rail junction at Apostolovo and threatened to isolate the IV and XVII Armeekorps in the Nikopol bridgehead. Hollidt was forced to abandon Nikpol on 7 February and retreat westward to avoid encirclement. Even when the 24. Panzer-Division was returned to Hollidt, it had lost most of its tanks and 55 per cent of its trucks in the fruitless march north to join the Korsun relief effort.

Meanwhile, the Soviets were able to replenish the 1st and 2nd Ukrainian Fronts within two weeks of the end of the Korsun battle and Zhukov was eager to press on and finish off Heeresgruppe Sud before it could be reinforced. However, Vatutin was badly wounded by Ukraininan partisans on 28 February and died six weeks later; Zhukov temporarily took command of the front. The loss of Vatutin was a serious blow to the Red Army since he had become one of its most skilled practitioners of combined arms warfare. In comparison, Konev and most of the other front commanders tended to rely more on firepower than manoeuvre or deception. Zhukov immediately began preparing for the next round and using his clout with the Stavka, he managed to acquire the 4th Tank Army (6 GMC, 10 GTC) from the RVGK; this formation was under the command of General-leytenant Vasily M. Badanov, who had led the Tatsinskaya Raid in December 1942. In addition, Zhukov was able to get replacements for the 1 TA and 3 GTA, although neither could be brought up to full strength.

On 4 March, Zhukov's 1st Ukrainian Front attacked the boundary between PzAOK 4 and PzAOK 1, while Konev's 2nd Ukraininan Front attacked the boundary between PzAOK 1 and AOK 8. Zhukov's three tank armies attacked east of Tarnopol and made good progress, despite the efforts of the *LSSAH*, 7.Panzer-Division and s.Pz.Abt.503 (13 Tigers) to block the advance. Konev had even more success, attacking the XXXXVII Panzerkorps and VII Armeekorps in the area south of Lisiyanka with the 2 TA and 6 TA. A total of five Soviet tank armies were involved in the operation. Without adequate armoured reserves to opposive the 5 GTA, Wöhler was compelled to retreat or face envelopment, but Hube held most of his ground, centred on Proskurov. In 10 days, Konev's forces advanced 90km toward the Dnestr River. Hitler ordered von Manstein to stand fast, even though it was apparent the front was collapsing. Zhukov's forces were on the outskirts of Tarnopol, which Hitler declared to be a fortress and ordered held.

In the south, Malinovsky's 3rd Ukraininan Front attacked Hollidt's AOK 6 south of Krivoi Rog on the morning of 6 March and the 8th Guards Army achieved a major breakthrough the next day. Demonstrating great agility, the 8 GA punched through the XXIX Armeekorps, shoving aside the burnt-out 23. Panzer-Division, which had only four tanks, one assault gun and six SPWs. Soviet tanks and cavalry – not seriously impeded by the mud – advanced boldly to AOK 6's headquarters in Novy Bug and overran many German rear-echelon units. The 23.Panzer-Division was virtually destroyed, losing all its maintenance, medical and logistic units, as well as many of its vehicles.[20] The Soviets then pivoted south to envelope five German infantry divisions from the IV Armeekorps and the 9.Panzer-Division. This trapped force was dubbed Gruppe Wittmann and since no rescue force was available, it was compelled to fight its way out of encirclement over the course of the next several weeks. Soon, all of AOK 6 was forced to retreat to avoid being cut off by fast-moving Soviet armoured spearheads. The 24.Panzer-Division fought a rearguard action, but lost over 800 men and one-quarter of its wheeled vehicles, which were immobilized by deep mud. By 13 March, AOK 6 formed a composite Panzergruppe with the remaining tanks of the 9., 23. and 24.Panzer-Divisionen – three tanks – to cover the retreat.[21] Fuel shortages plagued the Germans during the retreat, forcing them to abandon a great deal of equipment. *Totenkopf* ran out of fuel at Balta, just short of the Dnestr, on 27 March and when the Soviets overran the town, the division was forced to abandon over 60 tanks and assault guns, as well as 1,000 wheeled vehicles.[22] The last seven Tigers were blown up near Tiraspol by their crews on 2 April. By the time *Totenkopf* crossed the Dnestr into Romania, it had no tanks left.

Von Manstein expected the 1st Ukrainian Front to head west toward L'vov, so he strengthened Raus' PzAOK 4 at the expense of Hube's PzAOK 1. In fact, Zhukov and Konev struck southward on 18 March, breaking through on both of Hube's flanks. On 17 March, the 2 TA reached the Dnestr River at Yampol. On 20 March, Katukov's 1 TA re-entered the battle with 140 tanks and severed the last remaining links between Hube's army and Raus' PzAOK 4. At the same time, Konev unleashed Kravchenko's 6 TA, which captured Mogilev-Podol'skiy on the Dniestr. The PzAOK 4 was in retreat and Gruppe Neinhoff, with 4,600 troops, was encircled in Tarnopol by the 1 GA. With his flanks demolished, Hube began falling back toward Kamenets-Podol'skiy, but Katukov severed his communications to the west, then managed to seize a bridgehead across the Dnestr. On 27 March, the 10 GTC from Badanov's 4 TA captured Kamenets-Podol'skiy, which left Hube in a shrinking salient with his back to the Dnestr. He was cut off from the one remaining German-held bridge over the Dnestr at Khotin and the Luftwaffe began an airlift to supply him.

The encirclement of Hube's PzAOK 1 was the largest catastrophe facing the Wehrmacht since Stalingrad. Hube's army comprised over 200,000 troops in 10 Panzer-Divisionen (*LSSAH, Das Reich*, 1, 6, 7, 11, 16, 17, 19), one Panzergrenadier-Division (20), 12 infantry divisions, one artillery division, s.Pz.Abt.509 and s.Panzerjäger-Abteilung 88 (Nashorn).* Although the army only had 35 operational tanks when it was surrounded, the loss of the veteran personnel would effectively cost Germany half her trained tankers. After much arguing with Hitler, von Manstein finally convinced him that Hube had to break out of encirclement or Heeresgruppe Süd's front would collapse. Although it was possible that Hube could have crossed the Dnestr, this would have made it very difficult for von Manstein to establish a new front. Instead, Hube was ordered to attack westward, where a relief force would assemble near the town of Berezhany. Hube reorganized his forces for combat, dividing all his units into two main assault formations: *Korpsgruppe von der Chevallerie* (1., 6., 7., 11. 16, 19.Panzer-Divisionen and *LSSAH*, plus six infantry divisions) and *Korpsgruppe Breith* (*Das Reich* and *17.Panzer-Division*, plus seven infantry divisions). Unlike previous pockets where the entrapped forced remained stationary in order to receive air resupply, Hube did not intend to remain tied to airfields since he knew that Zhukov would soon assemble overwhelming forces around the pocket to prevent escape or rescue. Instead, Hube intended to fight his way through the Soviet encirclement and rely upon parachuted supplies. Having learned quite a bit about supplying encircled forces, the Luftwaffe sent a special team (*Kesseltrupp*) into the pocket equipped with air-ground

---

* On 27 January 1944, Hitler ordered the Sd.Kfz.164 'Hornisse' tank destroyer renamed as the 'Nashorn'. This vehicle was similar to the Sd.Kfz.165 'Hummel' self-propelled 15cm howitzer, since both were based on the Pz IV chassis.

radios, beacons and flares in order to mark drop zones as needed.[23] Hube ordered all unnecessary or damaged vehicles destroyed, in order to reduce his army's fuel requirements. On 28 March, Hube began attacking westward with *Korpsgruppe Breith*.

Badanov's 4 TA was the main force blocking Hube's escape, with his 10 GTC holding the vital road junction at Kamenets-Podol'skiy and the 6 GMC located just west of there. Although Badanov only had about 100 tanks left, he still had plenty of infantry, artillery and anti-tank guns with him. The 10 GTC formed a hedgehog in Kamenets-Podol'skiy which blocked the main routes across the Smotrich River, a tributary of the Dnestr. Rather than assaulting the Soviet strongpoint, the 17.Panzer-Division seized a crossing site over the Smotrich north of Kamenets-Podol'skiy and Hube's army crossed over there. In the process, the 10 GTC itself was temporarily surrounded at Kamenets-Podol'skiy and Badanov, trying to stop the German breakout, was badly wounded on 29 March. The experienced General-leytenant Dmitri K. Lelyushenko was brought in to take command of 4 TA, but there was little that he could do but try to delay the breakout.

Initially, Zhukov was over-confident about the Kamenets-Podol'skiy pocket and simply assumed that Hube's PzAOK would sit put. Instead of reinforcing Badanov, Zhukov sent Katukov's 1 TA to capture Chernovtsy on 30 March and focused most of his effort on preventing any German units from escaping south across the Dnestr. He also committed the bulk of the 60th Army to reducing the German fortress of Tarnopol, even though the garrison was less than 5,000 troops. Both Zhukov and Konev used their infantry armies to compress the northern side of the pocket, but paid little attention to the western side of the pocket. At the same time, Hitler was furious that both Heeresgruppe Süd and Heeresgruppe A were in retreat and he opted to sack both von Manstein and von Kleist, whom he had lost faith in. In the case of von Manstein, the relief was not unjustified since von Manstein had consistently failed to anticipate enemy actions since Kursk and seemed more interested in retreats than counter-attacks. In their place, Hitler substituted Generalfeldmarschall Walter Model to command Heeresgruppe Süd and Schörner to command Heeresgruppe A. However, the immediate impact on the battle was negligible and both army groups continued to retreat.

By 31 March, Hube was advancing steadily westward and pushing back Lelyushenko's over-extended 4 TA (part of which was still encircled at Kamenets-Podol'skiy). Recognizing that Hube was escaping westward and not southward as expected, Zhukov ordered Katukov to bring part of 1 TA back north of the Dnestr to assist 4 TA. Nevertheless, Zhukov did not move any significant infantry forces into this area to strengthen the defence, which enabled Hube's desperate forces to continue pushing westward. By 4 April, Hube's army was approaching the Strypa River at Buchach. Meanwhile, Model was assembling the relief force near Berezhany, 60km away, consisting of Hausser's II.

SS-Panzerkorps (9.SS-Panzer-Division *Hohenstaufen* and 10.SS Panzer-Division *Frundsberg*), schwere Panzerjäger-Abteilung 653 (with 28 rebuilt Ferdinands) and two infantry divisions. Hausser's two SS-Panzer-Divisionen had been training in France, but they were not fully equipped as Panzer-Division. Instead, each only had two companies Pz IVs and two batteries of StuG-IIIs, a total of 98 medium tanks and 88 assault guns. Nevertheless, by 6 April Hausser was attacking eastward toward Buchach to meet Hube.

In the end, the skill and desperation of Hube's troops to escape and Zhukov's failure to bolt the door decided the battle in the German favour. With the 6. and 7.Panzer-Divisionen in the lead, *Korpsgruppe Breith* fought its way through the Soviet cordon. Belatedly, Zhukov tried to shift six rifle divisions and the 2 GTC into Hube's path, but 17.Panzer-Division fended them off long enough for the rest of the army to reach the Strypa River. On 8 April, the 6.Panzer-Division and two Tigers from the s.Pz.Abt.509 fought their way into Buchach and shortly thereafter, linked up with elements of II.SS-Panzerkorps. It took almost a week for all of Hube's exhausted army to cross the Strypa River, but then it was able to form a new continuous front with PzAOK 4. In terms of equipment, PzAOK 1 was in extremely poor shape with barely two dozen tanks left (one Tiger), a few assault guns and seven Nashorns. The escape of Hube's PzAOK 1 from encirclement at Kamenets-Podol'skiy was one of the great operational achievements of the Second World War, since it prevented the complete collapse of the German southern flank, at least for the time being. While Winston Churchill – speaking of Dunkirk – was correct that retreats do not equal victories, the successful breakout of Hube's army was nevertheless a huge morale boost for the Wehrmacht.

There were two important tactical postscripts to the Korsun Pocket and Hube's Pocket, both of which reflected the growing importance of German armour being used to rescue trapped garrisons. In the first case, the survivors of Gille's *Wiking* division's breakout from Korsun were sent to the Cholm-Kovel region in eastern Poland to regroup. Barely a month after arriving in Poland, a new Soviet offensive by the 2nd Byelorussian Front's 47th Army encircled the city on 15 March, trapping over 4,000 troops. Although *Wiking's* troops were outside the pocket, they had negligible combat capability. Nevertheless, a relief effort was hastily organized. The II./SS-Panzer-Regiment 5 had just arrived at Cholm after re-equipping with Panther tanks, but only one company was combat-ready and it was committed to lead the relief effort. By 21 March, Soviet Sherman tanks fought their way into Kovel and the city could fall at any time. On 27 March, a scratch relief force was assembled at Lukov, west of Kovel, consisting of an SS Kampfgruppe (17 Panthers and III./SS-Panzer-Grenadier-Regiment *Germania*) and a Heer Kampfgruppe (7 StuG IIIs and Grenadier-Regiment 343). The direct route to Kovel led through a frozen marsh crossed by a railroad track, which was blocked by the 60th Rifle Division, a battery of anti-tank guns and mines. The Waffen-SS opted for the direct approach and attacked at midday on 28 March, during a blizzard. No artillery support was available due to communication problems – one of the most common forms of friction in war.[24] Soviet 76.2mm anti-tank guns were sited at a right angle to the road and managed to destroy three Panthers with flank shots into their thinner side armour. When the Panthers tried to manoeuvre off road, 10 of the remaining 14 became bogged down in the soft terrain, which halted the relief effort. Recovering 10 Panthers from bog-like terrain with only a single Bergepanther consumed more than a day and the Heer troops were not sanguine about trying to push further with such a small force. Nor did the column have any pioniers to clear mines along the road. Nonplussed, the SS Panzer-Kompanie commander opted to go on alone and with a column of just nine Panthers he boldly advanced through the Soviet lines on the night of 29–30 March, losing two to mines, but then reached the city. However, this effort failed to lift the siege and only added a handful of tanks to the trapped garrison.[25]

On 2 April, the rest of the II.SS-Pz.-Rgt.5 began arriving by rail with 59 more Panthers and a larger relief effort was assembled, including Kampfgruppen from 4. and 5.Panzer-Divisionen. On 4 April, the second relief attempt began and the Soviets desperately tried to stop it. Untersturmführer Renz, leader of the reconnaissance platoon from the II./SS-Pz.Abt.5, described the final lunge toward Kovel:

During our next forward move, we took a hit, which, luckily, only rattled our Panzer. My gunner reacted with lightning speed. I directed him, patting his shoulder with my right hand, exactly to the target. With 'Explosive shell – 800 metres – cluster of buildings, Pak position in front – fire!' we began the firefight. Our first shot was dead-on. A huge cloud of dust, mixed with fragments of trees and building material, rose into the sky. Being the point Panzer, I directed the fire of the whole 6.Kompanie by radio. Grossrock followed my gunner with the fire from his five Panthers, and within a few minutes we managed to stop the fire from the Paks and the tanks. Afterwards it was determined that we had destroyed several tanks, approximately ten Paks, and numerous heavy and light machine guns.[26]

After blasting their way through the cordon of tanks and anti-tank guns, the *Wiking's* Panthers reached Kovel on 5 April. However, only a tenuous line of communication existed to Kovel and since Hitler would not countenance evacuating the city, *Wiking's* limited forces were committed to widening the corridor for the next three weeks. The *Wiking* Panthers gradually pushed the Soviet infantry back from the western side of the city, but mines and anti-tank guns wore down the SS-Panzer-Regiment 5's strength.[27] Yet Hitler was pleased, since Kovel was held for another four months. As with Korsun, even when a relief effort was successful, the cost in armour was often much higher than the benefits gained.

The other major relief effort during this period was Model's attempted relief of Gruppe Neinhoff in Tarnopol. Model knew that it was important for front-line morale not to write-off trapped garrisons and once Hube's PzAOK 1 was re-integrated into the front he managed to assemble a fairly large relief force by 10 April and selected Hermann Balck's XXXXVIII Panzerkorps to command the operation. The main assault element was SS-Gruppenführer Wilhelm Bittrich's 9. SS-Panzer-Division *Hohenstaufen*, which contributed a battalion of Pz IVs (II./SS-Pz.Rgt.9), a battalion of StuG-IIIs, a reconnaissance battalion, a battalion of Panzergrenadiers in SPWs (III.SS-Pz.Gr.Rgt.19), five other infantry battalions and a self-propelled artillery battalion (6x Hummel and 12x Wespe). Significantly, two-thirds of *Hohenstaufen*'s infantry were on foot, lacking motor transport. In addition, the 8.Panzer-Division contributed Kampfgruppe Friebe (I./Pz.Rgt.10) with 21 Panthers and its SPW battalion (I./Pz.Gr.Rgt.79), s.Pz.Abt.507 added 12 Tigers and s.Pz.Jg.Abt.653 contributed 28 Ferdinands. Altogether, the relief force had 64 tanks, 27 assault guns and 2,000 infantrymen, although it was short of pionier support. Balck kicked off his attack on 11 April from a bridgehead over the Strypa River, but soon ran into stiff resistance from the Soviet 60th Army, which had deployed numerous anti-tank guns and mines along the route. Heavy spring rains turned the soil into mud so deep that German tanks 'bellied out' with their hulls, greatly reducing mobility. The 52nd Guards Tank Brigade from the 6 GTC (3 GTA) counter-attacked the German column with some of the new T-34/85 tanks, which was an unpleasant surprise for *Hohenstaufen*'s Pz IVs. Even two Ferdinands were destroyed with flank shots.[28] In six days of heavy combat, Balck's relief force advanced halfway toward Tarnopol, but lost 13 Pz IVs, two Tigers and 21 StuG-IIIs. The Germans claimed to have knocked out 74 Soviet tanks and 21 anti-tank guns.[29] In an impressive display of front-line leadership, Model personally came forward to evaluate the operation's progress, riding in a Sd.Kfz.251 command track. Nevertheless, it was clear by 15 April that the relief effort had bogged down short of its objective and the Soviets were rapidly reinforcing this sector with more armour. Model finally decided to abort the relief operation 8km short of Tarnopol and he ordered Gruppe Neinhoff to attempt a breakout operation before the town was overrun. Before dawn on 16 April, about 1,300 survivors of the garrison attempted to infiltrate through the Soviet cordon but only 55 reached the positions held by Balck's XXXXVIII Panzerkorps. Neinhoff was killed in the breakout, as were most of his troops.

Following the efforts to relieve Kovel and Tarnopol, the Germans gained a brief respite due to the spring thaw. Both sides were also exhausted by 10 months of near-continuous fighting. On 4 April, the OKH decided to redesignate Heeresgruppe Süd as Heeresgruppe Nordukraine, with control of PzAOK 1, PzAOK 4 and the 1st Hungarian Army. Heeresgruppe Südukraine was created to control AOK 8, AOK 6, AOK 17 (in the Crimea) and what was left of the Romanian army. Interestingly, the Wehrmacht no longer remained on Ukrainian soil and Heeresgruppe Süd had been split into two pieces. Model believed that once the Soviets rebuilt their tank armies their main effort in the summer would be directed against his army group around L'vov and he used his influence to push for strong Panzer reinforcements to rebuild his command.

Defence of the Dniester Line, 5 April–15 May 1944

By the beginning of April 1944, Heeresgruppe Süd appeared to be broken in two and the Stavka regarded the liberation of the Ukraine as nearly complete. Although all the Soviet fronts were worn down by months of heavy combat, Stalin was eager to continue a broad front advance to seize as much territory as possible before the Germans regained their balance. Given that all four tank armies in the 1st and 2nd Ukrainian Fronts were reduced to 25 per cent or less of their authorized tank strength, a prudent course of action might have been to focus the remaining combat power on one axis of advance and temporarily shift to the defence elsewhere. Yet Stalin was not interested in prudence. He was interested in gaining as much territory as quickly as possible, before the Allies landed in France. Stalin ordered Zhukov's 1st Ukrainian Front to continue advancing westward toward L'vov and Konev's 2nd Ukrainian Front to move south into Romania, which meant the two strongest Soviet fronts assumed divergent courses and would no longer be within supporting range. Stalin regarded Romania as a particularly tempting target due to the Third Reich's dependence upon the Ploesti oil fields and he believed that it was open for the taking.

On 5 April, the Stavka ordered Konev to advance into northern Romania with his 27th and 40th Armies, supported by Bogdanov's 2 TA, to capture the frontier cities of Jassy and Kishinev.[30] The Stavka ordered Malinovsky's 3rd Ukrainian Front to assist Konev with the advance into Romania, although the bulk of

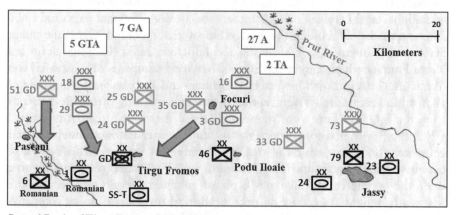

Second Battle of Tirgu Fromos, 2 May 1944.

Malinovsky's forces were focused on liberating the port of Odessa. Bogdanov could only field about 120 tanks between his 3 TC and 16 TC, but Stalin promised to send reinforcements. However just prior to Konev's offensive, the Stavka pulled Kravchenko's 6 TA back into reserve to refit, followed by Rotmistrov's 5 GTA, leaving very little armour at the front. Consequently, Konev's advance across the Dniester River into northern Romania began primarily with infantry on foot, supported by fewer than 200 tanks and a bare minimum of artillery support. In effect, the Stavka was repeating the same kind of mistake that it had previously made with Operations Star and Gallop in early 1943.

There was no doubt that the German and Romanian forces were disorganized after their precipitate retreat from the Ukraine, but Wöhler's AOK 8 was able to coalesce around Kishinev with five Panzer-Divisionen (*Totenkopf*, 3., 11., 13. and 14.Panzer-Divisionen) that proved to be a serious obstacle. At Jassy, the XXXXVII Panzerkorps concentrated *Großdeutschland*, 23. and 24.Panzer-Divisionen to block an advance by the under-strength 2 TA. In these sectors, the Germans were aided by rough terrain that favoured the defence and rainy weather that greatly slowed the Soviet advance. Inside Romania, the German units had simplified supply lines and received ample supplies of fuel and ammunition.

Nevertheless, the 27th Army advanced fairly rapidly into northern Romania, easily dispersing small Romanian rearguards and its 3rd Guards Rifle Corps (3 GRC) was able to capture the vital road junction at Tirgu Fromos on 9 April. Wöhler reacted by ordering *Großdeutschland* to conduct an immediate counter-attack in conjunction with the Romanian IV Army Corps to retake the town. Despite its involvement in heavy combat since *Zitadelle*, the *Großdeutschland* was one of the few mechanized units on the Eastern Front that the OKH had kept up to strength; in this, the fact that the division could recruit from across Germany, like the Waffen-SS, gave it an advantage over the Heer's other Panzer-Divisionen, whose replacements were derived from home Wehrkreis. By early April 1944, *Großdeutschland* was still a formidable force with about 45 operational tanks (a mix of Pz IV, Panthers and Tigers), 25 assault guns and 1,600 Panzergrenadiers.[31] Under the leadership of the firebrand Generalleutnant Hasso von Manteuffel, *Großdeutschland* conducted a rapid 40km march toward Tirgu Fromos, which caught the Soviet 27th Army completely by surprise. Von Manteuffel attacked with his Panzergrenadiers and Panzers on the morning of 10 April and recaptured Tirgu Fromos by evening, isolating three rifle divisions from the 3 GRC. Since von Manteuffel lacked the troops to surround the 3 GRC, the Soviet divisions were able to escape, but abandoned much of their equipment. Having cleared the area, von Manteuffel rapidly established a new defensive hedgehog around Tirgu Fromos, with his Panzergrenadiers digging in on the perimeter and his tanks kept as a mobile reserve. Once secure, von Manteuffel mounted an active defence for the next three weeks, using company-size armoured raids to keep Konev's forces off balance.

Surprised by the rebuff at Tirgu Fromos, Konev urged Bogdanov's 2 TA to push toward Podu Iloaie with 3 TC, 16 TC and two rifle divisions. However, the 24.Panzer-Division mounted a series of small armoured counter-attacks on 12–13 April that completely halted Bogdanov's advance. Likewise, the German armour concentration at Jassy fended off all efforts by Bogdanov to move in that direction as well. Further south, the XXXX Panzerkorps mounted a strong defence at Orgeev with the 3., 11. and 13.Panzer-Divisionen which slowed the 4th Guards Army's crossing of the Dniester. By mid–April, Konev was forced to shift to the defence across his front and await replacements to restore his dulled combat capabilities. Consequently, German tactical victories at Tirgu Fromos, Podu Iloaie and Jassy prevented Konev from pushing rapidly into Romania and gave Heeresgruppe Südukraine a short, but valuable respite.

Meanwhile, Malinovsky's 3rd Ukrainian Front succeeded in liberating Odessa on the morning of 10 April, but efforts to encircle the eastern half of AOK 6 with General-leytenant Issa A. Pliev's tank-cavalry mobile group (4 GMC, 4 GCC) failed.[32] Instead, Malinovsky pursued Hollidt's retreating AOK 6 to the Dniester River with four armies and managed to seize a number of small bridgeheads over the river before the Axis defence gelled. However, the Stavka pulled Pliev's cavalry group back to refit and Malinovsky was left only with the depleted 23 TC and a few tank brigades, which were insufficient to expand the bridgeheads. Instead, Axis resistance noticeably stiffened and AOK 6 fortified high ground overlooking the tiny bridgeheads and repulsed all of Malinovsky's attempts to break out for the next several weeks.

Embarrassed by his initial defeats at Tirgu Fromos, Konev used the last half of April to prepare for a second round. He brought up General-polkovnik Mikhail S. Shumilov's relatively fresh 7th Guards Army (seven rifle divisions and the 27 GTB) to be the main battering ram against Wöhler's lines to the west of Tirgu Fromos and Rotmistrov's partly-rebuilt 5 GTA to be the exploitation force. General-leytenant Sergei G. Trofimenko's 27th Army (seven rifle divisions and two tank regiments) would mount a supporting attack northeast of Tirgu Fromos, with Bogdanov's 2 TA ready to exploit a breakthrough. Rotmistrov would deploy the 18 TC and 29 TC with 231 tanks (incl. 183 T-34) and 87 self-propelled guns. In addition, the RVGK reinforced Rotmistrov with the 14th and 53rd Guards Heavy Tank Regiments, each with about 20 of the new JS-2 heavy tanks. Rotmistrov had also received some of the new T-34/85 medium tanks.[33] Boganov's 2 TA was considerably weaker, with the 3 GTC, 16 TC and 11 GTB having a total of just 98 tanks (75 T-34, 16 JS-2 heavy tanks, 5 JS-85 heavy tanks and 2 Churchills) and 23 self-propelled guns (18 SU-152 and 5 SU-85).[34] Due to the lack of combat-ready independent tank brigades, Konev was forced to use both 5 GTA and 2 TA in the infantry support role, which left him with no armoured reserve for exploitation. Nevertheless, Konev could commit nearly 500 AFVs in his two tank armies, which he believed provided him with a 4–1 or better numerical superiority in armour. Assisted by three artillery divisions, Konev expected to blast his way through Wöhler's front and push on deep into the interior of Romania.

In fact, Konev's offensive planning was based upon faulty intelligence. Kirchner's LVII Panzerkorps used the *Großdeutschland* to anchor the defence at Tirgu Fromos, but had to rely upon Romanian units to cover both flanks. The Romanian infantry was poorly equipped and suffered from poor morale, but Brigadier-General Radu Korne's 1st Armoured Division still had some fight left in it. In September 1943 Germany had begun to provide Romania with Pz IV tanks and Korne's division had several dozen Pz IVs and a dozen StuG-III assault guns, as well as some SPWs for its infantry. Von Manteuffel's *Großdeutschland* had 36–39 operational tanks (22 Pz IV, 6–7 Tigers and 8–10 Panthers) in Oberst Willy Langkeit's Panzer-Regiment, and the division still had a number of assault guns.[35] Generalleutnant Maximilian Freiherr von Edelsheim's 24.Panzer-Division, deployed at Podul-Iloaie, was also available to support Kirchner with 15 Pz IVs and nine StuG-IIIs.* Although *Totenkopf* had lost all its tanks and many of its vehicles during the retreat to the Dniester, it had just received some replacements and Wöhler ordered it to form a mobile Kampfgruppe as an operational reserve for LVII Panzerkorps; by evening of 1 May SS-Sturmbannführer Fritz Beiermeier formed a group consisting of 24 Pz IV tanks, II.SS-Pz.Gr.Rgt.6 and a battery of assault guns. The German troops had used the three weeks at Tirgu Fromos wisely, digging in deeply and laying minefields. For once, the Germans had something like a defence in depth and adequate mobile reserves. Furthermore, German intelligence knew where the enemy was about to strike.

At 0515 hours on 2 May, Konev began his offensive with a massive 60-minute artillery barrage that laid waste to some of the enemy's front-line positions. Then at 0615 hours, Shumilov's 7 GA attacked with eight reinforced rifle divisions, followed by waves of tanks from General-major Evgeny I. Fominykh's 29 TC. The Grenadier-Regiment *Großdeutschland* was hard hit and partly overrun, with at least one company nearly destroyed. Interestingly, even in an elite unit like *Großdeutschland*, Panzergrenadiers still relied upon the hand-delivered *Hafthohlladung* (hollow charge magnetic mine) for close-combat with tanks since the new Panzerfaust was not yet available in quantity.

However, Fominykh's tankers failed to spot a battery of concealed assault guns, which blasted the lead Soviet tank battalion from the point-blank range of 300 metres. Then von Manteuffel committed Langkeit's Panzer-Regiment *Großdeutschland* in an expertly-executed counter-attack, which virtually slaughtered the remainder of Fominykh's T-34s. As the Soviet attack ebbed, Langkeit's Panzers came under long-range fire from 13 JS-2 heavy tanks from the 14th Guards Separate Heavy Tank Regiment.[36] Langkeit brought

---

* Von Edelsheim commanded Panzergrenadier-Regiment 26 in the original 24.Panzer-Division at Stalingrad but was flown out of the pocket in November 1942.

up Oberleutnant Fritz Stadler's eight Tigers and the first battle between the latest Soviet and German heavy tanks began at a range of over 2,000 metres. Technically, the Soviet 122mm D-25T gun had better penetration than the German 8.8cm KwK 36 at this kind of range, but the Soviet tankers lacked the training to achieve accuracy over this distance. Von Manteuffel saw rounds from the Tigers strike the enemy heavy tanks, but they 'all bounced off.' The IS-2 had a much lower rate of fire than the Tiger and only eight BR-471 APHE rounds each, so they fired sparingly. Stadler decided to move in closer and probably told his crews to switch to Panzergranate 40 APCR with tungsten cores.* This time, from a range of about 1,800 metres, the Tigers were able to destroy four IS-2, which caused the rest to retreat. Langkeit aggressively ordered a company of Pz IVs to pursue the retreating enemy heavy tanks and they were able to close within 1,000 metres and knock out a few more with shots into the rear armour.

While von Manteuffel was focused on his left flank, two more Soviet rifle divisions and General-major Ivan A. Vovchenko's 3 GTC tried to overrun his Füsilier-Regiment. Langkeit sent his other company of Pz IVs to this sector and von Edelsheim also sent part of an armoured Kampfgruppe, which resulted in Vovchenko's tankers being hit on both flanks and losing more than 30 tanks in a one-sided action. Ironically, Shumilov's 7 GA achieved some success west of Tirgu Fromos, where the 8th Guards Airborne Division and the 18 TC succeeded in routing the Romanian 6th Infantry Division. However, Korne moved a battlegroup of his armoured division to prevent a complete collapse in this sector and Konev failed to reinforce his success here.

Northeast of Tirgu Fromos, the Soviet 27th Army attacked the right flank of Füsilier-Regiment *Großdeutschland* and a regiment from the 46.Infanterie-Division with three rifle divisions. Bogdanov supported the attack with about 120 AFV, including 16 JS-2s from the 6th Separate Heavy Tank Regiment. This attack achieved some success, penetrating over 5km into the German line, which caused Bogdanov to commit Dubovoi's 16 TC to exploit the perceived gap. Before noon, the JS-2s drove into the town of Facuti and began to engage German artillery and headquarters troops. This was a tense moment for von Manteuffel, whose own armour was fully engaged at this point. However, von Edelsheim committed both his Kampfgruppen, which attacked into Dubovoi's exposed flank with about 40 tanks and assault guns. Two of Dubovoi's brigades were shot-up, losing perhaps 40 tanks, and the rest of the corps was routed. Amazingly, Kirchner's LVII Panzerkorps had repulsed Konev's offensive and inflicted heavy losses upon the 2 TA and 5 GTA, amounting to about 150–200 tanks and self-propelled guns.[37] Out of about 36 tanks engaged, *Großdeutschland* lost six tanks destroyed and eight damaged.

---

* Most of the tungsten core ammunition had been withdrawn from service after Kursk due to shortage of this vital metal, but Tiger units still received some APCR rounds.

Konev refused to accept that Kirchner's defence around Tirgu Fromos was still solid and decided to renew the attack on 3 May. Massing his remaining armour, infantry and artillery, Konev tried to bash his way through Kirchner's lines on a narrower front, but the 8.8cm flak guns from *Großdeutschland* inflicted a 'tank slaughter' upon Rotmistrov and sharp counter-attacks by the *Großdeutschland*, 24.Panzer-Division and Kampfgruppe Beiermeier from *Totenkopf* repulsed every Soviet attack. After two days of combat, Konev had fewer than 200 AFVs still operational, but he tried again on 4 May; this final surge only resulted in more needless casualties and left's Konev's exhausted and depleted forces over-extended. He decided to shift to the defence and pulled Rotmistrov's 5 GTA back to refit. Bogdanov's 2 TA was reduced to just 35 tanks and 12 self-propelled guns.[38] Sensing the weakness of Konev's front-line units, Kirchner mounted two combined-arms counter-attacks with infantry, panzers and some air support on 7 May, which caught the Soviet 7 GA and 27 Army flat-footed. Both *Großdeutschland* and 24.Panzer-Division were able to recover some key terrain and inflict painful losses on Konev's forces. Following this success, both sides shifted to the defence in northern Romania.

However, the Stavka had hoped that Malinovsky's 3rd Ukrainian Front could mount an offensive across the Dniester from its small Tashlyk bridgehead and set the stage for a push toward Kishinev. Rather than used the depleted units already in the bridgehead, Malinovsky opted to bring up his relatively fresh 8th Guards Army (8 GA) and 5th Shock Army to take their places. It is always dangerous conducting a relief in place under the gaze of an alert enemy and the German 6.Armee (AOK 6), now under General der Artillerie Maximilian de Angelis, spotted what Malinovsky was attempting to do and decided to pre-empt it. General der Panzertruppen Otto von Knobelsdorff formed an assault group based around his XXXX Panzerkorps, comprised of the 3., 13. and 14.Panzer-Divisionen, two assault gun brigades and two infantry divisions. On the morning of 10 May, von Knobelsdorff attacked with all three Panzer-Divisionen on line after an artillery preparation and rapidly penetrated the Soviet perimeter of their bridgehead. General-leytenant Vasily I. Chuikov, hero of Stalingrad, commanded the 8 GA in the bridgehead, but his units were not ready to repel an attack by over 100 German tanks and assault guns. Chuikov had only 10 tanks in the bridgehead and his artillery was very short of ammunition. The Germans struck while Chuikov's divisions were still moving into the bridgehead and they were shattered. In three days of heavy fighting, von Knobelsdorff's Panzers greatly reduced the Soviet bridgehead and inflicted up to 30,000 casualties upon Chuikov's veteran 8 GA; thousands of Soviet soldiers were taken prisoner.[39]

Malinovsky attempted to reduce the pressure on Chuikov's battered 8 GA by ordering the 5th Shock Army to mount a supporting attack across the Dniester, but von Knobelsdorff's assault troops handily defeated this effort and inflicted 20,000 more Soviet casualties. With both Konev's and Malinovsky's fronts defeated, the Stavka had no choice but to postpone a major push into Romania until the summer months. Not only did Heeresgruppe Südukraine conduct a very successful defence, but Wöhler's AOK 8 even continued local attacks in June to disrupt Konev's forces north of Jassy. For the Red Army, once again the danger of continuing offensives with badly depleted forces was made evident, which played to the German strength of striking back at over-extended Soviet spearheads. It was also a very poor idea to use valuable tank armies in the infantry support role. For the Germans, the victory in defending the Dniester in April-May demonstrated the value of a mobile defence and was one of the last occasions where Panzer-Divisionen achieved a significant operational-level success.

Operation Bagration and its Aftermath, 22 June–31 August 1944

Contrary to popular Eastern Front historiography, the Stavka did not ignore Heeresgruppe Mitte during the winter of 1943–44 and mounted several major attacks against the Vitebsk salient held by 3.Panzerarmee (PzAOK 3) and against 4.Armee (AOK 4) at Orsha. Despite some tense moments, Heeresgruppe Mitte's central defences held, even if both flanks were increasingly vulnerable. Nevertheless, Heeresgruppe Mitte still suffered over 128,000 casualties between January and mid-June 1944, including 36,000 dead or missing. The drain of constant casualties and the influx of partly-trained replacements led to a stark reduction in the quality of many of the divisions in Heeresgruppe Mitte. Half of the infantry units were at 50 per cent strength or less, but each was expected to hold 20km or more of the front. Under Generalfeldmarschall Ernst Busch, Heeresgruppe Mitte settled into a *Stellungskrieg* (positional warfare) mindset and focused on building up impregnable defences. Each German division established minefields and obstacles to their front and alternate defence lines to their rear. The cities of Bobruisk, Mogilev, Orsha and Vitebsk were converted into strong defensive hedgehogs, intended to act as obstacles to any Soviet advance. The terrain in this area, replete with marshlands and forests, favoured the defence and made the large-scale use of armour seem improbable. Due to Soviet advances in the Ukraine, Heeresgruppe Mitte now held a large salient, centred around Minsk, which offered the theoretical advantage of using the 'central position' tactic which had worked well in the defence of previous salient, such as Rzhev. However in order for the tactic to work, the defender had to have mobile reserves.

In May 1944, Model began requesting that the OKH transfer him additional armoured formations in order to mount a counter-offensive to recover ground east of L'vov. In reality, Model simply wanted additional armoured reserves to deal with the next round of Soviet offensives and he was able to convince Hitler and the OKH that Heeresgruppe Nordukraine was likely to receive the enemy's main blow, rather than Heeresgruppe Mitte. Eventually, Hitler authorized the transfer of the LVI Panzerkorps (4. and 5.Panzer-Divisionen, s.Pz.abt.505 and Sturmgeschütz-Brigade 237) from Heeresgruppe Mitte to Heeresgruppe

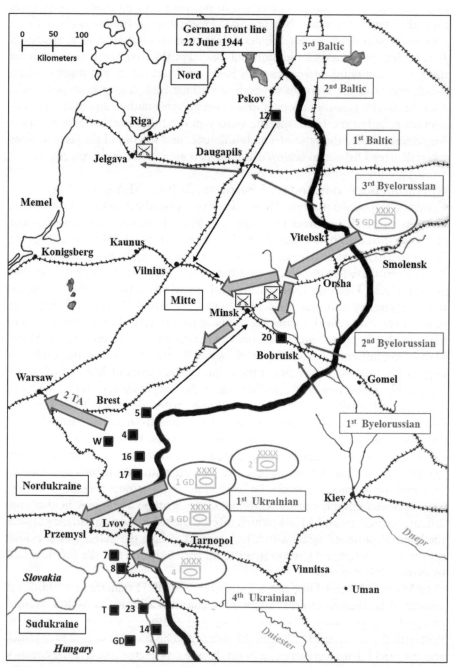

Advance of Soviet tank armies during Operation Bagration and Lvov-Sandomierz Offensive, June-July 1944

Nordukraine on 29 May, which effectively deprived the former of its primary armoured reserves. Instead, Heeresgruppe Mitte was left with only a single Panzer-Division in operational reserve – Generalleutnant Mortimer von Kessel's 20.Panzer-Division, which had a single Panzer-Abteilung with 71 Pz IVs. In addition, Heeresgruppe Mitte had s.Pz.Abt.501, with 20 operational Tigers.

Yet even if Heeresgruppe Mitte had retained the LVI Panzerkorps and been reinforced with additional armour, Germany's ability to conduct mobile operations was rapidly coming to an end due to the fuel crisis. The Third Reich had always been short of fuel, but the Allied bombing effort that began in April 1944 against German oil production facilities had an almost immediate impact upon the Luftwaffe and mechanized units. The Romanian oil fields at Ploesti were bombed repeatedly in April–June 1944 and production was curtailed by 80 per cent, while the attacks on synthetic plants deprived Germany of both fuel and synthetic rubber. Between March and September 1944, Germany's production of fuel for motor vehicles fell by 64 per cent, which immediately impacted the operational mobility of Panzer-Divisionen at the front.[40]

On 31 May 1944, the Ostheer had been reduced to only 955 operational tanks on the Eastern Front, of which 233 were Tigers, 238 were Panthers and 484 were Pz IVs.[41] The Ostheer had a total of 16 Panzer-Divisionen, seven Panzergrenadier-Divisionen and six schwere Panzer-Abteilungen. Only about six of the 23 mechanized divisions were still reasonably combat effective (*Großdeutschland*, 1., 4., 5. , 8. and 24.Panzer-Divisionen) while the rest were reduced to 25–40 per cent combat effectiveness. Noticeably, the bulk of the German armour was in the south: 606 tanks in Heeresgruppe Nordukraine, 190 in Südukraine, 86 in Mitte and just 73 in Nord. In contrast, the Red Army was now capable of committing over 6,000 tanks into battle across the Eastern Front, with large reserves ready to replace losses.

By early June 1944, Heeresgruppe Mitte had over 578,000 personnel assigned – 31 per cent of the entire Ostheer – although its actual front-line combat strength was barely 120,000 troops.[42] Busch's main forces consisted of Generaloberst Georg-Hans Reinhardt's PzAOK 3, General der Infanterie Kurt von Tippelskirch's AOK 4 and General der Infanterie Hans Jordan's AOK 9, which altogether had a total of 26 infantry divisions, two Luftwaffe Feld-Divisionen and three Panzergrenadier-Divisionen (18, 25, *Feldherrnhalle*). Busch also had Generaloberst Walter Weiss's AOK 2, which protected the boundary between Heeresgruppe Mitte and Heeresgruppe Nordukraine. Busch was fairly optimistic that the salient could be held due to the strong field works, since previous Soviet offensives had taken days or weeks to chew their way through less robust defences. Based upon past experience of Soviet efforts to break German defence lines, neither Busch nor the OKH anticipated that the Red Army would be able to create a breakthrough in more than one or two sectors, which could then be contained. The only really worrisome factor was the weakness of the Luftwaffe, since Luftflotte 6 only had 40 Bf-109G fighters assigned – grossly insufficient for air cover over Heeresgruppe Mitte.

Since Busch's mission was strictly defensive, most of the armour assigned to Heeresgruppe Mitte consisted of assault guns and self-propelled Panzerjägers. Aside from Mortimer's 20.Panzer-Division, the only other division with tanks was *Feldherrnhalle*, which had 20 Pz IVs and a battery of StuG-IIIs. Altogether, the PzAOK 3 had about 60 assault guns and one battalion of Nashorns (s.Pz. Jgr.Abt.59), the AOK 4 had 246 assault guns and two battalions of Nashorns (s.Pz.Jgr.Abt.655) and AOK 9 had 76 assault guns. This gave Heeresgruppe Mitte a grand total of 111 tanks, 382 assault guns and 100–120 tank destroyers (Nashorn and Marder).[43] It is significant that Heeresgruppe Mitte had no Panthers at this point – one year after they had been introduced on the Eastern Front – and still relied upon the Pz IV as its main battle tank. Although German industry had increased the production of the Pz IV tank to 300 per month, the latest Ausf J version was a step backward, since it omitted the turret motor to save space and weight; this meant that German tankers using this model now had to laboriously crank the turret around by hand – a huge disadvantage in battle. Busch could have massed his assault guns in mobile anti-tank reserves with 50 or more StuG-IIIs kept behind each army, but he allowed these assets to be split up into penny packets, generally a battery or a platoon assigned to each infantry division.

German intelligence expected that any new Soviet offensives against Heeresgruppe Mitte would likely focus on Vitebsk and Orsha, as they had in the past. However, since the OKH expected the main Soviet offensive would be against Model's Heeresgruppe Nordukraine that is where the bulk of the German armour was deployed. Thus Busch's army group was now like the French in 1940, expecting a predictable battle of position but getting a battle of manoeuvre for which it was unprepared.

On the other side, the Soviets had four fronts deployed against Heeresgruppe Mitte: Rokossovsky's 1st Byelorussian Front, General-polkovnik Georgy F. Zakharov's 2nd Byelorussian Front, General-polkovnik Ivan Chernyakhovsky's 3rd Byelorussian Front and General Ivan Bagramyan's 1st Baltic Front. After the liberation of the Ukraine, Stalin was eager to see Byelorussia liberated as well and he directed the Stavka to begin planning for a major summer offensive against Heeresgruppe Mitte. Zhukov was recalled to Moscow in late April and together with Vasilevsky and other members of the Stavka, they developed an outline for a grand offensive to be known as *Bagration*. Unlike previous Soviet offensives, *Bagration* was intended to be a massive set-piece battle with the resources needed to achieve a decisive victory. This time, Stalin did not rush the professionals but allowed Zhukov and Vasilevsky the time they need to amass overwhelming combat power against Heeresgruppe Mitte. While most of the 118 rifle divisions allocated for the operation were at only 60 per cent of authorized strength, the Soviets would still enjoy a 3–1 superiority in infantry.

This time, the Red Army would use all the tools of combined arms warfare in synchronization, in order to unlock the German defences. A massive amount of artillery support, including 13 artillery divisions, was provided for *Bagration*. Four air armies were deployed with over 5,000 aircraft, including 2,300 fighters – which would allow the VVS to completely dominate the airspace over the battlefield.

The Stavka intended to use infantry, artillery and airpower to smash through Heeresgruppe Mitte's front lines at multiple points, and then push its armour through to exploit deep into the rear. Zhukov and Vasilevsky were both familiar with Vladimir K. Triandafillov's pre-war theories of Deep Battle (*glubokiy boy*) and intended to use a similar approach in the conduct of *Bagration*. As part of the *Maskirovka* (deception) effort, the bulk of the Red Army's armoured formations remained with the 1st and 2nd Ukrainian Fronts, but the four fronts involved in Bagration were provided with six tank corps (1 TC, 1 GTC, 2 GTC, 3 GTC, 9 TC, 29 TC) and two mechanized corps (1 MC, 3 GMC), including Rotmistrov's 5 GTA which was quietly transferred from northern Romania to Chernyakhovsky's 3rd Byelorussian Front. These armoured formations had over 2,700 tanks. Soviet production was such that the Red Army could now begin to equip tank brigades entirely with T-34s and the T-70 light tanks began to phase out of service. About 20 per cent of the T-34s were the newest T-34/85 model, which was definitely superior to the Pz IV Ausf J. Some Soviet units were still equipped primarily with Lend-Lease armour, such as the 3 GMC, which had over 100 M4A2 Shermans and some Valentines and Churchills.[44] The number of JS-2 heavy tanks was still limited and only 80 in four regiments were available for *Bagration*. However, production of the Su-76M self-propelled gun was well advanced and over 1,000 SPGs would be involved in the offensive, as well as over 100 of the new JSU-122 which was capable of defeating Tiger tanks.

On 22 June, the four Soviet fronts began counter-reconnaissance and probing actions all along Heeresgruppe Mitte's front, stripping away its outpost line. Then at 0500 hours on 23 June, the Red Army unleashed a two-hour artillery preparation unlike anything the Germans had previously experienced. Most Soviet artillery units fired two basic loads of ammunition during the preparation, meaning that a battery of 122mm howitzers fired 640 rounds each.[45] Although well dug in, the front-line German infantry positions were badly battered. Around 0700 hours, the ground attack began with specially-organized assault groups moving forward to clear obstacles and eliminate forward German positions. Unlike previous offensives, the Red Army avoided sending large masses of infantry forward until forward obstacles were breached and ensured that these assault groups were provided with adequate engineer support. The new PT-34 mine-roller tank was employed for the first time in quantity and it proved a success at rapidly clearing lanes through minefields. Although the German forward defences in the AOK 4 and AOK 9 sectors was still strong enough to repulse the initial attacks, it was a different story in Reinhardt's

PzAOK 3 sector. The 6th Guards Army and 43rd Army from Bagramyan's 1st Baltic Front punched their way through the German IX Armeekorps defence west of Vitebsk while the 5th and 39th Armies from Chernyakhovsky's 3rd Byelorussian Front smashed the VI Armeekorps south of Vitebsk. By the end of the first day of *Bagration*, it was clear that the two Soviet fronts were attempting a double envelopment of the LIII Armeekorps in the Vitebsk salient.

Busch was at Hitler's headquarters when *Bagration* began and did not immediately grasp the scale of what he was up against. Hitler ordered 'no retreat' and Busch obeyed, without protest. In reality, it was really up to the local German commanders to decide how to respond to the Soviet offensive and thus the normal quick-thinking style of decision-making that characterized earlier German operations was not really evident in this situation. On 24 June, the Soviets increased the scale of artillery preparation in all sectors and this time, achieved small breakthroughs against AOK 4 and AOK 9, as well. The problem was that the German units were trying to hold too much frontline with too few troops, so inevitably the Soviet assault groups would find a weak spot. Near Orsha, the AOK 4 split the 20 Tigers of s.Pz.Abt.501 up across a wide area, trying to contain multiple enemy assault groups, but the dispersion into platoon-size packets robbed the Tigers of their ability to influence the battle. Although the Tigers, assault guns and Pak guns managed to knock out a significant amount of Soviet tanks, it was soon apparent that the Soviets were advancing much more quickly than thought possible. Reinhardt's sector was the hardest hit and his front collapsed first. For the Germans soldiers in the front line of Heeresgruppe Mitte, Operation *Bagration* struck like a tidal wave, inundating all their fixed defences at a terrifying rate.

Hans Jordan waited until 25 June before committing Kessel's 20.Panzer-Division and then sent it to deal with the enemy breakthrough south of Bobruisk, in the XXXXI Panzerkorps sector. Kessel's division did not move into combat as an integral whole, but in pieces, and it was surprised to bump into armour from the 1 GTC well behind the XXXXI Panzerkorps' HKL. Near the village of Slobodka, Panzer-Abteilung 21 claimed to have knocked out 60 tanks from Panov's 1 GTC, but lost about 30 Pz IVs. While Kessel's Panzers were tied up with Panov, the Soviet 3rd Army punched through the XXXV Armeekorps east of Bobruisk and sent the 9 TC to envelop the city. After just three days of battle, Jordan's AOK 9 was in serious trouble. In the middle of the German front, AOK 4 initially held together because it had some of the best units and Zakharin's 2nd Byelorussian Front did not have its own armoured exploitation force. Yet when both flanks began to give way on 25 June, AOK 4 began falling back toward the Dnepr River and Orsha was overrun on 26 June. Chernyakhovskiy sent Burdeiny's 2 TC down the Smolensk-Minsk highway in pursuit.

For Heeresgruppe Mitte, the real disaster occurred in the area in between VI Armeekorps and XXVII Armeekorps, where the 5th Army achieved a complete breakthrough when two German infantry divisions disintegrated. Choosing the right moment, Chernyakhovsky committed Rotmistrov's 5 GTA into the breach and this time, the Soviet armoured wedge advanced rapidly into the depth of the German defences, overrunning artillery and support units. The collapse of the VI Armeekorps left Reinhardt's right flank in ruins and Soviet infantry and armour moved in to encircle the LIII Armeekorps in Vitebsk. Reinhardt pleaded with Busch and Hitler to allow these units to retreat before they were surrounded, but this was refused. Instead, the Soviets surrounded LIII Armeekorps by 26 June and the formation attempted a breakout on 27 June that resulted in the loss of 30,000 German troops. Reinhardt's broken PzAOK 3 retreated westward toward Polotsk. Rotmistrov's armour poured into the German centre, wreaking havoc. The Panzer-Grenadier-Division *Feldherrnhalle* tried to act as a blocking force north of Orsha but it was easily batted out of the way, then encircled and destroyed.

By 27 June, it was obvious even to Hitler that *Bagration* was no normal Soviet offensive, since Heeresgruppe Mitte was giving way everywhere. Ignoring Busch's belated requests to retreat to save his armies from imminent encirclement, Hitler began to act irrationally. He ordered the 12.Panzer-Division (equipped with nine Pz III and 35 Pz IVs) transferred from Heeresgruppe Nord to reinforce Jordan's AOK 9, then relieved Jordan of command for his belated commitment of 20.Panzer-Division.[46] Yet before the lead elements of 12.Panzer-Division could begin arriving by rail, Rokossovsky began to complete his double envelopment of Bobruisk. In short order, the 20.Panzer-Division and the bulk of the XXXV Armeekorps and XXXXI Panzerkorps were surrounded. Kessel spearheaded a breakout effort on 28 June that managed to save part of his division and 12,000 German troops, but the rest were abandoned to their fate. When the 65th Army stormed Bobruisk on 29 June, two German corps and 70,000 troops had been killed or captured. Rokossovsky exploited his victory by dispatching a mixed armour-cavalry group east toward the rail junction Baranovichi, which would complicate the German ability to move in reinforcements against his flank.

With PzAOK 3 and AOK 9 virtually destroyed, von Tippelskirch's AOK 4 was unable to hold on the Dnepr and fell back rapidly to the Berezina River, abandoning Mogilev on 28 June. Only six out of 20 Tigers from s.Pz.Abt.501 made it across the Berezina; the rest either ran out of fuel or were damaged. The German infantry divisions were in even worse shape since they had very few motor vehicles and their artillery was towed by horses – so they could not outrun Soviet mechanized units. Rotmistrov's armour was hot on AOK 4's heels, stomping on retreating German columns and his vanguard was approaching the Berezina. The 78.Sturm-Division, one of the best infantry divisions in the Heer, was surrounded and destroyed near Orsha. As the Germans retreated, they were also pounded by VVS airstrikes, which killed two German corps commanders on 28 June (Pfeiffer of VI Armeekorps and Martinek of XXXXI Panzerkorps). The AOK 9 headquarters was also bombed, knocking out critical communications links. On the same day, Hitler sacked Busch and replaced him with Model, although this officer also retained command over Heeresgruppe Nordukraine.

By the time Model took command, Heeresgruppe Mitte was a broken, routed force that had almost no intact units left and was running for the rear. Reinhardt's PzAOK 3 was a loose fragment, gravitating toward the northwest, without connection to either Heeresgruppe Nord's AOK 16 or the rest of Heeresgruppe Mitte. Bagramyan's 1st Baltic Front pursued Reinhardt and, if it had possessed a tank army, the pursuit could have been decisive. In the centre, the remnants of AOK 4 and AOK 9 fell back toward the Berezina at Borisov then to Minsk, where Generalleutnant Karl Decker's 5.Panzer-Division and the attached s.Pz.Abt.505 (29 Tigers) were just arriving by rail from Kovel; this division had been recently rebuilt and had 55 Pz IVs and 70 Panthers.[47] Generalleutnant Dietrich von Saucken, a solid Prussian cavalry officer, was put in charge of Decker's division and a few other rear detachments and was given the difficult mission of holding the crossings over the Berezina as long as possible in order to save the two retreating armies.

One company of Tigers from s.Pz.Abt.505 detrained near Krupki, 36km northeast of Borisov, on the evening of 27 June and found itself immediately in contact with the lead elements of Vovchenko's 3 GTC from Rotmistrov's 5 GTA. Vovchenko's corps was primarily equipped with Lend-Lease tanks: 110 M4A2 Shermans 70 Valentine Mk IX and 16 T-34s.* On 28 June, the Tigers tried to make a stand against the mass of the 3 GTC, but it was like a rock against the sea; the Tigers knocked out 34 tanks but the Shermans flowed around both flanks and six damaged Tigers had to be abandoned. The next day, the Tigers knocked out another 21 enemy tanks but were quickly threatened with encirclement once their ammunition was nearly exhausted and they were forced to retreat. Reaching the Berezina River, the Tigers could not cross the bridge and had to await engineer support to reinforce the structure. Once across the Berezina on 30 June, the Tigers conducted a mobile delay action to slow 5 GTA while 5.Panzer-Division deployed.

Decker's Panzer-Pioniers wired the bridges over the Berezina for detonation while the divisional reconnaissance battalion screened along the river. However, the lead elements of the 5 GTA reached the Berezina and decided to bypass the 5.Panzer-Division roadblock at Borisov by gaining a small crossing north of the city. Several Soviet rifle divisions were right behind 5 GTA and also got troops across the river. No more German troops were coming, so Decker blew the bridges over the river. Once Rotmistrov reached the Berezina, he pushed the 29 TC across north of Borisov while the 2 GTC crossed south near Berezino. Since Decker's 5.Panzer-Division did not yet have its Panzer-Regiment on the Berezina, he was only able to fight a delaying action before abandoning Borisov on the evening of 30 June. By 1 July, Rotmistrov was across the Berezina in force and Heeresgruppe Mitte rear elements began to evacuate Minsk. Rotmistrov decided to conduct a double envelopment of the city, sending 2 GTC as the southern pincer and 29 TC and 3 GMC as the northern pincer. Once Panzer-Regiment 31 reached the front, Decker and von Saucken elected to fight a tank battle near Pleshchenitsy, 55km northeast of Minsk, to stop the northern pincer. The battle was fought in an area covered by forests and peat bogs, which complicated tactical mobility and reduced engagement ranges to under 500 metres. Decker's 5.Panzer-Divison fought a bitter action on 1–2 July and succeeded in stalling the northern pincer and inflicting considerable losses, but his own losses were heavy as well. On 5 July, the s.Pz.Abt.501 blew up its last Tiger and was withdrawn to Germany to refit.

However, 5.Panzer-Division could not hold off a tank army on its own and Burdeiny's 2 TC slipped around south of Minsk virtually unopposed and began entering the city early on 3 July. A brisk fight followed but the Germans could not hold the city and Minsk was liberated by the end of the day. Burdeiny's capture of Minsk isolated the remnants of AOK 4 and AOK 9 which were still east of the city and these formations were annihilated over the next few days. A breakout was attempted but very few units escaped the pocket and another 100,000 German troops were lost. Decker's 5.Panzer-Division fought a brilliant delaying action but after losing more than 80 per cent of its tanks, it was compelled to retreat. Model literally had nothing left to work with – three of Heeresgruppe Mitte's armies had been destroyed and the remaining fragments were too weak to hold anywhere. Without authorization from Hitler or the OKH, Model ordered his troops to fall back into Poland, realizing that his only option now was to trade space for time.

The collapse of Heeresgruppe Mitte created a cascading effect across the Eastern Front. Bagramyan's 1st Baltic Front boldly pushed toward Polotsk, which was overrun on 4 July. Despite frantic efforts by Model and Heeresgruppe Nord to recreate a frontline in this sector, Bagramyan and Chernyakhovsky's 3rd Byelorussian Front advanced into eastern Lithuania against minimal opposition. Vilnius was liberated on 13 July and Soviet armour was soon approaching Riga and the Baltic Sea, threatening to isolate Heeresgruppe Nord by 31 July. In the south, on 13 July Rokossovsky's 1st Byelorussian Front and Konev's 1st Ukrainian Front struck Heeresgruppe Nordukraine, which had been weakened by transfers to Heeresgruppe Mitte. Rokossovsky committed three tank armies (1 GTA, 3 GTA and 4 TA), which smashed through the PzAOK 1. By this point, large numbers of T-34/85s were available and they outclassed both the Pz IV and the StuG-III. It still took two weeks to achieve a complete breakthrough, but then L'vov fell on 27 July. Konev's and Rokossovsky's forces surged into southern Poland while PzAOK 1 and PzAOK 4 survived by falling back into the Carpathian Mountains. Bogdanov's 2nd Tank Army liberated Lublin then advanced toward the Vistula, but he was wounded on 21 July and General-major Aleksei I. Radzievsky continued the advance with the 8 GTC, 16 TC and 3 TC. On 27 July, the Soviet 8th Guards Army was able to gain a bridgehead over the

Vistula at Magnuszew, south of Warsaw. By the morning of 31 July, the lead elements of two Soviet tank corps were just east of Warsaw – which sparked the Warsaw Uprising by the Polish Home Army.

Due to the amazing success of *Bagration*, virtually the entire German front was in retreat and the Red Army was on the verge of a historic military triumph. However, Soviet logistics were strained by an advance of over 500km in one month, and it became apparent that there were not enough trucks and transport planes to keep the forward tank units supplied. Furthermore, the OKH was rushing reinforcements to Model, including 12 Volksgrenadier-Divisionen, the Fallschirm-Panzer-Division *Hermann Göring* from Italy and the 19.Panzer-Division from Holland. The *Hermann Göring* had 64 Pz IV and 31 of the new Jagdpanzer IV assault guns, while 19.Panzer-Division had 81 Pz IV and 79 Panthers – a remarkably strong force. Guderian, the new head of the General Staff, helped to orchestrate a counter-attack against the 2 TA with these two fresh divisions and *Wiking* and *Totenkopf* on the morning of 1 August. By massing over 170 tanks, the Germans were able to badly maul the 3 TC in four days of tank battles around Wolomin and force 2 TA to pull back 20km. For the only time during the Second World War, Stalin deliberately exaggerated the extent of the German victory and claimed that 2 TA could not advance to Warsaw until its losses were replaced. In fact, the Red Army had considerable strength on the Vistula by 5 August, but Stalin wanted the Germans to destroy the Home Army to pave the way for a communist dictatorship in post-war Poland.

Elsewhere, the madcap Soviet advances of July came to a halt in August. Outside Riga, Saucken conducted Operation *Doppelkopf* on 15–27 August, with the XXXIX Panzerkorps (4. and 12.Panzer-Divisionen) and XXXX Panzerkorps (5., 7, 14.Panzer-Divisionen) against Bagramyan's forces in an effort to reopen the rail line to Heeresgruppe Nord. After more than a week of fighting, the operation succeeded in capturing the town of Jelgava and re-opening land communications, despite the arrival of the 5 GTA. However, Hitler refused to allow Heeresgruppe Nord to retreat through the corridor and ordered them to remain in Estonia and northern Lithuania, so *Doppelkopf* proved a hollow tactical victory. The Germans were less successful in Romania, where the coup in Bucharest on 23 August led to Romania switching sides. In short order, AOK 6 was badly defeated and Malinovsky's forces were able to roll into Romania against negligible opposition. The loss of the oil from the Ploesti oilfields further exacerbated the Wehrmacht's worsening fuel crisis and ensured the end of large-scale mechanized operations.

In southern Poland, Konev's forces had secured a crossing over the Vistula near Sandomierz on 29 July and began feeding elements of Katukov's 1 TA into the bridgehead. Heeresgruppe Nordukraine mounted counter-attacks to eliminate the bridgehead, but without success. On 5 August, the reconstituted s.Pz.Abt.501 was sent to spearhead another counter-attack with 45 of the new Tiger II tanks. This was the combat debut of this new weapon on the Eastern

Front and it was a disaster. Forced to make a 50km road march from the rail head to the front, 37 of 45 Tiger IIs broke down due to faulty final drives. When the counter-attack actually began, it did not go well. A single T-34/85 from the 53rd Guards Tank Brigade (6 GTC/3 GTA), commanded by Leytenant Aleksandr P. Oskin, was camouflaged in a corn field and spotted a platoon of three King Tigers approaching in column along a road. Oskin fired BR-365P APCR rounds from a range of just 200 metres against the turret sides of the lead two Tigers and destroyed both with four rounds each; the turrets of both King Tigers were blown off. The third King Tiger tried to retreat, but Oksin pursued and pumped a round into its engine compartment, disabling it. In the one-sided action, 11 of 15 German King Tiger crewmen were killed, the rest captured.[48] The next day, the s.Pz.Abt.501 was forced to abandon another King Tiger, which was captured intact by the Soviets.

By the end of August 1944, the war in the East was decided, even though the Wehrmacht was able to temporarily create a new front. In an effort to get more tanks to the front, the OKH sent four Panzer-Brigaden, each with 36 Panthers, to the East in August 1944. These Panthers were the improved Ausf G model, which were less prone to engine fires, but the final drives still tended to fail after just 150km. In contrast, the Red Army was rapidly re-equipping its tank units with the T-34/85, which in competent hands could deal with any German tank. The Soviets not only had an overwhelming numerical superiority, but they were closing the gap in qualitative terms as well.

During the period June–August 1944, the Third Reich suffered catastrophic defeats on both the Eastern and Western Fronts. Altogether, the Wehrmacht suffered over 900,000 dead or missing in this period, which cost them the bulk of the combat veterans who had achieved the victories of 1940–42. After this point, the Wehrmacht could only continue to fight on for another eight months by scraping the bottom of the barrel. The Germans also lost 2,398 tanks in this three-month period, including 801 Panthers and 481 Tigers; these losses could not be replaced on a one-for-one basis because Allied strategic bombing on the tank factories and rail yards in Germany was finally causing a drop in German tank production. Without adequate fuel, veteran crews, spare parts or replacement tanks, the outlook for the Panzer-Divisionen was grim.

Compared to previous Soviet offensives, the Red Army did not pay an excessive price for its unprecedented gains during *Bagration* and the L'vov-Sandomierz operations; altogether 256,000 personnel dead or missing and 4,300 tanks lost. These losses would be made good in short order and the Red Army was gathering its strength for the final lunge into Germany.

Epilogue, September 1944–May 1945
Due to the drawn-out Polish rebellion in Warsaw, which the Germans were allowed to crush undisturbed, the Stavka decided to temporarily suspend operations in the centre of the Eastern Front and concentrate on the flanks.

The 1st Baltic Front struggled to sever Heeresgruppe Nord's lines of communication through Riga, but PzAOK 3 was reinforced and mounted another counter-offensive on 16 September with nearly 400 tanks – one of the last major German armoured operations of this size on the Eastern Front. However, the effort failed to remove the threat to the corridor and lost one-third of its tanks. The Red Army's tank units were now plentifully equipped with the T-34/85 and even the JS-2 was available in significant numbers. Every time the Germans managed to scrape together an armoured force, it ran straight into a wall of anti-tank guns and was constantly attacked by Soviet fighter-bombers. The Luftwaffe could no longer protect the Panzer-Divisionen. After absorbing the German counter-attacks, the 1st Baltic Front began its own massive offensive on 6 October, using the 5 GTA as its battering ram. The 3 PzAOK disintegrated and retreated into East Prussia, while the 5 GTA reached the Baltic on 10 October. By 15 October, Riga fell and Heeresgruppe Nord was isolated in the Courland Peninsula, where it remained for the rest of the war. The 4. and 12.Panzer-Divisionen were among the isolated units. Instead of evacuating these two armies by sea to reinforce the defence of East Prussia, Hitler ordered them to remain where they were, although some units were evacuated in January 1945. Amazingly, the Soviets decided to keep attacking the Courland Pocket all winter – even though it made little military sense – and lost over 1,000 tanks for minimal gains.

The other major focus for the Stavka was the Balkans. Romania was completely occupied by the end of September and the 1st and 4th Ukrainian Fronts advanced into Hungary, while the 2nd and 3rd Ukrainian Fronts marched into Bulgaria and Yugoslavia. The German PzAOK 1 and PzAOK 4 put up a stiff fight in the Carpathians, particularly at Dukla Pass in eastern Czechoslovakia in September. At Debrecen, the Germans managed a counter-attack that destroyed Pliev's mobile cavalry-mechanized group, although this was just a tactical victory. Since AOK 6 had been destroyed yet again in Romania, the OKH decided to form a new 6.Armee, even though it only had the decimated 13.Panzer-Division and a single infantry division. Pursued by Tolbukhin's forces, AOK 6 retreated into southeastern Hungary and by the end of October nearly half of Hungary had been overrun and Belgrade had been liberated. In November, Malinovsky's 2nd Ukrainian Front made a push for Budapest, but did not encircle the city until 26 December 1944.

Amazingly, Germany succeeded in recreating fronts in both the east and west, while their opponents outran their supply lines. Yet instead of using this respite to rebuild his forces in the East, Hitler decided to allocate his remaining armoured reserves for a grand, nonsensical counter-stroke in the West in the Ardennes. All the best armoured units went to the Ardennes, leaving mostly burnt-out or untried divisions in the East. Yet the Ardennes offensive failed and squandered Germany's last armoured reserves. In addition to ill-conceived counter-strokes, the Germans also decided to upgrade the *Großdeutschland* division to a corps-size formation, and the same was done with the *Hermann Göring* division; this was a foolish waste of resources on a few elite units while the rest of the Panzer-Divisionen were starved of replacements. The second division in Panzerkorps *Großdeutschland*, Panzergrenadier-Division *Brandenburg*, was poorly equipped and its Panzer-Regiment only had a single battalion equipped with a mix of Panthers, Pz IVs, Pz IIIs, assault guns and SPW half-tracks.[49]

In early January 1945, Hitler mandated that AOK 6 would mount a relief operation to rescue the trapped forces in Budapest, which included the 13.Panzer-Division, Panzergrenadier-Division *Feldherrnhalle* and Hungarian 1st Armoured Division. Operation *Konrad* was hastily organized, with the IV SS-Panzerkorps (*Totenkopf* and *Wiking*) making two efforts to break through to the city but failing. Even with the addition of the 23.Panzer-Division and King Tigers from the s.Pz.Abt.503, the third attack also failed. A small number of troops escaped the city in a breakout effort, but the rest of the garrison surrendered on 13 February. The quality of German replacements dropped off sharply by late 1944, as youths were conscripted to replace combat veterans. Even the Waffen-SS was scraping the bottom of the barrel: 16-year-old Gunter Grass was conscripted in autumn 1944 and sent to join the SS-*Frundsberg* division in Silesia in early 1945. Grass was assigned to a unit with three Jagdpanthers but was given no training and panicked in his first taste of combat.[50] Even as Germany deployed its best tanks and tank destroyers in the final hours of the war, it had few competent troops left to operate them.

Meanwhile, the German forces defending the Vistula were out-numbered 6–1 in armour, 5–1 in personnel and 8–1 in artillery. Indeed, the German defence in central Poland was little more than a reinforced screen. Zhukov and the Stavka spent months planning the Vistula-Oder operation and it was the best Soviet set-piece offensive of the war. Zhukov decided to use the Magnuszew and Pulawy bridgeheads as the springboards for the 1st Byelorussian Front's attack on the rebuilt AOK 9. He brought up Katukov's 1 GTA and Bogdanov's 2 GTA to serve as his exploitation forces. The offensive began on the morning of 14 January 1945 with an artillery preparation that shattered two frontline Volksgrenadier-Divisionen and Zhukov's troops advanced 20km on the first day. The AOK 9 committed its mobile reserve – the 19. and 25.Panzer-Divisionen from XXXX Panzerkorps – but their counter-attacks were too puny and uncoordinated. Zhukov committed Bogdanov's armour on the second day of the operation and it created a broad wedge in AOK 9's front. After four days of fighting, the German front broke wide open and Warsaw was occupied. In less than three weeks, Zhukov's forces shattered Heeresgruppe Mitte and Heeresgruppe A and advanced 500km to the Oder River. Soviet losses were relatively light, but Soviet logistics were still inadequate despite the influx of large numbers of American-made trucks.

In March 1945, the Germans mounted their last offensive in the East near Lake Balaton, south of Budapest with the 6.SS-Panzerarmee, transferred from the West. Guderian wanted to use this armour to stabilize the main front in the east, but Hitler was focused on recovering ground in Hungary. Operation *Frühlingserwachen* (Spring Awakening) employed virtually all the Waffen-SS Panzer-Divisionen (*LSSAH, Das Reich, Totenkopf, Wiking, Hohenstauffen* and *Hitler Jugend*), elements of four Heer Panzer-Divisionen (1, 3, 6, 23) and two King Tiger battalions against Tolbukhin's 3rd Ukraininan Front on 6 March. This operation saw the last major concentration of German armour, with almost 500 tanks (including 249 Panthers and 72 King Tigers) and 173 assault guns. After a brief initial period of success that achieved a 30km advance in two days, the offensive bogged down and was called off after 10 days. German material losses were crippling in this last offensive, leaving the panzer units involved in woeful state by mid-March.

The final campaign along the Oder River in April 1945 and the subsequent attack into Berlin was not the Red Army's finest hour. Instead, Zhukov allowed his rivalry with Konev to affect his decision-making and Stalin goaded both men into a sloppy offensive that relied on mass, rather than skill. Zhukov's decision on 16 April to commit the 1 GTA and 2 GTA into battle, even though the German defences on the Seelow Heights were still unbroken, resulted in massive Soviet casualties. Amazingly, Hitler had not anticipated a direct Soviet advance across the Oder and had left his best armoured units in Hungary, which left few Panzer units on the Oder. The SS-Panzergrenadier-Division *Nordland* and 10 King Tigers from schwere SS-Panzer-Abteilung 503 were the only veteran armoured units to fight in the final battle for Berlin. Instead of elite units, the approaches to Berlin were defended by extemporized units such as Panzer-Division *Müncheberg* and Panzer-Division *Kurmark*, which were divisions in name only. The final German stand on the Oder and in Berlin involved only small amounts of armour, mostly assault guns, but the fanatical defence inflicted enormous losses on the Red Army, including nearly 2,000 tanks. The widespread introduction of the Panzerfaust proved deadly in Berlin and the Soviet use of so much armour in the dense urban terrain was a tactical error. Nevertheless, Zhukov and Konev used their armour to batter their way into Berlin and brought an end to the Third Reich.

Conclusions

Both sides made tactical and operational mistakes in the conduct of armoured operations on the Eastern Front in 1941–45, but it was the Germans who made the strategic mistake of starting a war that they were not prepared to win. Furthermore, the Red Army learned a great deal more from its defeats in 1941–42 than the Wehrmacht learned from its victories. Both during and after the war, the Germans repeatedly tried to rationalize their defeat by pointing to the Soviet numerical superiority, as if it was somehow not fair. Yet the reason that the Red Army enjoyed a numerical superiority in tanks was due to the fact that its tanks were designed to be simple to produce and operate and easy to repair; they could also move lengthy distances without too many breaking down. This functionality of Soviet tanks was based on pre-war industrial decisions that were made with an eye to winning a protracted war. Both before and throughout the war, the Soviet oversight of tank development, production and evolution was much more professionally directed than on the German side. Unlike the Germans, who did not put a tank expert like Guderian in charge of overseeing the restoration of the Panzer-Divisionen until after Stalingrad, General-leytenant Yakov N. Fedorenko, head of GABTU, directed Soviet tank programmes throughout the entire war. Furthermore, Guderian was ignored on all the key decisions – such as the premature commitment of the Panther tank, the decision to attack at Kursk, the need to build panzer reserves – whereas Fedorenko played a key role in reconstituting shattered Soviet tank armies and ensuring that tank production stayed ahead of combat losses. Instead, the Germans opted for more sophisticated tanks that were produced in smaller numbers and were more difficult to maintain. The Germans also enjoyed producing small numbers of experimental designs such as the Ferdinand tank destroyer, whereas the Soviets had the discipline to focus on a few proven designs.

Certainly the most obvious mistake German tank designers made was to rely upon petrol engines rather than expending the effort to build a high-torque diesel engine, as the Soviets had. Fuel-hogs like the Panther and King Tiger were using 2–4 times as much fuel as earlier designs, just when Germany was running short of fuel. Hitler regarded the diesel engine as the preferred solution, but allowed himself to be dissuaded by technocrats who opined that it would take too long to develop and the war would be over before it was ready. Tied in with the mistaken reliance on fuel-inefficient petrol engines, the Germans became enamoured of mounting bigger and bigger guns on their tanks and Panzerjägers. The problem was that armoured vehicles over 45 tons were difficult to get across rivers, since German pontoon bridges were not intended for heavy tanks, and it was increasingly problematic for recovery vehicles to retrieve them on the battlefield. Thus, by 1943, German heavy tanks had difficulty getting across minor water features, which negatively impacted mission accomplishment on a number of occasions, such as Kursk and the Korsun relief operation. Germany needed a good 30–35-ton tank with a diesel engine and a long 7.5cm gun that could be built in quantity, but instead the Panzer-Divisionen were provided with tanks that increasingly failed to meet the operational requirements of *Bewegungskrieg*. Interestingly, many of the design features that the Germans found so interesting – such as interweaved road wheels – were abandoned by all post-war tank designers.

Another mistake which cost the Germans dearly was the diversion of so many resources to building Waffen-SS and Luftwaffe Panzer-Divisionen, which was done for political rather than military reasons. By late 1943 Himmler was outfitting more and more Waffen-SS units, many of which were of dubious quality. Guderian failed to stop this diversion of resources and most of the Heer Panzer-Divisionen were starved of resources and allowed to become second-rate formations by late 1944. After Kursk, the German combined arms team was increasingly broken as less infantry, air and artillery support was available.

Soviet leaders stuck with a conservative attitude toward tank design and production throughout the war and it paid off handsomely. By late 1943 the Red Army had six tank armies which contained up to 30 per cent of its available armour and a small cadre of veteran front leaders such as Vatutin, Rokossovsky, Bagramyan and Konev, who learned to employ these armoured fists to achieve operational-level victories. Yet the Red Army could not have smashed German army groups just with superior numbers – that method had failed repeatedly in 1941–42. Instead, the Red Army learned how to mass its artillery to achieve breakthroughs and to employ its engineers in mobility and counter-mobility roles. By the time of Kursk, the Soviets learned that a minefield covered by fire from concealed anti-tank guns was the best answer to the Tiger or Panther, yet the Germans never really improved their mine-clearing skills. The Soviet ability to quickly refit decimated tank armies and redeploy them long distances without being detected was another skill that contributed greatly to the Soviet victory over the Panzer-Divisionen. Soviet expert use of *Maskirovka* (deception) allowed the Red Army to gain the advantage of surprise again and again over German commanders who could not understand that their opponents were evolving.

The Soviet failure to invest in developing armoured personnel carriers for their infantry, better reconnaissance vehicles and mobile flak guns were serious technical mistakes that proved costly in battle, but Lend-Lease deliveries of US-made halftracks and reconnaissance vehicles helped to partly rectify this deficiency by the last year of the war. Could the Red Army have defeated Germany's armoured forces without Lend-Lease? This is doubtful for a number of reasons. Although the quality of many Lend-Lease tanks was poor, the quality of the trucks, halftracks and other support vehicles was not and without these vehicles, the Red Army's ability to conduct Deep Operations would have been severely impaired. Another factor is that the supply of aluminum, machine tools and other key raw materials enabled the Soviet Union to rapidly expand its tank production despite the loss of so much of its own territory and resources; without this assistance, Soviet tank production would likely have been reduced by one-third. It is highly unlikely that the Red Army would have had the mobility and the numbers necessary to conduct the sweeing advances of 1944–45 without Allied Lend-Lease aid.

Yet Soviet armoured tactics were undermined throughout the war by the lack of training provided to Soviet tankers in comparison to their opponents. In 1945, some Guards tank units were afforded special gunnery training, but for most of the war Soviet tankers went into battle with inadequate gunnery training and poor communications due to the limited number of radios. These limitations – which could have been mitigated – gave an enormous advantage to German tankers and help to explain many of the lop-sided kill ratios. Yet Stalin and his Kremlin cronies were not interested in improving military training since they regarded this as a step toward professionalism and elitism, which was dangerous for the authority of the party. Instead, Stalin accepted heavy losses as the price of victory and only cared about losses when it affected mission outcomes. Nevertheless, the Red Army eventually developed a veteran armoured force by 1945 that was capable of achieving any mission assigned and had surpassed the capabilities of the German Panzer-Divisionen even in their prime.

Appendix I

Rank Table

U.S. Army Rank	German Army Rank	Waffen SS Rank	Soviet Rank
General of the Army	Generalfeldmarschall	N/A	Marshal of the Soviet Union
General	Generaloberst	*SS-Oberstgruppenführer*	General Armiyi
Lieutenant General	General der Panzertruppe	*SS-Obergruppenführer*	General Polkovnik
Major General	Generalleutnant	*SS-Gruppenführer*	General Leytenant
Brigadier General	Generalmajor	*SS-Brigadeführer*	General Major
Colonel	Oberst	*SS-Standartenführer*	Polkovnik
Lieutenant Colonel	Oberstleutnant	*SS-Obersturmbannführer*	Podpolkovnik
Major	Major	*SS-Sturmbannführer*	Major
Captain	Hauptmann	*SS-Hauptsturmführer*	Kapetan
First Lieutenant	Oberleutnant	*SS-Obersturmführer*	Starshiy Leytenant
Second Lieutenant	Leutnant	*SS-Untersturmführer*	Mladshiy Leytenant
Sergeant Major	Stabsfeldwebel	*SS-Sturmscharführer*	N/A
First Sergeant	Oberfeldwebel	*SS-Hauptscharführer*	Starshina
Sergeant First Class	Feldwebel	*SS-Oberscharführer*	Starshiy Serzhant
Staff Sergeant	Unterfeldwebel	*SS-Scharführer*	N/A
Sergeant	Unteroffizier	*SS-Unterscharführer*	Serzhant
Corporal	Obergefreiter	*SS-Rottenführer*	Mladshiy Serzhant
Private First Class	Gefreiter		Yefreytor
Private	Oberschütze	*SS-Sturmmann*	N/A
	Schütze	*SS-Mann*	Krasnoarmeyets

Armour Order of Battle, 1 July 1943

German
Heeresgruppe Nord (Generalfeldmarschall Georg von Küchler)
16.Armee (Generalfeldmarschall Ernst Busch)
- o 18.Panzer-Grenadier-Division (Generalleutnant Werner von Erdmannsdorff)
- o Sturmgeschütz-Abteilung 184
- o 18.Armee (Generaloberst Georg Lindemann)
- o Sturmgeschütz-Abteilung 226
- o Sturmgeschütz-Abteilung 912
- o schwere Panzer-Abteilung 502

Heeresgruppe Mitte (Generalfeldmarschall Günther von Kluge)
3.Panzerarmee (Generaloberst Georg-Hans Reinhardt)
- • XXXXIII Armeekorps (General der Infanterie Karl von Oven)
  - o 20.Panzer-Grenadier Division (Generalmajor Georg Jauer)
- • Army Reserves:
  - o 8.Panzer-Division (Generalmajor Sebastian Fichtner)[1]

4. Armee (Generaloberst Hans von Salmuth)
- • Sturmgeschütz-Abteilung 270
- • Sturmgeschütz-Abteilung 667

2.Armee (Generaloberst Walter Weiss)

9.Armee (Generaloberst Walther Model)
XLVI Panzer-Korps (General der Infanterie Hans Zorn)
- • 7.Infanterie-Division (Generalleutnant Fritz-Georg von Rappard)
  - o 2./Sturmgeschütz-Abteilung 909
- • 31.Infanterie-Division (Generalleutnant Friedrich Hoßbach)
  - o 1.,3/Sturmgeschütz-Abteilung 909
- • 258.Infanterie-Division (Generalleutnant Hanskurt Höcker)
  - o 6./Panzer-Regiment 29 [Pz IV]
  - o 2./Panzerjäger-Abteilung 2 [Marder]

XXXXI Panzer-Korps (General der Panzertruppen Josef Harpe)
- • 18.Panzer-Division (Generalmajor Karl-Wilhelm von Schlieben)
- • 86.Infanterie-Division (Generalleutnant Helmuth Weidling)
  - o *schwere Panzerjäger-Abteilung* 654 [Ferdinand]
  - o Panzerkompanie (Fkl) 313
  - o Sturmgeschütz-Abteilung 177
- • 292.Infanterie-Division (Generalleutnant Wolfgang von Kluge) WIA 20 July
  - o *schwere Panzerjäger-Abteilung 653* [Ferdinand]
  - o Panzerkompanie (Fkl) 314
  - o Sturmgeschütz-Abteilung 244

- *schwere Panzerjäger Regiment 656*:
  - ○ Sturm-Panzer-Abteilung 216 [Sturmpanzer]

XXXXVII Panzer-Korps (General der Panzertruppen Joachim Lemelsen)
- 2.Panzer-Division (Generalleutnant Vollrath Lübbe)
- 9.Panzer-Division (Generalleutnant Walter Scheller)
- 20.Panzer-Division (Generalmajor Mortimer von Kessel)
- 6.Infanterie-Division (Generalleutnant Horst Großmann)
  - ○ 1.,2./schwere Panzer-Abteilung 505
  - ○ Panzerkompanie (Fkl) 312 (Leutnant Nolte)
- Sturmgeschütz-Abteilung 245
- Sturmgeschütz-Abteilung 904

XXIII Armeekorps (General der Infanterie Johannes Frießner)
- ○ Sturmgeschütz-Abteilung 185
- ○ Sturmgeschütz-Abteilung 189

Group Esebeck (9.Armee Reserve):
- 4.Panzer-Division (Generalleutnant Dietrich von Saucken)
- 12.Panzer-Division (Generalmajor Erpo Freiherr von Bodenhausen)
- 10.Panzer-Grenadier-Division (Generalleutnant August Schmidt)

2.Panzerarmee (General der Infanterie Heinrich Clößner)
LIII Armeekorps (Generalleutnant Friedrich Gollwitzer)
- 25.Panzer-Grenadier-Division (Generalleutnant Anton Grasser)
- 5.Panzer-Division (Generalmajor Ernst Felix Fäckenstedt)
- Sturmgeschütz-Abteilung 202
- Sturmgeschütz-Abteilung 904

Heeresgruppe Süd (Generalfeldmarschall Erich von Manstein)
4.Panzerarmee (Generaloberst Hermann Hoth)
- XLVIII Panzerkorps (General der Panzertruppen Otto von Knobelsdorff)[2]
  - ○ 3.Panzer-Division (Generalleutnant Franz Westhoven)
  - ○ 11.Panzer-Division (Generalmajor Johann Mickl)
  - ○ Panzer-Grenadier Division *Großdeutschland* (Generalleutnant Walter Hörnlein)
  - ○ 10.Panzer Brigade (Oberst Arnold Hans Albert Burmeister) Oberst Karl Decker
    - ▪ Panzer-Regiment 39 (Major Meinrad von Lauchert)
      - • Panzer-Abteilung 51
      - • Panzer-Abteilung 52
  - ○ Sturmgeschütz-Abteilung 911
- II.SS-Panzerkorps (General der Waffen-SS Paul Hausser)
  - ○ 1.SS-Panzergrenadier-Division *Leibstandarte SS Adolf Hitler* (SS-Oberst-Gruppenführer Sepp Dietrich)
  - ○ 2.SS-Panzergrenadier-Division *Das Reich* (SS-Gruppenführer Walter Krüger)
  - ○ 3.SS-Panzergrenadier-Division *Totenkopf* (SS-Brigadeführer Max Simon)

Armee-Abteilung Kempf (General der Panzertruppe Werner Kempf)
- III Panzerkorps (General der Panzertruppe Hermann Breith)
  - ○ 6. Panzer-Division (Generalmajor Walther von Hünersdorff)
  - ○ 7. Panzer-Division (Generalleutnant Hans Freiherr von Funck)

- o   19. Panzer-Division (Generalleutnant Gustav Richard Ernst Schmidt)[3]
- o   Sturmgeschütz-Abteilung 228
- o   Sturmgeschütz-Abteilung 393

6. Armee (General der Infanterie Karl-Adolf Hollidt)
- 16. Panzergrenadier-Division (Generalleutnant Gerhard Graf von Schwerin)
- Sturmgeschütz-Abteilung 203
- Sturmgeschütz-Abteilung 210
- Sturmgeschütz-Abteilung 243
- Sturmgeschütz-Abteilung 287

1. Panzerarmee (Generaloberst Eberhard von Mackensen)
- Sturmgeschütz Abteilung 209
- Sturmgeschütz-Abteilung 232
- Sturmgeschütz-Abteilung 901

XXIV Panzerkorps (General der Panzertruppe Walther Nehring)
- 5.SS Panzergrenadier Division Wiking (SS-Brigadeführer Herbert Otto Gille)
- 17.Panzer-Division (Generalleutnant Walter Schilling)
- 23.Panzer-Division (Generalleutnant Nikolaus von Vormann)

Heeresgruppe A (Generalfeldmarschall Ewald von Kleist)
17.Armee (General der Pioniere Erwin Jaenecke)
- XXXXIX Gebirgs-Korps (General der Gebirgstruppe Rudolf Konrad)
- 13.Panzer-Division (Generalleutnant Hellmut von der Chevallerie)
- Sturmgeschütz-Abteilung 191
- Sturmgeschütz-Abteilung 249

Reinforcements:
- August 1943
  - o   22 August: I./SS-Panzer-Regiment 2 [Panther] (SS-Hauptsturmführer Hans Weiss) for *Das Reich*
  - o   24 August: I./Pz.Rgt. 15[Panther] (Major Karl von Sivers) for 11. Panzer-Division
  - o   31 August: II./Pz.Rgt. 23 [Panther] (Major Fritz Fechner) for 23. Panzer-Division
- September 1943:
  - o   20 September: s.Pz.Abt. 506 [Tiger]
- October 1943:
  - o   2 October: I./Pz.Rgt. 2 [Panther] (Hauptmann Bollert) for 13. Panzer-Divison
  - o   20 October: 24. Panzer-Division (Generalmajor Maximilian Freiherr von Edelsheim) from Italy
  - o   25 October: 14. Panzer-Division (Oberst Martin Unrein) from France
- November 1943:
  - o   6 November: 25. Panzer-Division from Norway (Generalleutnant Adolf von Schell)[4]
  - o   7 November: s.Pz.Abt. 509 [Tiger]
  - o   9 November: *LSSAH*, including I./SS-Panzer Regiment 1 [Panther] (SS-Sturmbannführer Herbert Kuhlmann)
  - o   11 November: 1.Panzer-Division (Generalleutnant Walter Krüger), including I./Pz.Rgt.1 [Panther] (Major Ernst Phillip) arrives from Greece

- December 1943
  - o 5 December: I./Pz.Rgt.31 [Panther] (Major Hubertus Feldtkeller), attached to XI Armeekorps.
  - o III. SS-Panzerkorps (Obergruppenführer Felix Steiner)
    - 11.SS-Panzer-Grenadier-Division *Nordland*
    - 4.SS-Panzergrenadier-Brigade *Nederland*
- January 1944
  - o **Panzer-Grenadier-Division** *Feldherrnhalle* **from France** (Generalleutnant Otto Kohlermann)
- March 1944:
  - o 9.SS-Panzer-Division *Hohenstaufen* (SS-Gruppenführer Wilhelm Bittrich)
  - o 10.SS Panzer-Division *Frundsberg* (SS-Gruppenführer Karl Fischer von Treuenfeld)

Soviet
Leningrad Front (General-polkovnik Leonid A. Govorov)
- 5x Tank Brigades (1, 152, 220, 222; 30 G)
- 6x Tank Regiments (98, 260, 261; 31 G, 46 G, 49 G)
- 3x OTB (86, 116, 287)
- 1x SAP (1439)

Volkhov Front (General Kirill A. Meretskov)
- 6x Tank Brigades (16, 29, 122, 124, 185; 7 G)
- 5x Tank Regiments (25; 32 G, 33 G, 35 G, 50 G)
- 6x OTB (107, 500, 501, 502, 503, 507)
- 2x SAP (1433, 1434)

Northwestern Front (General-polkovnik Pavel A. Kurochkin)
- 2x Tank Brigades (60, 81)
- 10x Tank Regiments (27, 32, 37, 38, 65, 226, 227, 239, 249; 3 G)
- 4x OTB (150, 170, 514, 515)

Kalinin Front (General-polkovnik Andrei I. Eremenko)
- 4x Tank Brigades (78, 143, 236; 28 G)
- 2x Mechanized Brigades (46, 47)
- 2x Tank Regiments (105, 221)
- 1x OTB (171)

Western Front (General-polkovnik Vasily D. Sokolovsky)
- 13 Tank Brigades (94, 120, 153, 187, 196, 213, 256; 2 G, 10 G, 23 G, 29 G, 42 G, 43 G)
- 4x Tank Regiments (119, 161, 233, 248)
- 2x OTB (138, 520)
- 3x SAP: (1453, 1536, 1537)
- Under Front Control:
  - o 1st Tank Corps (General-major Vasily V. Butkov)
  - o 5th Tank Corps (General-major Mikhail G. Sakhno)

Bryansk Front (General-polkovnik Markian M. Popov)
- 1x Tank Brigade (68)
- 9x Tank Regiments (36, 82, 114, 231, 253; 11 G, 12 G, 13 G, 26 G)

- 6x SAPs (1444, 1445, 1452, 1535, 1538, 1539)
- Under Front Control:
  - 1st Guards Tank Corps (General-major Mikhail F. Panov)

Central Front (General Konstantin K. Rokossovsky)
- 2nd Tank Army (General-leytenant Aleksei G. Rodin)
  - 3rd Tank Corps (General-major Maksim D. Sinenko)
  - 16th Tank Corps (General-major Vasily E. Grigor'ev)
  - 11th Guards Tank Brigade
- 2x Tank Brigades (129, 150)
- 14x Tank Regiments (40, 43, 45, 58, 84, 193, 229, 237, 240, 251, 259; 27 G, 29 G, 30 G)
- 4x SAP (1442, 1454, 1540, 1541)
- Under Front Control:
  - 9th Tank Corps (General-leytenant Semen I. Bogdanov)
  - 19th Tank Corps (General-major Ivan D. Vasil'ev)

Voronezh Front (General Nikolai F. Vatutin)
- 6th Guards Army (General-leytenant Ivan M. Chistiakov)
  - 96th Tank Brigade
  - 230th and 245th Tank Regiments
  - 1440th SAP
- 7th Guards Army (General-leytenant Mikhail S. Shumilov)
  - 27th Guards, 210th Tank Brigades
  - 148th, 167th and 262nd Tank Regiments
  - 1438th and 1529th SAP
- 1st Tank Army (General-leytenant Mikhail E. Katukov)
  - 3rd Mechanized Corps (General-major Semen M. Krivoshein)
  - 6th Tank Corps (General-major Andrei L. Getman)
  - 31st Tank Corps (General-major Dmitri Kh. Chernienko)[5]
- 38th and 40th Armies
  - 86th, 180th and 192nd Tank Brigades
  - 59th and 60th Tank Regiments
- Under Front Control:
  - 2nd Guards Tank Corps (Polkovnik Aleksei S. Burdeinyi)
  - 5th Guards Tank Corps (General-leytenant Andrei G. Kravchenko)

Southwestern Front (General Rodion Ia. Malinovsky)
- 4x Tank Brigades (11, 115, 173, 179)
- 9x Tank Regiments (52, 141, 212, 224, 243; 5 G, 9 G, 16 G, 17 G
- 1x SAP (1443)
- Under Front Control:
  - 1st Guards Mechanized Corps (General-leytenant Ivan N. Russiianov)
  - 2nd Tank Corps (General-major Aleksei F. Popov)
  - 23rd Tank Corps (General-leytenant Efim G. Pushkin)[6]
  - 9th Guards Tank Brigade
  - 10th Guards Tank Regiment

Southern Front (General-polkovnik Fedor I. Tolbukhin)
- 2nd Guards Army (General-leytenant Georgy F. Zakharov)
  o 2nd Guards Mechanized Corps (General-leytenant Karp V. Sviridov)
- 5th Shock/28th, 44th and 51st Armies
  o 4x Tank Brigades (140; 6 G, 32 G, 33 G)
  o 1x Tank Regiments (22 G)
- Under Front Control:
  o 4th Guards Mechanized Corps (General-major Trofim I. Tanaschishin)[7]

North Caucasus Front (General-leytenant Ivan E. Petrov)
- 2x Tank Brigades (63; 5 G)
- 5x Tank Regiments (85, 244, 257, 258; 6 G)
- 2x OTB (75, 132)
- 2x SAP (1448, 1449)

Stavka Reserve (RVGK)/Steppe Front (General Ivan S. Konev)
- 4th Guards Army (General-leytenant Grigoriy I. Kulik)
  o 3rd Guards Tank Corps (General-major I.A. Vovchenko)
- 5th Guards Army (General-leytenant Aleksei S. Zhadov)
  o 10th Tank Corps (General-leytenant V.G. Burkov)
- 5th Guards Tank Army (General-leytenant Pavel A. Rotmistrov)
  o 5th Guards Mechanized Corps (General-major Boris M. Skvortsov)
  o 29th Tank Corps (General-major I. F. Kirichenko)
  o 53rd Guards Tank Regiment
  o 1549 SAP
- Other forces in Steppe Military District:
  o 4th Guards Tank Corps (General-leytenant Pavel P. Poluboiarov)
  o 3rd Guards Mechanized Corps (General-major Viktor T. Obukhov)
  o 1st Mechanized Corps (General-leytenant Mikhail D. Solomatin)
  o 2nd Mechanized Corps (General-leytenant Ivan P. Korchagin)
  o 93rd Tank Brigade
  o 34th, 35th and 39th Tank Regiments

Stavka Reserve (RVGK)/Separate Armies
- 3rd Guards Tank Army (General-leytenant Pavel S. Rybalko)
  o 12th Tank Corps (General-major Mitrofan I. Zin'kovich)[8]
  o 15th Tank Corps (General-major Filipp N. Rudkin)
  o 91st Tank Brigade
- 5th Mechanized Corps (General-major Mikhail V. Volkov)
- 18th Tank Corps (General-major Boris S. Bakharov)
- 25th Tank Corps (General-major Fedor G. Anikushkin)
- Tank Regimens (126, 127, 225)
- SAP (1547, 1548)

Moscow Military District
- 6th Guards Mechanized Corps (General-major Aleksandr I. Akimov)
- 11th Tank Corps (General-major Nikolai N. Radkevich)
- 20th Tank Corps (General-leytenant Ivan G. Lazarev)
- 30th Tank Corps (General-leytenant Georgy S. Rodin)
- 6x Tank Brigades (88, 92, 118, 144; 31 G, 34 G)

Volga Military District
- 9th Mechanized Corps (General–major Konstantin A. Malygin)
- 8x Tank Brigades (41 G; 2, 10, 14, 15, 116, 207, 254)
- 5x Tank Regiments (51, 61, 104, 154, 250)
- 6x OTB (126, 249, 258, 563, 564, 608)

Reinforcements:
- August 1943
  - 7th Mechanized Corps (General–major Ivan V. Dubovoi)
  - 8th Mechanized Corps (General–major Abram M. Khasin)

Front	Tank Armies	Tank Corps	Mechanized Corps	Tank Brigades	Tank Regiments	OTBs	Total Authorized Tanks
Leningrad				5	6	3	600
Volkhov				6	5	6	700
Northwestern				2	10	4	615
Kalinin				4	2	1	320
Western		2		13	4	2	1,200
Moscow MD		3	1	6			1,000
Bryansk '		1		1	9		560
Central	1	4		3	14		1,340
Voronezh	1	3	1	6	7		1,200
Steppe	1	4	4	1	4		1,545
Southwestern		2	1	5	10		1,140
Southern			1	4	1		420
North Caucasus				2	5	2	360
RVGK	1	4	1	1	3		1,000
Volga MD			1	8	5	6	900
TOTAL	4	23	10	67	85	24	12,900

Appendix III

Tanks on the Eastern Front, 1943–44

	Pz III L	Pz IVH	Panther A	Tiger 1	King Tiger
Introduced	June 1942	May 1943	August 1943	August 1942	February 1944
Weight (Metric tons)	22.7	25.9	44.8	57.0	69.8
Crew	5	5	5	5	5
Engine	HL–120TRM	HL–120 TRM	HL 230 P30	HL 230 P45	HL 230 P30
Horse Power	265	300	700	700	700
Suspension	Torsion Bar	Leaf Spring	Torsion Bar	Torsion Bar	Torsion Bar
Max Speed (kph)*	40/20	40/20	46/24	38/20	35/17
Fuel Type	Gasoline	Gasoline	Gasoline	Gasoline	Gasoline
Range (kms)*	155/95	210/130	250/100	100/57	170/120
Max Fording Depth (m)	0.8	1.2	1.9	1.6	1.6
Track width (cm)	40	40	66	72.5	80
Main Gun	5-cm KwK 39 L/60	7.5-cm KwK 40 L/43	7.5-cm KwK 42 L/70	8.8-cm KwK 36 L/56	8.8-cm KwK 43 L/71
Ammo Type	APCBC	APCBC	APCBC	APCBC	APCBC
	APCR	APCR	APCR	APCR	APCR
	HE	HE	HE	HE	HE
					HEAT
Ammo Quantity	78	87	79	92	84
Frontal Armor (mm)	50+20	50–80	60–100	100	100–180
Side Armor (mm)	30	30	40–45	80	80
Rear armor (mm)	50	20–30	40	80	80

Notes:
*On Road/Off-Road

Soviet Tanks

	T-70	T-34/76 Model 1943	T-34/85	KV-85	IS-2
Introduced	March 1942	April 1943	March 1944	November 1943	April 1944
Weight (Metric tons)	10	30.9	32.0	46.0	46.0
Crew	2	4	4	4	4
Engine	2x GAZ-203	V-2	V-2	V-2K	V-2
Horse Power	85 each	500	500	600	600
Suspension	Torsion Bar	Christie	Christie	Torsion Bar	Torsion Bar
Max Speed (kph)*	45/24	55/40	55/40	43/18	37/19
Fuel Type	Gasoline	Diesel	Diesel	Diesel	Diesel
Range (kms)*	360/180	432/365	360/310	160	150/120
Max Fording Depth (m)	0.9	1.3	1.3	1.6	1.3
Track width (cm)	30	55	55	70	65
Main Gun	45-mm L/46	76.2-mm F-34	85-mm ZIS S-53	85-mm D-5T	122-mm D-25T L/43
Ammo Type	AP	APHE	APHE	APHE	APHE-T
	HE-FRAG	HE-FRAG	HE-FRAG	HE-FRAG	HE
Ammo Quantity	90	100	60	70	28
Frontal Armor (mm)	45–60	47–70	47–90	75–110	100–120
Side Armor (mm)	35–45	52–60	60–75	60–65	90
Rear armor (mm)	35	47–52	47–60	60–65	60–90

Tank Production, 1943

Germany

| Month | MEDIUM | | | HEAVY | |
	Pz III	Pz IV	Pz V	Pz VI	TOTAL
January	46	163	(4)*	35	248
February	34	171	(18)	32	255
March	35	205	(59)	41	340
April	46	213	(78)	46	383
May	43	272	324	50	530
June	11	253	160	60	484
July	0	244	202	65	511
August	20	283	120	60	483
September	0	289	197	85	571
October	0	328	257	50	635
November	0	238	209	56	503
December	0	354	299	67	720
TOTAL	**235**	**3,013**	**1,768**	**647**	**5,655**

| Month | ASSAULT GUN | | | | TANK DESTROYERS | | | |
	StuG III	StuH 42	StuG IV	Sturmpanzer	Marder II Marder III	Ferdinand	Hornisse[1]	TOTAL
January	130	0	0	0	140	0	0	
February	140	0	0	0	89	0	14	
March	197	10	0	0	40	1	30	
April	228	34	0	20	34	30	41	
May	260	45	0	40	76	60	35	
June	275	30	0	0	82	0	35	
July	281	25	0	0	90	0	44	
August	291	5	0	0	62	0	16	
September	345	10	0	0	101	0	27	
October	395	11	0	0	141	0	42	
November	163	4	0	0	100	0	24	
December	306	30	30	10	75	0	37	
TOTAL	3,011	204	30	70	1,030	91	345	

* Note: The first production tranche of Pz V Panther tanks required re-building and were not issued until May 1943.

Key Industrial Decisions, 1943
- Hitler is impressed with the 128-mm gun and orders it mounted on either a Panther or Tiger as a tank destroyer.
- May 1943, Hitler approves the Maus super-heavy tank (188 tons) for production, which will divert resources from Krupp and Alkett for the next two years.
- August 1943, Pz III production terminated and facilities shift to Sturmgeschütz production.
- December 1943, Hitler approves Jagdpanzer IV for production against Guderian's objections. Krupp–Grusonwerk AG plant ceases Pz IV production in favor of Jagdpanzer IV.

Primary AFV Manufacturing Centers:
- Braunschweig (*Muehlenbau und Industrie* AG (MIAG), Pz III, StuG-III
- Nurnberg (*Maschinenfabrik* Augsburg Nurnberg AG or MAN), Pz III, Pz V
- Berlin-Marienfelde (Daimler-Benz AG); Pz III, Pz V
- St. Valentin, *Nibelungenwerke*, Pz IV
- Plauen *(Vogtlaendische Maschinenfabrik* AG or VOMAG), Pz IV
- Magdeburg (Krupp-Grusonwerk AG), Pz IV
- Hannover (*Maschinenfabrik* Niedersachen Hannover, GmbH), Pz V
- Kassel (Henschel & *Sohn* AG), Pz V, Pz VI
- Berlin-Borsigwalde (Alkett or Altmärkische Kettenwerk GmbH), StuG-III, StuH 42, Marder II
- Breslau *(Fahrzeug und Motorenbau*, GmbH (FAMO), Marder
- Duisburg, (Deutsche-Eisenwerke AG or DEW), Hornisse/Nashorn

Tank Engines:
- Friedrichshafen (*Maybach Motorenbau GmbH)*: Maybach HL 120 TRM; Maybach HL 230 P30 V12;
- Berlin (*Norddeutsche Motorenbau);* Maybach HL 120 TRM
- Berlin-Niederschönewide (assembly plant)
- Berlin (Daimler-Benz AG); Maybach HL 230 P30 V12
- Zwickau *(Auto Union AG):* Maybach HL 230 P30 V12

New tank models (3):
- April 1943, Pz IV Ausf H with new KwK 40 L/48 gun, improved frontal armor protection up to 80-mm but increased weight by 2.5 ton
- July 1943, Pz V Ausf D with long 7.5-cm KwK 42 L/70 introduced
- August 1943, Pz V Ausf A introduced

New assault gun models (3):
- March 1943, StuH 42 assault gun with 10.5-cm StuH 42 L / 28 howitzer starts mass production. Ten pre-production models were built in November 1942 and sent to Leningrad.
- April 1943, Sturmpanzer introduce with 15-cm StuH 43 L/12 howitzer on Pz IV hull, built by Deutsche Eisenwerke A.G.
- December 1943, StuG IV introduced

New tank destroyer models (2):
- February 1943, Nashhorn tank destroyer equipped with 8.8-cm Pak 43 L/71 on ?? chassis. Built by DEW (Deutsche-Eisenwerke AG) in Duisburg
- April 1943, Ferdinand tank destroyer introduced with 8.8-cm KwK 43 L / 71 gun, built at *Nibelungenwerke*

Soviet Union, 1943

Month	Light			Medium	Heavy				Total
	T-60	*T-70*	*T-80*	*T-34/76*	*KV-1S*	*KV-85*	*IS-1*	*IS-2*	*Total*
January	11	300	0	1,030	92	0	0	0	1,433
February	44	400	0	1,060	73	0	0	0	1,577
March	0	500	0	1,411	53	0	0	0	1,964
April	0	500	0	1,315	45	0	0	0	1,860
May	0	325	0	1,246	75	0	0	0	1,646
June	0	128	0	1,085	30	0	0	0	1,243
July	0	260	20	1,393	52	0	0	0	1,725
August	0	360	20	1,375	39	22	0	0	1,816
September	0	365	20	1,403	0	63	0	0	1,851
October	0	209	17	1,458	0	63	2	0	1,749
November	0	1	0	1,452	0	0	25	0	1,478
December	0	0	0	1,468	0	0	40	35	1,543
TOTAL	55	3,343	77	15,696	459	148	67	35	23,888

Month	SP Guns/Assault Guns					Total
	Su-76	*Su-85*	*Su-122*	*Su-152*	*JSU-152*	*Total*
January	25	0	32	0	0	57
February	N/A	0	100	15	0	N/A
March	N/A	0	100	90	0	N/A
April	0	0	75	75	0	N/A
May	0	0	100	25	0	N/A
June	N/A	0	100	85	0	N/A
July	N/A	3	72	80	0	N/A
August	N/A	100	36	84	0	N/A
September	N/A	152	0	84	0	N/A
October	N/A	162	0	84	0	N/A
November	N/A	166	0	42	0	N/A
December	N/A	176	0	4	35	N/A
TOTAL	1,908	761	611	668	35	4,019

Key Industrial Decisions, 1943
- 21 March 1943, Production of the Su-76 is stopped by GKO after only 170 built due to engine and transmission failures. The improved version, Su-76M, re-enters production in late May or June 1943
- August 1943, Phase-out of KV-1 heavy tank, shift to heavy assault guns and new IS-series heavy tanks
- October 1943, all light tank production programs are cancelled

Primary AFV Manufacturing Centers:
- Sverdlovsk/Plant 37, T-60, Su-76
- Gorky/GAZ Plant, T-70, Su-76
- Nizhniy Tagil/Stalin Ural Tank Factory183, T-34/76
- Chelyabinsk (ChTZ), T-34/76, KV-1, KV-85, IS-1/2, SU-152
- Gorky/Krasnoye Sormovo Plant No. 112, T-34/76
- Omsk/Lenin Plant 174, T-34/76
- Sverdlovsk/UZTM *Uralmash,* T-34/76, Su-85, Su-122
- Kirov/Plant 38, Su-76
- Mytishchi/Plant 40; Su-76

Tank Engines:
- V-2 Diesel engine (Zavod 75)

New tank models (4):
- July 1943, the T-80 light tank entered service as an improved T-70 with a two-man turret, improved armored protection and better horsepower, but was cancelled three months later.
- September 1943, the KV-85 heavy tank entered service as an interim design until the IS-1/2 heavy tanks were ready for production. Based upon a KV-1S hull, but using a new turret designed for the IS-series tank and armed with the 85-mm D-5T gun, a total of 148 KV-85s were built.
- October 1943, the IS-1 (or IS-85) heavy tank entered service, armed with the 85-mm D-5T gun, but these tanks were later re-equipped with the 122-mm D-25T gun.
- December 1943, the IS-2 heavy tank entered service, armed with the 122-mm D25T gun.

New SP/Assault gun models (3):
- February 1943, the SU-152 self-propelled gun entered service as a replacement for the KV-2. Originally designated as the KV-14, it mounted the 152-mm ML-20S gun-howitzer on the chassis of a KV-1S.
- August 1943, the SU-85 tank destroyer entered service, armed with the 85-mm D-5T gun on a T-34 hull.
- December 1943, the ISU-152 assault gun entered service as an improved replacement for the SU-152. It used the same ML-20S howitzer, but substituted the new IS tank chassis.

Armour Order of Battle, 21 June 1944

German

Heeresgruppe Nord (Generaloberst Georg Lindemann)

16.Armee (General der Artillerie Christian Hansen)

18.Armee (General der Artillerie Herbert Loch)

Armee-Abteilung Narwa (General der Infanterie Johannes Frießner)

- III. SS-Panzerkorps (SS-Obergruppenführer Felix Steiner)
  - ○ schwere SS-Panzer-Abteilung 103
  - ○ SS-Panzer-Grenadier-Division *Nordland* (SS-Gruppenführer Fritz Scholz)
  - ○ 20.Waffen-Grenadier-Division der SS (estnische Nr. 1) (Brigadeführer Franz Augsberger)
  - ○ 4.SS-Freiwilligen-Panzergrenadier-Brigade *Nederland* (SS-Brigadeführer Jürgen Wagner)

Under Heeresgruppe Nord control:

- 12.Panzer-Division (Generalmajor Gerhard Müller)

Heeresgruppe Mitte (Generalfeldmarschall Ernst Busch)

3.Panzerarmee (Generaloberst Georg-Hans Reinhardt)

2.Armee (Generaloberst Walter Weiss)

4.Armee (General der Infanterie Kurt von Tippelskirch)

- XII Armeekorps (Generalleutnant Vinzenz Müller)
  - ○ 18.Panzergrenadier-Division (Generalleutnant Karl-Ludwig Zutavern)[1]
- XXVII Armeekorps (General der Infanterie Paul Volkers)
  - ○ 25.Panzergrenadier-Division (Generalleutnant Paul Schürmann)
- Under Army Control: s.Pz.Abt. 501 (Tiger), s.Pzjr.Abt. 655 (Nashorn)

9.Armee (General der Infanterie Hans Jordan)

Under Heeresgruppe Mitte control:

  - ○ 20.Panzer-Division (Generalleutnant Mortimer von Kessel)
  - ○ Panzer-Grenadier-Division *Feldherrnhalle* (Generalmajor Friedrich-Carl von Steinkeller)
  - ○ 5.SS-Panzer-Division *Wiking* (Gruppenführer Herbert Otto Gille)

Heeresgruppe Nordukraine (Generalfeldmarschall Walter Model)

1.Panzerarmee (Generaloberst Erhard Raus)

- III. Panzerkorps (General der Panzertruppe Dietrich von Saucken)
  - ○ 1.Panzer-Division (Generalmajor Werner Marcks)
  - ○ 7.Panzer-Division (Generalmajor Gerhard Schmidhuber)
  - ○ 8.Panzer-Division (Generalmajor Werner Friebe)
  - ○ 17.Panzer-Division (Generalleutnant Karl-Friedrich von der Meden)
  - ○ 20.Panzergrenadier-Division (Generalleutnant Georg Jauer)
- XXIV Panzerkorps (General der Panzertruppen Walther Nehring)
  - ○ schwere Panzerjäger-Abteilung 653 (Ferdinand)

4.Panzerarmee (Generaloberst Josef Harpe)

- LVI Panzerkorps (General der Infanterie Johannes Block)
  - ○ 4.Panzer-Division (Generalleutnant Clemens Betzel)

o 5.Panzer-Division (General der Panzertruppe Karl Decker)
o s.Pz.Abt.505 (Tiger)
o Sturmgeschütz-Brigade 237

1st Army [Hungary] (Lieutenant General Károly Beregfy)
o 2nd Armored Division [Hungarian] Brigadier General Zoltán Zsedényi

Under Heeresgruppe Nordukraine Control:
o 2.SS-Panzer-Division *Das Reich*
o 9.SS-Panzer-Division *Hohenstaufen*
o 10.SS Panzer-Division *Frundsberg*
o 16.Panzer-Division (General-major Hans-Ulrich Back)

Heeresgruppe Südukraine (Generaloberst Ferdinand Schörner)
6.Armee (General der Artillerie Maximilian de Angelis)
• XXX. Armeekorps (General der Artillerie Maximilian Fretter-Pico)
o 13.Panzer-Division (Generalleutnant Hans Tröger)[2]
• XXXXIV Armeekorps (General der Artillerie Maximilian de Angelis)
o 10.Panzergrenadier-Division (Generalleutnant August Schmidt)
• LII Armeekorps (General der Infanterie Erich Buschenhagen)
o schwere Panzerjäger-Abteilung 93 (Nashorn)
• Army Reserve:
o 3.Panzer-Division (Generalleutnant Wilhelm Philipps)

8.Armee (General der Infanterie Otto Wöhler)
• LVII Panzerkorps (General der Panzertruppen Friedrich Kirchner)
o 14.Panzer-Division (Generalleutnant Martin Unrein)
o Panzergrenadier-Division *Großdeutschland* (Generalleutnant Hasso von Manteuffel)
o 24.Panzer-Division (General der Panzertruppe Maximillian Reichsfreiherr von Edelsheim)
o 3.SS-Panzer-Division *Totenkopf* (Gruppenführer Hermann Priess)
• IV Armeekorps (General der Infanterie Friedrich Mieth)
o 23.Panzer-Division (Generalleutnant Joseph von Radowitz)
• Romanian 4th Army

Under Heeresgruppe Südukraine control:
• 1 Rumania Mare Armored Division (Brigadier General Radu Korne)

Reinforcements:
July 1944:
• Fallschirm-Panzer-Division *Hermann Göring* from Italy
• 6.Panzer-Division from Germany
• S.Pz.Abt. 510 [Tiger]

August 1944:
• 19.Panzer-Division from Holland
• Panzer-Brigaden 101, 102, 103, 104 [Panther]

September 1944:
• Panzer-Brigaden 109, 110 [Panther]
• Fuhrer-Grenadier Brigade [Panther]

Soviet

Leningrad Front (General Leonid A. Govorov)
- 4x Tank Brigades (30 G; 1, 152, 220)
- 14x Tank Regiments (26 G, 27 G, 31 G, 46 G, 260 G; 27, 45, 82, 98, 124, 185, 221, 222, 226)
- 12x SAP (394 G, 396 G, 397 G; 806, 938, 952, 1198, 1222, 1238, 1439, 1495, 1811)

3rd Baltic Front (General Ivan I. Maslennikov)
- 3x Tank Brigades (7 G; 16, 122)
- 4x Tank Regiments (33 G; 51, 258, 511)
- 3x SAP (750, 768, 1433)

2nd Baltic Front (General Andrei I. Eremenko)
- 3x Tank Brigades (29 G; 78, 118)
- 6x Tank Regiments (37, 47, 81, 227, 239, 249)
- 4x SAP (991, 1199, 1453, 1539)
- Under Front Control:
  - 5th Tank Corps (General–major Mikhail G. Sakhno)

1st Baltic Front (General Ivan Bagramyan)
- 5x Tank Brigades (10 G, 34 G, 39 G; 143, 171)
- 2x Tank Regiments (2 G; 105)
- 1x SAP (1203)
  - 43rd Army (General–leytenant Afanasy P. Beloborodov)
  - 1st Tank Corps (General–leytenant Vasily V. Butkov)

3rd Byelorussian Front (General-polkovnik Ivan D. Chernyakovskiy)
- 5x Tank Brigades (2G; 28 G; 120, 153, 213)
- 1x Tank Regiment (63 G)
- 10x SAP (735, 926, 927, 953, 954, 957, 958, 959, 1435, 1445)
  - 11th Guards Army (General–leytenant Kuzma N. Galitskiy)
  - 2nd Guards Tank Corps (General–leytenant Aleksei S. Burdeyniy)
  - 5th Tank Army (Marshal Pavel A. Rotmistrov)
  - 3rd Guards Tank Corps (General–major Ivan A. Vovchenko)
  - 29th Tank Corps (General–major Evgeny I. Fominykh)
  - 3rd Guards Cavalry Corps (General–leytenant Nikolai S. Oslikovskiy)
  - Front Reserve:
  - 3rd Guards Mechanized Corps (General–leytenant Viktor T. Obukhov)

2nd Byelorussian Front (General-polkovnik Georgiy F. Zakharov)
- 4x Tank Brigades (23 G, 42 G, 43 G; 256)
- 1x Tank Regiment (233)
- 7x SAP (722, 1196, 1197, 1444, 1819, 1830, 1902)

1st Byelorussian Front (Marshal Konstantin K. Rokossovsky)
  - 2x Tank Brigades (1, 68)
  - 8x Tank Regiments (36, 42, 193, 223, 230, 231, 251, 259)
  - 16x SAP (713, 922, 925, 1204, 1205, 1206, 1221, 1295, 1812, 1821, 1888, 1890, 1897, 1899, 1900, 1901)
  - 3rd Army (General–leytenant Aleksandr V. Gorbatov)
  - 9th Tank Corps (General–major Boris S. Bakharov)

- 65th Army (General-leytenant Pavel I. Batov)
- 1st Guards Tank Corps (General-major Mikhail F. Panov)
- 1st Mechanized Corps (General-leytenant Semyon M. Krivoshein)

Under Front control:
- 8th Guards Tank Corps (General-leytenant Aleksei F. Popov)
- 11th Tank Corps (General-major Filipp N. Rudkin)
- 2nd Guards Cavalry Corps (General-leytenant Vladimir V. Kriukov)
- 4th Guards Cavalry Corps (General-leytenant Issa A. Pliyev)
- 7th Guards Cavalry Corps (General-major Mikhail P. Konstantinov)

1st Ukrainian Front (General Konstantin K. Rokossovsky)
- 1st Guards Tank Army
  - 8th Guards Mechanized Corps (General-major Ivan F. Dremov)
  - 11th Guards Tank Corps (General-leytenant Andrei L. Getman)
  - 64th Guards Tank Brigade
  - 11th Guards Tank Regiment
- 3rd Guards Tank Army
  - 6th Guards Tank Corps (General-major Vasily V. Novikov)
  - 7th Guards Tank Corps (General-major Sergei A. Ivanov)
  - 9th Mechanized Corps (General-leytenant Ivan P. Sukhov)
  - 91st Tank Brigade
  - 71st Guards Tank Regiment
- 4th Tank Army
  - 6th Guards Mechanized Corps (General-leytenant Aleksandr I. Akimov)
  - 10th Guards Tank Corps (General-major Evtikhii E. Belov)
  - 93rd Tank Brigade
  - 72nd Guards Tank Regiment
- 13th Army
  - 25th Tank Corps (General-major Fedor G. Anikushkin)
- 60th Army
  - 4th Guards Tank Corps (General-leytenant Pavel P. Poluboiarov)
  - 59th Tank Regiment
- 31st Tank Corps (General-major Vasily E. Grigoriev)
- 1x Tank brigade (150)
- 3x Tank Regiments (1G, 12 G; 39)
- 4x SAP (293 G; 1228, 1827, 1889)

2nd Ukrainian Front (General Rodion Ia. Malinovsky)
- 2nd Tank Army
  - 3rd Tank Corps (General-leytenant Vasily A. Mishulin)
  - 16th Tank Corps (General-major Ivan V. Dubovoi)
  - 11th Guards Tank Brigade
  - 754th, 1219th SAP
- 6th Tank Army (General-leytenant Andrei G. Kravchenko)
  - 5th Mechanized Corps (General-leytenant Mikhail V. Volkov)
  - 5th Guards Tank Corps (General-leytenant Vasily M. Alekseev)[3]
  - 156th Tank Regiment
  - 1494th SAP

- Under Front Control:
  - o 7th Mechanized Corps (General-major Fedor G. Katkov)
  - o 18th Tank Corps (General-major Vasily I. Polozkov)[4]
- 1x Tank Brigade (27 G)
- 2x Tank Regiments (25, 38)

3rd Ukrainian Front (General Fedor I. Tolbukhin)
- Under Front Control:
  - o 4th Guards Mechanized Corps (General-major Vladimir I. Zhdanov)
  - o 23rd Tank Corps (General-major Aleksei O. Akhmanov)
  - o 5th Guards Mechanized Brigade
- 1x Tank Brigade (96)
- 2x Tank Regiments (5 G; 52)
- 6x SAP (398 G; 864, 1200, 1201, 1202, 1891)

STAVKA Reserve (RVGK)
- 10th Tank Corps (General-major Matvei K. Shaposhnikov)
- 19th Tank Corps (General-leytenant Ivan D. Vasiliev)
- 20th Tank Corps (General-leytenant Ivan G. Lazarev)
- 1st Guards Mechanized Corps (General-leytenant Ivan N. Russiyanov)
- 2nd Guards Mechanized Corps (General-leytenant Karp V. Sviridov)
- 5th Guards Mechanized Corps (General-major Boris M. Skvortsov)
- 7th Guards Mechanized Corps (General-leytenant Ivan P. Korchagin)
- 8th Mechanized Corps (General-major Abram M. Hasin)

Coastal Army (General-leytenant Kondrat S. Mel'nik)
- 1x Tank Brigade (63)
- 3x Tank Regiments (85, 244), 257)
- 1x SAP (1449)

Front	Tank Armies	Tank Corps	Mechanized Corps	Tank Brigades	Tank Regiments	Total Authorized Tanks
Leningrad				4	14	600
3rd Baltic				3	4	250
2nd Baltic		1		3	6	500
1st Baltic		1		5	2	450
3rd Byelorussian	1	3	1	5	1	900
2nd Byelorussian				4	1	200
1st Byelorussian		4	1	2	8	1,200
1st Ukrainian	3	7	3	4	7	2,100
2nd Ukrainian	2	3	2	2	3	1,000
3rd Ukrainian		1	1	1	2	450
Coastal Army				1	3	150
RVGK		3	5		8	1,650
TOTAL	**6**	**23**	**13**	**34**	**59**	**9,450**

Reinforcements:
December:
- 10th Mechanized Corps

Tank Production, 1944

Germany

Month	Medium		Heavy		
	Pz IV	*Pz V*	*Pz VI Tiger I*	*Pz VI Tiger II*	*Total*
January	300	279	93	5	677
February	252	256	95	5	608
March	310	270	86	6	672
April	299	311	104	6	720
May	302	345	100	15	762
June	300	370	75	32	777
July	300	380	64	45	789
August	300	350	6	94	750
September	180	335	0	63	578
October	187	278	0	26	491
November	200	318	0	26	544
December	195	285	0	56	536
TOTAL	**3,125**	**3,777**	**620**	**379**	**7,901**

Month	Assault Gun				Tank Destroyers					
	StuG III	StuH 42	StuG IV	Sturmpnzr	Marder III	Hornisse Nashorn	JgPnzr IV PnzrIV/70	Jgpnzr 38	JgPnthr	Total
January	227	20	108	20	74	0	30	0	5	484
February	196	54	181	15	53	25	45	0	7	576
March	264	50	87	16	79	0	75	3	8	582
April	294	58	91	12	47	20	106	20	10	658
May	335	46	95	3	31	24	90	59	10	693
June	341	100	90	40	39	6	120	102	6	844
July	377	92	90	30	0	3	125	110	15	842
August	312	110	70	20	0	31	152	178	14	887
September	356	119	65	19	0	12	139	237	21	968
October	325	100	53	14	0	7	193	240	88	1,020
November	361	102	80	3	0	5	205	406	55	1,217
December	452	40	49	23	0	0	255	332	67	1,218
TOTAL	3,840	903	1,059	215	323	133	1,535	1,687	226	9,989

Key Industrial Decisions, 1944
- December 1943 – January 1944, Utilize Czech production facilities to mass-produce the Jagdpanzer 38 tank destroyer.
- Spring 1944, VOMAG ceases Pz IV production in favor of Jagdpanzer IV. Only Nibelungenwerke still producing Pz IV.
- August 1944, Hitler order Pz IV tank production to cease by the end of 1944 and shift production resources to the Jagdpanzer IV program.

Additional AFV Manufacturing Centers:
Jagdpanzer 38 (t)
- Prague, Boemisch-Märische Maschinenfabrik (BMM), began production in March 1944
- Pilsen, Skoda Werke, began roduction in July 1944

New tank models (1):
- March 1944, Panther Ausf G introduced.

New assault gun models (1):
- August 1944, the Sturmtiger entered limited service (18 built) after a long development period by Krupp and Alkett. It mounted a 380-mm rocket launcher on a Tiger I hull.

New tank destroyer models (5):
- January 1944, the Jagdpanzer IV was introduced. It mounted a 7.5-cm Pak 39 L/48 atop a Pz IV chassis.
- January 1944, the Jagdpanther entered service, mounting an 8.8-cm Pak 43 on a Panther hull.
- April 1944, the Jagdpanzer 38 was introduced as a low-cost supplement to use the Pz 38(t) chassis with a 7.5-cm Pak 39 L/48.
- July 1944, the Jagdtiger is introduced in limited numbers, mounting a 12.8-cm Pak 44 L/55 atop a King Tiger chassis. Total of 51 built in 1944.
- August 1944, the Panzer IV/70, which was an up-gunned variant of the Jagdpanzer IV armed with the 7.5-cm Pak 42 L/70 gun, entered serviced.

Soviet Union

| Month | Medium | | Heavy | |
	T-34/76	T-34/85	IS-2	TOTAL
January	1,220	25	35	1,280
February	1,180	75	75	1,330
March	889	328	100	1,317
April	176	992	150	1,318
May	186	1,001	175	1,362
June	177	1,034	200	1,411
July	102	1,119	225	1,446
August	154	1,175	250	1,579
September	2	1,236	250	1,488
October	0	1,239	250	1,489
November	0	1,242	250	1,492
December	0	1,196	250	1,446
TOTAL	4,086	10,662	2,210	16,958

			SP Guns/Assault Guns			
Month	*Su–76*	*Su–85*	*Su–100*	*Su–122*	*JSU–152*	*Total*
January	N/A	176	0	N/A	N/A	N/A
February	N/A	176	0	N/A	N/A	N/A
March	N/A	191	0	N/A	N/A	N/A
April	N/A	200	0	N/A	N/A	N/A
May	N/A	205	0	N/A	N/A	N/A
June	N/A	210	0	N/A	N/A	N/A
July	N/A	210	0	N/A	N/A	N/A
August	N/A	210	0	0	N/A	N/A
September	380	135	40	0	N/A	N/A
October	N/A	120	90	0	N/A	N/A
November	N/A	60	150	0	N/A	N/A
December	N/A	0	220	0	N/A	N/A
TOTAL	**7,155**	**1,893**	**500**	**493**	**2,510**	**12,551**

Key Industrial Decisions, 1944
- Production switched from the T-34/76 to the T-34/85 in April 1944 and T-34/76 production ceased entirely by September 1943.
- Chelyabinsk (ChTZ) ceased all T-34 production after March 1944 and switched entirely to IS-2 and ISU-152 production.

Notes

Chapter 1

1. Christopher W. Wilbeck, *Sledgehammers: Strengths and Flaws of Tiger Tank Battalions in World War II* (Bedford, PA: the Aberjona Press, 2004), pp. 18–23.

2. Thomas L. Jentz, *Panzertruppen: The Complete Guide to the Creation & Combat Employment of Germany's Tank Force, 1943–1945, Volume II* (Atglen, PA: Schiffer Military History, 1996), pp. 43.

3. Manfred Kehrig, *Stalingrad: Analyse und Dokumentation einer Schlacht* (Stuttgart: Deutsche Verlag-Anstalt, 1974), pp. 670.

4. Jentz, pp. 49.

5. Heinz Guderian, *Panzer Leader* (New York: Ballantine Books, Inc., 1968), pp. 234.

6. Samuel W. Mitcham Jr., *Hitler's Legions: The German Army Order of Battle, World War II* (New York: Stein & Day Publishers, 1985), pp. 387.

7. Guderian, pp. 237.

8. Guderian, pp. 239.

9. Meldung der Sonderkommission des OKH, 27 June 1941, NAM (National Archives Microfilm), series T-315, Roll 744, frame 729.

10. IIa, lib, Tatigkeitsbericht Verlustliste, Apr 1 - Oct 31, 1942, PzAOK 1, NAM (National archives Microfilm), series T-313, Roll 36.

11. Ernst Rebentisch, *The Combat History of the 23rd Panzer Division in World War II* (Mechanischsburg, PA: Stackpole Books, 2012), pp. 496–500.

12. Hans Schäufler, *Knights Cross Panzers: The German 35th Panzer Regiment in WWII* (Mechanichsburg, PA: Stackpole Books, 2010), pp. 203.

13. Armin Bottger, *To the Gates of Hell: The Memoir of a Panzer Crewman* (Barnsley, UK: Frontline Books, 2013).

14. Bottger.

15. Jentz, pp. 34.

16. Wolfgang Schneider, *Panzer Tactics: German Small-Unit Armour Tactics in World War II* (Mechanicsburg, PA: Stackpole Books, 2005), pp. 326.

17. Artem Drabkin and Oleg Sheremet, *T-34 in Action* (Barnsley, UK: Pen & Sword, 2006), pp. 128.

18. Otto Carius, *Tigers in the Mud* (Mechanicsburg, PA: Stackpole Books, 1992), pp. 3–20

19. *The United States Strategic Bombing Survey: The Effects of Strategic Bombing on the German War Economy* (Washington, DC: U.S. Government Printing Office, 1945), Tables 14, 15.

20. Lukas Friedli, *Repairing the Panzers: German Tank Maintenance in World War 2*, Volume 2 (Monroe, NY: Panzerwrecks, 2011), pp. 151.

21. Adam Tooze, *The Wages of Destruction: The Making and Breaking of the Nazi Economy* (New York: Penguin Books, 2006), pp. 552–589.

22. Tooze, pp. 569.

23. Walter J. Spielberger, *Panzer IV and its Variants* (Atglen, PA: Schiffer Military History, 1993), pp. 60.

24. Spielberger, pp. 80.

25. Tooze, pp. 152–154.

26. Steven J. Zaloga, *Panther vs. Sherman: Battle of the Bulge 1944* (Oxford: Osprey Publishing, 2008), pp. 13.

27. Michael Winninger, *OKH Toy Factory: The Nibelungenwerke, Tank Production in St. Valentin* (Andelfingen, Switzerland: History Facts, 2013), pp. 184–205.

28. Roddy MacDougall and Darren Neely, *Nürnberg's Panzer Factory* (Monroe, NY: Panzerwrecks, 2011), pp. 53.

29. Albert Speer, *Inside the Third Reich* (New York: Simon & Schuster, 1970), pp. 217.

30. Walter J. Spielberger, *Panther and its Variants* (Atglen, PA: Schiffer Military History, 1993), pp. 244.

31. Spielberger, *Panther and its Variants* pp. 244 and Thomas L. Jentz, *Germany's Panther Tank: The Quest for Combat Supremacy* (Atglen, PA: Schiffer Military History, 1995), pp. 89.

32. Spielberger, *Panther and its Variants* pp. 106.

33. Tooze, pp. 602.

34. Tooze, pp. 598.

35. Charles C. Sharp, *Soviet Order of Battle World War II, Vol. III* (Published by George F. Nafziger, 1995), pp. 4.
36. Charles C. Sharp, *Soviet Armour Tactics in World War II* (Published by George F. Nafziger, 1999), pp. 100–101.
37. David M. Glantz, *Colossus Reborn: The Red Army at War, 1941–1943* (Lawrence, KS: University Press of Kansas, 2005), pp. 224.
38. Glantz, pp. 223.
39. G. F. Krivosheev, *Soviet Casualties and Combat Losses in the Twentieth Century* (Mechanicsburg, PA: Stackpole Books, 1997), pp. 252
40. Drabkin, pp. 40.
41. Valeriy Zamulin, *Demolishing the Myth: The Tank Battle at Prokhorovka, Kursk, July 1943: An Operational Narrative* (Solihull, UK: Helion & Company Ltd., 2011), pp. 83
42. Charles C. Sharp, *Soviet Armour Tactics in World War II* (Published by George F. Nafziger, 1999), pp. 73–77.
43. Drabkin, pp. 80.
44. Drabkin, pp. 129.
45. Mark Harrison, *Accounting for War: Soviet Production, Employment and the Defence Burden, 1940–45* (Cambridge: Cambridge University Press, 2002), pp. 226. Also, A. Yu. Yermolov, *Gosudarstvennoe upravienie voennoy promyshlennostyu v 1940-e gody: Tankovaya promyshlennost* (Saint Petersburg: Aleteyya, 2012), pp. 188.
46. Sergey Ustyantsev and Dmitri Kolmakov, *Boevye mashiny uravagonzvoda tank T-34* (Media-Print, 2005), pp. 86.
47. Mikhail Kolomiets and Ilya Moshchanskiy, *Tanki Lend-liza 1941–1945* (Moscow: Eksprint, 2000).

Chapter 2
1. Wilhelm Tieke, *The Caucasus and the Oil: The German-Soviet War in the Caucasus 1942/43* (Winnipeg: J. J. Fedorowicz Publishing Inc., 1995), pp. 232–237.
2. Tieke, pp. 145–48, 250.
3. Ernst Rebentisch, *The Combat History of the 23rd Panzer Division in World War II* (Mechanicsburg, PA: Stackpole, 2012), pp. 205.
4. Veterans of the 3rd Panzer Division, *Armoured Bears: The German 3rd Panzer Division in World War II, Volume II* (Mechanicsburg, PA: Stackpole Books, 2013), pp. 113–115.
5. Ibid. pp. 131–132.
6. Tieke, pp. 298–299.
7. David M. Glantz, *Endgame at Stalingrad, Book 2: December 1942 – February 1943* (Lawrence, KS: University Press of Kansas, 2014), pp. 408.
8. Glantz, *Endgame at Stalingrad*, pp. 403.
9. Glantz, *Endgame at Stalingrad*, pp. 441.
10. Robert A. Forczyk, *Panzerjäger vs. KV-1: Eastern Front 1941–43* (Oxford: Osprey Publishing, 2012), pp. 69.
11. Glantz, *Endgame at Stalingrad*, pp. 444.
12. Glantz, *Endgame at Stalingrad*, pp. 403.
13. Glantz, *Endgame at Stalingrad*, pp. 485.
14. Ewald Klapdor, *Viking Panzers: The German 5th SS Tank Regiment in the East in World War II* (Mechanicsburg, PA: Stackpole Books, 2011), pp. 132–133.
15. Rebentisch, pp. 217.
16. Wolfgang Schneider, *Tigers in Combat, Volume I* (Mechanicsburg, PA: Stackpole Books, 2004), pp. 74.
17. Schneider, pp. 121.
18. Rebentisch, pp. 231.
19. Jentz, pp. 32.
20. Rebentisch, pp. 231.
21. Klapdor, pp. 141.
22. Klapdor, pp. 142.
23. Friederich W. von Mellenthin, *Panzer Battles: A Study of the Employment of Armour in the Second World War* (New York: Ballantine Books, 1971), pp. 250.
24. Pavel Rotmistrov, *Stal'naya gvardiya* [Steel Guard] (Moscow: Voenizdat, 1984), Chapter 3.
25. Robert Forczyk, *Tank Warfare on the Eastern Front 1941–1942: Schwerpunkt* (Barnsley, UK: Pen & Sword, 2013), pp. 244–246.
26. Samuel W. Mitcham, Jr. *Hitler's Legions: The German Army Order of Battle, World War II* (New York: Stein & Day Publishers, 1985), pp. 378.

27. Jentz, pp. 31.
28. Vasiliy M Badanov, *Glubokii tankovyi reid* [Deep Tank Raid] in A.M. Samsonov (ed.) *Stalingradskaya epopeya* (Moscow: Nauka Publishers, 1968), pp. 625–640.
29. Erich von Manstein, *Lost Victories* (Novato, CA: Presidio Press, 1982), pp. 389.
30. Steven J. Zaloga, P*anzer 38(t)*, (Oxford, Osprey Publishing, Ltd. 2015), pp. 32–33.
31. Richard N. Armstrong, *Red Army Tank Commanders* (Atglen, PA: Schiffer Publishing, 1994), pp. 163–164.
32. John Erickson, *The Road to Berlin* (London: Cassell, 2003), pp. 33.
33. Franz Kurowski, *Sturmgeschütz vor!* (Winnipeg: J. J. Fedorowicz Publishing, Inc., 1999), pp. 39.
34. Paul Carell, *Scorched Earth: The Russian-German War 1943–1944* (Atglen, PA: Schiffer Publishing, 1994), pp. 280–82.
35. Schneider, pp. 74.
36. David. M. Glantz, *The Battle for Leningrad 1941–1944* (Lawrence, KS: University Press of Kansas, 2002), pp. 270.
37. Schneider, pp. 75.
38. Website: http://bdsa.ru/documents/html/donesyanvar43.html.
39. Armstrong, pp. 57.
40. David M. Glantz, *From the Don to the Dnepr: Soviet Offensive Operations December 1942– August 1943* (London: Frank Cass, 1991), pp. 93.
41. Glantz, *From the Don to the Dnepr*, pp. 106.
42. Glantz, *From the Don to the Dnepr*, pp. 108.
43. Von Manstein, pp. 416–417.
44. Klapdoor, pp. 178.
45. Hans-Joachim Jung, *Panzer Soldiers for 'God, Honor, Fatherland' The History of Panzerregiment Großdeutschland* (Winnipeg: J. J. Fedorowicz Publishing, Inc., 2000), pp. 39.
46. Rudolf Lehmann, *The Leibstandarte, Volume III* (Winnipeg: J. J. Fedorowicz Publishing, Inc., 1990), pp. 47.
47. George M. Nipe, Jr., *Last Victory in Russia: The SS-Panzerkorps and Manstein's Kharkov Counter-offensive February-March 1943* (Atglen, PA: Schiffer Publishing, 2000), pp. 87.
48. Ia, KTB, SS-Panzer-Korps, *Darstellung der Ereignisse as 5.2.1943*, NAM (National Archives Microfilm), Series T-354, Roll. 120.
49. Will Fey, *Armour Battles of the Waffen-SS 1943–45* (Mechanicsburg, PA: Stackpole Books, 2003), pp. 5.
50. Lehmann, pp. 88–89.
51. Wolfgang Schneider, *Tigers in Combat, Volume II* (Mechanicsburg, PA: Stackpole Books, 2004), pp. 83–84.
52. Lehmann, pp. 96.
53. Nipe, pp. 126.
54. Lehmann, pp. 66.
55. Nipe, pp. 217–218.
56. Lehmann, pp. 150–151.
57. Lehmann, pp. 151.
58. Lehmann, pp. 152–153.
59. Jung, pp. 47.
60. Hans Schäufler, *Knights Cross Panzers: The German 35ᵗʰ Panzer Regiment in WWII* (Mechanicsburg, PA: Stackpole Books, 2010), pp. 210–213.
61. David Glantz, *Atlas and Survey, Prelude to Kursk: The Soviet Central Front Offensive, February-March 1943* (Self-Published, 1998).
62. Schäufler pp. 213–217.
63. Schäufler pp. 219–220.
64. Von Hardesty and Ilya Grinberg, *Red Phoenix Rising: The Soviet air Force in World War II* (Lawrence, KS: University Press of Kansas, 2012), pp. 165–222.
65. Elena Zhiltsova and Vasily Stoyanov, *Na Kubanskom platsdarme: tankovyye boi na Kubani, 5 fevralya-9 sentyabrya 1943 goda* [*On the Kuban Bridgehead: Tank Battles in the Kuban, 5 February – 9 September 1943*] (BTV-MN, 2002).
66. Tieke, pp. 345.
67. Hans-Ulrich Rudel, *Stuka Pilot* (New York: Bantam Books, 1984), pp. 85–94.
68. Friedrich von Hake, *Der Schicksalsweg der 13. Panzer-Division 1939–1945* [*The Destiny of the 13. Panzer-Division*] (Eggolsheim, Germany: Dorfler im Nebel Verlag, 2006), pp. 163–164.
69. Jentz, pp. 43.
70. Edward Bacon, 'Soviet Military Losses in World War II,' *Journal of Slavic Military Studies*, Vol. 6, no. 4 (December 1993), pp. 623.

71. Erich Hager, *The War Diaries of a Panzer Soldier: Erich Hager with the 17th Panzer Division on the Russian Front 1941–1945* (Atglen, PA: Schiffer Military Publishing, 2010), pp. 113–119.
72. David M. Glantz and Jonathan M. House, *The Battle of Kursk* (Lawrence, KS: University Press of Kansas, 1999), pp. 21–23.
73. Schäufler pp. 221.
74. Lukas Friedli, *Repairing the Panzers: German Tank Maintenance in World War 2*, Volume 1 (Monroe, NY: Panzerwrecks, 2010), pp. 152–156.
75. Guderian, pp. 249–250.
76. 'Einsatzbereite Pz. u. Stu.Gesch. Ost.', Gen. Qu. Insp. D. Panzertruppen, NAM (National archives Microfilm), series T-78, Roll 145, Frame 76020.
77. Niklas Zetterling and Anders Frankson, *Kursk 1943: A Statistical Analysis* (London: Frank Cass Publishers, 2000), pp. 27–31.
78. Zetterling, pp. 22.
79. Valeriy Zamulin, *Demolishing the Myth: The Tank Battle at Prokhorovka, Kursk, July 1943: An Operational Narrative* (Solihull, UK: Helion & Company Ltd., 2011), pp. 43.
80. David M. Glantz and Jonathan M. House, *The Battle of Kursk* (Lawrence, KS: University Press of Kansas, 1999), pp. 76.
81. Zamulin, pp. 40.
82. Zamulin, pp. 54.
83. Karl-Heinz Münch, *The Combat History of German Heavy Anti-Tank Unit 653 in World War II* (Mechanicsburg, PA: Stackpole Books, 2010), pp. 57.
84. Jung, pp. 131.
85. Robert Forczyk, *Kursk 1943: The Northern Front* (Oxford: Osprey Publishing, 2014), pp. 73–74.
86. Zetterling, pp. 34–35.
87. Didier Lodieu, 'La Panther-Abteilung de la 9. Pz.-Div. ou la II./Panzer-Regiment 33 puis la Panzer Abteilung 51 Historique du Pz.-Rgt. 33,' *39/45 Magazine*, No. 169, July 2000.
88. David M. Glantz and Jonathan M. House, *The Battle of Kursk* (Lawrence, KS: University Press of Kansas, 1999), pp. 84.
89. Glantz and House, pp. 96.
90. Jung, pp. 115–116.
91. Zamulin, pp. 97–99.
92. Lehmann, pp. 215.
93. Zetterling, pp. 207.
94. Glantz and House, pp. 102.
95. Glantz and House, pp. 105.
96. Mikhail E. Katukov, *Na ostrie glavnogo udara* [*On the Point of the Main Attack*] (Moscow: Military Publishing House, 1974), pp. 220–222.
97. Zamulin, pp. 132.
98. Zamulin, pp. 141.
99. George M. Nipe, *Blood, Steel and Myth: The II. SS-Panzerkorps and the Road to Prochorowka, July 1943* (Stamford, CT: RZM Publishing, 2011), pp. 199.
100. Zamulin, pp. 123–124.
101. Christer Bergström, *Kursk, The Air Battle: July 1943* (Hersham, UK: Ian Allan Publishing, 2007), pp. 66.
102. George M. Nipe, *Blood, Steel and Myth: The II. SS-Panzerkorps and the Road to Prochorowka, July 1943* (Stamford, CT: RZM Publishing, 2011), pp. 208.
103. Nipe, pp. 237.
104. Zamulin, pp. 167.
105. Nipe, 267–268.
106. Robert Forczyk, *Panther vs T-34: Ukraine 1943* (Oxford: Osprey Publishing, 2007), pp. 56.
107. Nipe, pp. 216.
108. Zamulin, pp. 192–193.
109. Zamulin, pp. 241.
110. Zamulin, pp. 276.
111. David M. Glantz and Jonathan M. House, *The Battle of Kursk* (Lawrence, KS: University Press of Kansas, 1999), pp. 169.
112. Zamulin, pp. 330.
113. Zamulin, pp. 336–337.
114. Nipe, pp. 318–319.
115. Nipe, pp. 331–332.
116. Zamulin, pp. 440.

117. Lehmann, pp. 238.
118. Zetterling, pp. 187, 207.
119. Zetterling, pp. 188.
120. Didier Lodieu, *III. Pz. Korps at Kursk* (Paris: Histoire & Collections, 2007), pp. 102–103.
121. Bergström, pp. 78.
122. Didier Lodieu, *III. Pz. Korps at Kursk* (Paris: Histoire & Collections, 2007), pp. 120.
123. Paul Carell, *Scorched Earth: The Russian-German War 1943–1944* (Atglen, PA: Schiffer Publishing, 1994), pp. 91.
124. Zamulin, pp. 547–548.
125. Grigoryi A. Koltunov, 'Kursk: The Clash of Armour,' *History of the Second World War* (Marshall Cavendish, 1973), pp. 1384.
126. David M. Glantz, *When Titans Clashed: How the Red Army Stopped Hitler* (Lawrence, KS: University Press of Kansas, 1995), pp. 167.
127. George M. Nipe, *Decision in the Ukraine: Summer 1943, II SS and III Panzerkorps* (Winnipeg: J. J. Fedorowicz Publishing Inc., 1996), pp. 63–64.
128. Zetterling, pp. 199.
129. Zetterling, pp. 220–221.
130. Sergei M. Shtemenko, *The Soviet General Staff at War 1941–1945* (Honolulu: University Press of the Pacific, 2001), pp. 162.
131. David M. Glantz and Jonathan M. House, *The Battle of Kursk* (Lawrence, KS: University Press of Kansas, 1999), pp. 232–234.
132. Bergström, pp. 88–89.
133. Münch, pp. 51.
134. Bergström, pp. 91.
135. Wolfgang Schneider, *Tigers in Combat, Volume I* (Mechanicsburg, PA: Stackpole Books, 2004), pp. 225.
136. Bergström, pp. 93.
137. Rudel, pp. 101.
138. Münch, pp. 54–55.
139. Jung, pp. 143.
140. Rebentisch, pp. 281.
141. George M. Nipe, *Decision in the Ukraine: Summer 1943, II SS and III Panzerkorps* (Winnipeg: J. J. Fedorowicz Publishing Inc., 1996), pp. 99–102.
142. Schneider, Vol. II, 118, 158.
143. Bergström, pp. 118.
144. George M. Nipe, *Decision in the Ukraine: Summer 1943, II SS and III Panzerkorps* (Winnipeg: J. J. Fedorowicz Publishing Inc., 1996), pp. 190.
145. Rebentisch, pp. 285–286.
146. Ian Michael Wood, *Tigers of the Death's Head: SS Totenkopf Division's Tiger Company* (Mechanicsburg, PA: Stackpole Books, 2013), pp. 50.
147. Wolfgang Vopersal, *Soldaten, Kämpfer, Kameraden: Marsch und Kämpfe der SS Totenkopf-Division, Vol. III* (Bissendorf, GE: Biblio-Verlag, 1999), pp. 433.
148. Nipe, pp. 218–219.
149. Vopersal, pp. 441.
150. Nipe, pp. 252.
151. David M. Glantz and Jonathan M. House, *The Battle of Kursk* (Lawrence, KS: University Press of Kansas, 1999), pp. 245.
152. Andrei L. Getman, *Tanki idut na Berlin [Tanks Go to Berlin]* (Moscow: Nauka, 1973), pp. 113–114.
153. Walter Rahn, 'Fighting Withdrawal of Kampfgruppe von Sivers as Floating Bubble in the Vorskla Valley from Tomarovka via Borissovka-Grayvoron-Pirasevka-Kirovka as far as Akhtyrka in August 1943,' unpublished paper by former orderly officer of Panzer-Abteilung 52.
154. David M. Glantz, *From the Don to the Dnepr: Soviet Offensive Operations, December 1942 – August 1943* (London: Frank Cass Publishers, 1991), pp. 286.
155. Getman, pp. 119–120.
156. Jung, pp. 147.
157. Getman, pp. 125.
158. Nipe, pp. 281.
159. Getman, pp. 127.
160. Glantz, *From the Don to the Dnepr*, pp. 313.
161. Schneider, Vol. II, 159.
162. Schneider, Vol. II, 39.

163. Jentz, Volume 2, pp. 110.
164. Jentz, Volume 2, pp. 136–137.
165. Vasily P. Istomin, *Smolenskaya nastupatel'naya operatsiya 1943* [*Smolensk Offensive Operation 1943*] (Moscow: Military Publishing House, 1975).
166. Veit Scherzer, *113. Infanterie-Division, Kiew – Charkow – Stalingrad* (Jena: Scherzers-Militaer-Verlag Ranis, 2007), pp. 260.
167. Istomin.
168. Istomin.
169. Sherzer, pp. 256.
170. Dmitry F. Loza, *Fighting for the Soviet Motherland: Recollections from the Eastern Front* (Lincoln, NE: University of Nebraska Press, 1998), pp. 21.
171. Krivosheev, pp. 262.
172. Artem Drabin and Oleg Sheremet, *T-34 in Action* (Barnsley, UK: Pen & Sword, 2006), pp. 68.
173. Rebentisch, pp. 296.
174. Rebentisch, pp. 303.
175. Rebentisch, pp. 305.
176. Jentz, Volume 2, pp. 114–115, 284.
177. John Erickson, *The Road to Berlin* (London: Cassell, 1983), pp. 122.
178. Aleksandr D. Tsirlin, P. Biryukov, V. P. Istomin and E. H. Fedoseyev, *Inzhenernyye voyska v boyakh za Sovetskuyu Rodinu* [*Army Corps of Engineers in the Battle for the Soviet Motherland*] (Moscow: Military Publishing, 1970), Chapter 8.
179. Aleksandr A. Maslov, *Fallen Soviet Generals: Soviet General Officers Killed in Battle, 1941–1945* (London: Routledge, 1998), pp. 109.
180. Maslov, pp. 109.
181. David M. Glantz, *The History of Soviet Airborne Forces* (London: Routledge, 1994), pp. 265–272.
182. Kirill S. Moskalenko, *Na Yugo-Zapadnom napravlenii* [*In the Southwest Direction*] (Moscow: Nauka, 1969), pp. 34–37.
183. Rolf Hinze, *Crucible of Combat: Germany's Defensive Battles in the Ukraine, 1943–44* (Solihull, UK: Helion & Co. Ltd., 2009), pp. 61.
184. Münch, pp. 70–71.
185. Hager, pp. 127–128.
186. Rebentisch, pp. 308–309.
187. Rebentisch, pp. 309.
188. Jung, pp. 155–156.
189. Armstrong, pp. 359–360.
190. Rebentisch, pp. 310.
191. Jung, pp. 156.
192. Rebentisch, pp. 314–316.
193. Hinze, pp. 136, 142–143.
194. Werner Haupt, *Die 8. Panzer-Division im 2. Weltkrieg* (Eggolsheim: Podzun-Pallas Verlag, 1987), pp. 310, 316.
195. Ilya B. Moshchanskiy, *Trudnosti Osvobozhdeniya* [*Lost Liberation*] (Moscow: Veche, 2009), chapter 2.
196. 'Einsatzbereite Pz. u. Stu.Gesch. Ost.', Gen. Qu. Insp. D. Panzertruppen, NAM (National archives Microfilm), series T-78, Roll 145, Frame 76020.
197. Hugh Trevor-Roper, *Hitler's War Directives 1939–1945* (Edinburgh: Birlinn Ltd., 2004), pp. 218–224.
198. Schneider, Volume I, pp. 346.
199. Hinze, pp. 146.
200. Kirill S. Moskalenko, *Na Yugo-zapadnom napravleniy* [*On the Southwest Direction*] (Moscow: Military Publishing House, 1979), chapter 6.
201. Hinze, pp. 149.
202. Hinze, pp. 151.
203. Stephen Barratt, *Zhitomir-Berdichev: German Operations West of Kiev 24 December 1943–31 January 1944* (Solihull, UK: Helion & Company Ltd., 2012), pp. 73.
204. Armstrong, pp. 70.
205. Barratt, pp. 77, 83–91.
206. Krivoshein, pp. 262.
207. Zetterling, pp. 147–148.
208. Jentz, Volume 2, pp. 110.
209. Barratt, pp. 73.

Chapter 3

1. Wilhelm Tieke, *Tragedy of the Faithful: A History of the III. (germanisches) SS-Panzer-Korps* (Winnipeg: J. J. Fedorowicz Publishing, Inc., 2001), pp. 28.
2. Steven H. Newton, *Retreat from Lenningrad, Amy Group North 1944/1945* (Atglen, PA: Schiffer Military History, 1995), pp. 27–28.
3. Otto Carius, *Tigers in the Mud: The Combat Career of German Panzer Commander Otto Carius* (Mechanichsburg, PA: Stackpole Books, 2003), pp. 43.
4. Carius, pp. 57.
5. Tieke, pp. 66–68.
6. Armstrong, pp. 209.
7. Armstrong, pp. 362.
8. Hinze, pp. 174.
9. Tsamo RF, Fond 236, opis 2673, delo 311, list 12, 39, 64, 85.
10. Armstrong, pp. 417.
11. Dmitry Loza, *Commanding the Red Army's Sherman Tanks* (Lincoln, NE: University of Nebraska Press, 1996), pp. 3.
12. Zetterling, pp. 99.
13. Zetterling, pp. 74.
14. Zetterling, 83.
15. Zetterling, pp. 96.
16. Douglas E. Nash, *Hell's Gate: The Battle of the Cherkassy Pocket, January-February 1944* (Stamford, CT: RZM Publishing, 2005), pp. 91.
17. Nash, pp. 252.
18. Nash, pp. 267.
19. Zetterling, pp. 277.
20. Rebentisch, pp. 344–345.
21. Rebentisch, pp. 346.
22. Wood, pp. 143–144.
23. Helmut Schiebel, *A Better Comrade You Will Never Find: A Panzerjäger on the Eastern Front, 1941–1945* (Winnipeg: J. J. Fedorowicz Publishing, Inc., 2010), pp. 113.
24. Will Fey, *Armour Battles of the Waffen-SS, 1943–45* (Mechanichsburg, PA: Stackpole Books, 2003), pp. 74.
25. Klapdor, pp. 250–262.
26. Fey, pp. 80.
27. Klapdor, pp. 271.
28. Münch, pp. 213.
29. Velimir Vuksic, *SS Armour on the Eastern Front 1943–1945* (Winnipeg: J. J. Fedorowicz Publishing, Inc., 2005), pp. 97.
30. David M. Glantz, *Red Storm over the Balkans: The Failed Soviet Invasion of Romania, Sring 1944* (Larence, KS: University Press of Kansas, 2007), pp. 39.
31. Jung, pp. 204.
32. Glantz, pp. 120–122.
33. Glantz, pp. 192.
34. Glantz, pp. 194–5.
35. Jung, pp. 210.
36. Glantz, pp. 228–229.
37. Glantz, pp, 249.
38. Glantz, pp. 272–273.
39. Glantz, pp. 317.
40. Rolf Hinze, *To The Bitter End* (Philadelphia: Casemate, 2010), pp. 69.
41. Jentz, Volume 2, pp. 205.
42. Walter S. Dunn, Jr., *Soviet Blitzkrieg: The Battle for White Russia* (Mechanichsburg, PA: Stackpole Books, 2008), pp. 61.
43. Samuel W. Mitcham, Jr., *The German Defeat in the East 1944–45* (Mechanichsburg, PA: Stackpole Books, 2007), pp. 10–14.
44. Mikhail Baryatinski, *Sredniy tank 'Sherman', Vmeste i protiv T-34 [Medium Tank Sherman: With and Against the T-34]* (Moscow: Eksmo, 2006), pp. 67.
45. Steven Zaloga, *Bagration 1944: The Destruction of Army Group Centre* (London: Osprey Publishing, 1996), pp. 42.
46. Mitcham, pp. 48.
47. Mitcham, pp. 27.

48. Steven Zaloga, *T-34/85 Medium Tank 1944–1994* (Oxford: Osprey Publishing, 1996), pp. 11–12.
49. Eduard Bodenmüller, *Diary of a Tank Gunner in the Panzer Regiment of the Brandenburg Panzergrenadier Division, February 1945* (New York: Europa Books Inc., 2004), pp. 61.
50. Gunter Grass, *How I Spent the War: A recruit in the Waffen S.S.*, The New Yorker, June 4, 2007.

Appendix II
1. Fichtner had been in charge of the Heereswaffenamt Wa-Prüf 6 in the critical years of 1937–42, where he played an important role in panzer development programs. Fichtner was badly wounded in mid-September 1943 and put in the Fuhrer-Reserve. He was arrested by the Gestapo after the 20 July Plot and spent two months in detention before being released, but saw no further service.
2. General der Infanterie Dietrich von Choltitz listed as commander from 6 May until 29 August 1943
3. Committed suicide when caught behind enemy lines, 7 August 1943.
4. Relieved of command on 15 November 1943.
5. Killed in action, 18 August 1943.
6. Killed in action 11 March 1944.
7. Killed in action, 31 March 1944.
8. Killed in action, 24 September 1943.

Appendix IV
1. Name changed to Nashorn in January 1944.

Appendix V
1. Committed suicide, 6 July 1944.
2. Captured in Romania, 1944.
3. Killed in action, 25 August 1944.
4. Killed in action, 28 August 1944.

Bibliography

Department of the Army Pamphlet No. 20–290, *Terrain Factors in the Russian Campaign*, July 1951.

Richard N. Armstrong, *Red Army Tank Commanders* (Atglen, PA: Schiffer Publishing Ltd, 1994).

Stephen Barratt, *Zhitomir-Berdichev: German Operations West of Kiev, 24 December 1943–31 January 1944* (Solihull, UK: Helion & Company Ltd., 2012).

Evgeni Bessonov, *Tank Rider: Into the Reich with the Red Army* (Philadelphia: Casemate, 2003).

Artem Drabkin & Oleg Sheremet, *T-34 in Action* (Barnsley, UK: Pen & Sword Ltd, 2006).

Lukas Friedli, *Repairing the Panzers: German Tank Maintenance in World War 2, Volume 2* (Monroe, NY: Panzerwrecks, 2011).

David M. Glantz and Jonathan M. House, *The Battle of Kursk* (Lawrence: University Press of Kansas, 1999).

David. M. Glantz, *The Battle for Leningrad 1941–1944* (Lawrence, KS: University Press of Kansas, 2002).

David M. Glantz, *Colossus Reborn: The Red Army at War, 1941–1943* (Lawrence, KS: University Press of Kansas, 2005).

David M. Glantz, *From the Don to the Dnepr* (London: Frank Cass, 1991).

David M. Glantz, *Red Storm over the Balkans: The Failed Soviet Invasion of Romania, Sring 1944* (Larence, KS: University Press of Kansas, 2007).

Heinz Guderian, *Panzer Leader* (New York: Ballantine Books, Inc., 1968).

Werner Haupt, *Die 8. Panzer-Division im 2.Weltkrieg* (Eggolsheim: Podzun-Pallas Verlag, 1987).

Aleksei Isaev et al., *Tankovyi Udar: Sovietskie tanki v boiakh 1942–1943* [Tank Attack: Soviet Tanks in Battle, 1942–1943] (Moscow: EKSMO, 2007).

Hans-Joachim Jung, *Panzer Soldiers for 'God, Honor, Fatherland' The History of Panzerregiment Großdeutschland* (Winnipeg: J. J. Fedorowicz Publishing, Inc., 2000).

Mikhail E. Katukov, *Na Ostrie glavnogo udara* [*At the Point of the Main Attack*] (Moscow: Voenizdat, 1974).

Ewald Klapdor, *Viking Panzers: The German 5th SS Tank Regiment in the East in World War II* (Mechanicsburg, PA: Stackpole Books, 2011).

Ernst Klink, '*Heer und Kriegsmarine*' in Militärgeschichtliches Forschungsamt (ed.), *Das Deutsche Reich und der Zweite Weltkrieg*, Band 4: *Der Angriff auf die Sowjetunion*. (Stuttgart: Deutsche Verlags-Anstalt,1987).

Franz Kurowski, *Sturmgeschütz vor!* (Winnipeg: J. J. Fedorowicz Publishing, Inc., 1999).

Rudolf Lehmann, *The Leibstandarte, Volume III* (Winnipeg: J. J. Fedorowicz Publishing, Inc., 1990).

Erich von Manstein, *Lost Victories* (Novato, CA: Presidio Press, 1982).

Hasso von Manteuffel, *The 7th Panzer Division: An Illustrated History of Rommel's ‚Ghost Division' 1938–1945* (Atglen, PA: Schiffer Military History, 2000).

Friederich W. von Mellenthin, *Panzer Battles: A Study of the Employment of Armour in the Second World War* (New York: Ballantine Books, 1971).

George M. Nipe, Jr. *Blood, Steel and Myth: The II. SS-Panzerkorps and the road to Prochorowka, July 1943* (Stamford, CT: RZM Publishing, 2011).

George M. Nipe, Jr. *Last Victory in Russia: The SS-Panzerkorps and Manstein's Counter-offensive February–March 1943* (Atglen, PA: Schiffer Military History, 2000).

Erhard Raus, *Panzer Operations: The Eastern Front Memoir of General Raus, 1941–45* (Cambridge, MA: Da Capo Press, 2003).

Ernst Rebentisch, *The Combat History of the 23rd Panzer Division in World War II* (Mechanicsburg, PA: Stackpole Books, 2012).

Pavel Rotmistrov, *Stal'naya gvardiya* [Steel Guard] (Moscow: Voenizdat, 1984).

Gustav W. Schrodek, *Die 11. Panzer-Division: Gespenster-Division 1940–1945* (Eggolsheim: Dörfler Verlag GmbH, 2004).

Wolfgang Schneider, *Panzer Tactics: German Small-Unit Armour Tactics in World War II* (Mechanichsburg, PA: Stackpole Books, 2005).

Wolfgang Schneider, *Tigers in Combat, Volume I* (Mechanicsburg, PA: Stackpole Books, 2004).

Dmitri Shein, *Tanki vedet Rybalko. Boevoi put' 3-i Gvardeiskoi tankovoi armii* [Rybalko's Tanks Lead: Battles of the 3rd Guards Tank Army] (Moscow: EKSMO, 2007).

Valeriy Zamulin, *Demolishing the Myth: The Tank Battle at Prokhorovka, Kursk, July 1943: An Operational Narrative* (Solihull, UK: Helion & Company Ltd., 2011).

Niklas Zetterling and Anders Frankson, *The Korsun Pocket: The Encirclement and Breakout of a German Army in the East, 1944* (Philadelphia: Casemate, 2008).

Niklas Zetterling and Anders Frankson, *Kursk 1943: A Statistical Analysis* (London: Frank Cass Publishers, 2000).

Georgy K. Zhukov, *The Memoirs of Marshal Zhukov* (London: Jonathan Cape Ltd, 1971).

Aleksandr M. Zvartsev, *3-ya gvardeiskaya tankovaya* [3rd Guards Tank] (Moscow: Voenizdat, 1982).

Index